AN ALTERNATIVE VISION

An Interpretation of Liberation Theology

by Roger Haight, S.J.

PAULIST PRESS
New York, Mahwah

Chapter 1 appeared originally as "The Suppositions of Liberation Theology," *Thought* 57 (June, 1983) 158–69.

Chapters 2 and 7 contain some material from Roger Haight, "Spirituality and the Concern for Social Justice: A Christological Perspective," *Spirituality Today* 34 (Winter, 1982) 312–25.

Library of Congress
Catalog Card Number: 84-61974

ISBN: 0-8091-2679-6

Published by Paulist Press
997 Macarthur Boulevard
Mahwah, N.J. 07430

Printed and bound in the United States of America

CONTENTS

in Gratitude to
My Former Colleagues and Students
at the Jesuit School of Theology in Chicago

PREFACE

This book grows out of a long-term interest in and sympathy with the liberation theology that has emerged in Latin America. Since 1973 on a variety of occasions and in various cultural settings I have taught some of the fundamental texts expressing this interpretation of Christianity and discussed them with students. Almost invariably, but especially in North America, the reaction to this theology is ambivalent. On the one hand North Americans can experience the inner truth and power of this literature. The fundamental insight behind liberation theology is correct and it stimulates Christian energy. On the other hand this theology jars with the immediate external social and cultural situation of North America, so that it is not easy against this background to completely assimilate this vision. The rhetoric and the language, the symbols and the experience behind them, are not readily received by people whose experience is formed by the general social context of the north and its churches.

The point of this book is to help this process of assimilation. It is an attempt to "translate" liberation theology into a cultural context that extends beyond Latin America. The intention is to try to transcend the particularity of the concrete imperatives that lie behind the genesis of liberation theology and, at the same time, to *include* them but on a more general and abstract level. The basis for this move is the conviction that liberation theology is an expression of the truth of Christianity and Christianity's vision of human life and existence, and that this vision of truth is not exclusively for Latin America. Of course it must be recognized that since it has been written by a North American, this book will inevitably take on another particular viewpoint and the limitations that go with it. In any case the point is that the book is designed for an audience outside of Latin America.

A second goal of this book is that of presenting liberation theology as a unified whole. Such an attempt is risky business and may be pre-

1

mature since liberation theology today represents an already vast and rapidly expanding body of literature, and one that is not designed systematically. At certain points liberation theology systematically resists systematization. Moreover all liberation theologians are not saying exactly the same thing at every turn. In the face of these cautions it still seems reasonable to try to approach this theology from a wholistic point of view. And while there are any number of ways in which a view of the whole might be approached, I have chosen to take up the challenge in the rather traditional way of bringing together liberationist material under the headings of some of the basic doctrines of Christian belief. In effect the presentation reflects an outline for a doctrinal systematics even though I have made no special commitment to the order of presentation.

The result of trying to fulfill these goals is thus a short theological introduction to Christian faith in terms of the content of this faith, its beliefs or doctrines. Such an ambitious project has inherent difficulties and limitations. Indeed on rereading this volume I am somewhat appalled by what is not said, by explanations not given, by the rapidity and sometimes superficiality with which some crucial issues are treated, by the limits, unclarity and even false impressions that the text may convey. Every chapter provides an example of subject matter that deserves fuller analysis.

But there is a positive value to such a short introduction to the liberationist interpretation of Christian faith. And this lies precisely in the effort to see this theology as a whole so that its main positions on a variety of issues can be interrelated as integral parts of a single vision.[1] The vision that is mediated with Christian faith is both given us, and thus gratuitously received, and at the same time active, a function of the world-constructing and meaning-giving insight of mind and imagination. This vision construes the world and human existence both as it is and in a new way. It fills empty three-dimensional reality with the meaning that comes from an experience of God and God's rule, real or potential. It sees not only what is but also what ought to be, what might be, what can be.

The liberationist vision of reality stands within the prophetic tradition of the Judaeo-Christian community. Relative to other accounts of Christian faith and belief it is an alternative vision. Liberation theology is certainly a modern theology, one that translates and reinterprets Christian symbols in dialogue with our contemporary world and culture. But it is at the same time counter-cultural; it calls into question society and culture as it actually is; it mediates God's word and will to unbelief and sin. And this prophetic word is addressed not only to the world but also and especially to the Church wherever it exists in an easy relation with society and culture.

Finally, this book contains no explicit analyses of the social, cultural and economic spheres of human existence. It does not employ the social disciplines of history, economics, sociology or political science. This may seem strange for any work on liberation theology. The decision not to enter this mode of reflection explicitly is largely due to my own lack of expertise in these disciplines. It is in no way an expression of any view that these analyses are unessential for a full understanding not only of liberation theology but also of human existence itself, both as it is at any given time and as it is in itself. At this point, then, I simply claim the necessity of a division of labor and encourage those who may penetrate deeper into liberation theology and its consequences through the mediation of these disciplines. But I am also convinced that one can gain some basic understanding of liberation theology *theologically,* and that one does not have to be educated in any one of these disciplines or schools within them to appreciate this theology.

In sum, then, the purpose of this volume is twofold. It is hoped that it may be useful for those students of the liberation theology of Latin America who are seeking to integrate this theology into the categories and patterns of thought of a more general and wider cultural and theological framework. And secondly it is meant to be an introduction to what Christian faith offers us in our time, namely, an alternative vision.

INTRODUCTION

Faith is a fundamental human phenomenon. It may be said that all human beings live by faith when faith is seen as the centered and centering concern lying at the core of each personality. Such a faith becomes explicitly religious when this ultimate concern involves God. Religious faith is consciously being in the presence of or standing before God in the course of living one's life. As such, faith is existential. Belief on the other hand is quite distinct from faith and may be looked upon as the content of faith. The distinction between faith and belief stands out when one speaks of beliefs in their objective or propositionally stated forms in contrast to the deeper existential commitment that constitutes faith. Although distinct, faith and belief are inseparable. For faith is also cognitive and thus implicitly contains some content which may be drawn out by reflection and analysis. What I have called vision lies at the conjunction of faith and belief and is associated with the imaginative function of the human mind.[1]

The phrase "an alternative vision" implies a change or reinterpretation of faith's vision. Just as demythologization involves remythologization, and deideologization involves reideologization in the hope that where the former ideology was oppressive and malign the latter will be liberating and benign, so too liberation theology is a new interpretation of faith's vision. One way of seeing how this alteration of faith's vision took place is by an analysis of the beliefs or doctrines that thematize and express this faith and its vision. In the reinterpretation of those beliefs which follows there are several concepts at work which are fundamental to the whole enterprise. Four such notions in particular influence the method of analysis and underlie the theological language at every point. It will be helpful then to introduce these basic concepts at the very outset and to show how they influence the development of the whole argument.

First of all and of central importance through this essay is the term "freedom." Freedom is used to refer to various levels of the phenomenon of human existence. And at its deepest level and meaning freedom points to that which makes human existence specifically human. It is a descriptive term that indicates the nature of the defining characteristic of being human. As such it takes on a substantive meaning. Human beings are not something else that also happens to be free; rather human beings are freedom. This term is based on the self-evident and self-authenticating personal experience of all persons of their own freedom, and from this it is postulated that an elementary freedom lies at the core of human existence itself. Thus at this primary level the term "freedom" is a substitute for what in medieval philosophy was called "soul" or what today is often referred to as "the human spirit." It is of course one thing to say that human existence is freedom, and it is quite another thing to determine the quality of that freedom, just how free human beings are. The point here is not to argue that human existence consists in some total freedom. The freedom that is human existence is a freedom in the world, a freedom immersed in the physical and material structures that limit and at the same time help to release it, that both determine it and serve as the basis for their own transcendence.[2]

Besides this depth dimension of freedom as a form of being, the term also refers to the exercise of freedom in the myriad forms this may occur. It is partly true that freedom, as a dynamic and existential concept, points to a reality that only exists insofar as it is exercised and actualized.[3] Such activity may be recognized at a variety of levels and degrees. At its most elementary level freedom is manifest in some degree of self-consciousness, that is, reflective consciousness where freedom is the bending back of consciousness on itself. And this reflective awareness is coupled with self-determination or some degree of autonomy and self-actualization. Both knowing self-awareness and self-actualization are expressions of freedom. And out of these elementary structures and extending well beyond them freedom becomes actualized in the myriad forms of human understanding, designing and creative actuation that constitute human culture.

The freedom that constitutes human existence, in both its substantive and its dynamic existential sense, has three dimensions which are determined by three relationships. By virtue of its self-transcendence and self-consciousness, freedom is related to itself; it bends back on itself. By virtue of its being an autonomous self in the physical arena which is not the self, freedom is related to the world. And by virtue of the finite character of the world and the self in it, freedom stands in relation to the transcendent, that is, to God. Human existence itself is constituted in this triple relationship. And thus a phenomenology of human freedom, both as knowing and as autonomous self-actualization, will reveal these three relationships and hence three dimensions of human freedom or existence.[4] Human existence as freedom in three dimensions, its personal, social and transcendent qualities, is one of the central building blocks in the argument of this book.

Another concept that governs the whole structure and argument of this essay at interpretation has to do with method in theological reflection. And this is the idea of correlation and the method of correlation. The principle governing this commonly recognized structure of theological interpretation is self-evident. If theological truth is to be intelligible, it must, like any other truth, be mediated and formulated in terms that are themselves intelligible. And to achieve this intelligibility the understanding and language of theology must correspond with some form of actual human experience and be integrated with the current common human experience that constitutes our understanding of reality. Understanding in theology must correlate with our knowledge and understanding of our situation in the world. This does not imply that God does not confront the present situation through the tradition of the concepts that mediate Christian revelation from out of our past and within our present situation. In fact Christian tradition does stand in opposition to and challenge much of modernity. But to say that is to insist that God's word be related to the present situation and be intelligible to it.[5]

In this work there is a correlation between anthropology, that is, an understanding of human existence as freedom in its three dimensions, and the Christian tradition of faith and belief that mediates God's revelation. The dynamics of this correlation is generated out of the experience that human freedom is a question to itself, and that in itself it provides no answer for itself concerning its ultimate destiny and its purposefulness in the world. This question receives an answer in Christian revelation and tradition. And in order to explain the full relevance of this answer one must look at it in such a way that it be seen to address the full range of human experience, that is, all three dimensions of human freedom. The basic logic of this interpretation of Christianity, then, is that it is a correlation between Christian tradition and the three levels of human existence or freedom. God's revelation in the Christian tradition addresses human existence as self-conscious and personal freedom, as world-conscious and historical freedom, and as God-conscious and transcendent freedom.

A third key concept for this interpretation of the Christian vision is referred to by the term "focus." By focus I mean a subjective or existential concern of critical importance and centrality that predominates over all other concerns. The idea of a focus also has an objective meaning in this text, one that will be illustrated further on in relation to Jesus

Christ, and it will be obvious when the term is used in this fashion. But the primary methodological import of the term "focus" lies in its stemming from an overriding existential concern.[6] However a focus in this sense is not an exclusive concern, not one that eliminates other problems and interests. On the contrary, the image of a focus is meant to convey comprehensiveness, a concern that includes other imperatives and draws them into itself. The argument of this book is that there is such a commanding existential crisis today that should serve as the focus for interpreting the meaning of Christian faith. And this crisis concerns the meaning of human existence or freedom itself precisely in its social historical dimension.[7]

The correlation that governs the interpretation of Christian doctrine in this book is one that responds to all three dimensions of human freedom while at the same time attending to the principal focus that arises out of our current situation. As a result there is a constant tension in this presentation which reflects actual experience today. The tension is between two poles of our experience. The first is a demand for an adequate and integral understanding of the Christian message, one that responds fully to human existence or freedom in all of its dimensions; the second is a demand that the Christian message provide meaning in particular for the question of social existence and freedom because the urgency of this crisis, often passed over or neglected in traditional dogmatics, calls the credibility of the whole Christian message into question. The tension then is between comprehensiveness and focus in Christian interpretation of itself. The introduction of this tension into this book is meant as a corrective to some readings of liberation theology that see it governed by a thematic monophysitism, that is, as concerned exclusively with this-worldly social issues. It is also meant as a corrective to those Christian theologies which either have something to say about every human problem and thus lack any focus or where an actual focus has not come to terms with the urgency of the crucial problem of our times, namely, that of social freedom and the commitment of our personal and transcendent freedom to historical issues, the problems we share as a race.

A fourth concept that is consistently at work in this presentation is that of symbol. The term refers specifically to religious symbols and in it is implied a religious epistemology. A religious symbol is some finite thing of this world which mediates transcendence to human consciousness. A religious symbol may be a concept or an idea, a word or a text, but it may also be a thing such as a sacred tree or mountain; it may also be a human person or action or historical event. The structure of a symbol can be discerned from the way it functions epistemologically. All knowledge of God is knowledge that is mediated through the world. There is no immediate knowledge of God precisely because God is transcendent and other than the world while all human knowledge, like freedom itself, is bound to and mediated through the world. Even what appears to be "direct" experience or knowledge of God is really a mediated immediacy because it cannot be had apart from the existence of human freedom in the world and its determination by the world and society. But at the same time experience of transcendence is real, and what is experienced is experienced as precisely transcendent or other than the finitude which mediates it. Thus the structure of the religious symbol itself appears as polar: It has its own finite integrity and identity in itself; it is not the transcendent. And at the same time it both points beyond itself to what is other than itself and transcendent, and it participates in this transcendence insofar as it renders it present or mediates it to human awareness. This polar structure of not being that which it points to, of being a finite self-identity which nevertheless participates and shares in the transcendent other which it in turn makes present, is similar to the analogy of being, and thus symbolic knowledge is similar to the analogy of faith knowledge.[8]

As was said, religious symbols may be words and concepts, or they may be things or persons. This work deals with some of the fundamental conceptual symbols of Christianity such as God, Spirit, creation, the Kingdom of God and so on. But it is not our task here to investigate the origin of these symbols, a task that is more properly that of biblical and historical theology. Rather this introductory essay looks at Christianity as a community of faith which is in part held together by a tradition of basic religious symbols, a collection of many symbols the most important of which are contained in the creed and its central doctrines. The book is thus an interpretation of these symbolic doctrines. It is also an interpretation of symbols that in addition to being conceptual are also historical realities such as the sacraments, the Church and principally Jesus Christ. In the latter case, Jesus is not merely a conceptual symbol, a myth or a kerygma, but a person. Especially in the sections on Christology Jesus Christ is interpreted primarily on the basis of the fact that Jesus was a concrete person in history who, as the source of Christian faith, also became the this-worldly objective focus for the Christian's faith in God. Jesus was one who in his self-identity as a human being made God present to the world and human consciousness. Thus Jesus Christ is the central real symbol for Christian faith in God.[9]

In sum, these four concepts and principles underlie the development of this liberationist interpretation of Christianity. They are in brief a notion of human existence as freedom existing in three dimensions, the idea of correlation as a structure for theological reflection, focus as a determining subjective or existential concern which objectively has Jesus as its central this-worldly referent for faith in God, and finally the concept of symbol which provides an overarching epistemological theory of how faith is historically mediated. As for the structure of this interpretation, it is divided into two parts. The first, Chapters I to IV, is methodological and deals with several of the issues that have just been mentioned. The second part, Chapters V to XII, is constructive and consists in essays that provide the outline for an alternative vision in terms of some of the basic doctrines of Christian faith.

Chapter I is an introduction to the world of Latin American liberation theology. There are of course many different ways in which such a task might be accomplished short of living on that continent and participating in the liberationist movement. By now most people are familiar with the genesis of this theology and its principal authors. Thus I have chosen to look at the theology of liberation as a whole and to try to define it simply by enumerating some of its major principles, suppositions and axioms. Without some awareness of and sympathy for these basic and constitutive characteristics of liberation theology one will not really be able to understand what is going on in it.

Chapters II and III set up the methodological tension between the focus of liberation theology and an adequate comprehensive view of human existence or freedom. Chapter II argues that the problem and concern underlying liberation theology is not merely a local and particular phenomenon; the crisis to which liberation theology is responding has universal dimensions and impact. Thus all human beings participate in it, and they do so in such a way that it constitutes the general crisis of our time. This crisis concerns the very meaningfulness of our corporate social this-worldly human existence. But in responding to this issue an adequate and integral theology must attend to the whole of human existence or freedom. Thus Chapter III presents a schema for an anthropology that includes all three levels of human freedom simultaneously as the paradigm for self-understanding that enables a comprehensive reinterpretation of Christian symbols.

Chapter IV is on faith and it serves as a bridge to the constructive argument of the book. Faith is a general anthropological category with a specific Christian manifestation. It seems impossible today to consider Christian faith and revelation as totally discontinuous with other religious experiences and traditions. But at the same time Christian faith is a particular historical phenomenon which is defined by the event of Jesus Christ. Thus the form of Christian faith is Christic; the human being Jesus is its objective this-worldly real symbolic focus.[10] But what is crucial for an understanding of faith today is its distinction from belief or a merely cognitive acceptance of a set of doctrines. Faith must be seen first of all on its deepest anthropological level as an existential mode of human freedom itself, one which embraces both knowledge and action, belief and doing, so that all separation between Christian dogmatics and Christian ethics is overcome. All Christian ethics, whatever the historical source of its content may be, becomes informed by Christian faith and its vision and hence its beliefs.

Chapter V begins a constructive interpretation of the doctrine of God from a liberationist perspective. This chapter does not argue to the existence of God, nor is it a systematic analysis of the nature of God.[11] Rather it presupposes the perspective of Christians who have entered and belong to a community of tradition. This tradition is in part made up of a collection of symbols that disclose and define who God is. This chapter simply enumerates some of these classical Christian symbols and interprets them by describing how they open up a vision for faith and freedom in our current situation.

Chapters VI and VII deal with Christology, first with the data and structure of Christology and then with the reinterpretation of the significance of Jesus Christ for Christian life today. Here more than anywhere the apologetic structure of a method of correlation is demanded. Thus within the context of a general anthropology that implicitly requires faith, Christology looks at the genesis of the specifically Christian faith that has its source and historical mediation in the human being Jesus. Given the structure and data for Christology that are laid out in Chapter VI, Chapter VII outlines how this material for Christology must be reinterpreted for the imagination of faith today if it is to respond to our situation and provide meaning for human existence in it by opening up a world of possible meaning for the commitment of Christian freedom.

Chapter VIII deals with the third constitutive symbol of Christian faith, God as Spirit. It is frequently said that Christian theology lacks a developed doctrine of the Spirit. Part of the problem here is that consideration of the Spirit of God has been overly associated with the doctrine of the immanent Trinity. Whether this is true or not, the systematic hypothesis underlying this chapter is that Roman Catholic theology does possess a highly developed theology of the economy of the Spirit of God under the title of the theology of grace. By contrast the traditions of the Reformation have a highly developed theology of the Spirit even while the term "grace" is more closely associated with the economy of God's Word, Jesus Christ. This chapter unites the two symbols, grace and Spirit, and borrowing from the Roman Catholic theology of grace offers a description of the effects of the working of God's Spirit. It also borrows from the Protestant theology of grace and of the Spirit and tries to preserve the anti-Pelagian theme which is at the core of Reformation theology. This is a particularly crucial point since one of the implicit religious criticisms of liberation theology is that it appears to some as intrinsically Pelagian and as undermining the Christian conviction that God alone saves. The effort here then will be to show that the work of the Spirit of God is pure grace, the pure grace of God manifest in Jesus Christ. But the effects of the operation of the Spirit are precisely to release freedom from bondage, to open it up and free it for commitment on all its levels, but with a special focus on ethical action in the social arena.

Chapters IX and X deal with the Church and its sacraments. Following the lead of the Second Vatican Council's redefinition of the Church as open to the world and society, Chapter IX retrieves the New Testament symbol of mission as, along with others, constitutive of the Church. When the comprehensive sacramentality of the Church is viewed concretely, existentially and historically within this context of a mission to and for the world, the new demand for an historical understanding of the efficacy of the sacraments, developed in Chapter X, falls into place. Moreover the doctrines of the Church and the sacraments are seen to be entirely consistent with the doctrines of Jesus Christ and the Spirit of God.

Chapter XI deals with the ministry of the Church. But once again, because so many concrete issues and problems are encountered in this area, none of which can be adequately handled in a short discussion, it becomes necessary to look beneath all these specific issues for foundational principles that govern all ministry in all its forms. Christian ministry emerges out of freedom grasped by faith; it is service to and for human freedom on all of its levels. This simple formula defines all Christian ministry after the pattern of Jesus Christ and through the structures of the Church. Although there are fundamental tensions that govern the structure of Christian ministry, so that each form of ministry and every exercise of it requires prudential judgment, still Christian ministry is always in the service of freedom. And because of the crisis of our time and situation there is a religious exigency that all ministry take account of and attend to the social nature of human existence.

And, finally, Chapter XII concludes this volume with a sketch of the spirituality implied in or at the basis of this alternative vision, the spirituality to which this theology leads. The principle operative in this chapter is that spirituality is synonymous with what is called "the Christian life." Spirituality is a term that is comprehensive so that it includes both understanding and behavior in all its forms. If one has a specific faith and religious vision, it informs the totality of one's life and not simply an aspect of it. And, conversely, one's real faith is something like a fundamental option that is constituted by one's praxis. One's faith is synonymous with one's spirituality when spirituality is understood as the Christian life and the sum total of one's understandings and beliefs and decisions and actions. The liberationist spirituality that is outlined in this chapter in the concrete and descriptive terms of a person's fundamental attitudes and behaviors is thus a fitting summary and conclusion for this alternative vision.

Chapter I
THE SUPPOSITIONS
OF LIBERATION THEOLOGY

In the phrase "liberation theology" the word "theology" does not quite have the same connotation as it does in a name such as "Scholastic theology." Scholastic theology points to a finished theological system in which the language is more or less stable and in which all of the major doctrines have been examined. In contrast, liberation theology is still what may be called a movement. It is not yet a systematic theology. Although there have been other very similar theological movements, such as the theology of the social gospel earlier in this century,[1] liberation theology is still barely nascent and has scarcely reached the level of methodological refinement and of execution in content and scope of other theologies of the past.

The movement of liberation theology, moreover, is not a unified whole; it is not a school and the term "liberation theology" is not univocal. There are many liberation theologies and many authors who are not all saying the same thing. There are liberation theologies not only in Latin America, but also in Asia (in the Philippines and India), Africa, and the United States. And the political theology of Europe may be considered a not too distant cousin. But we shall restrict our consideration to the liberation theology as it has unfolded in Latin America.

In spite of this still unstable quality of liberation theology, which indeed may be a virtue and not a vice, one can still discover certain fundamental experiences and themes, as well as basic presuppositions and principles, that are more or less common in all of liberation theology and either guide its thinking explicitly or are implicit in it. This chapter will consist in an analysis of some of these general characteristics of liberation theology. Thus this analysis will not at all be a thorough or complete examination of this theology, and intends little more than an enumeration of these experiences, themes, suppositions and principles as a help toward a critical appreciation of the actual content of liberation theology. The point of this chapter is simply to isolate these themes as a help to further analysis and constructive interpretation. At the same time we hope to show the degree to which liberation theology is a thoroughly modern theology.

Probably the most basic and fundamental experience underlying liberation theology is *the experience of poverty*.[2] Poverty here does not mean the noble and dignified state of a simple life of physical hard work in which the basic necessities of life are won by toil but without any superfluity or luxury. Nor does it have anything to do with the vow of poverty that Christian religious take. Poverty here means destitution: it is the lack of the basic necessities of human existence, food and drink, clothing, shelter and home, medical care, the lack of any of which causes death. And the phrase "the experience of poverty" does not refer merely to the fact of the existence of such poverty nor the experience of those who suffer from it. Rather the reference here is to the reaction that is being experienced more and more throughout the world in the face of the existence of this destitution and to its degree and extent. It is an experience all at once of outrage, of condemnation of this condition, and of guilt at allowing it to continue. This guilt implies human responsibility. Thus included in this experience of poverty is the realization that it is caused by human beings. There is a connection between wealth and poverty, a causal interrelationship between the extraordinary wealth of the developed sectors both inside and outside of Latin America and the extensive poverty that prevails there.

The poverty or destitution that is pointed to here is a worldwide reality and the meaning of the term is the same everywhere. Moreover the reaction to it described here is a growing worldwide cultural experience. But for liberation theology this experience of poverty is a *religious* experience. This can be seen at two points. Negatively, this poverty is experienced as against the will of God. Not only does God not accept this poverty, God wills the opposite. Secondly and consequently, the experience of this poverty contains a deep moral imperative for the Christian conscience. Working to help the victims of poverty is experienced as constitutive of being at one with God as a Christian. The term "the people," which refers to the vast majority who are poor, is very clearly a religious symbol in liberation theology.

It is impossible to over-emphasize this experience or the fact that it is crucial for understanding liberation theology. Just as this is a fundamental generative experience for this theology, so too an appreciation or sympathy for what is going on in this theology is dependent upon some sharing in this experience.

The experience of historicity, of sharing in an *historical conscious-ness,* is a presupposition of liberation theology even as it is latent in the way it experiences poverty.[3] Historical consciousness is an awareness of being in time and that the present is a product of the past. It is a pro-found experience of the relativities and differences of ways of thinking and acting in different times and places. This is implied, for example, in the demand of liberation theology that Christian understanding or the-ology become relevant or related to the specific problems of human life that constitute the Latin American reality. This consciousness does not allow us to imagine God's providence as a set plan for the unfolding of human history in any detailed or particular sense. Historicity implies that the course of human events is open and undetermined. To some extent at least human history is in corporate human hands.

Thus intimately connected to historical consciousness, if not simply an aspect of it, is the experience of *autonomy and freedom.*[4] The term "autonomy" is used positively and not in an anti-religious sense here; it refers to the experience that we human beings are responsible for his-tory. Society and culture are constructed by human beings and not totally preconstituted by a created pattern of nature. And hence the pat-tern and structure of social life can be changed by human planning and initiative. Without this supposition massive poverty might be under-stood as some form of fated necessity which is to be endured passively because it was not in human control.

The term "freedom" points to the personal and collective exercise of choice and creative initiative that is not inhibited by external force or suppression. More and more this freedom, both personal and collective, is being looked upon as one of the highest if not the highest of all human values. From existentialism we have learned that to be human is to be a center of creativity, of deliberate choice, decision, commitment and action, that is always making things anew. In this framework, to be less free or to have the potentiality of freedom cut off and stifled by oppres-sion or poverty is literally dehumanizing; it is an attack on the essence of people's humanness. These lines of thinking are implicit in liberation theology.[5]

Another supposition of liberation theology is the experience of *sec-ularization.* This word and its variants have many meanings, all stem-ming from the autonomy of the social and political spheres from reli-gious authority.[6] The world today does not run on the basis of religious authority. Certainly liberation theology is aware of this. But there is another aspect of secularization and the experience of it that is charac-teristic of this theology, and this is the broad and general perception of *the importance of this world,* the importance of human history, of life in it and of the human institutions that govern it. It is the experience of "being at home" in the world.[7] This may be understood in contrast to the particular religious experience of otherworldliness, the feeling that we do not really belong here but in another world. The experience referred to here is not contrary to religious experience; it simply says that while we are in this world this is where we belong. This is our world, the only world we have at this time, and it is important, even supremely important. Liberation theology considers this world and Christian life within it with utter seriousness.

From what has been said it is very easy to understand why and how one of the chief characteristics of liberation theology is that it sees itself as explicitly *contextual and related*. Every theology of course is contextual or dependent on a specific historical situation. In liberation theology, however, an explicit goal is to directly link its understanding to its particular situation.[8] Arising out of the experiences already mentioned, this theology is driven by the imperative that Christian faith and its understanding be related to the concrete situation or context in which the Christian life is lived. In Latin America this means an historical situation of massive poverty, a situation in which the freedom of millions is suffocated by the actual reigning structures of social life. Thus liberation theology grows out of a concrete and particular historical experience and tries to formulate its understanding of Christian faith in such a way that it will in turn impel a Christian life that is engaged in the problems of everyday life in history and society.

Closely related to its contextual relatedness is another characteristic of liberation theology which may be called its *historical viewpoint*.[9] This historical viewpoint is a characteristic of its point of departure, its theological method and the framework in which its content is understood. With Vatican II Roman Catholic theology has been released from an authoritarian point of departure and from a kind of theologizing that consists in an objective analysis of purely objective data and meanings based on authority. The point of departure of liberation theology is the actual historical situation in which this theology is written and the experience of a concern and involvement of Christians in that situation. Its method is a form of the *method of correlation:* out of lived historical experience it poses questions to the tradition of Christian understanding that ask for responses that illumine precisely the situation of the questioners. Because of the circular character of hermeneutics, the responses to these questions which constitute the doctrine or content of liberation theology have a decidedly historical character. Christian doctrines in liberation theology are ways of understanding concrete historical human experience. They are not doctrines or understandings of supra-historical realities except insofar as these transcendent mysteries impinge on historical life and bear meaning for how we live life in this world.[10]

Liberation theology is also *existential,* although not in the sense of an existentialism that is centered on the religious experience of individual persons or one whose affirmations do not transcend actual subjective experience. The existential quality of liberation theology is another way of referring to its concern for actual concrete human existence and the necessity that theological understanding have bearing on, carry meaning for, and make sense to actual human existence.[11] The poor are not merely a collective mass. They are individual people: individual children in and around the city of Lima; particular families on the Andean Altiplano; specific groups of people in Guatemala. Liberation theology is also existential insofar as it is marked by a high degree of urgency. This urgency comes both from the situation of suffering that it addresses and from an impatience with other theologies that do not share the same underlying experiences. Thus liberation theology is often polemic, not only against society but also against the Church and other theologies insofar as they fail to meet the exigencies of historical life. For this reason it sometimes bears a strident rhetorical and moralistic tone. These qualities, then, should be judged from within the context of the experience which they reflect.

A way of summing up much of what has been said thus far and at the same time characterizing further the method of liberation theology would be to say that it operates out of a *broader context for theological thinking* than has been traditional in Roman Catholicism at least. The world and human history and experience of life in the world constitute the horizon for this theology.[12] This is, after all, the situation of Christianity and Christian life itself. Involved in the adoption of this horizon is an "uncentering of the Church"[13] as the sole provider of data and criteria for theological understanding. Christian sources must be combined with other sources of knowledge and experience from history at large. Moreover the Church and Christianity itself tend to be seen dynamically as relational and functional within the broader context of the world and history. Christian doctrine is not the private segregated understanding of a sect within but apart from history. The whole point of Christianity and faith's understanding of the world is to communicate itself and be of service to the whole race and its history.

Another implicit experience of liberation theology, especially in its desire to be related to its situation and of service to history, is what may be called the recognition of *the challenge of Marxism.*[14] To appreciate this one has to realize that outside of the more affluent societies of the West, which is the traditional home of Christianity, the Marxist under-

standing of history provides a serious rival or at least a challenge to traditional Christianity. The social analysis and the ideals that underlie
Marxism and other secular humanistic theories of human existence have
won converts from Christianity who bring with them an altruistic and
religious fervor. And the promise of Marxism appears more credible
against the background of Christian, or at least the West's, failure; it
promises the third world what the Christianity of the first world has
failed to accomplish.[15] That liberation theology has experienced deeply
this challenge is reflected in the fact that many proponents of liberation
theology have adopted Marxist social and historical analysis and language. This is an attempt to coopt into Christian understanding the values and truths contained in Marxism.

A further characteristic of liberation theology, then, is its *use of
social analysis* or social sciences in its theologizing.[16] It is certainly true
that Greek philosophy has ceased to be the exclusive dialogue partner
in Roman Catholic theology, which has in fact become more and more
eclectic in recent years. Typical of liberation theology is its use of social
analysis and the bringing of this to bear in mediating theological understanding. This is both a strong point and a weakness in this theology,
for while it helps to integrate theological understanding with actual concrete life and its structures, it still is not clear methodologically *how*
social analysis enters into *theological* understanding. Philosophy has
consistently dealt with the problem of transcendence. Exactly how any
particular social analysis is more than a necessary ancillary discipline to
theological understanding is part of the present problematic of liberation theology. But at present the social sciences are mediating a broader
and more comprehensive view of human existence. And since anthropology is constitutive of all theological statements when a method of correlation is employed, the social dimension of human existence released
by these sciences has a direct bearing on theological understanding. This
will become apparent in the following point.

One of the presuppositions and constant themes of liberation theology that has been contributed by the social sciences concerns *the
social nature of human existence.* The importance of this premise of
the social dimension or character of human life can be seen at three
points. First, the human person is constituted by society. Like no other
creature the human person must learn, and the process of socialization
is a factor that governs human thinking and acting at every point. Liberation theology has learned from social science that it must be critical
of the unquestioned assumptions of any given social milieu since they
determine our most basic ideas, values and behaviors. And certainly this
has a bearing on theology. Second, the social character of human exis-

tence means that no person is simply a private individual existence but also lives in relation to others. The human person is dependent on others and influences others simply by being and acting. This radical interdependence on an interpersonal level and on the larger social level of the interrelation of peoples and societies is fundamental to liberation theology. Liberation theology "thinks" in a socially relevant fashion. Third, from social science one learns *how* autonomous human freedom creates the social structures and institutions within which we live, and with its analyses shows the various factors and groups which support and sustain them. The recognition of the fact of this dependence of social institutions on human will and freedom is responsible for such categories as "institutional" and "social" sin and these are basic terms in liberation theology. And, finally, all of this has direct bearing on Christian ethics and spirituality, that is, on how the Christian life is led.

The term *solidarity* is a major symbol in liberation theology.[17] "The people" are a *solidum,* a community, a whole, and individuals are urged to join and be united with and committed to the others. The impetus of this ideal is a desire that more and more people take on and share the common experience, values, interests and problems of the greater proportion of the community. This extremely vital value in liberation theology points to a deeper ontological truth that should be characterized as a theological supposition, namely, the unity of the human race. Despite enormous cultural differences between peoples, both across the span of recorded history and the spectrum of differentiated situation and ethos today, there is some transcendental unity to the human family. Human beings journey through this life in this world together. This solidarity is being brought home to us in striking ways in the twentieth century; our ontological oneness is assuming ever more concrete and historical forms. In today's world we are willy-nilly the "keepers" of our brothers and sisters. Thus the symbol of solidarity is one that echoes our real human experience, both locally and globally, in a positive ideal form.

A strictly theological supposition of liberation theology concerns *the universal availability of God's saving grace.* Due especially to the work of Karl Rahner and the affirmations of Vatican II, this position is almost taken for granted in Catholic theology today.[18] But when formally adopted as a theological axiom, this position has several important consequences. First, it is really behind the move of uncentering the Church which was mentioned earlier. Second, it grounds theologically a much more positive view of human history as a whole as the broader arena of where God is active and may be found. Third, it confirms theologically the importance of concrete everyday human life in the world as the place where God's grace is most decisively encountered. This last idea will recur under the theme of liberation spirituality.

Very closely related to the position on grace and an extended notion of the Kingdom of God, in fact on the basis of them, liberation theology assumes or tries to establish *the close relation between liberation and salvation,* if not their identity.[19] Here liberation is taken to include in its meaning social, economic and political release from oppressive structures. And God's saving grace is seen to affect not just a person's psychology and spiritual intentions and motivations but the whole of human existence. While the ultimate meaning of salvation as final and definitive beyond history is not lost sight of, liberation theology is mainly concerned with how salvation in Christ affects human existence and life here and now in this world. In this linking of salvation and liberation, the strictly theological datum from the content of faith and the social realities of secular life in history and this world meet in a dramatic way. This point, then, of uniting the symbol and experience of salvation with historical liberation is a central element in liberation theology in which many of the points already mentioned come to fruition.

Shifting now to the area of spirituality or the Christian life, liberation theology maintains implicitly or explicitly that *the essence of Christianity consists in love.*[20] God's revelation and address to the human race in Jesus is a manifestation and confirmation of an absolute love of God for human beings that in turn releases love into history and asks for love in return. The way that union with God is constituted in this world is in or through the dynamics of self-transcending love displayed in history. This may seem obvious enough, but it takes on more significance if it is set over against a view of Christianity as a knowledge to be protected in some form of orthodoxy. Obviously this should not be taken as an attack on the importance of human existence being in truth. But it is a shift for Roman Catholicism at least to see that this truth is secondary and only relevant insofar as it is in the service of the works of love.

Finally, the spirituality or understanding of the Christian life that emerges in liberation theology is one that *links love with the demands of justice,* in particular, social justice.[21] The exigency for social justice is the initiating experience of this theology. And thus it may be seen to come full circle in interpreting Christianity in such a way that that demand will be met by an authentic understanding and living of the Christian life. An integral Christian spirituality will involve a love of neighbor that displays itself in the public and social sphere, and its general form will consist in the effort to replace unjust and oppressive social structures with liberating ones.

This sketch of the presuppositions of liberation theology may fittingly conclude with a consideration that is very basic but that may be overlooked by interpreters of this theology. Liberation theology is a modern and secular theology. It begins with analysis of society and ends with a conception of the Christian life that is immersed in the world and the problems of society. But at the same time this theology is not simply a reaction to culture and society's evils. Its real basis and grounding lie in deep religious experience and intuition. And this can be seen at two points or in two axioms. First, in the Christian conception of things love and union with God depend on love of the neighbor. Second, in our day real love of neighbor must unfold in a social context.

First, the principle that liberation theology proposes relative to our union with God comes out of the deep and radical question: Exactly how are we united with God? The question is not simply how we know God, or how we know that we are united with God, but how is this union constituted? What *makes* us united with God?

The response of liberation theology to this question is that we are ultimately united to God through our being united with the neighbor; we love God through loving the neighbor.[22] This answer comes from the whole of the New Testament as well as specifically from various parts of it. One thinks of the counsel of John that a person who says he loves God and does not love his neighbor is a liar. The two great commandments of love of God and love of neighbor are one; they do not flow one from another but are one. To put this principle in its most radical form, it may be said that we can only truly love God by loving the neighbor; we cannot love God except by loving the neighbor.

Without developing this point further as it should be, it can be illustrated with two propositions that seem self-evident on the basis of the New Testament. First, if a person says he loves God and performs all his religious duties faithfully, but does not love his neighbor, he is not really united with God. Second, if a person truly loves his neighbor and displays this in his actions, even though he denies God and maintains that he does not love God, he is really united with God. When one adds to this principle the truism that love displays itself in action not words, one has the groundwork for a deep religious spirituality of moral commitment and action on behalf of the neighbor.

Second, love of neighbor today must unfold in a social context. Here many of the presuppositions mentioned in this analysis come to the fore. Because of our historical consciousness and sense of responsibility for history and its social structures, and because of the fact of interdependence and the social nature of human existence that postulates that we all participate in the social structures that are in place, and because of the influence of social structures on human lives, love of neighbor today must include a concern for those social structures that keep human lives in bondage and unfreedom and a concern for creating new liberating social institutions.

A justification for this position in Christian tradition and sources may be found in the prophetic tradition of Scripture. The passages from Isaiah and Amos and others are well known: "I do not want your sacrifices, I want social justice," says the Lord. But it is most important to see that a return to these sources is not a question of proof texting, not an argument from these texts directly, for one could find texts that indicate the opposite. These texts should be regarded as containing a revelation; they disclose the nature of God to Jewish and Christian faith. In or through these texts liberation theology experiences a God who is utterly and intrinsically concerned about human life and welfare, and who condemns every human agency or structure that is injurious to God's own people. Consequently an "option for the poor" and social engagement on behalf of the marginated are actions according to the will of God, actions that place the actor in union with God by a moral union of wills that is ontologically supported by God's grace. This religious basis underlies and suffuses the whole of the argument of liberation theology.

Given these experiences, suppositions and principles that together help to define the "world" of liberation theology, we may now ask how these themes interact to form a method for theological understanding. An interpretation of the method of liberation theology will be the subject of the next two chapters.

Chapter II
THE PROBLEM OF HISTORY
AND THE FUNDAMENTAL
STRUCTURE OF THEOLOGY

Liberation theology, like any theology, is built on a whole host of suppositions and principles that continuously enter into its argument and suffuse its understanding of reality. In the last chapter I enumerated some of these suppositions in order simply to bring them to the surface as a help to understand this theology. In this chapter I shall extend the analysis of liberation theology further by interpreting what might be called its fundamental logic. In what follows I will try to draw the lines of the elementary structure of this theology in terms of the most basic issue and insight around which all the suppositions and principles revolve. What I propose to show is that most generally liberation theology is a Christian response to the central problem of our times, the problem of the meaning of history.

Before moving ahead with this, it may be helpful to reflect briefly on the intentionality of this interpretation itself. It was said earlier that the theme of these chapters is the attempt to look at liberation theology systematically. To the extent a theology becomes systematic and coherently argued, it should at the same time take on a more universal character and scope. Thus one of the points of this chapter is to see the problem to which liberation theology is a response from a broader and wider cultural perspective than one that would be limited to a Latin American or even a southern point of view.

One of the claims of liberation theology is that it is not merely another particularly focused theology. It is not of the same character, for example, as a theology of work or a theology of play. Rather liberation theology intends to have a bearing on the way all Christian theology is formulated; liberation theology addresses and seeks to have an impact on the whole of Christianity. As Gutiérrez has said, the question to which liberation theology responds has to do with the meaning of Christianity itself.[1] If this be the case, as I believe it is, then one has to say that it is not just or simply a local theology. Liberation theology has implications for Christianity as such and hence for a more general theological interpretation, and not merely for Latin America or the third world.

There is always a tension between particular experience and expression of it on the one hand, and the universal implications of that experience on the other. The supposition here is not that liberation theology as developed in Latin America is not a local theology adapted to that context and situation. It is a particular interpretation of Christianity. But it is not merely that. Nor is it being implied here that liberation theology as it has been developed in Latin America can be internalized in other places of the world without adjustments. The particularities of liberation theology and its rhetoric and language do not exactly fit other historical situations. But what is being said here is that liberation theology has a universal dimension as does all truth, and that this universal or worldwide character can be ferreted out and disclosed.

It may be thought that the universal dimension of liberation theology is to be found within the phenomenon of mass poverty, suffering and oppression to which it is a response. Although poverty and social injustice are unevenly distributed, these phenomena are certainly worldwide. Thus there is more than a small degree of truth in this view; liberation theology responds to the universal dimensions of human sin that are everywhere manifest in the social oppression of human beings. But at the same time there are some indications that liberation theology is sectarian. In this reading liberation theology would not appear as a universally applicable interpretation of Christianity. Some questions which give rise to this feeling need to be answered. For example, is the liberation movement and its theology addressed equally to the poor and to the rich? In some places in Latin America middle class Christianity remains untouched by liberation theology; this view of Christian faith is not directly addressed to these sectors, so that in many ways there exist two distinct churches with two quite distinct interpretations of what it means to be a Christian. Is liberation theology, because of its concern for the poor, really an interpretation for a specific class, or a third or southern world phenomenon where poverty and oppression are quantitatively more acute, visible and demanding? Again, liberation theology has been criticized theoretically for being partisan, and to this extent un-Christian. One thinks of such slogans as "God is on the side of the poor."[2] This chapter will try to respond to these questions by looking for a level of common contemporary human experience, of both the wealthy and the poor, of people of, at least potentially, every continent to which the liberationist interpretation of Christianity corresponds.

Liberation theology must begin to open itself up to the whole world. It must begin to generalize its vision. At this moment the main issue should not be the attempt to differentiate this theology off from the theologies in other parts of the world, notably northern theology. By and large liberation theology is beginning to find a certain sympathetic response in Europe and North America, at least among some segments of the Church. Thus liberation theology should be placed in dialogue with other theologies that share common suppositions, and bridges should be built in the light of common experience and common problems. Liberation theology cannot survive as a merely local theology.

The project here, then, is to see liberation theology as not merely attached to the problems and factors that were responsible for its genesis in the concrete situation of Latin America, at least not insofar as they are local and particular. It is an attempt to see the basis of the liberationist interpretation of Christianity in a deeper and hence broader common human and cultural experience. This is not a negation of the particular and real problems to which liberation theology is a response. Rather it is a reaffirmation of them but from a higher point of view and a broader cultural context that seeks to be inclusive.

To begin I will recall the actual historical genesis of liberation theology in Latin America and some of the perceptions that accompanied this development. Any interpretation of liberation theology should also account for and be faithful to these initial self-defining phenomena. The argument will then gradually broaden or expand the horizon of interpretation in an effort to define the problem or crisis of our time in which all human beings participate, which all of us share. And, finally, one will then be able to see the "whole" of liberation theology as a response to this fundamental human dilemma or issue. In other words, the most fundamental logic or structure of the liberationist interpretation of Christianity is to be seen in its attempt to respond to the general and common human crisis of our age.

THE GENESIS OF LIBERATION THEOLOGY

Historically liberation theology arose in Latin America as a human response to the large-scale human suffering that is so manifest there.[3] Liberation theology in its first moment was and is a reaction, a reaction against the naked poverty that assails the lives of so many human beings in the southern continent. Thus it arose as a theology of the poor, for the poor, on the side of the poor, committed to the liberation of those who are literally in capitivity. The poverty in question is not merely the poverty of each individual person, but also a social condition of masses of people. Moreover this condition is not a question of fate or natural necessity. It is due rather to human causes, to cultural, social and political factors which can be identified and which can be changed. Thus liberation theology is concerned with human oppression, and its development has been closely tied with social analysis, and in Latin America with the theory of dependence. Although the various theories of dependence may be convincing, and as important as these analyses in fact are, it is also important to realize that liberation theology does not itself depend on them. The ultimate validity of no theology depends on a social or economic analysis of human existence. The primary human response that generated liberation theology positively speaking is concern for the poor.[4]

This reaction to concrete human beings who are suffering, now seen as together constituting a vast social fact and condition, is not merely an emotional experience. Involved in this experience is a perception and judgment concerning nature, human existence and being itself. In its first moment this judgment is negative. In general terms, but relative to the particular situation, the content of the judgment may be expressed in the following way: "This should not be the case." Thus judgment may be colored with sentimental emotion or outraged anger, but in either case its underlying theme is epistemologically certain: human beings should not, and a fortiori should not be forced to, live in conditions that are dehumanizing, that is, which attack the very foundations of life itself and life that is characteristically human. At bottom this human reaction, perception and judgment is ontological. However implicitly it makes a statement about the reality of our finite world and the nature of human life in it.[5]

This negative judgment implies as well a positive affirmation, since the very certainty of the negation lies over against a positive horizon that allows the negative to appear as precisely negative. Why should not human beings live like lower forms of life? Why should not the segment of humanity which has power allow or force other people to suffer? The implied response is the conviction that the human person has something of an autonomous and absolute value. Poverty that attacks human life itself is itself to be attacked. Human existence is essentially constituted as free, as reflective and self-determining, as critical and creative. Oppression that kills the possibility and the actuality of freedom, that suppresses this potentiality and attacks human life at its essential point, should itself be aggressively resisted. The fundamental intuition behind this judgment is one that sees the humanity of human existence lying in or as constituted by freedom and considers this freedom sacred.

These perceptions are not necessarily Christian, and Gutiérrez reports that at the outset of the liberation movement in Latin America many who were not Christian considered the concern for liberation at odds with the established Church and with Christianity itself as they knew it. Some Christians in turn felt that one had to choose between an active involvement with the poor and commitment to Christianity and the Church.[6] In other words, this concern for the poor is first of all a profound human response, based on a conviction and human aspiration with a long human tradition. And over against this, the Church at any given time may become detached from this tradition and from its actual historical situation; in its theology and institutional structure it may actually become an obstacle to human liberation on a corporate or social historical level. And this is in fact the criticism of the post-Tridentine and colonial Church made by liberation theologians. But, once again, this negative perception reflects and fuels a positive desire and a demand of Christian faith to bring Christianity, the Church and its theology into relation to the actual contemporary historical situation of poverty and human suffering that are due to the oppression of social injustice. Liberation theology was thus born of faith, but within a broader cultural movement based on human aspirations for freedom.

The genesis of liberation theology can be explained by the most obvious and prosaic formulas concerning doctrinal development. Liberation theology in Latin America is simply the inculturation and reinterpretation of Christianity in terms of the actual or contemporary historical situation and experience of that continent. As such the genesis of liberation theology reflects a law that has become more and more operative in an explicit way in modern culture since the Enlightenment. With the breakdown of an extrinsicist notion of this-worldly religious authority, unless a Church and its authority can illumine concrete actual historical experience, it becomes in that same measure irrelevant and negligible. It loses comprehensibility; it does not make sense. Positively, Christian theology must address common social human experience in each age and culture. This implies that Christianity must be reinterpreted in terms corresponding to and illuminating the problems or crises of each age.

THE PROBLEM UNDERLYING LIBERATION THEOLOGY

What is the problem or issue that underlies liberation theology? In responding to this question an effort will be made to reach beyond and beneath the actual historical oppression that characterizes Latin America and increasingly so much of our world. In order to show the universal significance of liberation theology one must try to find the more general and anthropological and universally religious issue which a theology addresses. As a first probe into this question, it may be said that the antitheses between southern and northern theologies, which it is claimed are addressing different fundamental religious issues, may be seen rather in terms of complementarity and correlativity.

To begin, it is good to recall the changes that have occurred in theology in the past leading up to the present. In the modern period philosophy shifted from an objective and a physical or naturalist point of view to a subjective and anthropological one. And gradually through the nineteenth century theology too in its liberal form became more and more based on religious experience and less on external authority. Theology became more aware of the historicity of human experience and the close relation that Christianity and the Church in their actual forms bore to history and the world. By and large these currents were prevented from having an impact on Roman Catholic theology until the eve of the Second Vatican Council. During the nineteenth century the Catholic Church seemed to cut itself off from modern, secular and intellectual culture. The First Vatican Council, with its emphasis on authority, and the condemnation of modernism, with its implicit fear of development and change, are two of the landmarks of this retrenchment. By contrast, Vatican Council II marks a significant turning point if not reversal for the Church and its theology along this line of development. And the document on the Church in the modern world is the focusing symbol for the opening up of the Catholic Church to the modern world, toward history, society and the problems raised by modern culture.

In the theology that has followed the Council, Sobrino sees two distinct lines or currents that underlie contemporary theology which are defined by two different sets of problems. Both are signals of a crisis of religious faith in God. The first comes from the experience of the autonomy of human existence, which is seen or formulated in terms of secularization, knowledge, science and technology over against God. Typically modern experience raises the question and the problem of belief: Can one believe in a scientific age? Can God be known at all? Does one need God? In a sense this crisis is symbolized by Immanuel Kant and the problem of religious knowledge he left for western thought. The other problem is symbolized by Karl Marx. The context of this crisis is the perception that history and society are ruled by material and economic laws, if not also motives. Not only is social human existence autonomous from God, but religion plays a negative function in being a factor in the oppression that characterizes history. Here the problem is not simply one of belief, but one of confronting the situation of oppression and human misery that history and society have bequeathed us. Liberation theology is concerned with this second problem; the academic theology of the northern countries is concerned with the first.[7]

There is some truth to this analysis. There is a level at which one can see that these distinct questions are thematizing the two different kinds of theology in question. But at the same time these two divergent themes can and should be mediated and even merged; on a deeper level one can see how they converge. On the one hand, the problem of belief or faith in God is not a problem of rational knowledge; it is recognized today that commitment to God does not lie there alone. The question of faith is not decided by an extended argument or a book that claims to have demonstrated that God is or that God-talk is meaningful. Rather it depends almost solely on whether Christian faith as a social or public phenomenon is meaningful. Increasingly people will believe or not believe to the extent that systems of belief are experienced by people as meaningful or not for their human lives. But on the other hand, the problem of oppression and human suffering is also a problem for belief in God. Human suffering has always been the greatest mortal threat to the doctrine of God, and the experience today of the massive character of that suffering is the greatest block to any belief in a provident Creator God. Issues such as the nature of God and God's providence need explanation. If one is dealing with theology, the problems of God and belief in God and problems of human suffering and oppression are in no way divergent themes; today they merge and include each other.

Gutiérrez too has proposed, and often repeated, that theology in the developed nations is fundamentally different from liberation theology. Like Sobrino, he sees northern theology as dominated by the problem of faith in a secularized and even materialistic consumer society and culture. How is one to mediate God to a satisfied society? The problem of Latin American and liberation theology is not the problem of God or faith in God. Rather it is the problem of the non-person, the oppressed and disenfranchised, and how Christianity responds to them in their situation.[8]

There is an obvious truth in this observation as well. It appears in the contrast between the deeply engrained cultural religiosity of the majority of ordinary people in Latin America and the degree to which a large portion of people are sophisticatedly agnostic or atheistic in the more technologically advanced northern cultures. It is also manifest in the degree to which believers in our culture wrestle with skepticism and doubt.

But on a deeper level these two problems also can be seen to merge. This is so because once again the non-person in God's creation and under God's providence does challenge acceptance of these doctrines and ultimately faith in God himself. The retort that it is human beings that cause oppression and not God, although true enough, does not relieve the mystery. The doctrine of creation implies a total and absolute dependence of the whole of reality on God, so that the very existence of evil, and especially the moral evil that lies embedded in each and all of us, is profoundly disturbing to the questioning mind. The human recognition of and submission to a sense of guilt implied in the doctrine of sin do not adequately remove the mystery of human suffering. The existence of moral evil and human suffering must somehow be acknowledged and incorporated into one's belief in God, and this amounts to a problem for any belief in God.[9]

On the other side, however, liberation theologians have pointed out how religion itself and the Christian Church have contributed to this oppression. Liberation theology has shown the degree to which some forms of Christian faith are still a source of deep conservativism, both personal and institutional, relative to oppressive structures and social change. In attempting to mediate God, to explain who and what God is and what faith in God entails, has northern theology attended to the oppressive and dehumanizing possibilities in religious faith? While liberation theologians have not felt the need to argue to the existence of God in a religious culture, they have at least meditated deeply on the nature of God and Christian faith.

In sum, on the one hand oppression and the problem of the non-person is an intrinsic challenge to any faith in God. Liberation theology should see this and deal with these issues on a critical level. Liberation theology has shown that massive poverty and social oppression on a continent dominated by Christianity and the Church for four centuries is a scandal to Christian faith. It has to deal with the depth of that scandal to Christian and Church commitment on a level that goes beyond popular religiosity. On the other hand, northern theology must be critical of the concept of God it attempts to mediate and of the institutions it implicitly defends in so doing. One cannot deal with faith in God today without dealing with the very notion and concept of God in relation to human suffering and oppression. Theology has to include the contemporary phenomena of massive human suffering and oppression into its reflection on the causes of skepticism and unfaith. In short, the problem of human suffering is also the problem of God for theology. In other words, the theological issues of our time come to a focus in the problem of history as a history of suffering, oppression and liberation.

THE PROBLEM OF THE MEANING OF HUMAN HISTORY

What is the problem of history? It has been implied that the problem of history is the common broader cultural crisis to which the theologies of both the southern and northern tiers must respond. In what follows I shall try in a brief statement to explain why this is the common cultural and human context for all of Christian theology today. In effect the problem of history is really the problem or question of human existence itself, when human existence is seen from the point of view of historicity and participation in a common social process.

We may begin by looking back at some of the suppositions that are characteristic of modern culture and which are presuppositions common to both liberation theology and much of contemporary theology. I pass over some of the more general suppositions seen in Chapter I which are also important here, such as acceptance of a certain secularization, a recognition of the value of life in this world, and the practical character of theology. But more central to the discussion here are the following three ideas: first, freedom as the essence of human existence; second, the historical character of human existence; third, the social character of human existence. In all of this the term "human existence" applies equally to the individual person and to the whole of human existence taken generally or corporately.

Let us assume with liberation theology that the essence of human existence may be described as freedom. Over against the animal world, the human form of existence is free. Rationality is essential to this difference, but rationality may be taken as intrinsic to human freedom, constitutive of it and in service to it. To be human is to be free. Human existence is the ability to stand back from matter and nature, to transcend it even in ourselves, the ability to consider, judge and make decisions, to create new things, to take responsibility, to change, to make oneself and the world different, and, if possible, better. Freedom is both self-fulfillment and surrender to ideals and values outside of the self. Of course freedom may be seen as both potentiality and actuality. But freedom becomes actual, historical and real in its exercise, in the achievement in one degree or another of what the potentiality is for.

Second, this human existence is historical; it unfolds concretely in or through time. Freedom does not occur all at once, but is a potentiality that becomes a reality through nurture over time; it grows and develops. It needs exercise, practice, new experiences and discipline. It is at once open-ended but limited by time and space and the life cycle; it has a beginning, a fullness and a tapering off. It moves through time toward an end in the Christian view of things, and fulfillment is not to be seen as occurring completely or only out of this world. Rather freedom has a value and an appointed fullness and purpose even as it moves through time.

Third, human existence is also essentially and inescapably social. This is so because we are open subjects always in conscious dialogue with the world and other human beings. We are individuals with a personal and unique center, but we are also just as absolutely subjects whose central ego is shaped and formed into what it really or actually is through interchange with the world and especially other people. Human existence occurs and unfolds in solidarity; we are what and who we are through our relations to others taken as individuals and collectively as society.

Now the problem of human existence appears when the free, historical and social human phenomenon is looked at in the concrete terms of its actuality which is so characterized by poverty, by oppression of freedom and by sheer human suffering. What is most important here is the *extent* of this suffering, that is, in terms of the quantity and masses of people who are victimized, and the *degree* of it, that is, its quality and the level of actual crippling and mortal effects this suffering attains. In other words, human suffering characterizes or is the lot of an enormous portion of the human race. The problem of human existence appears when one compares essential human existence with the concrete and actual reality of human existence.

First, what does it mean to say that human existence is freedom if so many human beings are in fact not free? If human beings are immersed in nature, as Freire puts it, and have a fated reality and view of life, what does freedom mean in this situation?[10] If huge proportions of humankind are bound to the material world, to the task of searching for food, clothing and shelter each day, not in the forest but in urban centers throughout the world, what does freedom mean in their regard? If there is any freedom in such human existence, if there is any responsibility and decision making, is it any different from that which would be exercised in captivity? If freedom implies a being directed or attracted by some goal, something ahead that one can choose and strive for, and it is this that gives meaning to human life, what meaning can life with no options have? The freedom of countless human beings does not reach the level of actuality in the sense of autonomous, self-conscious and deliberate activity. Due to their actual social situation, the potentiality itself of freedom becomes ever more hardened by deprivation, deadened by mechanical routine and numbed by suffering.[11]

Second, human existence is freedom over time; it becomes what it is and is to be through and over time. What does human existence mean in those innumerable lives that are choked off or ended at birth, before five years old, before ten, before the end of adolescence? And what does human freedom mean for those adult lives which have no dimension of time because life is an endless repetition within limits that are perceptible, that is, literally defined in terms of space and the objects that surround them? A future dimension is essential to time, and hence to freedom. Human existence or life or freedom without a future is static, dead-ended and to that extent unfree, for it lacks in the concrete that openness to what is new and ahead of it which is the potentiality itself of freedom that is characteristically human. At this point eschatology gives no relief to the problem of the meaning of historical existence in this world. The affirmation of an absolute future that occurs after this life and outside this world does provide grounds for hope. But it offers no explanation for this-worldly history as such. If the question concerns the actual meaning and value of time spent in this world, talk of an absolute future as its only saving hope in fact compounds the problem, for it implicitly ratifies the meaninglessness of human life in time.

Third, the decisive point is seen in the fact that all human beings share in this general situation because all share a common human existence. This philosophical and Christian conviction of the unity of the human race is gradually becoming an empirical historical datum. We are mixed up with one another socially on a global scale. Human existence is interdependent existence, and that interdependence is becoming actual in new and unprecedented ways. Each of us is part of the race; all of us participate in a common human nature that is an historical existence. And now the enormous variety of human groups throughout the world are directly influencing each other. Human solidarity has become actual. Thus social oppression, mass poverty, and intense human suffering raise questions of the meaning of human existence for everyone and in a new and personal way.

This point may seem subtle but it can be illustrated in terms of the Christian hope for final salvation. Individual people cannot say that their lives have meaning because they are going to be saved in the end even if others are not. One cannot affirm, one has absolutely no ground for affirming, one's own possible salvation without affirming the possibility for all. To do so would involve a denial of the most basic Christian truths. It would contradict the Christian view of God loving all equally. It would implicitly deny that one is part of a common humanity, that one shared in common human sinfulness. It would be an assertion of my worth and the non-worth of other human beings. On what grounds could such an attitude be possible? How could one hope for one's own personal salvation and at the same time be willing to expect that this possibility was not open to all or expect that it would not be fulfilled in the greater portion of humankind?

One need only shift this logic to the question of the meaningfulness of human existence within history itself. Thus similarly one cannot affirm that there is meaning in my human existence, even though the human existence of half the race seems meaningless, pointless, valueless, leading nowhere, absurd. If one participates in a common human existence, then the value, worth, importance and meaningfulness of each one is called into question by the massiveness of the seeming senseless existence of so many of us. Any assertion or conviction of my personal salvation here and now, and a finding of a complete fulfilled personal human existence, that is, over against and in spite of the actual condition of the larger segment of human beings, is illogical, and, one must suspect, egoistic and grasping. It can only be achieved by a compartmentalization of consciousness, a shutting out of and a refusal to engage a major and obvious sphere of reality.

It should be clear at this point that the issue of the social existence of humanity is a theological problem. Anthropology and theology become one at this point. The existence of vast amounts of human suffering and oppression, of fated and unfree existence, calls into question both the meaning of human existence itself and the reality of a God that is claimed to grant it meaning from the outside. The sheer existence of massive unfree and closed human existence demands an inquiry into the nature of God, Creator and provident.[12] Moreover, the continuance of this actual and real situation calls into question the reality of the salvation mediated by Christ, at least relative to our historical existence. The temptation is to surrender to the problem, and to consign it to Fate. Surely a personal God could not cause by creation the huge amounts of poverty and suffering that are witnessed today. And even if God is not the cause of this situation, if a great deal of this suffering is due really to human beings preying on others, what relevance, what utility does God have in and for this actual situation? Many today opt for the Stoic solution, mediated to us again by the Enlightenment, and so courageously expressed by Freud at the end of his *The Future of an Illusion*.[13] Freed from a transcendent God, freed from the mystification of evil,[14] human beings may attack human suffering in the name of the immanent god of reason. Yet this is not really a solution and we are left with a dilemma. For without God, how is one to then justify any intrinsic value of human existence? Where are any grounds for the ideals of fraternity and sorority that we wish to project on and into corporate human existence to be found, since they are so obviously lacking in reality?

The problem for Christian theology today may be summed up in the following way, borrowing terms from Paul Tillich. Tillich wrote that the tradition of Christian theology could be understood in terms of three problems that underlie the great epochs of Christian thought.[15] The classical period of the Fathers stretching through the medieval period was characterized by the problem of mortality and death. It saw salvation in eternal life and incorruptibility. The Reformation period was preoccupied with guilt and saw salvation in God's gracious forgiveness witnessed to in Christ. Today's crisis, he said, in an age of historical consciousness, pluralism and relativity, is the crisis of meaning. This he understood in a personalist existential way. I am suggesting that today we realize that existence is social historical existence and that the crisis of meaning arises out of the seemingly meaningless existence that society and history has imposed on the majority of the human race. This requires a new explanation because it is a scandal even for those who accept God, Christ and salvation understood as eternal life. The problem of human existence is the problem of historical social existence in which we all share. Thus this is not only a problem of the poor. It is a problem of meaning for every thinking person who pauses to consider it.[16]

A RESPONSE TO THE PROBLEM OF HISTORY

The previous paragraphs explained how the problem underlying liberation theology may be seen as generalizable. This issue is not just the problem of Latin America, but the problem of human existence itself, of all human beings. It is the sharp threat that actual historical and social human existence is indeed without any ultimate meaning or value, however much private meaning and personal satisfaction individuals might grasp at for themselves and those immediately around them here and now by shutting out the larger questions and issues. In response to this crisis it is possible at the outset to outline in very general terms the response to this problem that is contained in Christianity according to the liberationist interpretation of it. The most basic structure of liberation theology can be seen as a response to this problem. That response consists in two elements. The first is God and the second is the salvation of God, as revealed in Jesus Christ, and understood as a process of humanization.

First of all, liberation theology, like all Christian theology, affirms that God is the ground of the meaning of human existence and hence of historical existence. As the ground of actual existence, and not just of being as such, God is the basis of the meaning of that existence. This must be accepted in faith and trust; the acceptance of the existence of

God does not wipe away the problem that has been described, but must be affirmed in the face of it in faith and in doubt at the same time. However one must say more about God since the concept of God has been used in the past to accentuate the problem.

God, according to Christianity, is one who is concerned for human existence. This is the witness of the whole biblical tradition which finds its climax in Jesus. From our point of view, in accordance with what God has revealed of God's own self in the Christian tradition, God is love-for-human-beings. The situation of human existence, therefore, may also be viewed as a problem for God in the sense that the situation is not according to God's plan or active will. Rather God offers the race salvation from this situation. The very being of God then is both Creator and Savior, from the very beginning, and not just since the time of Jesus. The whole of history, in spite of its apparent meaninglessness and in the face of it, is, or at least could be, a history of salvation. The question is: In what does this salvation consist?

The salvation that God offers must be understood in anthropological terms. This appears inescapable epistemologically. It is impossible to conceive of other terms in which it could be thought. In such terms salvation appears as the completion and fulfillment of human existence. Salvation in its most general or basic terms would consist in the fullness of human freedom—not only the introverted satisfaction of freedom's delight in total good, but the opening up of the human spirit to an absolute submission and responsible commitment to what is absolutely valuable. This is the classic response of a Greek, medieval and teleological interpretation of salvation, and at this broadest and most fundamental level, recast in terms of human freedom, it probably cannot be improved upon.

However this formulation as it stands is not sufficient; it does not by itself guarantee a meaning to historical human existence. On the contrary, it may precisely undermine that meaning. In itself it is an affirmation of fullness of life after human existence in this world is over, at the end and outside of history. But what we seek and demand is a meaning to social existence here and now, in the actuality of the world as it unfolds in time. To affirm meaning only outside of history is precisely to negate any ultimate value or meaning to life in itself as we presently experience it. Salvation then must have a meaning that can be read in historical terms; it must also be understood within the fabric of historical life itself and not simply beyond it.

Human existence, it was said earlier, stretches out through or across time. Human existence as historical therefore is a process or movement.

As such, history and human life can only have meaning if it has a direction, and its intrinsic purpose is its direction. In this scheme of things, salvation appears as the direction and goal toward which history is moving; salvation is life's purpose. But this means, reciprocally, that the salvation which is the goal of history is not merely external to history; it is at the same time internal and active within it. Salvation is not just an extrinsic term outside human history; it is also its intrinsic motive, its reason for being, and its meaningful or meaning-giving power. Salvation is not just a goal but also a process, or a possible process, within history itself. There cannot be complete discontinuity between history and its goal, or else the process of history and living human life in it would be intrinsically valueless. Whatever the discontinuity between history and final salvation may be, it is not total, and salvation is also operative within concrete history itself.

To interpret that salvation further, liberation theology portrays it as identical with a process of humanization. Humanization here means a movement toward a greater degree of human freedom, the essence of what it means to be human. In this it agrees with a variety of secular humanisms. But whereas the ground for such an affirmation or interpretation is unclear in secular humanism, liberation theology finds its ground in God as God is revealed in the actual life of Jesus of Nazareth and confirmed in the experience of his resurrection. The process of humanization occurs in history when human freedom is opened up and allowed to expand in possibility and option, rational deliberation and choice, the discovery of truth and value that leads to creative action. Because the essence of human existence is freedom, the process of humanization is liberation, the process of becoming free and responsible. Salvation in this world, in history, is liberation, and its ultimate goal is final liberation and freedom.

It should be recalled that this formulation is stated in very general and objective terms. To say that salvation in history is a process of liberation is equivalent to talking about objective salvation, or to talking about salvation objectively. Nothing has been said yet about subjective salvation, how one appropriates and participates in this inner meaning and substance of history.[17] But, finally, one can see here that the term "liberation" in response to the question of the meaning of history has a much profounder meaning than that which a contrast to the idea of "development" or a "theory of dependence" would assign it. It describes a process that may give meaning to human existence itself when viewed historically and socially.

THE SALVIFIC MEANING OF HISTORY IN PRAXIS

Up to this point it may seem quite arbitrary to assign salvation as the absolute end of history and to project it as the active substance of history in the face of its obvious and apparent negation. But for liberation theology it is apparent that this salvation is at work in history. Why or how is this the case? The response to this question is probably the most significant insight that liberation theology has to contribute to the real problem of history or historical human existence. According to it, the meaning of history assigned to it by Christianity lies in or is constituted by praxis.[18]

In the light of the experience of historicity and our historical consciousness, history appears today as arbitrary in the past and open-ended into the future. There can be no complete philosophy of history, it is often said, until history is completed. The logic of history, then, and the inner meaning of historical life, both ours personally and that of the race over its millennia, are really created or constituted by history itself. The idea of providence as a prefabricated plan that is simply being unfolded is unacceptable to contemporary consciousness. Such a conception could not be reconciled either with human experience of history or the Christian conception of God. History's meaning is really created for us by ourselves, by human beings, as we swerve headlong out of the past and into the future.

If this be the case, it follows that the meaning of history, that is, the meaning of collective human freedom, will only appear in history when human beings create that meaning. It follows that the Christian meaning of history, which consists in its liberation and salvation, is only real to the extent that it becomes actual. Or to put this in less Pelagian terms, salvation only occurs, or only actually becomes the meaning of history, when human beings are its agents.[19] Without actual efforts at a process of humanization and liberation, not only would the affirmation of such a process be gratuitous and unfounded, but that salvation would not even exist. At least a salvation that responded to the problem of history would not exist. Morally good, free and integral human individuals might exist, who thus appeared as apparently "saved," but precisely insofar as they did not participate in a struggle to alleviate the inhuman conditions that mark the lot of the majority of the human race, they would actually testify once again to the senselessness of *social* and *historical* human existence by their standing apart from these problems.[20]

In the light of historicity and the existential openness of historical processes, then, two things become clear. The first is the meaning of the term "praxis"; the second is the reason why theory and praxis are bound together in Christian theology. Praxis does not simply mean action, behavior or practice. Rather it means a particular form of historical behavior, not of course blind or unmixed with reason or theory. Its meaning supposes the broad and general truth that history is in some degree in human hands, that it is moved neither by blind fate, nor by a closed set of laws, nor by a predetermined providence. History is open and in some measure can be directed by human beings. Moreover this history is meant to move in the direction away from human imprisonment, enslavement and oppression of human freedom toward greater liberty and personal and social freedom. Praxis is behavior that is a participation in this movement of history; it is a practice or behavior or struggle to increase freedom in society.[21]

Second, theory and praxis are bound together in the Christian liberationist affirmation of salvation within history. That salvation is affirmed and is real and is experienced as such when one is actually engaged in work for increased social justice and freedom. It would be arbitrary to affirm salvation in history if one did not experience it. But one experiences it precisely in and by participating in its actuality within history. Salvation is the substance of meaningful history for those who participate in this process. The theory of Christian salvation in history cannot be separated from the actuality, and the actuality is only apparent in praxis.

CONCLUSION

What has been said in this chapter can be recapitulated in a very few words. The effort has been to generalize beyond the Latin American context the germinal insights of liberation theology. This has been done here with respect to the problem which accounts for the rise or the genesis of liberation theology. Liberation theology developed as a reaction against and a Christian response to the problem of the suffering of the poor in Latin America. Can this theology also be seen as a response to a more general and human crisis? Is not liberation theology a response to the human and hence theological crisis of our time, namely, the problem of history?

The problem of history is the problem of human existence itself, and of God, once human life is seen concretely in its historical and social reality. That problem appears when one looks at what Metz has called the underside of history and the actual extent of human suffering and oppression that exists in our world today. That problem has become intensified for us today; it is a permanent intrinsic scandal to Christian faith. But the liberationist interpretation of Christianity does present a response to that problem from within faith itself, one that is self-consistent, and, although apparently incredible to one who stands outside of faith, convincing to those who share this faith. But here faith involves a form of praxis, a mode of being and acting in the world. This response says in the name of Jesus Christ that God is essentially Savior and that this salvation is operative as a process of humanization or liberation within history. This salvation gives meaning to history because it leads toward eternal life and because it gives meaning to history here and now as something that is meant to increase the capacity of human freedom itself. This humanization process will lead to absolute or final human fulfillment or freedom. But the condition for affirming this experientially, meaningfully and with conviction is praxis, that is, participation in the historical movement itself.[22]

In sum, if there is a central and centering problem for the whole of Christian theology today, it is the crisis of the meaning of human history. This issue is comprehensive, and it encompasses and unifies the problematic underlying both northern and southern theologies. The fundamental logic and structure of a liberationist interpretation of Christianity for our time, then, can be seen as a response to this crisis. It says that salvation given by God is a process of humanization in this world, in history. Moreover this is actually experienced insofar as one participates in this process by some form of praxis. That is, the actual involvement in this process constitutes the experience of it. And, finally, Jesus Christ, as the focusing symbol of specifically Christian faith in God, is the reference point for this conviction or ultimate concern. Given this elementary structure for Christian understanding today, in the next chapter I will look at the method of theology that is implied in it.

Chapter III
METHOD IN THEOLOGY IN THE LIGHT OF LIBERATION THEOLOGY

In the last chapter it was proposed that the problem of history is the human and theological crisis of our epoch. The massive human poverty and oppression in our time, both the amount of it and the degree of the damage it does to human life, calls into question the very meaning of human existence and hence our faith. This chapter will consider the method of the theology that has to reckon with this problem.

To begin it will be useful to say a word about theology itself. Theology as it is understood here is not simply talk about God. Nor is theology simply reflection on faith, either subjective faith or faith understood as the doctrines that make up the content of Christian religion. Nor is the definition that makes theology reflection on the praxis of faith sufficient. Theology is better defined as reflection on reality in the light of Christian faith. Since faith informs the whole of a person's human life, theology seeks to understand the nature of the whole of human existence, the world and God in the light of the symbols of Christian faith. By far the greater portion of theological literature is not directly about God. Theology moreover is a discipline and has always been understood as such. Therefore pragmatically theology is what theologians do, and in general that may be understood as the disciplined or methodical reflection on reality in the light of Christian faith. Although all intelligent Christians reflect on their faith at one time or another, and implicitly are doing so all the time, it would be confusing to say that every Christian is a theologian. Hence the disciplined, systematic or methodical character of theology is understood as a presupposition in this inquiry.

If theology is disciplined inquiry, the question of the method that is employed becomes extremely important. However the term "method" itself can be understood in a variety of ways. For example, it is often used to refer to how the development of an argument unfolds as this

43

would be reflected in the outline of a work or a table of contents. Method in this case refers to the approach taken to a subject, or the order in which topics are treated. It is an organizational concept. But method here is used in a much deeper sense to indicate the fundamental structure of theological understanding and statement. Method in this sense refers to the way one understands, the suppositions of theological knowing and how these are brought to bear on the very sources of Christian affirmation. So basic is this question that it will influence the content of theology, that is, precisely the way it is understood. "The method used in arriving at the truth is itself a forward step within the bounds of truth."[1]

The question of method in theology is a very complex issue, and in a short space it cannot be expected that this issue will be dealt with adequately. The intention here is to treat this question very generally and to point to a very basic methodological structure that is commonly agreed upon among contemporary theologians. Even when there is disagreement in detail, the fundamental structure of theological method that will be described here is usually at work. Once again, the aim is to seek a level of general acceptance even though this will leave a great number of nuances unattended and further important questions unanswered. In the first part of this chapter some of the major themes concerning method in theology from liberation theology will be enumerated. The main burden of the argument will be to explore how these may be integrated into a wider cultural and theological context. And in conclusion I will point to the general direction that a reinterpretation of the major Christian symbols will take when it assumes a liberationist method.

METHODOLOGICAL THEMES
FROM LIBERATION THEOLOGY

What are some of the methodological principles that underlie liberation theology? An enumeration of a number of the themes or axioms that govern the method of liberation theology is easily accomplished since liberation theology has from the beginning been quite self-conscious about its method.[2] This will not of course add up to a reconstruction of the method used in liberation theology; the point is simply to isolate and to underscore some of the major axioms or principles which are frequently cited as important in determining the structure of this thought.

First, it has already been seen that liberation theology in general is a response to the problem of the non-person in history. It is a response to the problem of history that is manifest in the social injustice and oppressive poverty that marks Latin America. Gutiérrez has further defined the problem underlying liberation theology in a series of questions all of which have as their underlying theme the relation of Christianity and Christian faith to human history and society.[3]

Second, the theory of dependence is another major theme in liberation theology that has a direct bearing on its method. This theory is the point of departure of many liberationist works, and often the term "liberation" is defined in this context.[4] In a word the theory of dependence sees the Latin American world in a dependent and oppressive relationship to the centers of the capitalist world. Moreover this structure is internalized within the dependent countries where the wealthy few, who are the agents of the industrialized centers, maintain a system that keeps the masses in a dependent and oppressive poverty. Insofar as these concepts of dependence and liberation describe the reality of Latin America specifically, they provide a good example of a particularist point of departure for theology. And this raises the question of whether or not this particular situation or reality might be rethought on a more general and even anthropological level. Is this dependence and bondage characteristic of human existence itself so that it may be used as a question for understanding Christianity beyond the boundaries of Latin America?

Also the use of the theory of dependence is one example of a more pervasive methodological characteristic of liberation theology, namely, its use of social science and analysis in theological reflection and construction.[5] Theology, of course, is always influenced by its social and historical situation. But liberation theology allows disciplined social, political, economic and cultural analyses to explicitly enter into and come to bear on theological understanding. Theological understanding is thus related to the actual social and historical condition in which the reflection is done.

Third, the symbol of liberation itself is of course a central one in liberation theology. In a sense, the very nature of Christianity is being reinterpreted through the lens of the symbol of liberation. Thus the term "liberation," because it is so fundamental, functions at a number of different levels and illumines the experience of a number of different spheres of existence and reality. Gutiérrez, for example, has delineated three overlapping spheres or levels to which the symbol "liberation" refers. Liberation is a response to the problem of dependence; it points to freedom from concrete social oppressions. Liberation is also a more generalized symbol, pointing to a general theory of human history, the core of which is a process of humanization that is also a process of liberation. On a more strictly theological level, the symbol of liberation is used as an explicit hermeneutical principle for interpreting the meaning of Christian salvation. Salvation is a form of liberation, a liberation not exclusive but inclusive of the other spheres of liberation. They all interact.[6] In all of this, it is important to recall that the term "liberation" is being employed as a very profound religious symbol to interpret the central mystery of Christian grace and salvation. As such it is a rich and polyvalent symbol and its meaning cannot be reduced to a definition. What Gutiérrez has done is simply to isolate and then interrelate general spheres of meaning.

Fourth, the notion of praxis is central to the method of liberation theology. Theology has been defined as "critical reflection on liberation praxis."[7] In this understanding, faith itself is understood as constitutive of this praxis; and reversing this, liberation praxis is understood as constitutive of Christian faith which is itself a mode of life. Therefore theology is reflection on faith, the lived life of faith. This is a thoroughly consistent view of the nature of theology. It is also quite traditional if one recognizes that Christianity is primarily an historical movement consisting of the concrete lives of Christians that make up the corporate life of the Church. Theology through history is reflection on the corporate lives of Christians. But the shift occurs when Christian praxis is seen in terms that were discussed in the last chapter. Praxis is not just any behavior, but rather praxis for corporate liberation in society. Is there not some ambiguity here? The question might be asked whether other forms of faith, or forms of human behavior and practice that are informed by faith, might also be the basis of theological reflection. Can there not be a monastic theology or a theology based on the centering practice of the liturgy, both of which would lead in other directions? Thus there appears to be a circular argument, if not a begging of the question, when liberation theology defines itself as reflection on liberation praxis in order to understand Christian faith as a response to oppression. Can this point of departure for theology be justified in broader anthropological terms?

Fifth, the notion of a prior option for the poor is a very influential notion or theme in the method of liberation theology, defining as it does a kind of decisive attitudinal supposition for the whole theological enterprise. It is present in all of liberation theology but has been defended at length by Juan Luis Segundo.[8] On one level this prior option for the poor makes complete sense. If one accepts as central for today the problem of the meaning of history in the light of continued oppression, then the very acceptance of that as a problem involves a willingness, a desire and even a commitment to work against that oppression in favor of its victims. But on the level of an option understood as a concrete decision for action, such a decision, if it is to be responsible, already presupposes an analysis of social issues and an understanding of Christian faith that would make such a commitment grounded and effective. In short the question concerns the nature of this option and how it relates to theology in an a priori fashion.

Sixth, liberation theology is often described as precisely a method for doing theology. Less a body of content, it is an ongoing process of theological reflection that is structured by a continuous circle of action-understanding-action, or praxis-reflection-praxis. Out of the lived situation of ministerial and corporate liberation praxis, new insights and understandings are generated which lead back to praxis. On one level, the personal, this process may be understood as resting on a theory of knowledge and anthropology that is similar to that of the pragmatism of Maurice Blondel or of William James. On another level this process is accomplished by a community of subjects as in a basic community. Or it may even be used to describe the growth in awareness of a whole culture or society; it characterizes the general structure of the progress in knowledge of humanity. In liberation theology this process is quite narrowly defined in terms of the local or Latin American situation, but it may be understood more generally to apply to other situations as well. "Like every theology, it must be open to serving all human beings because that is part of its ecclesial essence."[9]

There are a good number of other things that should be said concerning method in liberation theology. The impression should not be given that with these points one has somehow summed up liberationist methodology. Still, given these themes and principles from liberation theology, the task here will be to see them in a broader cultural context. The movement will be a double one. It will extrapolate or project from these axioms in order to formulate a common understanding of method in theology in their light. And it will try to provide a general description of method in theology as it is commonly accepted today in such a way that it is informed by, is faithful to, and incorporates within itself these principles.

METHOD IN THEOLOGY IN THE LIGHT OF LIBERATION THEOLOGY

I would take the fundamental structure of some form of a method of correlation as generally characteristic of current Christian theology. This correlation involves bringing together two poles or areas of research, contemporary experience and the sources of Christian theology from the past. In what follows, then, I will look at each of these poles successively.

The Method of Correlation

The term "a method of correlation" is closely associated with the theology of Paul Tillich who, in his three volume *Systematic Theology,* outlined the method he uses in the work and labeled it a method of correlation.[10] Broadly described, Tillich saw the method of systematic theology consisting in a formulation of the question of human existence in the light of contemporary experience and philosophy to which the Christian message of revelation provided an answer in terms of its central symbols. Here the term "correlation" should not be understood in a strict Tillichian sense, neither as formulated by him as in principle a method of question and answer nor according to his actual execution of the method. Rather correlation simply means that adequate and intelligible method in theology today requires that the two poles of contemporary human experience, including religious experience, and of history, especially the record of the originating experiences of Christianity as found in Scripture, be held together in dialogue, tension, correlation with each other.[11] Indeed this method, formulated in these broad terms, has characterized all of the creative theology of the modern period beginning with the end of the eighteenth century. Even the theology of Karl Barth is a response to human culture, albeit a negative one, which contains far more borrowing from his contemporary world than his principles admit.

The first pole or element of a contemporary theology then is contemporary experience. The human experience referred to here is not simply personal experience, although that is not excluded. Rather it refers to a critical appropriation of more general human experience. It involves an analysis that tries to ferret out the common dimensions of human experience today. It would involve not only examining the psychological structures of our experience, but also the socially and culturally mediated aspects of human thought and experience. It would involve criticism of the common assumptions that are always at work in our experience and which are provided us by society and its ideologies. Moreover, since contemporary human experience forms the context and matrix for all our human understanding, one must begin theological understanding at this point. And, consequently, the first norm for any viable theology will be its adequacy or intelligibility relative to contemporary human experience.

The second pole or element of contemporary theological method consists of the Christian sources. These are the records of Christian experience in the past, especially Scripture and more particularly the New Testament. Since Christianity is an historical phenomenon, an adequate understanding of it necessarily includes an understanding of its genesis in history. And at the same time, these documents from the past, both Scripture and the whole history of Christian thought and experience, project forward toward the future a conception and a vision of human life in history. This tradition, then, is the very data of theology, that which has to be interpreted for today. But in so doing, theology must be faithful to the Christian message, to the inner meaning and logic of Christian teaching, even while that is being brought to bear on contemporary experience. A second norm for theology, then, must be fidelity to the Christian message as it appears in its sources.

The method of correlation, which is the bringing together of these two poles of the past and the present in a mutual dialogue and a constant tension, is not a mechanical process. It is not a step by step procedure which when followed yields automatically relevant and true results. Rather correlation is simply descriptive of the structure of theology and theological statement. If in fact it is followed by most theologians today, it becomes obvious that such a method allows for a great deal of variety in how it is actually carried out and great differences in result. Liberation theology uses a method of correlation, as is evident from all that has been said.[12] It is a basic hermeneutical structure, a method of interpretation and reinterpretation that requires fidelity to Christian sources and adequacy to human existence as it is experienced today. In all of this, there may be a general fear that beginning with our own contemporary experience and allowing our questions to be the interpreting factor of the meaning of the Christian message may intrinsically distort that message, since in general questions determine the response or interpretation that is given. This is indeed a danger, but it is also the price that must be paid, the risk that must be taken, to have an intelligible theology in our time. At the same time this caution is also a reminder that the Christian message from out of the past can confront and call into question our contemporary human experience. This is a theme from a theology of the Word such as Karl Barth's that has perennial value even within a method of correlation.

Contemporary Experience, Anthropology, and the Question for Christian Sources

Much of what may be called typically modern or contemporary human experience has already been seen in the analysis of the suppositions of liberation theology, for this is a thoroughly modern theology. How much of this experience comes to a religious focus was seen in the analysis of the problem of history, or of historical human existence to which liberation theology is a response. In that movement it was shown how our human experience today comes to a focus in the question of the meaning of human existence itself. But if human existence is a question to itself, a question that seeks an ultimate or absolute meaning-granting response, then the nature of human existence itself should be more carefully or systematically analysed. In a method of correlation in which theology begins with an analysis of human experience, anthropology becomes the hermeneutical condition for understanding the meaning of Christian revelation. And if a theology is to make any claim at comprehensiveness, the anthropology that underlies it must consist in more than simply a series of commonly recognized experiences. The Christian message should be seen in relation to a more adequate and systematically coherent and comprehensive view of human existence. Once again it is only the general and governing structure of such a systematic anthropology that will be presented here.[13]

Human existence can be understood comprehensively as freedom. The human spirit, that which makes the human human and the person a human person, is freedom. Human existence is conscious freedom in matter and in the world. But this freedom is also in bondage and captivity; it is limited and bound and even oppressed in its very condition of being free spirit. And this bound freedom can be seen at three levels, each one of which is constitutive of human reality itself. These three levels are the individual, the interpersonal and social, and finally the transcendent elements that constitute human existence.

The first aspect of human existence and at the same time level of human freedom is the individual or the strictly personal dimension of human life. Here is located the uniqueness of every individual person and his or her personal identity. I am not someone else. Potentially at least each person has an autonomy and responsibility for the self that are inalienable; each is a center of responsible activity, reflection, choice, decision and creativity through which a person makes himself or herself to be what each one is. At the same time, however, even at this level, human existence is limited and in bondage. The human spirit is dependent on matter; or, more descriptively, the human person is bound and determined by the human body and the surrounding physical world of nature. We are who we are because of the physical, biological and psychological determinants that make us this way and not another. Nor are we free to be anything else. The laws and determinants of nature which structure our freedom are ambivalent; they both limit freedom and release it; the nature both within and outside of the human spirit is the tool or instrument or material with which freedom operates. But physical and natural determinations can also choke off freedom and hold it prisoner. Freedom on the personal level, then, is a relative concept; some are more free than others.

The second aspect of human existence and level of human freedom is the interpersonal and the social. We are open subjects; our freedom opens out to the world in knowing and acting so that our being is being-in-relation-to-others. Spontaneous interpersonal relationships and especially the social relationships that are forged in larger groups and over time are meant to increase and release further the freedom of the human spirit. Human existence is lived in solidarity, and without the interpersonal and social structures, and the memory and socialization and routinization that they presume, life would be an impossible chaos. Social structures are meant to and really do nurture and promote the freedom and creativity and ensure the existence of human beings. As an example, one has only to think of the complex system of food supply in a large city. But there is also a great relativity in the freedom generated and afforded by the social structures of human life. Social structures vary greatly among themselves and promote human freedom unevenly; and in any given social arrangement people participate in very unequal ways. The same structure may afford great opportunity for human development for some and at the same time, and by this very fact, suppress the freedom of others, crushing it in the direction of non-existence.

The third aspect of human existence and level of human freedom is its transcendence. The freedom of the human spirit can and does stand outside itself or extend beyond the self, beyond the limits of society and the world, and reaches toward infinity. Here one sees the radicality and the depth of human freedom. It transcends the self by submitting itself to values and ideals, and implicitly to the ground of these ideals which is transcendent and absolute. This transcendent quality of human freedom is seen in the implicit logic of the basic trust that human beings possess in life itself. This trust postulates both a transcendent ground for human existence and a desire to be continuously and fully. We do not wish to cease to be. But this radically expansive character of human freedom, that reaches outward to what is true and good absolutely speaking, is also held in bondage. There is the bondage of mortality and death that is obvious enough. But also our freedom is bound by the judgment of our own ideals. We are condemned by the very ideal of the absolute good that our freedom reaches out for. All and in varying degrees are imprisoned in a radical concupiscence and selfishness; we do not and we cannot surrender absolutely to the good in itself outside of ourselves.

In short, we are not what we can be and know we ought to be. This is the doctrine of sin, and once again it shows that freedom on the level of transcendence is also a relative concept.

This analysis of human existence as personal, social and transcendent is an attempt to schematize elements for an anthropology in the light of contemporary experience. Obviously enough such a schema is very abstract. The analyses of psychology, sociology and actual religious experience are needed to probe these levels further and to give an account of their actuality in different locales. It should be noted further that human existence as it is envisioned here is one; it is an encompassing notion. Thus all the levels and dimensions of it are of one piece. We are not individual persons apart from our social dependencies and transcendent longings. Society is constituted by individuals; society also projects and lives by a transcendent mythos, however implicit or unreflected. Our ideas of transcendence are socially formed even when they are unique and personally formulated ideals and goals. And insofar as this threefold analysis of human existence as freedom in bondage may be seen as a framework for a transcendental anthropology,[14] it also forms a question once again of the meaning of human existence. In other words, the bondage of human freedom on all its levels is also the question that human existence is for itself, one that looks for an ultimate answer in the revelation of God that Christian faith takes the Christian message to be.

The answer to the question of human existence, therefore, should have bearing on all levels of human existence and of human enslavement. Christian revelation or the Christian message is addressed to human existence and the whole of it.[15] It must therefore illumine all of its dimensions. It has something to say not only to each dimension of human life, but also to the passivity and activity within each dimension, both to human bondage and to the direction of the exercise of freed freedom, both to weakness and to strength, to impotence and to power. Examples of the variety of concrete situations within the open schema of the levels of existence could be multiplied indefinitely. On the personal level, revelation should provide meaning for the personal human life that has no chance for freedom because of mental illness, as well as for a fully developed, powerful and autonomous personal freedom. On the social level, Christianity should respond to those groups of people who find themselves enslaved by social structures as well as direct a message to the beneficiaries of society and the directors of our corporate destiny. Christian faith should proclaim a God that both relates to our sin and at the same time draws our freedom out of itself toward completion. The message of Christianity has to be understood as multifaceted to correspond to the multiple dimensions of human existence and the variations within them.

Methodological Focus

A theology that is comprehensive must deal with the Christian message insofar as it illumines the totality of human existence. But at the same time, a theology that is unified, coherent and relevant to a particular epoch in history must have a certain focus. The metaphor and analogy of a focus suggests a centering concern that organizes and directs the attention in theological reflection and construction. A focus for a theology then is the dominant interest, passion and concern, the unifying theme that holds the whole of it together as a coherent vision. But this centering of concern should not be construed as exclusive, as excluding other concerns. Rather, like the lens that draws rays of light to a center, but without blocking any of their light, so too a centering concern of a theology should organize and unify theological data thematically, but without negating the legitimate concerns represented by other and lesser problems. Thus in no sense should a focus operate in such a way that it leaves out of its ken other aspects of human existence or fails to illumine the whole spectrum of human problems.

The focus of any theology, although mediated by the subjectivity of the theologian, cannot be arbitrary. Rather, it arises out of and is determined by the historical situation. The focus of a theology thus should not be determined merely by the personal and in this sense subjective experience of the individual theologian. It should emerge rather out of the conditions of the world and history and a shared human experience of them. Practically speaking, this means that it will be in tune with the community of theologians who are themselves corporately in touch with the Christian and human community in the broadest possible way. If a theology is to be adequate to the experience of the generation of people it addresses, it must reflect the general concern and problem experienced by that generation.

The focus of a theology, then, cannot and should not be just any particular problem. By definition, if the theology is to be comprehensive, then the focusing issue or crisis must itself be all embracing; it must be deep enough to shed light on the whole Christian message; it must be broad enough to carry implications for the whole of human life and every aspect of human existence. Much of current theology that seeks to be adequate to contemporary human experience is not, simply because it lacks focus. Although some theologies in their comprehensiveness say something about a whole host of specific problems, they do not communicate a unified vision that gives Christian faith an identity that is precisely responsive to our current situation, that is, in a profound way that touches the depth of human anxiety rather than a whole host of more incidental worries.

In the last chapter it was argued that the problem or crisis of our time is the problem of the meaning of historical human existence. This problem did not arise all at once, especially not with the genesis of liberation theology in the 1960s. This profound crisis of meaning has been growing since the period of the Enlightenment, and the human suffering against which it is a reaction is as old as the human race. But that suffering seems to be increasing in geometrical proportions in relation to the increase of human population and the sophistication of human technology by which we are able to oppress and inflict pain on other human beings. Roman Catholic theology has only awakened to it theologically since the Second Vatican Council. The problem of our contemporary human experience and existence is that of the crisis of meaning in social historical existence, and thus this problem should be the focus of today's theology. If this problem is indeed the commonly experienced crisis of our time, then unless a theology addresses this issue, it will not really be relevant or adequate to our period of history. This centering focus, it must be repeated, should not rule out other problems and other aspects for understanding human existence or Christian revelation today. But it does provide a center of gravity for that theological task. The question of the meaning of social historical human existence is precisely a focus because it is seen as threatening the sense of the whole Christian message. Hence this problem is one for the whole of theology and for theology everywhere to the extent that it pretends to be adequate to contemporary experience.[16]

A method of correlation, then, implies that Christian revelation be approached through anthropological self-awareness. It requires a comprehensive view of general human existence, yet one that is also unified and focused in terms of the situation of humanity in the world now. Theology thus involves a constant tension, a tension between comprehensiveness in relation to the whole of human existence and its problems and adequacy in relation to the critical issue of the age. When the problem of historical existence is assumed as the focusing issue for theology today, then theology will be seen to incorporate into itself the methodological themes that have been outlined earlier from liberation theology. But at the same time, these themes must be understood in the wider context of a comprehensive anthropology. Unless this is the case, the resultant interpretation of Christianity will be one-sided and limited; it will not be comprehensive.

Thus the methodological principles enumerated earlier from liberation theology may be restated in such a way that they appear as both adequate and comprehensive to the whole theological task. First, the problem of theology is that of the non-person. But this is also the problem of all individuals, as well as a problem of society as a whole, and it is a problem of transcendence. Second, the theory of dependence reappears in theology, but it is given a wider meaning because it is understood as having a deeper anthropological base and a threefold significance relative to human bondage. Third, and similarly, the symbol of liberation must respond to every level of human existence. Fourth, an anthropology of freedom incorporates into itself the liberationist concern for praxis because freedom is only fully freedom in its exercise. Christianity must be interpreted in such a way that it gives meaning for human living in society and for the exercise of freedom on a personal, social and transcendent level. Fifth, an a priori option for the poor is implicit in the focusing problem of theology today, because the very existence of massive poverty and oppression is the ultimate scandal to faith itself. One must be committed to overcoming this in the very desire to discover the meaning of human life. This option is relevant to every individual, to society, and it engages the question of transcendence. And finally the circle of action-reflection-action may be seen as integral to the hermeneutical process of the method of correlation. The method of correlation involves bringing the question of human existence that arises out of the problem of history into dialogue with Christian sources so that they may illumine contemporary experience and stimulate Christian behavior today.

To summarize, the method of correlation describes the structure of theological understanding; it is not a mechanical process, but defines the ingredients that are necessary if disciplined reflection is going to understand the Christian message in a way that is both relevant to today's world and faithful to Christian revelation. The first pole of that method requires a systematic understanding of contemporary human existence in anthropological terms that transcend any particularist problematic. If human existence is understood as freedom today, that freedom is seen as possessing three distinguishable dimensions that interpenetrate each other. The question of human existence, then, although it extends as far as each human questioner, also has these three dimensions and the Christian message should be interpreted inclusively in terms of all three. But at the same time the problem or crisis of meaning due to the social condition of human existence today requires a focus within these three dimensions of human freedom and provides an overall context for theology today. No understanding of Christian faith today as merely a response to the question of individual or strictly personal and transcendent freedom can have meaning for human existence today without also responding to the scandal of social and historical oppression and suffering. The question for Christian sources, then, is this: How does the Christian vision provide salvation from the bondage of human freedom on all levels of its existence, but especially relative to our social and historical existence?

Revelation and the Question for Our Interpretation of Historical Human Existence

In a method of correlation the first pole of interpretation, namely, contemporary common human experience, poses a question to the sources of Christianity which contain or mediate revelation. At the same time and reciprocally, these sources of revelation from the past, precisely as revelatory, mediate a question for our interpretation of ourselves, our humanity, our life and our understanding of our corporate historical existence. In other words, a method of correlation is dialogic, and as a method of theology it must allow room for the judgment of the transcendent God on our contemporary self-understanding as that judgment is mediated through the revelatory symbols of Christian faith.

Once again, it is most difficult to discuss revelation and its sources adequately in the course of a couple of pages. Both what is said so schematically and what is not said may in the end be either trivial or misleading. Yet in spite of this it is necessary to say something.[17] Thus in what follows I shall make at least four points which seem essential as presuppositions for any contemporary theology. The first concerns the nature of revelation as a form of religious experience. The second relates to the need for critical historical work in theology over against the error of fundamentalism. Third, the limitations of historical theology have to be insisted upon in the light of the constant need for new interpretation, the proper task of theology. Finally, I would insist on the ongoing revelatory power of Christian symbols and the fact that they continually pose challenges for our new and further self-understanding.

To begin, revelation is a form of human experience. This may be assumed as an elementary epistemological truth and axiom. Revelation has always been considered by Christians as the word of God. But that word of God must "appear" in human consciousness to be heard. There should not, therefore, be any antithesis between human religious experience and revelation.[18] Revelation is thus primarily an existential concept; in its primary meaning it refers to an experiential and ongoing phenomenon. Only secondarily does revelation refer to the objective expressions of this revelation that is constituted in experience.[19]

A sufficient portion of the religious experience that is at the source of Christianity found its way into written form or texts. And Christian texts are the most common source of all Christian theology. They are the written and hence permanent objectifications of the originating and ongoing Christian experience and revelation. And as such they are the common basis and source of ongoing Christian theology. This is especially true of the New Testament which is both the oldest and therefore closest in time to the source of Christian revelation, Jesus, and also the very origin of the record of revelation relative to all of the texts that come after it. All of the texts of the Christian tradition are part of the sources of Christian theology and are actually used as such. But the New Testament is the privileged source, the norm and the ultimate basis for theology.

Second, then, these texts are the source for theological reflection on the meaning of Christian revelation. But because revelation experience is a form of human experience, and all human experience is historically and culturally conditioned, so too are these texts which mediate revelation to us. For this reason, in order to understand them one must in a first step approach them historically and critically. A critical historical method is required if one is to arrive at their intrinsic originating meaning or sense. This can only be understood in a first instance as partly a function of their historical circumstances, or of a religious experience that occurred within an historical context. Thus one can lay down as a first axiom the need for incorporating the results of critical historical research into an adequate theology. A theology that lacked this component would be at worst fundamentalistic and at best deficient in its credibility for today.[20]

The need and especially the actual use of a critical historical method as a first step to understanding the sources of Christian revelation has a significance for theology that is often ignored or overlooked in practice. The implications here can be seen as both positive and negative. Positively, an historical critical re-creation of Scripture and the history of Christian statement and report opens up a whole world of the past. Meaning and significance are disclosed in a completely new way when seen in context, within the structure and pattern of a different socio-cultural milieu. Old texts come alive with meaning. To the extent that a past culture can be opened up to us, in the same measure one can resonate more deeply with the past experience that generated our historical tradition. Negatively, however, historical method uncovers past experience precisely as past, and as such it is quite different than current experience. The very work needed to recover the meaning that is ensconced in past historical forms dramatizes the fact that that meaning is different from present understanding. Moreover past expressions of meaning appear as limited, culturally determined, contextually particular and not universal. The expressions of revelation from the past are relative; they are related to the past.

All of this adds up to the impossibility of fundamentalism in theology. Fundamentalism stands for the direct application or use of past religious statement as normative or authoritative for the present without the mediation of interpretation on the basis of current experience. Of course fundamentalism in its more obvious forms seems so hostile to the discipline of theology that this scarcely needs mention. Yet much of theology remains fundamentalistic, and this is a constant danger because of the need of theology to appeal to scriptural sources. Indeed much of liberation theology appears to be fundamentalistic in its use of Scripture and biblical theology.[21] Because of our historical consciousness, theology cannot make its point by simply quoting Scripture. Biblical as well as any other historical theology in itself has no direct theological relevance for the present if it is not mediated by and to contemporary experience.

But, third, this last statement does not undercut the normativity of originating revelation. Original Christian revelation that lies within and beneath its record and expression is still the criterion for Christian theology. Besides adequacy to contemporary experience, a second criterion for Christian theology is fidelity to Christian revelation as that is manifested primarily in Scripture and secondarily in ongoing Christian tradition, where tradition stands for the whole corporate life of the Christian movement. The point of the rejection of fundamentalism is the positive demand that our tradition of Christian symbols be mediated to us today by interpretation or reinterpretation. Indeed the method of correlation is such a method of reinterpretation. This reinterpretation occurs within the actual encounter, confrontation and correlation between current common experience of reality and human existence and the vision, in all its multifarious detail, pluralism and richness, that is contained especially in the Scriptures but also in Christian tradition.

When contemporary systematic and constructive theology looks to the past it is confronted with an enormous array of data. The Old and New Testaments, the history of Christian life and thought, present a mass of material that cannot be controlled by any single human being, and cannot even be absorbed consciously in a whole community. But still, practically speaking, it is also true that there are certain common denominators, points of continuity, common threads of experience and expression, central and unifying symbols around which the whole Christian message, both biblical and traditional, revolves. A religious symbol, here, refers to a thing, person, event, word or concept that points beyond itself to the infinite and transcendent and through which people become aware of God. Such symbols from the Christian tradition are, for example, God, creation, providence, covenant, Jesus the Christ, the Kingdom of God, salvation, redemption, the Spirit, grace, the Church, resurrection. There are of course innumerable symbols in Scripture and tradition since religious language is itself symbolic language. But there is also a certain order of importance to biblical symbols, since some are closer to the center of the Christian message than others. This is shown by the emergence early in Christian history of the creeds which are attempts at a summary statement of Christian revelation or faith in terms of its central symbols or doctrines.

Given these central Christian symbols, the whole of Christian theology rests on one huge assumption, one which is at the same time absolutely fundamental to the whole enterprise. This is the idea that these symbols from the past, from an alien culture, from a limited and particular social context, from a single tradition, are relevant beyond these limitations both for our present and potentially for all human beings, that is, universally. In other words, these symbols, which express an original revelatory experience, are not confined to the past; their whole meaning cannot be explained by their historical genesis; the meaning they had and which can be uncovered by historical critical method does not exhaust their significance for today. Rather these symbols since their genesis have consistently looked forward and possessed a power of meaning for the future. Their exact meaning for today can only be determined by the mediation of reinterpretation.

This leads to the last point on revelation, namely, that these symbols do have a power to challenge, mold and shape our current human experience, and that it is the task of theology to demonstrate this. It may be mistakenly assumed that the dynamic element of theology lies exclusively in the first pole of theological method, in contemporary experience and the new questions it poses for past sources and symbols. This is not the case. The symbols of Christian revelation also pose a question for and to human experience today. On the one hand, they are the data and object of Christian theological reflection and interpretation. But on the other hand, on the basis of their long life within the historical community, they contain "in themselves" content and meaning for the religious imagination, and thus in some measure determine the content of Christian faith now and into the future. No matter how open and polyvalent a religious symbol is, thus allowing for a pluralism of interpretation, it is not open to every possible interpretation. God, the will of God, God's justice, Jesus Christ—these symbols challenge human consciousness and conscience today. They contain an inner power that criticizes contemporary experience, tells it what it means to be human, and brings to bear upon our lives the judgment of the transcendent God. This is the function of any religious symbol, and it is the task of theology to mediate this transcendent power to our contemporary religious experience within our contemporary historical situation, especially relative to the issue of our corporate social existence.

THE DIRECTION OF THEOLOGICAL REINTERPRETATION

To conclude this all too brief statement on the structure of theological method and revelation, as these appear from the point of view of the liberationist interpretation of Christianity, I shall try to point the direction in which this method is leading today. What will be the general thrust of Christianity, the contours of its global meaning, if it is reinterpreted for our day under the influence of the problematic of historical human existence? The response to this question will serve to indicate the direction in which the following chapters of this book will go. And at the same time it will serve to reassert the initial thesis, namely, that the relevance of liberation theology extends far beyond the southern continents. Methodologically the themes that influence and govern liberation theology, and the direction in which they lead, can be preserved in a more generally defined and universally conceived statement concerning theological method, that is, when theological method is formulated in the widest possible current cultural context.

There is less dispute today over what the sources of theology are than over the manner in which they are to be interpreted. In the structure for theology presented here there are two elements that are most important, both in themselves and especially in the tension in which they must always be kept. The first consists in the adequacy with which one understands human existence. The rhetoric of liberation theology tends in the direction of seeing the human reality exclusively in social terms. But the anthropology that lies behind one's interpretation of the relevance of the Christian message for today must be adequate to all the levels and dimensions of human existence precisely in order that the full richness of the Christian message and experience be accommodated. The Gospel appeals to the whole of human existence and hence touches all the levels of human freedom.

The second element consists of the focus of contemporary theology which is defined by the problem of our age. The image or metaphor of focusing is meant to illustrate a process in which the multiple dimensions of Christian experience are in no way minimized or any one of them excluded, even though they are at the same time seen in relation to and having a bearing on a central and centering problem. This is the profound crisis of our time and culture, the problem of meaning for the whole of human existence when it is viewed historically and socially. This problem simply cannot be excluded from the Christian vision. Nothing ultimately meaningful can be said about individually personal and private salvation, or about ultimate individual or corporate salvation outside of history, without addressing the implications of these for social existence now. Unless this is consistently done, that is, unless the meaning of Christianity at every level is consistently brought to bear on this problem, a scandal remains that calls whatever meaning that is found on the other levels into question.

Given this structure for theological method, it may now be asked: In what directions will the interpretations generated by this method lead? A very general response to this question may be seen in terms of some of the central symbols and doctrines that summarize Christian faith.

First, regarding faith and revelation, these concepts will be understood existentially and historically as involving concrete experience within a social context. Revelation and faith will be seen to involve personal commitment to God that motivates the manner in which one lives one's life; faith includes behavior and practice. But human life is inescapably lived in society. In the light of the focus of the problem of our time, the liberationist axiom that Christian faith provides a basis and an imperative for some form of liberation praxis will be justified; and since theology is reflection on Christian faith, liberation praxis will appear as a peculiarly relevant source for Christian theology today.

Second, God in the biblical tradition has always been understood as being concerned for human existence. God is Creator, provident and saving, the God of the covenant. God is God for individuals and for people in society. The Scriptures need little reinterpretation to depict God as responsive to the problem of the non-person and the crisis of meaning in historical human existence. And, as was said, this is the problem of every individual as well because it attacks the basis of personal faith in God.

Third, the current emphasis in Christology consists in uncovering the historical Jesus who is the Christ and interpreting his salvation in historical terms. The message and life of Jesus, together with the New Testament and traditional interpretation of his person and salvation, will be seen as opening up new possibilities for human existence understood as freedom in history, and on all levels. The meaning of Christ will thus address freedom and bondage that is personal, social and transcendent. The Christian meaning of liberation will not be seen as stemming from a social theory of dependence, but from the meaning of Jesus as the Christ for the liberation of human freedom from bondage in all of its dimensions. But at the same time this liberation will be seen in terms that come to a focus on the crucial problem of our time, the social problem of human suffering and unfreedom due to oppression.

Fourth, the symbols of the Spirit, grace and subjective salvation all point to the same reality, the immanence and effectiveness of God's working of salvation in people. The Spirit makes Christ's message of God's salvation actual in history. These symbols will tend to be understood in terms of an actual process of liberation, the release and opening up of human freedom toward completion. The term "salvation" itself releases meanings that are closely akin to liberation. The Spirit of God which is grace will be seen as operative in every level of human freedom; the freedom *from* personal sin by forgiveness will always be seen to involve a released freedom *for* and *in* society and history. Thus liberation will remain a central symbol in theology.

Fifth, the Church is a community of disciples of Jesus the Christ, and disciples constitute the Church. A theological method whose focus is the problem of history will tend to see the Church itself as a continuation of the mission of Jesus to the world and in service to humanity in history. And in a situation of extensive human oppression, such a Church will naturally have a bias and prior option for the neighbor who is poor and oppressed. In theory, this option is not against the rich but is meant to be especially the option of the wealthy and influential.

Sixth, the end of history is the final salvation of the Kingdom of God. Insofar as it is the end of history, it is reached through the process of history itself, although this is to be understood in a way that does not deny grace or discontinuity between our history and God's promise. This process involves conscious human participation whose natural rhythm, both personally and communally, can be understood as a continuous circle of action-understanding-action. As a general characterization, this also describes the history of the community's life of faith and the process of theology moving unevenly toward the end of time.

In sum, a theological method of correlation that includes both an anthropology that tries to respond adequately to common human experience at all levels and an historical focus determined by the crisis of meaning for our time will incorporate the themes of liberation theology and at the same time join common cause with other theological movements sharing a more generally formulated methodology. The following chapter will discuss the structure of the faith that receives Christian revelation as that is portrayed in liberation theology.[22]

Chapter IV
THE THEOLOGY OF FAITH AND ULTIMATE CONCERN FOR JUSTICE

Anyone trying to unravel and explain the view of faith that underlies liberation theology runs into a major obstacle, at times an almost impenetrable barrier. What seems obvious, indeed self-evident, to people dedicated to the cause of social liberation from oppression in its various forms is simply not so appreciated in wider Christian circles where faith is either undisturbed or unexposed to the scandal of massive human suffering.

This difficulty of communicating or mediating in a convincing manner a conception of Christian faith that is significantly different from other prevalent views has a number of layers. Faith is ultimately an existential reality that only becomes self-consciously appreciated in the experience of it. One cannot explain freedom in a really persuasive way to one who has never experienced it. And it is even more difficult to mediate a different understanding of something which is already viewed, albeit from a narrower perspective, in a quite coherent fashion. Perhaps the most telling obstacle to an appreciation of the liberationist theological understanding of faith lies in other theologies of faith and their presuppositions. In the main, most theologies of faith carry the common supposition that faith links the individual person directly to God and that this bond is intimately connected with or mediated through, or even identified with, belief. Faith is ultimately some form of belief in God, and one that is mediated through objective beliefs about God. Thus from the viewpoint of the theology that represents those Christians who are untouched by grave social oppression even though they may and do suffer other attacks on their humanity, from the point of view of the majority of Christians who are not poor, the liberationist movement appears isolated and sectarian. And the conception of faith that underlies liberation theology will be viewed as at best a particular and somewhat peculiar understanding corresponding to a specific school or situation, and at worst as purely rhetorical in its wider claims.

The intention of this chapter is to present the liberationist concept of faith in a more general and universally relevant context. But due to the brevity of the presentation, it can consist in no more than an outline for a direction which an adequate analysis might take. In general, a convincing liberationist theology of faith would first have to criticize the inadequacies of prevailing theologies of faith. It would then have to mediate its alternative through careful conceptual analysis. And, finally, I believe that the acceptance of another view of faith would ultimately depend on some sort of crisis and conversion, not only because it would require a shift in a fundamental paradigm, but also because faith is the most personal and existential dimension of Christianity itself, even for the theologians who analyze it.

In what follows, then, I shall first enumerate some of the suppositions, principles and themes that lie behind the liberationist view of faith. Given these themes from liberation theology, the project will be to represent a more generalized view of the nature of Christian faith that is at the same time faithful to these, that is, one that both incorporates them and preserves them even while presenting a theology of faith from a more general and transcultural point of view. The positive development here will have four parts. The first will present a global situational context in the form of a problem to which any theology of faith today must respond. Second, faith in general and Christian faith in particular will be presented as a human existential reality. Third, it will be shown that all faith is historically mediated, and that today, in accordance with Christian tradition, that mediation is to be seen in terms of the neighbor. And, finally, it will then be explained why a concern for justice in the world should be the form of all contemporary Christian faith.

FAITH IN LIBERATION THEOLOGY

Up to this time, the liberation theology that has appeared in Latin America has not singled out the doctrine of faith for extended and pointed discussion. Liberation theology is far from being a systematic theology in which each of the major doctrines of Christianity is treated in depth and correlated coherently or systematically in relation to all the other doctrines. But at the same time the issue of the nature of faith is implicitly dealt with in the whole of liberation theology and in every part of it. And explicit statements about faith and the Christian life are scattered through all of this literature.

An accurate and full characterization of the nature of faith in liberation theology would have to begin with and take into account the more general presuppositions of this theology which govern its whole perspective. These are quite extensive and determinative. For example, a profoundly religious concern for the poor underlies the whole of liberation theology and colors every theological assertion. Liberation theology also presupposes the importance of life in this world as opposed to an exclusively other-worldly perspective. It has noted the appeal of Marxist ideas and has tried to incorporate certain elements of a Marxist analysis of history into the Christian vision. And its explicit design is to interpret all of Christian experience and doctrine into terms that relate it to the situation of Latin America. While these and other suppositions of liberation theology are important for understanding its view of faith, I wish to single out five other principles or themes that have an even more direct bearing on its theology of faith.

First of all, liberation theology assumes an existential and historical point of view in addressing the question of faith. Although at first sight it may seem difficult to imagine any other way of dealing with faith, still this observation does have some bearing on the issue. Faith is looked upon as a lived reality; it is not seen primarily in terms of the object of faith *(fides quae)*. Its first definition, therefore, is not an assent to or acceptance of objective truths. Faith is the existential Christian attitude that lies beneath Christian lifestyle and behavior; it is the motivating factor which guides the Christian life. A point of entry into the liberationist theology of faith, therefore, would be first of all descriptive and phenomenological. It would examine the personal and collective historical commitment of people involved in the liberationist movement. Conceptual analysis and definition of what faith is in objective terms would always have this existential reality as a point of reference.[1]

Second, faith in God in liberation theology is intimately linked and sometimes identified with love, and this love is extended to love of neighbor.[2] Often the paradoxical assertion is made that faith in God so includes a love of neighbor that they may be considered as identical. The connection between faith and love of neighbor is not of course new in the Christian tradition. But when the connection of these two themes is pushed to the point of identity, when one asserts that faith which includes a love of God *is* love of the neighbor and vice versa, one has a new radicalization of Christian doctrine that is often rejected. The issue here is not one of mere semantic confusion.

Liberation theology often conceives of faith as a form of praxis, or as identical with praxis.[3] Another version of the same assertion is the definition of theology as reflection on liberation praxis. Traditionally theology has been understood as faith seeking understanding. In the liberationist formula, this would become "praxis seeking understanding." Even aside from the fact that praxis in liberation theology means a certain kind of practice, namely, one that is for liberation in the public and social sphere, this identification of faith with action appears startling. Is not faith faith and action action? Is this some kind of Kantian reduction of faith to morality, or at least an implicit Pelagianism?

At the center of specifically Christian faith is Jesus Christ, and thus Christian faith is Christic in structure. It is natural then to find key themes for the nature of faith in Christology. Especially in the Christology of Jon Sobrino, faith appears as a practical way of life.[4] The essence of one's response to Jesus Christ, and hence of the whole Christian life, is discipleship. Thus once again the inner animating principle of Christian life, namely faith, is conceived in terms of commitment, following, behavior, doing and action.

And, finally, this mode of life is even further specified. A following of Christ involves making one's own central concern the Kingdom of God that Jesus preached and for which he lived. Moreover this Kingdom of God is interpreted in historical and not merely either immediately personal or eschatological terms. Thus one has a concept of Christian faith that directs human behavior in a rather clearly defined direction. It is not any kind of commitment to God, but one that takes the form of a commitment to social amelioration.[5]

These themes govern the liberationist theology of faith. In what follows we shall try to generalize upon them, to articulate the broad lines of a theology of faith that includes them, but is at the same time relevant to all Christians and not simply those who live in Latin America.

THE PROBLEM OF FAITH TODAY

It has been pointed out repeatedly that the focus of Christian faith has changed in the course of Christian history. In different periods the ultimacy of the human questioning out of which faith emerges anthropologically has taken on different forms.[6] And even more pointedly the different forms of faith that are manifest obliquely in the history of theology and implicitly in culture have been charted.[7] It should be accepted in principle, therefore, that our own period in history should demand its own distinctive form of faith. Whether by "our own period" is meant "right now," or whether it should include the whole of the twentieth century or the whole post-Enlightenment epoch should not concern us here. The question is whether or not there is a crisis for faith peculiar to our time.

Objectively a good case can be made for the view that the human crisis of our time lies in the massive amount of human suffering and our new appreciation of it. On the one hand, human suffering has been compounded in our day in terms of absolute numbers to a degree never before realized in the history of the human race. And on the other hand, we as a race are aware of this suffering in a completely new way. For we are conscious today that a great deal of this human poverty and oppression is not due either to nature or to fate but is caused by human beings. However inevitable human suffering in itself may be, however hardened and unchangeable the death-dealing structures of oppression may seem, however intricate and complicated the political determinants of human misery for large groups of people certainly are, they still involve corporate human will and freedom. Certainly Christian faith, being a Christian today, must respond to this objective problem.

But there is still a deeper question which Christian faith itself and any theology that seeks to either justify or understand it must address. This is the question of whether religious faith in general and Christian faith in particular may not be dysfunctional in the face of the objective historical problem. The question is not a new one. Enlightenment figures of the eighteenth century questioned faith as undermining personal responsibility, the freedom of criticism and the autonomy of human action. And purely secular humanism in both the nineteenth and twentieth centuries saw faith in God as a projection that kept human freedom in a kind of bondage of illusion and dependence. But whether the issue is new or old it is breaking in upon corporate or general Christian consciousness today in a way it never did before. In the past Christians were always able, aided by theology, to find a strictly personal meaning for personal faith, but in a way that often led to privatization and individualism. This is considerably more difficult today.

The force of this problem for a theology of faith appears when it is brought face to face with the objective issue of the massive human suffering witnessed in the world today. It also lies, as I see it, in a subtle combination of fact and theory, neither one of which alone would be sufficient to bring the problem home. On the one hand, faith is attacked in its actual performance. But the recitation of the evils done in the name of Christian faith, the usurpation of divine authority to subjugate human consciences and freedom, religious persecution and wars, inquisitions and crusades, are not enough in themselves to threaten what religious faith should be. In fact religious faith has led to fanaticism when it became politically conscious and to indifferentism when privatized. But these facts are counter-balanced by the saints and the good accomplished through the motivation of their authentic Christian faith. On the other hand, faith is attacked theoretically. The internal structure of faith itself, that of an absolute dependence and reliance on God, is said to undermine by its very nature human responsibility. By relating us absolutely to the transcendent we are necessarily, by an inner logic, alienated from our taking charge of the world with an absolute concern, an ultimate concern for other people, for their freedom and our own. But one may respond that the lack of any such concern is really due to a faulty notion of God. All atheism is a rejection of some particular notion of God. In reality God is concerned with human life, and faith in that God is precisely not alienating. The Christian God is the God of freedom.

It is only when fact and theory are taken in conjunction that the question of faith can become a real and, one must say, authentic suspicion. If one assumes an existential and historical point of view, it is less easy to distinguish what faith has been and too often is from what it ought to be. If by and large Christians behave no differently than others, and Christian nations and cultures betray no practical difference in their social relations, it is likewise difficult to say that Christian faith makes a difference in human life in other than the private sphere. Especially in the light of the objective historical and global social crisis of humankind mentioned at the outset, one has to recognize at least the possibility that, on the level of lived faith as opposed to the level of public exhortation, Christian faith is at best neutral. Moreover that question may become a positive suspicion when one observes the overwhelming tendency of the intensely personal habit or act of faith to become individualized and privatized. Is it not true that one's absolute or rock-bottom hope in God for my salvation and that of others in an eternal future intrinsically militates against our ultimate or even penultimate concern for the world, for others in society, here and now?

This problem or this suspicion is the question to which a theology of faith must respond today. A first response would consist in a clearer notion of the God who is the object of Christian faith. But in itself such a response would not be sufficient, not only because of the difficulty of determining the inner nature of God, but also because one is still left with the issue of the internal logic of Christian faith. These two issues, of course, are not separable. In what follows, an outline for a theology of faith will be sketched in relation to this problem, which, in a more particular form, is the problem addressed by liberation theology and the problem outlined in Chapter II.

THE EXISTENTIAL DEPTH OF FAITH

This first probe into the nature of faith will deal with faith in general and especially with what should be called more properly authentic religious faith. And this might begin with some remarks concerning the psychological manifestation of faith.

Psychologically faith appears as a centered and centering act or attitude of the human personality.[8] Even before it is considered as religious, faith performs a unifying and integrating function within a person. For example, William James describes the personality as a conglomerate system of ideas, aims, intentions and feelings all with their specific objects or goals. In religious conversion one aim, one interest, one passion, one idea, one concern becomes so stable and dominant that all others are subordinate to it. Thus faith may be seen as an habitual, permanent, stable and controlling center of human energy. It integrates the human personality because all other aims and intentions are subordinate to it.[9] Since the varieties of faith are so great, there does not seem to be any single psychological source for faith; no specific experience, no common emotion, no one argument, no single faculty accounts for it. But at the same time psychology can point to a single theme that underlies all faith, such as a tendency of the personality to seek unity, harmony and completeness.[10]

Faith then is a completely normal and common human phenomenon; it is an attitude that bestows a unity of meaning to the whole of one's life, one's knowing, valuing and acting. For this reason faith appears or may be described as a centering or integrating act or stance toward life. And since it does not seem to come from any specific "faculty" or mode of human reacting, one might suspect that it comes from another deeper region of the person. Thus it may be described as a centered act, one that ultimately flows from the depth of one's being.

If one is to try to find and characterize a common basis for understanding this common human phenomenon called faith, the attempt must unfold on the plane of transcendental anthropological analysis. While such an analysis or explanation of the anthropological grounds in common human experience for the experience of transcendence would be out of place here, still something must be said about this in any account of faith.[11]

Faith most fundamentally is a response of one's whole being to the question of one's own being and of being itself. This is the question that human existence and everyone's being is in itself to itself. Why am I? Whence am I? And whither? What is my being for? Faith is most basically a response of one's whole being to these issues; it is the act and

perduring self-disposition of acceptance of, affirmation of and commitment to a ground of one's own being and implicitly that of human existence itself. This is what is meant by Tillich when he characterizes faith
as ultimate concern.[12] And on this most general level, which is also the
most concrete, several more things can be said about faith. Every adult
human being must live by faith because some answer, whether it be
authentic or inauthentic, is inevitably given to these questions. One cannot escape a response to the question of one's destiny. It always receives
some answer implicitly.[13] Moreover, further analysis will reveal that
faith, when it is seen as ultimate concern, contains a criterion that is
internal or intrinsic to itself. An ultimate concern should only be
bestowed in the direction of the truly ultimate or absolute. And, finally,
the very "turning toward" and "recognition of" the Absolute as the sustaining whence and whither of human existence is always spontaneous
and given. This graced quality of authentic faith is universally recognized in religious experience[14] and is expressed by Tillich in the passive
formula of "being grasped by ultimate concern."[15] Authentic faith
always has as its object the ideal, that which is "above one," that which
is, finally, absolutely transcendent even while it is immanent.

Faith is not an undifferentiated whole. Every clear analysis of faith
shows that it has a certain structure and that it unfolds in various forms
and at different levels. In order to illustrate this, let us suppose that one
can distinguish three spheres within the human person, three distinct
modalities of human consciousness.[16] There is the sphere of knowing, the
realm of consciousness and knowledge of the world. Quite distinct from
this is the sphere of willing and doing, also a form of consciousness
toward the world, but more characterized by initiative and activity. But
there is still another level of consciousness, which may be called the level
of elemental freedom, and which is both distinct from and prior to the
others. This primary level of consciousness is consciousness-present-to-
itself, although not as an object. By what appears as a direct self-presence or immediacy, human consciousness is aware of itself as an elemental freedom contained within itself.

These three spheres of human existence are not separable; human
existence is one. But they do share a certain distinctiveness and autonomy. Knowing is not the same as willing, and neither of these two is the
same as the inner and apparent immediacy of one's being-present-to-
oneself, even though this latter consciousness is implied in both the consciousness of knowing and willing as an a priori.

Faith, insofar as it is authentic faith in relation to the transcendent,
has its basis and foundation in the first, deepest and most fundamental
form of human consciousness. It is at this level that the term "faith"

most properly applies. Faith is one's conscious being in relationship to the transcendent, to God. But this faith never exists as it were alone or isolated on this level. Faith always comes to expression in some symbolic objective form, either conceptually or linguistically. It also concretizes itself in some form of reaction, response, action, willing or doing. One may call the manifestation of faith in its objective symbolic and in some measure cognitive form "belief." And the expression of faith in willing and action may be termed "spirituality."

The purpose of these distinctions is to help uncover the structure of faith and the relationship between its several layers and dimensions. From them one can see that faith is not the same as belief. A person may have all sorts of beliefs, either created by the self or simply accepted from others, without any underlying experience of faith. Faith is always existential and demands in some measure an experience of transcendence. But given faith, it necessarily is or becomes objectified to itself; it is expressed in some symbolic conceptual form that can be formulated into a belief. Faith, then, has a cognitive dimension; it is an awareness of the transcendent. But it is not the same as the knowledge of anything finite in this world. Thus it is accurate to say that faith is not knowledge, and that the content and the validity (in the sense of their meaning or sense) of the beliefs that represent faith ultimately depend on the actual faith experience from which they are derived.[17] In parallel fashion, neither faith nor belief is identical with the willing and action that responds to faith experience and thus expresses it. One can will and perform religious activities heteronomously without the least religious experience of faith. And there can be genuine moral activity that is not explicitly religious. But faith experience of the transcendent necessarily expresses itself in a conscious willing and action, even if the action is some form of mystical or contemplative decision of surrender, a decision to allow oneself to dwell or rest in the experience. This active dimension of faith is of course precisely a response to something that is prior and gratuitously given. Moreover it is not blind but is guided or directed by the concepts or symbols that make up faith's belief structure and bring faith to the level of thematic clarity.

This analysis of the structure of faith illustrates both the existential and the historical character of all religious or authentic faith. Faith in its most profound source or elementary form relates back to a transcendent and religious experience. Faith is the ultimate response of our being to being itself. Even though it has an intrinsic transcendental anthropological basis, and even though the elemental freedom of the human spirit is itself a capacity for faith, faith itself is something that happens or occurs spontaneously. Faith is not something that can be rationally mediated with necessity or in any way controlled. Our faith is ultimately not within our control. All faith expresses itself in beliefs, but these beliefs can never be identified with the faith they express. Beliefs never comprehend and cannot adequately represent the transcendent object of faith experience which faith itself is aware of precisely as transcendent. As important and essential to faith as beliefs may be, a willing response to and an active expression of faith is even more essential to the authenticity of faith. For the action of spirituality is the principle that manifests the reality of faith itself.[18] If faith is an experience, an act and a permanent and pervasive attitude that governs the whole of one's life and being, then both the actuality or reality of faith and its quality will primarily be revealed or manifested in one's faithful action or response to the originating experience. Ultimately, despite the power of actual religious experiences in our lives, despite our stated beliefs, and despite our explicit commitments, we cannot really be sure of the quality, steadfastness and direction of our most basic faith. To what do we actually submit as the ground of our being? In the long run, faith in its actuality is the logic of human action. Faith is historical; it is that which plays itself out in the life of each human being.[19]

To summarize the argument thus far, it may be said that authentic faith has been described as a form of religious experience that has an existential character. This faith experience has a structure and in its most fundamental nature it should be characterized as a depth experience of awareness and response of our own being in relation to the absolute and holy mystery, God, who is the ground of being itself. This faith experience is always accompanied by symbolic objectifications of that which is experienced, namely beliefs, which have their validity precisely as expressions of faith experience. Therefore the assertions of faith are not assertions of knowledge. But the primary and humanly authenticating expression of faith is spirituality, one's conscious, willing and active response to the object of faith. In all of this, faith is to be seen not so much as a single act but, as Aquinas expressed it in Aristotelian language, a habit. Faith is a permanent disposition or quality or direction of a person's elemental freedom or spirit in relation to God.[20] In more contemporary phenomenological terms which point to the same reality, faith may be seen as a superactual value response, that is, a response to the transcendent that is consistently operative and directive or fundamentally influential in one's life even when it is not consciously attended to, not explicitly a motivating factor.[21] Or in still other contemporary terms, faith may be seen as lying beneath or within one's fundamental moral option insofar as that commitment rests upon an experience of and is formulated in terms of the transcendent mystery. Faith is not one's practice or action, but it is found primarily *in* one's action; it is the inner logic of human action. Faith in this sense is historical.

THE LOVING CHARACTER OF CHRISTIAN FAITH

In the first probe into faith it was shown that faith has an historical and moral character. This does not suggest in any way that faith can be reduced to morality in some neoKantian or even Pelagian sense. But it does imply that responsibility, willing and action are intrinsic, and not external or extrinsic, to the full historical reality of faith. In this section I shall deal with specifically Christian faith. With two distinct approaches I wish to indicate the loving character of Christian faith, that is, how love of other human beings is also intrinsic to or an essential part of Christian faith.

An appreciation of the loving character or nature of Christian faith ultimately depends on a recognition of the principle that all faith is historically mediated. Although faith may be described as having its anthropological source in a transcendental or universal openness or capacity of elemental human freedom for faith, and even a drive toward it,[22] and although primitive faith experience has a seemingly immediate quality of God-being-present to our own sheer being-present-to-ourselves, still faith is always historically mediated. This is necessarily the case because of the radical bondedness of the human spirit to matter, to the physical world, to a concrete and specific history. As a result there is no pure or universally identical religious faith; religion is always and necessarily mediated through the world and a concrete particular historical situation.[23] Whatever the universal structure of faith may be, actual faith is always mediated through the world, through the symbols and concepts, the things, places, persons and events of history.[24]

As a consequence of its mediated character, religious faith is necessarily characterized by other subsidiary forms. The notion of a "form of faith" is a highly abstract idea that refers to the *historical* shape that faith inevitably takes. These forms exist on a great variety of levels. One can discern the originating form of any historical religion. Here the originating symbols, the founding experience of a faith as mediated through its founding symbols, determine the specific self-identifying form of a faith. Beyond that one can distinguish other more "accidental" forms of faith by indirect analysis by examining the constellation of symbols, the corporate expressions, the theological representations and the social and ethical manifestations of a given religion at any particular time.[25] There are also different psychological forms of faith, over either the spectrum of the human cycle of growth or a spectrum of types related to different levels of maturity or self-transcendence.[26] Ultimately faith will exist in a unique and different form in every single religious person. But beneath the variety of forms in any given religion one can distinguish its elementary, basic or founding form in its originating, historical symbolic person or event.

For Christian faith the concrete symbol in this world, the elementary and structuring medium of faith, the revelatory event and mediating objective form through which faith as it were ascends to God as its transcendent object, is Jesus of Nazareth. Jesus Christ is the revelatory medium of specifically Christian faith as distinct from other religions or forms of faith; the life, teachings, death and resurrection of Jesus reveal and disclose to Christian faith the God who is the ground of being, render this God "available" or present to history in an external and symbolic way, and thus structure that faith. It is not that Jesus is the object of faith, at least not directly; God alone is the object of faith. But Jesus is the essential and fundamental symbol, focal point and determining and informing factor of the Christian form of faith.[27] The founder becomes the center of faith itself. Christian faith is Christic.

Beyond this fairly obvious observation it is most important to recognize exactly *how* Jesus Christ is the founder and determining factor of Christian faith. While this is more properly a question for Christology, some basic principles are necessary for the argument here. Historically and as a matter of fact, it is the man Jesus who was the source and origin of Christian faith. This means that it was the actual consciousness of Jesus, that is, his own consciousness about himself, the world and God, and the actual way in which he lived his life, taught and went to his death, that together constitute the historical foundation of Christian faith. This is true genetically even though we know very little historically about Jesus' actual consciousness, and know this only indirectly through his teachings and the way he lived his life. It is also true in spite of the fact that the only immediate sources for our knowledge of Jesus and for our faith are the confessions and consciousnesses *about* Jesus contained in the New Testament and the other earliest pieces of Christian literature. All of these sources, however, although they are first in our cognitive approach to knowing something about Jesus, are still derivative from the man about whom they were written. Because all New Testament confessions are about the man Jesus and God at work within his life, including the statement that God raised him, the elemental structure of all New Testament faith statements have their own basis in Jesus. The structure of faith today is the same as it was in the New Testament period; it is Jesus of Nazareth who accounts for the historical nature of faith because he is at the basis of the genesis of this faith; it is his actual historical life that is the historical basis for the structure of Christian faith.

On the basis of these principles governing the most basic structure of specifically Christian faith, one can easily demonstrate its essentially loving character. We *know* with a very high degree of historical probability that Jesus taught a self-sacrificing love of God and a love of neighbor as integral to our relation to God. We also know that he displayed this teaching as the fundamental logic of his own life. He went around doing good. It is precisely because of *this,* and its extraordinary degree, that he was remembered at all by his friends after his death. Jesus was not remembered because of his teaching alone, without the reality principle that authenticated his own faith. It was he who disclosed God's presence and power, and not merely his words. Moreover, the faithful remembrance of him in its first moment actually consisted in entering into "his way" of life, of following him, of being a disciple. And it was these disciples who generated out of their discipleship the primitive or first "doctrinal" or belief statements about their relation to God through him, and hence his relation to God and God's relation to him.

Discipleship or the following of Jesus, then, was the first mediating factor of Christian faith. It was the factor that explains the genesis of Christian faith and hence its elementary structure. It consisted and consists in allowing the pattern or logic of Jesus' life and teaching to disclose or reveal a relationship to God *through* a taking on or participating in this mode of life and of being-in-the-world. The revelation that Jesus was to others lay in his life. And the acceptance and response of faith to this revelation is an entering into this pattern which is essentially a life of love and doing good, not simply for one's friends, but for the "others," the outsiders.[28]

Another approach to the essential loving quality of Christian faith consists in examining more carefully the ethical teaching of Jesus, which has been consistently carried forward by Christian tradition, that the love of God and love of neighbor are inextricably entwined. It may be supposed here that in an integral existential faith the distinguishable virtues of faith, hope and love of God are all united in one holistic response. The unity of these three virtues or attitudes may be explained in a variety of ways.[29] The point however is that it is generally accepted that genuine faith includes hope in and love of God, that considered attention to any one of these virtues already implies the others. Christian faith then *is* love of God, in spite of other aspects such as holy fear and so on; and love of God *is* faith. The problem is to see the intrinsic relation of these to love of other people.

There is a level of faith at which it becomes apparent that the paradoxical statements that love of God *is* love of neighbor, and that love of neighbor *is* love of God, are true.[30] In order to appreciate this, however, one has to be willing to suspend the obvious sense that God is not other people nor are they God. In other words, there is a common or obvious objective and thematic sense in which this identity cannot be drawn. Rather the conflation is made on the basis of implied reasoning; each authentic love, either of God or of the neighbor, totally includes the other by implication. Objectively this can be shown by simply averting to the fact that one cannot love God wholly without including in that love all that is of God, especially all other people who are God's own. Similarly, an authentic love of other people implies a love for what makes them be and be as they are, their ground of being, God. The same conclusion can be seen subjectively through an analysis of implied intentionality. The direction of the self-surrender that is implied in the authentic love of others and even another leads to God as its necessary grounding reason. And a comprehensive self-surrender to God must radiate out toward all God's beloved.

Once again, the point of this analysis may be clearer than the analysis itself. Faith is self-transcendence, a going out of and beyond the self in response to a gratuitous and initiating disclosure of God to human experience. And this self-transcending response is necessarily mediated through history in one's concrete situation. In other words, as a perduring habit, disposition and attitude, Christian faith is not mediated once and once for all in the past, but is continually being mediated throughout one's historical life. The single most important ongoing historical mediation for faith and love of God is the other people who as much as ourselves (one must say more than ourselves) are God's, and in whom God is found as it were immediately at hand. The Christian God is immanent to the world as Creator and Spirit. But human existence is immersed in matter and relates to God through the world. Human beings cannot break free of the world or transcend it except through the world and in relation to other human beings. A person who loves and trusts the world and history with authentic self-transcendence has already been opened up to God's world and to God. And when a person's attitude is confirmed in closure to history and God's people, this is closure to God despite any other narrowly religious intentions or beliefs. The neighbor then is certainly the test and the criterion of authentic self-transcendence vis-à-vis God. But even more, the "others," he and she and they, are the privileged near-at-hand mediating vehicle through whom, by responding precisely to *them,* we respond to God. It is true that while we are in history the only way we can love God authentically is through the neighbor.[31] And inversely it may be said that all authentic self-transcendence toward the neighbor points to God as both its source and its direction. Thus it is as legitimate to say that we are justified by love as to say we are justified by faith, because love of the neighbor includes faith in God as much as faith in God includes love of neighbor. Both are equally gratuitous.

In what follows, I shall examine the form which the love of neighbor that is integral to faith should take.

JUSTICE AS THE FORM OF CHRISTIAN FAITH

The final step in this outline for a constructive theological interpretation of what faith should be today in the light of themes from liberation theology deals with a major theme in contemporary theological literature, the relation between Christian faith in God and social justice in this world. In much of this writing it never becomes quite clear how an objective social condition marked by justice or injustice enters intrinsically into faith, which is ultimately an existential human phenomenon. Often the connection appears as finally extrinsic; faith in God remains something that can be integrally explained without reference to social conditions. At best faith leads outside itself to a concern for social justice, but this concern is not intrinsic to faith itself. The point here then is to show why a concern for justice is an intrinsic quality of Christian faith itself, so that no explanation of Christian faith that neglects this quality or form is an adequate representation of it.

The term "justice" has many meanings and most of them are objective. For example, justice is a quality of the external dealings among people according to right order and equity.[32] And there are a variety of kinds of such justice from interpersonal retributive justice to social justice. Or justice may refer to a quality of a person's behavior if it corresponds to the reasonably discerned right order of things. But beyond these empirically based and practical determinations of justice, one can ask further for the ontological basis for every concept of justice. Justice and any concept of it ultimately is grounded in the form or structure of being itself, in the element, despite historical chaos, of stability, order, rationality, coherence, consistency and continuity in being. Here the form of being is taken in its Aristotelian and ontological sense of that which makes beings what they are; human beings are not objects, plants or animals. Persons as personal beings are the ground of justice. One's reaction to being should be according to the way things are, according to the nature of being. And since persons are equal, personal and free in the order of being, justice is ultimately an objective form that requires human valuing, response and action to correspond to the equality, personality and freedom of a person or persons.

From this basis, Tillich's axioms that justice is the form of love and faith's love works through justice make sense. Any response toward another person or group of persons should be formed, normed and structured by the structure of being itself. Or, in phenomenological language, a value response should correspond to the in-itself value of the thing responded to.[33] Justice in this ontological sense is not added to by love; rather love works *through* justice, or according to it. Justice is the medium of love and indeed at this basic level is the criterion and judge of love. Of course there are degrees of love that may go beyond even ontological justice; but the point here is that justice on this elementary plane is a vehicle and norm that utterly transcends, because it is more basic than any concept of justice as legality, established sets of human criteria, or mere external law. In its ontological sense justice is a structure of being which is intrinsic to human existence itself that governs and ought to motivate both from without and from within human responses to others.

From this it easily follows that a concern for justice is an intrinsic and constitutive element or form of Christian faith. The focus of attention in this claim is precisely on the existential and intrinsic quality of faith and thus on the interior motivation and attitude that should qualify a person of faith. Faith's love for the neighbor should be informed by a concern, indeed an ultimate concern, that other human beings be as they ought to be. Moreover, it is specifically a concern for social justice that is being referred to. No Christian has ever doubted faith's demand for personal honesty in dealing with others. But it is fairly recent in the history of the race that we have come to an awareness of the dependence of social situations on personal freedoms taken collectively and the dependence of personal freedom on social situations. This insight is not found in the New Testament, nor even in the prophetic literature in the way it is possessed today. And thus to appreciate that a personal concern for strictly social justice is an intrinsic form or disposition that is part of the structure of faith needs to be mediated or learned. On the one hand, then, the concern for justice for whole groups of people who are marginated, alienated and oppressed into social bondage and suffering as an intrinsic form of faith is a new teaching corresponding to a new historical consciousness and social awareness characteristic of our time. It depends on a realization of social interdependence, of social structures and situations as changeable human structures, of the ways in which all people participate in these situations. But on the other hand, this insight is continuous with and does not go beyond the teaching of Jesus concerning the Kingdom of God and his manifestation of the informing power of this symbol in his life.

In sum, then, one must say that a concern for social justice is an intrinsic form of authentic Christian faith, because it is the determining form that structures faith's love for other human beings. Moreover, the centrality and urgency of this is augmented when one recalls the primacy of the moral dimension of faith as the indicator of faith's reality and authenticity.[34] Active concern for other human beings on a social level, though never to the exclusion of concern for the other levels of personal and transcendent freedom, constitutes real union with God by an implied faith. And all faith that lacks this concern as its form is incomplete and suspect.

CONCLUSION

In conclusion, it might be asked whether this outline for a more generalized theology of faith preserves the values and themes contained in liberation theology. Certainly the whole effort here has been to preserve an existential and historical view of Christian faith as the core of actual Christian life and spirituality. With liberation theology, the theology of faith outlined here would also insist that faith in God includes love of neighbor, a love of neighbor in the actual social situation in which our fellow human beings are found. One should love most those who are most in need and according to their need.

There is a sense in which faith is praxis and even in which theology is Christian praxis or spirituality seeking understanding. This is true because of the principle of inclusion; faith is implied in authentic dedication to the neighbor. But unfortunately these blunt formulas often cause more confusion than conviction, and their truth is often obscured in these paradoxical expressions. This chapter has tried to preserve a certain autonomy for a level of faith experience that appears as mediated immediacy, a dimension of religious disclosure and response corresponding to mediated immediate self-consciousness. Without this structure faith becomes confused with either knowledge of this world or morality. But at the same time it must be insisted that no "pure faith" exists as such in history; faith is always mediated and expressed through, and is intimately connected with, knowledge of this world and moral or ethical responses to it. The way one responds to the world is ultimately the reality principle of authentic faith. Thus the value affirmed in liberation theology is preserved here.

And, finally, Christian faith may be characterized, again by metonymy, as discipleship. This is so because the original and originating form or structure of Christian faith is adherence to the man Jesus as the place where God has been disclosed to us in history. And the first and primary way of adhering to God through Jesus Christ is by entering into the disclosive pattern of his life, a life characterized by love. As in liberation theology, this view of faith would embrace the symbol of the Kingdom of God, which was central to Jesus' view of the world and his life and teaching, as one that discloses for us today a new vision of Christian faith's internal responsibility of concern for the socially oppressed.

It is difficult to summarize the Christian vision of reality in terms of faith without taking account of the content of faith. But at least one can show how Christian faith may be seen as a response to the problem of the possibility of the dysfunctionality of religious faith in the context of the problem of human history. Faith is an existential relationship to God; it involves the whole of a person's being and every phase of his or her life, since it is that ultimate concern that lies beneath and flows into everything that one does. Faith is commitment, surrender, decision, acceptance, striving, obedience, passion, interest, direction, love and action. It defines what or who one is in the world, what one does in the world, and how one lives in history; one's action is the expression of one's faith.

In the face of the problem of human existence today, authentic Christian faith is not dysfunctional. It is shaped most essentially by its Christic form, so that the paradigm for personal life is the pattern of Jesus' own life. The meaning and meaningfulness of life is disclosed in this person. Jesus' own life, from what we know of it, was itself grounded in and shaped by the Kingdom of God that he preached and lived for. Thus this social ideal or utopia of peace, harmony and fulfillment for all human beings, based on equality under God and justice among themselves, informs authentic Christian faith.

Actual faith must be mediated historically and lived out historically as well. This historical life of faith involves love of God and love of God's own. Since God is not immediately available to human beings in this world, the darkness of faith relative to God is illumined by the exigencies of our direct relationship to God's people. Thus a relationship to God demands a relationship to other people, and one's being concerned with justice for God's people *is* a being-in-relation-to-God. The objective norms of and demands for social justice constitute the form or structure through which the Christian response to God is to be lived out. Inauthentic Christian faith may be an obstacle to the process of humanization and liberation in history, but authentic Christian faith is precisely a response to oppression and human suffering insofar as it is a concern for it and a struggle against it. This is the faith that saves and the faith that constitutes the reality of a person's being united with God.

These four chapters have dealt with fundamental issues in liberation theology, its focusing problem, its method, and the conceptions of revelation and faith that underlie it. The second part of this book, beginning with Chapter V, will consider constructively the content of Christian faith as this is mediated to us by some of Christianity's basic symbols and doctrines.

Chapter V
THE IMAGE OF GOD AND
THE PROBLEM OF HUMAN EXISTENCE

This chapter begins a constructive account of the content of Christian faith in the light of liberation theology. And it seems fitting that this should start with the image or concept or idea of God.

When one takes up the problem or issue of God, often enough it is the question of the existence of God that is being addressed. Does God exist? The problem of God signifies the task of mediating credibly that God is, or at least the meaningfulness of talk about God. By contrast, a theological account of the doctrine of God is frequently dedicated to a systematic inquiry into the nature of God, the essence and the qualities and attributes that are to be predicated of God's being and person.

This chapter, however, will do neither of these things, but will fall rather somewhere between the two. I am impressed by Segundo's suggestion that it may be far more important, because it is a prior issue, to determine what is meant by the image, idea, concept, notion or the very symbol of God before one tries to establish God's existence.[1] Thus there will be no argument here for the existence of God, but only discussion of various symbols or predicates for God and ideas about God from the Jewish-Christian tradition that make appeal to contemporary experience. Nor will all of these symbolic qualities of God be subjected to a second more rationalized and systematic treatment that would try to account for the reality of God ontologically.[2]

The main portion of this chapter will deal with a correlation between our contemporary experience of the problem of human history and the data from Christian sources concerning God. In this correlation there are always two questions being asked. The first is this: In the light of our experience today, and from the standpoint of the meaninglessness with which our own history confronts us, what sense can we make out of the traditional symbolic language about God? And the second is the dialogic response which is also a question: What are we to make of our situation, of ourselves and our history, in the light of the symbols through which God is mediated to Christian consciousness? The first question will be addressed by a survey of some of the major symbols concerning God that make up our Christian language about God; the second will be handled by a commentary on some of the major issues that have arisen in our time concerning the relevance of God for our human history and for human participation in it. But these two questions are not separable. They are circular issues and both are actually operative even when attention seems to be focused on the one or the other.

But this whole discussion is also part of the larger project of trying to understand the dynamics of liberation theology. The goal in this as in other chapters is both to interpret theology in the light of the liberationist interpretation of Christianity, and to interpret liberation theology in a broader cultural context. I shall begin then by once again enumerating some of the suppositions, principles and axioms of liberation theology that have bearing on its theology of God.

GOD IN LIBERATION THEOLOGY

The whole of liberation theology is informed by a sense of historicity and a consciousness that all of reality, especially human reality, exists in time. And this supposition has most significant consequences for its theology of God. The world and people in it constitute a history; human existence is an historical existence which is a constant movement ever productive of novelty and change. The perspective here may be contrasted with a classical consciousness that is impressed by and fixed within a framework of the stable, repetitious, constant, continuous and unchanging aspects of order in the world. The importance of an historical consciousness is not that all of these continuities are denied. It lies rather in the fact that the relationship of God to an historically changing world will be differently conceived from the relationship of God to a static and fixed world. Hence an historical consciousness affects quite radically one's image of God, of God's nature and the way God relates to the world and to human beings. God's creation is not a finished product; the world is history, signifying that God's creation is being prolonged by the agency of human freedom.[3]

In liberation theology God is conceived of as related to, concerned about, and involved with the world, not just as a static system, but as historical event, interaction and continual movement. The God of liberation theology is the God of the Jewish tradition who acts in history. As the God of the covenant, God "will be the God who becomes acquainted and related through history, through the involvement of liberty with liberty, of person with person."[4] The idea that God acts in history, however, is not understood naively in such a way that God is a doer in history, or that God does for human beings what human beings are themselves called upon to do. God has left the running of the world to human freedom; but God is present as an empowering force as Spirit.[5]

One of the primary images for God in liberation theology is "Savior." God is Savior, and the salvation that God communicates is closely linked with liberation on the various levels that were seen earlier. The saving quality of God, God's saving relationship to human beings, is not something that began with the event of Jesus. It is of God's nature to be Savior, and Gutiérrez unites God's saving intention and action with God's creation and creative will.[6] Segundo insists that the Christian understanding of salvation history must be extended outward, away from seeing it as a particularist history, to allow it to embrace the total history of humanity. In other words, the scope of the theology of God must reach as far as the scope of God's nature as Creator and Savior, and God's effectiveness should be related with the whole of history in a saving way. Essentially Segundo sees the historical process of salvation as one of humanization, and since the human is constituted by freedom, this process is one of liberation, or the release of freedom from bondage for creativity.[7]

Salvation in liberation theology is not limited to a salvation that occurs outside of this world and its history. While final or ultimate salvation testified to by Christian tradition is in no way minimized, that is, its other-worldly and qualitatively different character, still this salvation is also bent back so as to become operative and effective within history itself. This salvation is, as was said, closely linked with the freedom that characterizes human existence, so that it is seen to consist in a process of liberation that is also a process of humanization. Thus despite the absolute, definitive and eschatological quality of ultimate salvation, there is still and also a continuity between salvation in this world and salvation beyond history. In other words, the category of the Kingdom of God, God's eschatological saving action, has bearing upon our history here and now.[8] Indeed there is a causal connection between the effects of the use of freedom in this world and history and what will remain in the end time.[9] Liberation theology maintains "that human beings, both as individuals and as political beings, are already building up the Kingdom of God here and now in history."[10]

In liberation theology God is on the side of the poor. The several lines of thought that lead in this direction make this conclusion quite logical. In searching for a response precisely to the apparent meaninglessness of historical existence because of the ruinous effects of poverty and oppression on human life, liberation theology naturally sees God as being concerned with the victims of history. God is the Savior of all, but such a Savior could not but be on the side of those who are most in need because of the exploitation of others. Liberation theology often gives the impression that God is exclusively for the poor and the socially marginated, those who suffer. But in its more careful expression it views God as the God of all and the release of people from oppression a liberation of the oppressor as well.[11]

If God relates to the world as to a history, then human beings in their turn relate to God through history, through historical situations, persons and events. The shift from a classical to an historical consciousness also has dramatic results here. God is not known on the basis of reason alone, because God is not a static knowable thing. Since God is in an active relation to a changing world and a human reason that is also changing, God is always experienced anew. "In reality our God is known only with the movement and process of de-alienation, creation, and love that God's own self enkindles in human beings. God is never known prior to, or outside of, that process. No heavenly signs point God out to those who do not scrutinize the ambiguity of history in search of their common liberation."[12] One comes to know God through God's revelation, and the epistemology of this consists basically in attending to the events of the liberation in history and interpreting them.[13]

To summarize, the notion of God in liberation theology is suffused by a consciousness and a concern for historical human existence. God is seen as related to history, as operative in it as Savior, for a salvation that consists in a liberation and humanization in history, and a history whose constitutive events are causally related to and partially constitutive of final eschatological salvation. God's intention in our situation is primarily concerned with the poor and oppressed. And as for our knowledge of and being related to God, this is mediated back toward God through history and the events of saving liberation in it. These themes do not exhaust the doctrine of God in liberation theology. But together they serve to indicate the general idea of God that is operative in this theology, more explicitly in some theologians, more implicitly in others. The task at hand now will be to see if these themes are relevant and applicable to a theology that addresses the notion of God from a wider cultural perspective.

REVELATION AND SYMBOLS OF GOD

Before enumerating and interpreting some of the classical symbols that mediate and structure Christian consciousness of God, some remarks on the nature and status of these symbols are necessary. How do these symbols relate to revelation? How do they represent the Christian's faith-knowledge of God? It is important to have some idea of the nature of these symbols as a context for the discussion of particular cases.

It was said in Chapter III that revelation is a form of human experience; revelation occurs within and is itself a kind of human religious experience. Of course the nature and specific qualities of this religious experience should be explained at greater length. But even without this some conclusions can be drawn immediately from the fact that revelation is being considered existentially as being mediated through human experience.

First, because revelation is mediated through human religious experience, it is always tied to the world and to history. Human existence may be looked upon and defined as conscious and free spirit which is itself bound to matter, the world, the material and the physical, the domain of nature and history. There is no human experience at all and hence no knowledge apart from the world. Consciousness and awareness are always consciousness of something, and that something, even when it is transcendent, is always connected with our material and physical determinants, our concrete imagination. In short, revelation is always bound to the world and to history.

In the case of specifically religious experience which is also tied to the world, that which mediates human knowledge of transcendence and of God is the religious symbol. There is no "immediate" knowledge of God; it is always mediated through the world, and those things, or events, or persons, or situations, or texts which mediate God to our consciousness are what is meant by a religious symbol. There are two things which characterize a religious symbol. The first is that as a finite reality in this world the religious symbol has a consistency and intelligibility in itself. As a finite piece of our world, the religious symbol has its own finite integrity which makes it what it is and hence understandable in itself. But on the other hand, the religious symbol points beyond itself; it opens up and discloses transcendence, that which is other than itself and which infinitely surpasses it. Thus there is a dialectical quality to all religious symbols: although they have a self-consistency in themselves, they are perceived to point beyond themselves and disclose what is completely other, the God who is transcendent and infinite. And, inversely, that which is completely other and transcendent is disclosed in and through that which is its mediating symbol. The transcendent that is revealed by any particular symbol, then, is disclosed within human experience precisely as transcending the symbol; it is the whole

of the transcendent that is mediated. But at the same time that wholeness and transcendence is limited, specified, focused and thematized by
the finite constitution of the mediating symbol.

Because revelation is a form of human experience and hence is tied
to this-worldly religious symbols, it is also historical. And because revelation always occurs in some point of history, it is always contextual or
related to the particular cultural circumstances in which it occurs. Of
course, in one sense, it is obvious that revelation to human existence
could not occur any place else but in history. Where else could it occur?
But the point here is that it is only in our small and yet bewildering
world and in our short but very arbitrary history that we have the possibility of discovering anything about God. In spite of the limitedness of
our world and our history, they present us with myriad and contradictory "revelations" of God.

From the historical character of revelation, once an existential point
of view is assumed, it also follows that special revelation is really the
primary or first and basic category for revelation, as opposed to natural
or general revelation. All revelation and knowledge of God is based on
special revelation. All revelation has the limits of the historical conditions that are at its origin and the contextuality of its continued interpretation. All our ideas about God are ultimately particular and historically conditioned. This conclusion can be and should be modified by the
discovery of a transcendental or universal dimension within all authentic revelation. But this transcendental dimension must always be held
in tension with the special, particular, historical quality of the religious
symbols that mediate it.[14]

Because revelation is a form of human experience, that which is
experienced of God in revelation is always experienced as related to
human existence. Epistemologically one cannot experience God outside
of this world, or outside of one's own experience; God cannot be experienced as God is in himself, so to speak. Within human experience, God
is always disclosed precisely in relation to the one who experiences God.
This is not to say that there is not an objective quality to human experience; the object of human knowing does stand out precisely as other
than the self. But apart from the fact that God cannot be experienced
as an object and still be God, the in-itself quality of what is experienced
in human knowing is never complete. God is always disclosed to human
experience in relation to human life and its historical condition.[15]

Religious symbols are potential disclosures of God; they are disclosive or revelatory of God. They are not descriptive accounts of God as if
God were an object in this world. In terms of knowledge measured by
science and what we know of things in this world, we actually know very

little about God. God is not known at all in any ordinary sense of the term "knowledge."[16] Rather God is disclosed to the religious imagination. Knowledge of God presupposes a religious imagination and is a religious experience. Disclosure means that these symbols mediate or open up to human capacity for transcendence an experience of the absolute mystery we call God. Only in and through such an actual experience can one speak analogously of any knowledge of God.

Finally it is most important to realize that this disclosure of God is also a disclosure of one's self and of human existence. A revelatory experience of God also illumines the nature of humanity precisely as it stands before God. The human experience that is a consciousness of God in a certain way is also a human experience that is conscious of itself. A consciousness of being in relation to God in a certain way, or of God in relation to us, is also a consciousness of oneself and thus a knowledge of oneself as a being-in-relation-to-God in a certain way. Thus knowledge of God is knowledge of oneself, and revelatory or disclosive experience of God is also a revelation of what it means to be human.[17]

For Christians the primary, normative and definitive symbol of revelation in history is Jesus. There are many other revelational symbols in the Judaeo-Christian tradition, both leading up to Jesus and in the New Testament tradition that followed his historical life. But Jesus, in his life, death and resurrection, is *the* mediating criterion and norm, at least in the negative sense that nothing can contradict the logic of Jesus in what Christians assert of God.[18]

We can summarize these brief suppositions concerning revelation in the following way. All revelational experience of God, and all the symbols that express that knowledge of God, point to God insofar as God is related to human existence. Even when God is experienced as totally other and transcendent, this is a human experience of God over against an implicit awareness of ourselves. This experience, moreover, is always embedded in our being-present-to-the-world; God is experienced in the world, and the object of this experience is always expressed in terms or symbols drawn from human life in the world. And since the experience of revelation is historical, so too are the symbols that express it contextual. This is said without in any way undermining the transcendental character of the human experience of God in authentic revelation. Thus, finally, the knowledge of God that is mediated through revelation is at the same time a knowledge of human existence, of ourselves, in relation to God. This last theme has bearing on all of the symbols that shall be considered in what follows and especially when the question of the relationship between God and human existence is considered.

GOD IN THE SYMBOLS OF CHRISTIAN REVELATION

What are some of the symbols or traditional predicates that are used to describe God as God appears to Christian faith? There is no systematic order to these symbols and in most cases they will be seen to have overlapping meanings and connotations. Nor is there any attempt here to be exhaustive. What is said here is not argumentative; nothing is being proved or demonstrated; the appeal is strictly to experience. When we speak of knowledge of God, we are not in any way referring to knowledge in the same sense as knowledge of things in this world. Religious experience and the faith that receives revelation are not objective knowledge in the common or ordinary sense of the phrase. Without saying that faith and revelational experience are purely subjective, and without denying that faith is in contact with God, this faith "knowledge" is *sui generis,* one whose ultimate authority lies within the experience itself. The following, then, is not an objective description of God, but a description of how God is disclosed to us in the symbols of Christian revelation.

God is first of all *transcendent.* God is the one and holy one; infinite glory and majesty surround the nature of God; God is God. Rudolf Otto referred to the object of religious experience as the *mysterium tremendum et fascinans,* the abyss of mystery and power before which the human subject both stands at a distance in awe and is attracted by fascination.[19] To say that God is transcendent is to recognize God as completely or totally other; God "goes beyond" all that one knows or can know—beyond the world, beyond every limited form of being. God is infinite. Although there must be some common ground between God and human existence, for otherwise there would be no contact with or discussion of God at all, still God has consistently been represented in the Christian tradition as totally and qualitatively transcendent and different from human existence.

God is *Creator.* The symbol and doctrine of creation corresponds to the human experience of being totally and absolutely dependent on a source of being outside of the self and ultimately outside of the world. Creation says that our being, including the very being of everything that is, has no reason for being in itself, but being thrown into existence it remains there because of the power of God. The symbol reinforces God's transcendence; God is the source, the origin, the sustainer of being; not simply in the beginning, but at every moment of time God holds what is in being. Here the word "absolute" has a place. We are all held in existence by a network of relationships to other things and the world on which we are dependent. But we are absolutely dependent on God whose power is the power of being itself of everything that is.[20]

Moreover we are created out of nothing, not out of God's substance or of some previous stuff. The alternative to the being that is by God's creative power is nothing. God is the power of being itself.

The symbol of creation has further connotations in Christian thought. In creation God creates precisely that which is other than God. Although that which is created is held in existence by God, still creation is precisely not God. From our perspective, then, creation is a symbol that demythologizes and secularizes the finite world; the finite world is not God. In itself the world is not sacred and the worship or surrender of oneself to any part of it apart from God is idolatry. Moreover, the creation myth also discloses God as handing over to human existence control and stewardship for the world. Human existence, too, is relatively autonomous vis-à-vis the world and invited to be co-creator of the ongoing process of creation that is history. This experience is a subtle one and contains levels: as part of creation, we are, like all else, absolutely dependent on God. Yet as conscious and free and other than God, we share and enjoy a freedom and autonomy relative to the rest of creation even while being still absolutely dependent on and responsible to God. Our very freedom and autonomy, which are real, are at the same time gifts of God and absolutely dependent on God.

God is *immanent*. God is experienced not only as the transcendent source or origin of being, but also as its inner ground. God is the ground of being. This is the other side of the symbol of creation. God does not only create the world as the potter forms the pot, so that it stands outside and away, distant and independent from God. God is God's creative power, and this power is the intrinsic sustaining force of what is. God is the within of things, not in the sense of being identical with that other which God has created, but in the sense of being intrinsically and causally present to all that is. Thus, inversely, all things are within the sphere of God; they exist in God's power or simply in God.[21] A symbol for this in the Scriptures is "the Spirit of God" which points to the power of God that is immanent and life-giving to all that is and especially all that lives. In sum, the dominant image of God is not that of a God outside of creation and looking down at it objectively and from afar. Rather as transcendent God is not anywhere but is immanent and present everywhere there is being.

God is also *personal*. The clearest manifestation of this in the Scriptures are the Psalms. For God in the Judaeo-Christian tradition is one to whom one prays, to whom one speaks or talks and addresses petitions and every other human sentiment. God is not a neutral cosmic principle, blank and blind, but a subject, infinitely transcendent to be sure, but also immanent and a conscious intentional subject nonetheless, with whom human beings enter into personal relationship and who consequently relates to us. This is true not only of individuals but also of groups. The great Old Testament symbol of the relationship of God with a people is the "covenant." The human experience underlying this symbol is a sense of favor, grace and predilection in God's sight. There could be a great danger in this symbol if it were not balanced with a sense of sin, or if it acquired a note of exclusiveness in addition to intimacy. The transcendent quality of God postulates that God is personally related to all single persons, to all identifiable groups and to all at the same time and equally. God's covenant is with the world.

God is also *provident*. Logically the doctrine of providence is not very distant from that of creation; in fact, all of the previous symbols are reasserted when one says God is provident. For providence discloses God's personal creative power, and God's transcendence and immanence, not just statically at any given moment but in the context of time, process and history. Providence is God's ruling power not just over what is but also over becoming, over the events of everyday and of total history as well, the movements of nature and natural process and the actions of human beings. For nothing at any time is independent of God's creative and life-giving power. And since God is personal and intelligent, and nothing exceeds God's power, God foresees the possibilities of the future so that potentially nothing escapes that power. This is not the same as fate or a set pattern that merely runs its course. Predicated of God, providence means the foreknowledge and care of a parent, the looking after and direction that does not enter into competition with the human freedom and autonomy that God after all established. What is experienced here is awareness that nothing really happens independently of God but all is under the guidance and ken of God's wisdom and power.[22]

God is *love*. Innumerable symbols in the Scriptures point to God's love. Jesus speaks of God as Father, a symbol which does not point to the sex of God, since God transcends this specificity, but to the loving care of the parent for his or her children. And in John the equation is drawn explicitly; God is pure love.[23] This indicates that God is totally *for* all that is created, especially human existence, because it is totally God's own. The power of God relative to individuals and the race taken as a whole is not exercised as force but precisely as love. God appeals to human freedom, drawing it out of itself into a mutual relation of a responding love on our part. But God's love is faithful and constant.

This is a major theme in the symbol of covenant and extends throughout the Scriptures. In a Greek framework of thought God was conceived of as immutable. When this is transferred to the historical context of the Judaeo-Christian conception of God relating personally to human existence across history, God is disclosed as utterly constant in love even while human behavior and response are fickle, changeable and irresponsible. God is not just an arbitrary love; love describes God's nature; God is intrinsically and essentially love relative to creation and the human race.

But God is also *Judge*. This disclosure is mediated through the prophets. There is no question here of an argument from texts in an objective way. What is revealed in the prophets' condemnation of social injustice is a God who does not accept this situation. The view of God as Judge and one who exercises judgment really flows from God's nature as lover. God wills the good of all. This God cannot but stand in judgment against human oppression and injustice toward any of God's own people.[24] This is one of the clearest and most powerful disclosures of who God is. God is not a selfish God concerned with human cult and ritual, nor even with worship, if it in any way coincides with the neglect of other human beings who are God's own. This symbol of God's judgment is too often passed over precisely because it cuts through and negates a great deal of the inauthentic religious experience that implicitly tries to grab hold of and possess God. One cannot cling to God against God's will, and the will of God is manifested in the prophets as being for all; it is an extension of God's care and intimacy for every single person. God's will is for the wholeness, completeness and fulfillment of that which God creates and sustains; it is consequently against every form of human diminishment. A response to God, therefore, must be according to the nature and the will of God. An authentic love for God must also be a love for what is God's and for what God loves. Since our human response to God can only be exercised in and through the world, it is absolutely impossible to escape our relationships to fellow human beings in this response.

In Jesus the revelation of the prophets is picked up in the symbol of the *Kingdom of God*. In its subjective form, this is the rule of God in the world, God's power, which is the power of love, that heals, cures, makes whole and leads to human fulfillment. It is God completely for all human beings without any exclusion and a preference for those who suffer most precisely because they suffer most. In its objective form, the Kingdom of God is the Kingdom of human fulfillment, the utopic Kingdom of peace and harmony, of justice and joy. To enter God's Kingdom one must take on attitudes and qualities of the God who has been disclosed to us, of loving care for other human beings. The constant tradition in the Scriptures, then, is that to know God, that is, to have faith, is to do God's will. This is not an arbitrary slogan but the existential reality of the way things are and the only way they can be. The will of God is not an arbitrary law or a set of regulations extrinsic to the logic of human living. One is in contact with the living God, one loves God, one is united with God in this human life, by finding God within the creation and history to which God is immanent. This is the tradition of Jewish law, of Wisdom and of the Kingdom of God. Human existence is united with the transcendent God precisely by living a human life in accord with the will of God, and this will is the logic of human existence itself. Moreover, this will is summed up in the disclosure that God is totally for the full human existence of all people.

But God is also *absolute mystery*. This is so first of all because God is transcendent. God totally escapes the power of the mind to know him in any "objective" way, that is, as an object. God cannot be possessed or contained by the human mind. To say that God is absolute mystery is to surrender to the fact that, in spite of all that has been said up to now, God escapes us; we do not know God as God is; we can only formulate concepts about God on the basis of these disclosive experiences that point to how God stands in relation to our religious experience.[25] But this mystery goes still deeper, for it is not really a problem of knowledge at all. The mystery of God is profoundly existential, and this is disclosed in the symbol of Job. In spite of the fact that God is disclosed as immanent, powerful, provident and faithful love for all, who wills only the fulfillment of human existence, a person such as Job, who is presented as innocent, has his life crushed by suffering over an extended period of time and is led to the brink of death. And all this transpires under the eyes of the God whose image I have described. This is the existential mystery of God and it leaves the human mind without any logical explanation; intellectually we are left with the limp confession that God's ways are not our ways.[26] But this submission of the mind does not define a total existential response to this mystery. Job is the model of a spirituality of expostulation. He does not accept evil and he will not allow any concept of God to justify it or explain it away. A spirituality of expostulation complains to God; it will submit to no orthodoxy that allows for injustice; within the context of submission and obedience to God, it argues and fights against the reality of God's creation and history because it knows that the injustice, evil and suffering that characterize human life ultimately have no right to exist in the name of the very God who seems to allow it.

But, finally, God is *Savior*. From first to last, God as Creator is already Savior. This affirmation corresponds to the deepest human trust that human existence does have meaning and makes sense in spite of the evil and human suffering that so deeply characterize it. Once again, this is not an arbitrary dimension of God relative to the human condition. God is always Savior relative to the human reality because, from the beginning, being human has always basically involved finitude, suffering and death. Relative to human life, as far as our human minds can take us, God must be Savior to be God, or else, in the light of God's absolute mystery, none of the other qualities of God make sense. This is reaffirmed by Jesus in terms of the Kingdom of God. God is Savior in the end when the Kingdom of God will finally come. And God is Savior now by the power of God's Spirit which is the power of God's love, healing and curing. But this theme of salvation will be developed further in the discussion of Jesus as the Christ and in relation to the problem of sin.

To sum up here we must confess that we do not know God. But God is experienced and the symbols of the Christian tradition try to express what God is like. God is first of all God, utterly transcendent; paradoxically God is experienced as totally other than what we gropingly affirm that God is. In spite of this transcendence and mystery, God is at the same time experienced in relation to us; God is Creator, immanent, provident, loving and faithful; God's care extends to every single human being. But the more these intimate, personal and loving relationships are affirmed, the greater the paradox becomes, for God appears strangely and sometimes dramatically absent from the lives of many. And God also appears as Judge, as judgment upon our irresponsibility and sin. The relation between God and human existence is a dialectical one. God is both immanent and transcendent; and human reality is both absolutely and intimately bound to God and at the same time alienated from God and even alone. The bridge of this paradox is God as Savior.

GOD AND THE PROBLEM OF HUMAN EXISTENCE

Having looked at some of the symbols by which Christians identify God, I now wish to take up some special questions that will enable us to probe a little more deeply the notion of God against the background of the problem of human existence. It is important here to recall the many suppositions mentioned at the outset concerning liberation theology. To a large extent these are the suppositions of modern and contemporary theology as such. Modern theology is existential; it takes historical consciousness seriously; it assumes experienced freedom and human autonomy as values; it admits the legitimacy of a certain secularization. But these have at the same time raised questions relative to traditional theology which reflects a different cultural situation, and these problems should be explained and mediated. Finally, in trying to understand the relation of God to the problem of human existence today, it should be kept in mind that the problem includes a variety of levels simultaneously. But at the same time, the problem comes to a focus in the question of the meaning of socio-historical existence. In what follows, then, I shall raise the issue of the relation of God to human existence by considering and trying to answer some questions that bear on this more general problem. All of these questions are raised by liberation theology, but a response to them has implications for theology generally.

The first question concerns how God relates to human history. How does God relate to the world and history? From our perspective it must be said that God is completely turned toward, concerned with and involved in human history. There is no other way that God can be conceived by human beings; the very talk of God presumes God's being related to and involved in human life if our talk and experience is not to be mere projection into the air. Human history is God's; God created and sustains all that is by being immanent to it. The symbol and doctrine of creation and providence imply that God is within the whole of what is so that the whole of human history unfolds as it were within God's sustaining power. For us, God is within the world and not simply transcendent to it. From our perspective, then, God is entirely related to the world and to everything in it.

This Christian affirmation, however, has taken on a new dimension today in the light of the problem of human existence. Given the amount of human suffering that one sees socially, that is, involving masses of people, one cannot simply say that history is God's in an unqualified way. This would amount to an impossible barrier to faith in the God responsible for *this* history. In fact insofar as one affirms that history is God's, one must also assume a spirituality of expostulation; one may and should complain to God for this history. But at the same time the affirmation that history is God's in a total and comprehensive way cannot mean an evasion of human responsibility for history. In large measure human beings have made history the way it is, and we are responsible for much of the human suffering that we witness. Although God sustains history in existence, much of it unfolds against God's will. God has given history over into the hands of humanity to fashion as co-creators, and the affirmation that God is the Lord of history must be balanced with a sense of personal responsibility for that part of creation that is in our control.

Secondly, then, how does human existence and activity relate to God? We have already seen that that relationship is characterized by absolute dependence in being. But although God sustains human existence completely in being and action, God has also granted human beings a certain relative autonomy; we are not God but stand over against God and are endowed with a freedom to take a conscious stand for or against what is absolutely other and good. And this can be done in no other way than through the world and through concrete history. God is immanent in finite reality, and human existence is tied to the world and history; while we are alive, then, there is absolutely no other way to encounter God than in everyday life in the world. Psychologically, the attempt to go to God directly by bypassing daily life and responsibility in concrete history is an error. The encounter with God and the forging of a relationship with God are accomplished concretely by all human beings by the way they live the whole of their lives according to their capacities and in their particular historical situation. The relationship will be different for those whose life is dominated by passivity in comparison with those whose freedom is more active. But in either case, one's relationship to God, positively toward union or negatively toward separation, is accomplished by the way one lives one's concrete life in history.

How, then, are politics related to religion? Most of the ambiguity of this question lies in the ambiguity of the terms used. The word "politics" as it is used by both political and liberation theology refers to the general sphere of arranging and negotiating human life on the public and social level. The political sphere is the running of our common historical and social existence and not merely groups striving for public office and power in society. Religion too has at least two very different senses. Religion may be taken in the root sense of the ways in which human beings are bound to or united with God. Or it may mean institutionalized religious practices and organization. It is clear that human social behavior, which is an integral dimension or part of human existence itself, has everything to do with religion in its root or primary sense. As was just said, human beings are united to God through the decisions and behavior that define their whole stance to the world and reality as such. The moral commitments and actions that human beings take in the social sphere are an intrinsic part of and help define how they stand before God. It is impossible to separate one's political concerns and actions from one's being-related-to-God.

The next question would concern the relation then of religion to politics. Here we take religion in its second meaning as organized religious behavior and institution. We have already seen how God relates to the world and hence to social and historical life and how the social behavior of every person helps define one's relationship with God. The question here really deals with the institutions and organizations that structure one's religious life. In primitive and less differentiated societies, religion and religious values colored every phase of human and social life in an integral system. In our own industrialized and urban cultures, which are more and more characterized by pluralism in religious belief and the separation of religious authority from the secular sphere, religion has tended to be relegated to the strictly private sphere of an individual's personal convictions or to the limited social sphere of the practice of worship and cult in common. If religion is seen to have a bearing on common social life, what concerns it is usually limited to issues of personal freedom and the values that apply to personal and family life. But this is a distortion of Christianity because it implies a distortion of religion in the primary sense of being in relation to God through the whole of our lives. Religious cult and symbol, preaching and practice, that do not have a direct bearing also on social life are faulty in terms of the Christian symbols for understanding our relationship with God because they suggest that one can be united with God by bypassing or going around social responsibility in the world and history.

Christianity is intimately bound up with moral life, and this includes life in society. Even on an organizational level and from a minority position, the Christian Church as the institution embodying and standing publicly for what it "knows" of God through Christian symbols should address public issues of social injustice. Exactly *how* religious authority, or, better, Christian leadership should be exercised in a secular and pluralistic world is a complex issue which cannot be resolved here. But what is often seen in privatized religion is not an adequate or authentic Christian solution. Christianity is defined so narrowly that it is practically limited to the personal sphere of private or family values, personal well-being and personal union with God. Then intervention in society is reduced to protecting those interests and values. And in so doing it bypasses and neglects the central human issue of our time, one which is also God's issue, namely the problems of massive social injustice, oppression and suffering of God's people. And, worse, by failing to address these issues with a prophetic ministry, it actually sacralizes the social systems in place.[27] In contrast to this, one may say that the purpose of organized Christianity is to mediate God to the world symbolically. And the will of God is for the good of all people both as individuals and in society. The message and influence of Christianity in society, therefore, should reflect the prophetic concern precisely for the well-being of all and of all *in society,* in the whole of their historical existence.[28]

Yet it still seems as if the very notion of God relativizes history and renders every social constellation ambiguous in the light of God's Kingdom. This is a major theme in political theology. But from the point of view of liberation theology it seems to rob historical activity of all its urgency which for it would be fatal in the light of the amount of current social oppression. If there are values on both sides of this question, then there is need for a double assertion. On the one hand, it is clear that the symbol of God's transcendence and creation does deabsolutize history. History is not God but precisely other than God. Human existence is thus freed from any particular history as an absolute, freed from ultimate fear or worship of any social system in this world. No historical plan or system is absolute or normative. But on the other hand, freedom, which is a release, is also a freedom for, a freedom to be exercised in creating or maintaining a just social system for the benefit of all. God has not only relativized history but also made it the field for the co-creativity of human freedom.[29] It will be shown below that the exercise of this *creativity* takes on an "absolute" value when it is seen constructively in relation to the Kingdom of God.

What is the relation between God's providence and action in history on the one hand and human freedom on the other? This problem has vexed Christian theology over the millennia and ultimately its solution is shrouded in mystery. This is the cosmic problem of God's omnipotence and the creativity of human freedom.[30] The problem arises from two seemingly different experiences. On the one hand, we experience our own autonomy and freedom in history. Moreover, even religiously, the experience of the Christian God of creation is the experience of a God who has made creation other than God and given it over to human stewardship. Yet on the other hand, we also experience the immanence of God and God's providence, and even speak of God acting in history. If God indeed does effect what happens in history and consciously intends what is effected, how can one really speak of human responsibility and freedom? Does not such language really lead to passivity and acceptance before the currents of events and ultimately to fatalism? A tentative and immediate solution to this problem may be seen in the concept of the "self-limitation of God."[31] God is omnipotent and the ground of all that is; at any given moment God holds reality in existence and provides the possibility for every immediate future. But God does not specifically determine the future; God does not effect *what* comes to being in human history. This is a self-limitation of God's own power. God acts in the present, preserving it and all its potentialities in existence, but God does not act in history to determine the human future; this power has been given over to human freedom and responsibility. This paradoxical concept of the self-limitation of God does not ultimately solve the problem because it remains paradoxical. But at least it preserves the inner elements of the double religious experience, the sacrality and importance of human freedom and the absolute dependence of it on God's creative and sustaining power.[32] In sum God does not act in history in place of human agents. God's providence is God's *presence* to human activity.

If God does not act in history to specifically determine the future, what then is to be said of the will of God? Is history as radically open as we experience it to be? Or is there a will of God that human beings can say they are following when trying to determine history in one way or another? The will of God has consistently been the subject of distinctions in theology. For example, it is often said that God actively wills the good that occurs in history; God merely permits with a passive will the evil. If one accepts the self-limitation of God relative to the future, one would have to say as well that the continuing future is not forged by any specific or determining will of God. One would have to speak of an open will of God. Here it might be useful to speak of the general intention and will of God that is for the good of all human beings and for history itself. This is God's will for human salvation, for the increase of freedom of all and for human completion and fulfillment. But God does not will the specific events of human history; these are left to the creativity and will of human beings. And these exercises of human willing and deciding and accomplishment, both personally and socially, may be more or less in agreement with the general will of God. Once again, such a distinction would preserve both the will of God and the inner responsibility and seriousness of human freedom. But at the same time, it would desacralize many popular conceptions of spirituality about "doing God's will." What we do during our human lives is our own will, and this may correspond in some degree but always imperfectly to the general will of God for the good. Historical decisions are always ambiguous, both subjectively in their motivation and objectively in their effects. There is no specific will of God for each individual. At best human beings may strive to shape their own decisions according to God's general will, but they always come up short.

Another major question regarding the relation between God and human history, and perhaps the major question for the Christian vision of God, concerns the relationship between final salvation and the movement of human history. This has been framed accurately by Bonino and Segundo as the question of the continuity and discontinuity of history with the Kingdom of God.[33] Once again, to affirm either the total continuity or the total discontinuity of history and God's ultimate purpose for history would eviscerate the Christian message. The Christian symbol of the Kingdom of God is clear on the one pole of the tension; the Kingdom of God is God's work, one that totally transcends human capacity now and in the future. But at the same time, by a negative logic and by some of the conclusions reached earlier, one has to say that human freedom plays a part in the fashioning of this Kingdom. If that were not the case, human freedom would be without any ultimate value beyond the here and now, and hence life here and now would not have any ultimate meaningfulness. This logic forces us to conclude that there is a causal relationship between the Kingdom of God and the positive values that are realized here in history by human freedom. That which is created by human freedom in human history and which has value according to God's criteria will be resurrected.[34] This position gives human activity a share in the absolute value of God's future and makes history as a project "absolutely" important, or at least a question of ultimate life or death.[35]

And, finally, one has also to ask the ultimate question for Christian faith of whether or not a belief in God's final and transcendent salvation is not an intrinsic distraction from a concern for social transformation and justice. This is especially the case today when more and more theologians are beginning to postulate not only the universal possibility of salvation but the salvation of all pure and simple. This question is important for several reasons. First of all it is hard to deny that an absolute conviction about final salvation, especially my personal salvation, could be such a distraction; it does after all guarantee my salvation no matter what.[36] And, secondly, given this inner problem and temptation, it is hard to deny that this doctrine has and still does undermine an absolute concern or ultimate urgency for ameliorating the life of others in this world. Thus the charge of Marxism and other secular humanisms that faith in God undermines a commitment to society and history becomes a real threat for Christian doctrine and faith, and ironically for many Christians themselves. It appears that Christians who consider this matter have to live with this historical possibility and danger. One way of overcoming the problem, of course, is to limit the salvific power of God. Salvation will only be for those who act morally and are obedient to God's open will that we be concerned for the neighbor in history. If one does not, one will be the victim of ultimate death. But this is to make Christianity a threat and revelation a message of fear. This hardly seems compatible with the revelation of a God who is pure love. Without denying that God's universal love is the norm for human life and thus a judgment on human behavior that neglects the neighbor, still the response to God that Christian revelation invites is one of love. And the only way one can respond lovingly to God in history is to lead a life in history in accordance with God's open will for the good of all here and now. But the whole dynamic of this is simply an invitation of God's love.

CONCLUSION

In Chapter IV it was stated that religion in general and Christianity as well could be in fact an obstacle both to the discovery of meaning for our corporate social history and to the actual project of overcoming the scandalous suffering that is inflicted on a huge number of human beings by other human beings, by ourselves. The quality of Christian faith itself that was argued for in the last chapter was a first essay at overcoming this dysfunctionality. But it was incomplete insofar as it presupposed some content to faith. This chapter has attempted to present a view of God, faithful to and consonant with the Jewish and Christian tradition, that responds to this problem. This has been an essay at disclosure and manifestation, of constructing an image of God based on religious experience that is also focused for our time through the classic symbols of tradition.[37] The God of our tradition is the God of the prophets, a God who is totally for human existence in love, and for that very reason a God who is profoundly concerned with human suffering and critical of the humanly constructed social conditions that cause it. God is on the side of the poor and of those who suffer, and God challenges and invites all those who believe in God to take this side as well.[38] God is both transcendent and immanent; God criticizes and energizes; and the witness of faith in this God also denounces what every human being of good will will denounce, and announces or reveals a vision of what could be in the utopic terms of the Kingdom of God.

This discussion has been a correlation between the Christian image of God and the problem of human existence. I shall conclude here by examining the problem of human existence on its three levels to see how the Christian image of God responds to that problem comprehensively.

First of all, human existence is constituted as a personal freedom. But this individual and strictly personal freedom is a relative concept because it exists along a spectrum that leads from sheer or mere potentiality to a fully developed and active exercise of it. On the one extreme of a fully realized human freedom, the God of Christianity provides a goal or a direction for that freedom; it indicates what freedom is for. It is for the building up of the Kingdom of God in history. At the other extreme of a freedom completely submerged in matter or nature so that it is little more than a potentiality, this appears as something that should not be and hence an evil. The existence of evil in the world remains a mystery. But the vision of God and God's ultimate salvation affords at least the possibility of a solution, a solution that would be impossible without any concept of God. Moreover, this God also directs other freedoms toward care for those less fortunate in this world.

Human existence is also social existence and the exercise of social freedom. But the quality of human existence understood as freedom also varies greatly in societies along an axis from oppression and fated existence on one side to openness, opportunity, options and the exercise of power and influence on the other. The mere existence of God does not give meaning to our social history. But the vision of a God who is against every form of human oppression, and who is an invitation to exercise love in history according to God's intention for history, and who provides a goal for that exercise, does provide ultimate meaning for human existence within the bounds of history itself. And this is true equally as a rationale for the personal exercise of freedom in the social sphere and as a mythos for our corporate decisions and ideals.

And, finally, the human spirit is transcendent freedom. It reaches out toward an absolute. To this human quest the revelation of God promises the response of fulfillment and eternal life. But this is to be understood properly. The salvation that God offers is an invitation from love to love; it is an invitation to a salvation that begins now with a response of love that is realized through action in the world and history. It is difficult to imagine how one could have confidence in the reality or cogency of the message of Christian revelation except within an actually loving faith. How could one hope in a salvation at the end of one's history without participating in the process that leads there?

Chapter VI
THE STRUCTURE AND DATA
OF CHRISTOLOGY

In the last chapter, I spoke of God's relation to human existence and of the reciprocal relation between human activity in history and God. For Christians, Jesus is the paradigmatic example of God acting in history. The immanence and action of God in our world and history comes to a focal point in Jesus: God is at work in Jesus. Jesus, precisely as an actual human being or person who lived in a point of time in history, is *the* symbol, the point of mediation, for understanding and being in contact with God.[1] Understanding of what this means should build on what was said before. The symbols of God's immanence and creative presence in the world and human life, especially of God's Spirit as the inner life-giving power of God, of God's will for the good of all leading to salvation, should not be left aside in the Christological discussion. Indeed they will take on fuller meaning in the paradigmatic case of Jesus.

This chapter and the next will add up to no more than an outline. Together they will merely indicate a direction in which Christology should move in the future. These Christological discussions will raise some of the many complex issues involved in reflection on Christ without being able to develop fully or adequately the positions taken on them. Thus they constitute an outline for a possible Christology, one that tries to be adequate to the problem of human existence as this has been defined, and to the many insights of liberation theology, but one that must be open as well to the current general ferment and discussion in this area of theology.

If one stands back and reflects on the very phenomenon of Christology itself (Where does Christology come from?), it becomes immediately evident that the basis of it is Christian faith, the actual faith life of individual Christians throughout the ages in community up to the present. This tradition has a beginning in time, and as a corporate phenomenon in the present this community experience is the basis, grounding supposition and source for Christology. This common Christian faith has two elements or components. The first is the historical appearance of Jesus. The second is the Easter experience which was at the same time the initial community's experience of Jesus risen, its interpretation of who he was and its faith reaction to God in and through him. This composite datum, Jesus and the faith interpretation of him, both in its origin and in its continuity to the present, is the basis for Christology. It is also the norm and criterion for an adequate Christology. In other words, a Christology, to be adequate, must account for, "explain," or express coherently the fact that Christians experience Jesus as the privileged concrete symbol and point of contact with God.

As to the question or issue that is addressed in Christology, it could be important to distinguish mutually interdependent spheres of concerns which are usually intertwined. On the more general level of Christian theology the question that Christology addresses concerns the meaning or content contained in the faith commitment to God that is focused in and through Jesus Christ. What is the meaning of reality if Jesus is God's Christ or Messiah? What does Jesus Christ disclose concerning God, human existence, the world and history? How does Jesus Christ shape and inform faith? And what is the content of specifically Christic faith as opposed, for example, to the faith of other religions? These questions are the concerns of the whole of Christian theology. Responses to these questions are found in the various doctrines and theologies that emerged with Christian faith. One might also say that the solutions to these issues are found germinally or reductively in Jesus Christ as the center of Christian faith. But, more specifically, two other questions, which are implicit in these general questions, have become the more focused issues of Christology. The one concerns the work of Christ: What did Jesus Christ accomplish for the human race? Ordinarily the investigation of this question is called soteriology. The other focuses on the person of Jesus himself as the Christ: What is the status of the person Jesus Christ? Who do we say that he is? This last question has been the particular focus of Christology for so long that it is regarded as the specific Christological question.

This essay in Christology will deal primarily with the specific Christological questions that bear on the saving work of Jesus Christ and his person. The wider Christological issues will also be addressed, but derivatively as arising out of the way that Jesus Christ is understood as Savior. The development is divided into two parts. In the first, this present chapter, I shall deal with the structure of Christology and its strategy and method. This issue is most important because, since the time of Strauss in the nineteenth century and even before him, and more acutely in the twentieth century with the general acceptance of the various kinds of historical criticism of the New Testament, there still remains at the present time an important debate on the very theological structure of Christic faith. The second part, Chapter VII, will be concerned with an attempt at a constructive interpretation of Jesus Christ and Christic faith for today.

Since the overall goal of this book is to generalize on the insights of liberation theology, this chapter will begin with a brief mention of some of the main principles and themes of liberation Christology. This will be followed by an attempt to define the appropriate strategy and method of Christology that is coherent with the structure of Christic faith. The greater portion of this part of the Christological discussion will be given over to a description of the data from which an interpretation of Christ for today must work.

THE PRINCIPLES OF LIBERATION CHRISTOLOGY

All of the suppositions of liberation theology as a whole, the axioms and methodological principles that were schematically outlined in Chapter I, come to bear spontaneously in a special way in Christology. These should certainly be kept in mind. But looking specifically at the Christology of liberation theology one can see certain distinctive moves that characterize and structure its understanding of Jesus Christ. In an effort to analyze this Christology the following six of these principles may help to define the liberationist point of view.

The method of liberation Christology is governed by a *hermeneutics arising out of a social context and concern.* The explicit intention of liberation Christology is to ask how Jesus Christ is relevant to the historical situation of poverty and oppression of large masses of people in Latin America. It is not a "neutral" Christology. Rather it sees the meaning of Jesus Christ against the background of a concrete problem, but at the same time reflects a transcendental human questioning concerning the meaning of history, its suffering and human participation in it.

Liberation Christology's prime although not exclusive focus is on *the historical Jesus.*[2] In this it joins the movement of modern Christology "from below" which understands Jesus Christ beginning with the life of Jesus of Nazareth. Two things should be noted about this approach. First, it may be understood over against or as opposed to a beginning with or a methodological primacy of the Christ of faith, especially as that is confessed in the classical Christological dogmas. Second, this methodology determines the very structure of Christian faith's understanding of Jesus Christ. The Christ of faith who is glorified and thus universally available to Christian experience because associated with God can assume an infinite variety of meanings for an infinite variety of religious experiences of him. Liberation Christology attempts to break through this radical pluralism or relativity by seeking a normative understanding of the meaning of Jesus Christ in the actual concrete life of the historical Jesus.[3]

The central category for liberation Christology is the *Kingdom of God*.[4] And both because the Kingdom of God was the central message of Jesus' preaching and because of liberation Christology's concern for the problems of history and society, this Christology sees *a strict correlation between the Kingdom of God and the project of liberation.* This is the decisive point in liberation Christology, just as it is for liberation theology in general and as it was for the social gospel movement earlier in this century. Jesus is related to the Kingdom of God, and the Kingdom of God is seen not simply in extra-historical terms but in eschatological terms that also have a bearing now on history. And what today is called liberation is part of the history of the Kingdom of God.

Because of liberation theology's turn to an existential and historical interpretation of Christian truth, it focuses not simply on the fact of Jesus but on *the dynamic unfolding of the actual life and history of Jesus.* Jesus is not simply considered as a person in whose person God appeared and was revealed. Rather, over and above this, for liberation Christology the way this revelation occurs is dynamically in and through the action of Jesus, the way he lived his life. In liberation Christology this concrete human history assumes a primacy over incarnation, cross and resurrection (although these are not excluded) in understanding Jesus Christ.[5]

Also, in liberation Christology *the work of Christ, salvation, is historicized.* This is another major shift relative to classical or traditional theories of objective redemption and salvation. The saving work of Christ is not something that was accomplished once for all in the past, although this theme is not totally excluded because the ontological definitiveness of the Christ event is maintained. Rather, salvation is an ongoing historical process, both objectively and subjectively considered, which Jesus initiated and his followers continue. Moreover, as was mentioned in Chapter I, the Christian symbol of salvation is conflated with the symbol of liberation. The history of Christian salvation is a history of liberation. And this liberation should be understood in such a way that it includes a being freed from oppressive historical, cultural, social, economic and political structures. These themes are at the very heart of liberation theology and they reflect back especially on Christology.

Finally another major theme in liberation Christology is *the follow-ing of Christ.*[6] The imitation of Christ is of course a classical Christian theme. But in liberation Christology it is given a new central focus. Fol-lowing Christ is following and imitating Jesus in his service of the King-dom of God, and this constitutes the essence of being a Christian. The key term here is discipleship. It takes priority over orthodoxy and understanding who the person of Jesus Christ is. In it lies the very con-dition of the possibility of understanding Jesus Christ and the essence of Christian spirituality as well, that is, *how* we are united to God in Christ.

Once again, I wish to try to preserve these themes of liberation Christology and their urgency in what follows, but at the same time I shall place them in the broader context of the problem of human exis-tence itself. The point is to show that these are not particularist but rather universal themes and concerns. How does Jesus Christ inform Christian faith so that faith in turn may provide meaning for human existence on the three levels of its freedom-in-bondage? How does Jesus Christ define and mediate for us what is authentically human given the triple tension of human freedom: a liberation of individual personal free-dom that is also finite, limited and often submerged by physical and psychic oppression; of a corporate freedom that is also the victim of instruments of social oppression; of an open and self-transcending free-dom that is also bound by mortality, estrangement and the guilt of sin? But before proceeding to the responses to these questions, one must first determine the procedure of Christology and the data with which it works. It is this task, largely methodological, that will constitute the main preoccupation of the rest of this chapter. Then in the following chapter, relying on these considerations concerning method and data, a more constructive interpretation of Jesus Christ will be presented.

THE STRATEGY, METHOD
AND STRUCTURE OF CHRISTOLOGY

The choice of a strategy for a Christology that will be adequate for our contemporary situation depends on one's assumptions and one's appraisal of that situation. As to an appraisal of the current situation, it would be out of place at this point, and is not necessary, to engage in an extended description of the world and contemporary culture. It may be taken for granted here that Jesus Christ must be reinterpreted for our age. The principle that underlies this essay is that every such reinter-pretation of Jesus Christ, and hence every adequate Christology today, must include an apologetic dimension.

The term "apologetics" is taken to indicate a viewpoint or strategy in one's theological thinking that gears the argument to the culture in which one lives. In the early Church this was seen as a missionary point of view; theology in terms of its audience was often a dialogue with a surrounding culture that was not Christian.[7] Today the Church finds itself in an analogous situation because it is a minority in a pluralistic world culture.[8] And precisely to the degree that it is a global culture, reflecting the ideas of enlightenment and modernity, it is less and less religious. The difference between ourselves and the early Church is that, insofar as this world's culture is secular and our own, Christians share much of its outlook and many of its values. The term "apologetic" today, then, has a double force. It means that an explanation or account of Jesus Christ is not only an explanation of him for others; an apologetic point of view is also required for our own understanding. The strategy of Christology, then, is apologetic, and even when Christology is properly called systematic and defined by a Christian audience, to be adequate to our current situation it should bear this apologetic dimension.[9]

It follows from this that a methodic interpretation and account of Jesus Christ must begin with the human being Jesus. Jesus of Nazareth is the point of departure for our theological understanding of Jesus Christ. This may be understood as distinct from beginning the properly theological interpretation of Jesus Christ with either the Christian dogmatic interpretations of Jesus as found in tradition or the kerygmatic understandings of Christ as found in the New Testament. The supposition is that these are the very interpretations that need reinterpretation today. It was said earlier that the basis of Christology is faith in Jesus as the Christ. In this sense Christology will always derive from Christian experience both past and present. But it is this experience that in theology must be explained. Theology therefore is not simply confession, but an attempt to critically analyze and render comprehensible to contemporary culture and to ourselves Christian claims that on the face of it often seem to defy intelligibility.

That such an historical point of departure corresponds with the apologetic import that Christology ought to bear is easy enough to see. In apologetics one attempts to appeal to common human experience. Now it is a universally accepted fact that Jesus was a man who lived in a specific period of time in history and about whom we can know something. This is admitted by everyone who has cared to consider the matter; Jesus' life became a public affair and knowledge of this event is something that Christians and others share in common. Indeed, we as Christians also *know* that Jesus was a man who lived in Palestine at the beginning of the Christian era. The word "know" is stressed here precisely in contradistinction to "believe." While there is a sense in which the acceptance of Jesus' humanity becomes an element of faith for the Christian,[10] that Jesus was a concrete human being of flesh and blood like other human beings is something we positively know. Thus the Christian may and should assume as a matter of course what even non-Christians do; this is something which we hold in common even as partners in a secular culture and history. To explain Jesus Christ to others and to ourselves we must begin with Jesus of Nazareth. In short, an apologetic approach to Christology realizes and concedes that what all human beings share in common is the humanity of Jesus, that is, the life this man lived among us as that can be retrieved and known through an historical and critical research.

This point of departure for Christology needs some further qualification if it is not to be misunderstood. First of all, it has already been said that the whole Christological enterprise rests on Christian faith and its commitment to Jesus as God's Christ. This faith is never absent from the Christological project. It is not held in suspension by some fictitious methodic doubt by the inquirer. But methodologically it is put in parentheses in an apologetic point of departure of a properly mediated or systematically presented theological analysis. To recognize this is simply to accept a distinction between Christic faith and the task of theology which is to critically examine this faith in order to render it intelligible and credible to oneself and to others. The more thoroughly faith is reflectively mediated, the more is its content potentially disclosive of the ultimate dimensions of reality.

Secondly, that one does not or should not begin with the kerygmatic presentation of Jesus Christ as found in the New Testament may sound ambiguous, since these accounts are for all practical purposes the only or exclusive sources we have for speaking about the historical Jesus at all.[11] We know practically nothing about Jesus that is not given us through the New Testament's confessional witness. But at the same time, it is not difficult to distinguish between the use of these confessional statements as records through which one can uncover something about Jesus by critical historical method, and the use of these confessions precisely as confessions as the point of departure for, and their content as the premise of, one's theological argument. The latter would not be an appeal to common experience, but a statement of one's confessional stance.

Yet another ambiguity lies in the question of what can be known about Jesus through such a use of critical history, and of the quality of that knowledge relative to Christological conclusions. There has been a great deal of shifting of ground on this rather fundamental issue in the modern period. The nineteenth century was given to writing biographies or lives of Jesus; in the twentieth century after Bultmann it was not uncommon to say that we could not know anything about Jesus other than the fact that he lived; and in our own day one finds a new quest for the historical Jesus, which, while considerably more modest than the original, is still convinced that we can know something historically about Jesus of Nazareth. But it is the common opinion and commitment of contemporary exegetes today that historical method can uncover, as it were behind the texts, a more or less accurate portrait and a "substantial" account of Jesus.[12] The thesis that is presented here is that what can be known about Jesus is to some extent, although not in its details, necessary for Christology.

Still further distinctions are necessary in a proper understanding of an historical approach to an understanding of Jesus Christ. For example, one must be clear about the fact that no historical portrait of any living person is identical with the historic reality of that person. This is true generally and therefore a fortiori in the case of a person who lies behind such highly confessional documents. From this point alone it becomes evident that one cannot equate or reductively identify the comprehensive reality of Jesus with the portrait that an historian provides. And this would become an even more serious error when one considers the quality of the portrait that an exclusively historical interpretation of Jesus must necessarily provide because of the nature of the discipline. It is generally accepted that history alone could never establish anything more than a human portrait of Jesus. The position reflected in this essay is that we can actually know very little about Jesus as an individual when what we know is compared with the complex fullness of any human life and thus of Jesus' as well. But what we do know of Jesus is sufficient for Christology.[13] However from this it should not be concluded either that Jesus can be reduced to what the discipline of history can recover concerning him, or that an historical account of Jesus will in any way prove or show him to be the Christ. The contention thus far is simply that an apologetic approach to Christology must begin with a consideration of Jesus of Nazareth.

A method that begins with the historical Jesus reflects or corresponds to the structure of Christology. In the final analysis, Christology concerns or is about Jesus.[14] Traditionally all religious faith and Christian faith in particular has as its object the transcendent mystery, God. Insofar as it is Christian, this faith has as its this-worldly axis and centering symbol the person of Jesus who appeared in history.[15] Thus Christianity, apart from its being essentially a way of life, does not consist in being merely a message about God; it is not even the message of Jesus.

Rather the mode of life and message of Christianity has its source and origin and also its intrinsic basis in the life of Jesus. In other words, Jesus as an actual person is part of the Christian message. And the particular discipline called Christology looks precisely to the person of Jesus and asks the critical reflective questions of how that person and the course of his life are to be understood. Christology, then, is about Jesus of Nazareth. And it would ultimately be impossible to have a Christology in the strict sense, that is, as contrasted with a general Christian message, if one could not say anything about Jesus. It is not just that Christology would hang in thin air; it would not have the referent required for it to be Christology at all.[16]

The strategy, method and structure of Christology dictate a certain procedure in its being carried forward. The particular human being who lived two millennia ago was accepted by Christian faith to be the Christ of God, and is interpreted and understood this way by Christians today. Therefore, to understand *this* fact, namely, the fact of faith in Jesus, one must study the genesis of this faith historically. How did it come to be? Quite obviously the historical origin or source of the genesis of this faith in Jesus was Jesus himself. It would be difficult to imagine any other historical source for this faith. Having come to be, this Christological faith came to expression and displayed a certain content concerning God, Jesus and the relation between these two. Formal Christology begins with faith's recognition of Jesus as the Christ in the Easter experience, and it has a history in the continuing report, record, expression and witness to this faith beginning with the New Testament and continuing right up to our present day. This is the data of Christology; it is retrieved by historical research, and in it one has one of the bases for interpreting the meaning of Jesus for faith today. The other basis, in a method of correlation, would consist in an interpretation of our contemporary situation.

In this process, one which is followed by many of the Christologies that are being written today, one can see a common pattern of procedure. The material on which investigation begins is the text of the New Testament since that is both the original and originating written witness in our possession to both the historical Jesus and the primitive community's faith stance toward him. A first step then would be to look behind the text with the historical critical tools of research to discover the man Jesus to the extent that this is possible. A second move would be to examine the resurrection or Easter experience which is the genesis itself of specifically Christic faith, the beginning of the Christian movement, and, in embryo at least, the beginning of the Christian Church. A third step would require an examination of the meaning of the various expressions of that new faith in Jesus as the Christ of God. The New Testament is the record of a variety of Christologies and understandings of God, human existence and the Christian life. This investigation would be called New Testament Christology or the history of the Christologies of the New Testament. A fourth step would be to look at the various Christologies that have been formulated by the Christian community after the New Testament period. This would include especially the central conciliar statements, but also the general history of the doctrine and theology of Christ. To put this in another way, the New Testament is a founding and constituting document; it looks both backward and forward. Behind it is Jesus which it interprets in the light of Easter faith. We can know something about this Jesus through the use of critical historical method, so that the historical Jesus becomes the basis of a Christology that is mediated critically and apologetically by the discipline of theology. In front of it is the future Christian community. For this ongoing Christian community the New Testament provides the first interpretations of Jesus as the Christ which are an inspiration to the community, a source for the continuing interpretation of Jesus, and also, as will be shown further on, another norm for understanding who Jesus is.

The final step in Christology would be constructive. It would consist in the reinterpretation of Jesus Christ and his meaning for today in the light of the situation and questions of contemporary culture. With varying weight all that has preceded this interpretation provides the data for such a reinterpretation, which, it must be assumed, should be faithful to the data it interprets. Thus the underlying apologetic structure, which is one of correlation corresponding to the inner logic of Christic faith itself, becomes apparent in this procedure. Christology is the continuing interpretation of Jesus. In the following section of this part of our discussion we shall deal with the first four areas of Christological research. The point will not be to develop these areas in an original manner or in any detail, but simply to point out some of the issues that have arisen and the conclusions that have been arrived at in recent years.

THE DATA FOR CHRISTOLOGY

The Life and Death of Jesus

A few decades ago many Scripture scholars felt that one could affirm practically nothing definite about Jesus. The documents we possess concerning him, namely the New Testament, are inflated and religiously symbolic expressions of the faith of the earliest Christian communities and reflect not Jesus as he had been during his own lifetime, but rather the situation and struggles of these various communities themselves as they sought for autonomy and identity. Without denying this, scholars today are confident that the accounts of Jesus, especially in the Synoptic Gospels, but not excluding John, are still based on memories of Jesus, and, hence, using a variety of techniques and criteria, one can make some general but historically authentic statements about Jesus. There is even a consensus about certain features of his life. This material may be divided into three broad areas: Jesus' message, his manner of life, and his death.

The central message of Jesus' preaching was the Kingdom of God. Actively or dynamically understood this is the rule of God, the effective action of God in the world that would change the actual situation of human suffering by putting an end to history or radically changing it by the establishment of a new order. Jesus thought that this would occur shortly. What would be established objectively would be the hoped-for condition that marked the end of all human suffering, a situation of peace, reconciliation and human fulfillment. Jesus' preaching was thus a challenge to be converted to this rule of God and to lead a life that was congruent with it.

Much can be said also about the broad lines of Jesus' life. He went around doing good; the miracle stories reflect this. He associated with people who were considered socially as sinners and outcasts; he often interpreted the law in favor of people and according to the higher principle of the rule of God which implied the love of God for all. He spoke of a God who forgave sin and declared sins forgiven in God's name. For him the whole of God's law and will could be summarized in two commandments that are really one: Love God and love your fellow human beings. In general Jesus' life is depicted as one lived totally for God, but for a God who is totally for human life and its fulfillment. And behind all this, some exegetes reasonably postulate a powerful religious experience of intimacy with God that expressed itself in Jesus' term of address to God, "Abba."

The important thing here is to see the message and the behavior of Jesus as one. Together they define the "logic of his life" which led to antagonism principally with the religious authorities of Palestine. And the spiral of this confrontation led in turn to his execution, by the Romans, to be sure, but he was handed over by the Sanhedrin. One may postulate that Jesus approached his death freely in the sense of dedicated loyalty and fidelity to his experience of God and his understanding of the Kingdom of God. Historically the life-death cycle appears as a failure because he was rejected by the people he preached to and his closest disciples seemed to fall away in the end in discouragement.

The Easter Experience

There are many things that may be said about the resurrection. But at least these two questions should be kept distinct: historical or religious philosophical statements about the resurrection experience itself and theological statements about the content of the experience or what is revealed in it. The first question is really a kind of bridge to the second.

The historical questions ask what the experience of the resurrection was, on the assumption that all revelation is a form of religious experience and that theological statements have their grounding here. At the death of Jesus, one sees on one side seemingly discouraged and scattered disciples. And on the other side one sees an enthusiastic group of disciples preaching Jesus risen. What happened to effect this change? It is generally agreed that the Easter experience is a form of faith experience. It did not have as its cause or object an empirical historical event like the resuscitation of a corpse. The resurrection can only be "perceived" by or in faith. Thus the resurrection is not an objective proof or apologetic datum that leads to faith; it is rather an experience of faith itself. The empty tomb stories, and the appearance stories, are thus symbolic expressions of a new faith experience of the disciples.

The theological content of this experience and hence what is asserted in the resurrection stories is that Jesus is risen, Jesus is alive, Jesus is taken up to God, Jesus is glorified and exalted by God. The faith experiences then are not mere subjective feelings, but are intended as assertions of reality. Something real although transcendent is disclosed in the experience of the resurrection so that faith is not the cause of the resurrection but rather "Jesus alive" is the cause of the experience.[17] This is the assertion of the New Testament stories. In fact, then, the Jesus affair did not end with his death because Jesus was experienced as alive in the sphere of God. God had vindicated and ratified the message and the life of Jesus of Nazareth.

Under the impact of this experience Christology properly so called begins. And this Christology is marked or characterized by two shifts or developments. First, in the light of the Easter experience that recognized Jesus as risen, the disciples begin to reinterpret or understand in a new light the Jesus of Nazareth with whom many had been associated. Obviously they were helped in this reflection both by the memories of Jesus and by the Jewish Scriptures and traditions that shaped the whole religious outlook of both Jesus and themselves. And, second, the message of Jesus became intimately linked and even identified with his person. Jesus did not preach himself, and it is becoming increasingly probable that he did not assign himself any messianic status. But since Jesus was now grasped as the risen one of God, reflection naturally merged his message of the Kingdom with himself as God's bearer or mediator of that reality. This is Christology, the attempt to understand who Jesus as the Christ is.

New Testament Christology

The whole of the New Testament is in a sense a reflection on, or at least a reflection in the light of, the experience that Jesus is the Christ of God. It is a reflection on the person of Jesus Christ, and, in close correlation with this, on the work of Christ, what Jesus did on earth and does as risen Lord. It is also a reflection on the implications of this, for example, on the life to be led on the basis of faith in Jesus as the Christ. The important thing that exegesis and biblical Christology have shown is that the New Testament is pluralistic in its response to these questions; it contains many different Christologies which cannot be reduced to one single conception. The books and individual passages in them represent different communities, or different traditions of reflection, or different avenues of approach in explaining the content of the common faith that Jesus is the Christ. These Christologies did not arise all at once but have a developmental history linked with the concrete circumstances of the different communities. What they all share in common, however, is that they are expressions of a faith in God focused exclusively in or through Jesus.

Most are familiar with the most common Christological symbols insofar as they have become a permanent fixture of Christian language. The work of Christ is mainly seen in terms of revealing and some form of redemption or salvation. "He died for our sins." And regarding the person of Jesus, he is the Messiah or Christ, the Savior, the Lord, the Son of God, or the Word of God (Logos). Along an axis that is not necessarily chronological, the titles and conceptions regarding the status of Jesus get higher and higher toward divinity itself. Jesus as the Christ is finally seen as pre-existent and sharing in the divine life of God.

In one sense, one sees in biblical Christology the complete or full structure of Christology. The historical Jesus who is remembered is, in the light of the faith experience of his being raised, interpreted as himself the bearer and mediator of divine salvation. And hence he is affirmed to share a certain divine status. The experience of the resurrection, then, is the bridge between the historical Jesus and Christological reflection, not just chronologically, or genetically, but also structurally. In one sense the experience of the disciples of Jesus risen and that

of Christians today is not so different.[18] But while the structure is complete, it is open, because it has relevance for ongoing Christian life in
history. The texts of the New Testament are themselves symbols that
open up to a future in history. The interpretation of Jesus is thus an
ongoing history of interpretation.

The Council of Nicea

The history of the interpretation of Jesus Christ has continued after
the New Testament period up to our day. The history of the Church's
doctrine on Christ and the theological traditions of Christology are all
data for contemporary Christology. There are of course some conciliar
statements and doctrines that are more important than others, and the
single most important is that of Nicea in the year 325. The Council of
Chalcedon (451), which contains the fuller and better known classical
statement of the doctrine of Christ, really presumes Nicea which is a
statement concerning Jesus' divinity. Ironically, Chalcedon was con-
vened in a crisis that needed a solution which would reaffirm Jesus'
humanity in a way that would balance with the Nicene assertion of his
divinity. In other words, that which must be assumed today, namely
Jesus' humanity, had to be defined in the fifth century. This startling
fact should warn us of the distance between the patristic period and our
own.[19]

Nicea cannot be understood without tracing the history that led to
it. In the course of that history the symbols "Logos" and "Son of God"
which point to Jesus' divine status were the controlling ones. But against
the assertion that Jesus Christ in his origin and pre-existence was less
than God, Nicea affirmed that the Logos or Son of God was strictly
divine, one in substance with the Father. The statement explains the
divine status of Jesus by affirming directly that the Word or Logos or
the Son that was incarnate in the historical person Jesus was no less
than God. And this statement became a credal norm for Christological
confession for the whole of Christianity. A negative result of this was to
shift the focus of Christology to the person of Christ and to his divinity
and to lessen a soteriological concern, at least overtly, for the work of
Christ, and especially the historical career of Jesus, as the starting point
of Christology.

Like the New Testament itself, this norm for belief must be
respected in any Christology. But at the same time, since it too is an
historical statement, it must also be reinterpreted in a language more
fitted to our culture, without losing its underlying intentionality. The
norm for orthodoxy cannot simply be the words of a proposition, since

what is being expressed by word-symbols transcends the verbal expression. Moreover, as historical statements they are limited by their historical context and suppositions and thus ultimately more relevant to a past culture than our own. Ultimately, the norm for orthodoxy lies within the dynamics and logic of Christian faith itself, and this is constituted and defined by the absolute Christian commitment to Jesus himself as the normative symbol for understanding God and the reality of human existence, in fact, for understanding reality itself.[20] That commitment *itself* implies that God was present and active in Jesus in a unique way. That is orthodox which expresses, explains and protects that faith commitment and praxis. Thus, what Nicea affirmed, namely that no less than God was at work in the life and person of Jesus, is already implied in the existential faith criterion.[21]

These are the data for Christology presented in the barest schematic form. They consist in the life of a man and a growing history of reaction to him and interpretation of him. These two elements, the actual life of Jesus and the interpretation of him, are completely inseparable for us today. We cannot arrive at any historical knowledge of Jesus except through the New Testament interpretation. And, genetically, Jesus, his teaching and the way he lived his life made an impression on the people of his time, and it is this impression, expressed in extraordinarily different ways, that we possess. But it is precisely the inseparability of the New Testament message and the person behind it that has given rise to a certain confidence that there is continuity between message and person. To put it analytically, in the New Testament interpretation of Christ there was at work an historical imagination, a *memoria Jesu,* even when this was being religiously "inflated" in the light of the new faith that was constituted in the resurrection experience.

The reason for this perhaps over-long and exaggerated emphasis on method in Christology lies in the fact that something crucial is at stake here. Method should be seen as corresponding to the fundamental structure of one's understanding of that which is being understood. At stake then is the structure of Christology, how Jesus Christ is to be understood and interpreted today. The thesis proposed here is that the material focus of the specific Christological concern, as opposed to the more general systematic concern of the meaning of the Christian message, is Jesus of Nazareth, the human being Jesus. The primary and specialized concern of Christology deals with Jesus. If there were no Jesus, there could be no Christology. If Jesus did not make an impression on his disciples and others, there would have been no Christology. If Jesus were not a religiously attractive figure, if there were absolutely nothing extraordinary about his life, there would have been no Christology. If Jesus did not live according to his message, his message is dubious. It is certainly true that without the experience of the resurrection there likewise would be no Christian faith and without its reality that faith would be in vain. But it is Jesus who was raised. And if Jesus did not live according to God's will, the assertion of *his* resurrection is quite unintelligible and even meaningless. Jesus was raised because of the way he lived his life. It would be difficult from our position in the world to assign any other possible logic to that event.

The structure of Christology is such, then, that all specifically Christological thinking has its material focus in the actual life of Jesus of Nazareth. This demands an historical point of departure (through the discipline of history) and an historical logic in understanding Jesus the Christ. It is as important to note what this does not mean as what it does. It does not mean that history as a discipline can show Jesus to be the Christ. Nor is it a question of being able to say many things about Jesus. Actually we know very little about him. Rather the point at issue is the locating of the exact center of Christianity in a this-worldly symbol and seeing, with the whole of Christian tradition, that the *axis mundi* of Christian revelation and faith is an empirical historical event, a concrete person of history. Jesus of Nazareth is the grounding source and this-worldly material basis of Christian imagination. This does not make this historical Jesus, that is, Jesus as he can be known today through the discipline of history, the exclusive norm of all Christian theology; Jesus did not reveal his resurrection, and there are too many other sources for Christian theology to make such a claim. But it does mean that our historical knowledge of Jesus is *in some sense* a norm for specifically Christological issues.[22]

The normative quality of our knowledge of the historical Jesus is seen precisely in the structure of Christology itself, in the fact that the Christian imagination's medium to God, or God's revelation to us, occurred in and is focused through Jesus. Negatively this implies that one cannot make statements about Jesus Christ that contradict what we know of Jesus historically, as not a few from the history of Christology plainly have. A religious symbol is open and polyvalent, but this does not mean that it is open to every imaginable interpretation. Jesus is in some degree a negative norm for Christology. And, positively, statements of faith about the risen Christ should likewise be bound to Jesus as their subject. All that we know of the risen Christ, even in faith, aside from the fact of the resurrection, is bound to and related back to Jesus as the one who was raised.[23] In this sense, revelation about Jesus Christ is no exception to the transcendental conditions of all revelation and faith knowledge which are bound to the world and to history. Christian statements about Christ always lead back to their subject, Jesus of Nazareth.[24]

In conclusion, then, these methodological considerations will have a great deal of bearing on Christological interpretation today. Presumably, the point of Christian theology is to render intelligible to our contemporary world the meaning of the faith vision that was mediated through Jesus Christ and the bearing that it has on human existence today. In Christology this task will be done by focusing on the Jesus of history and seeing how his life, which led through death to resurrection, releases salvific meaning, and, because of that, responds to the question of why he is called the Christ.

Chapter VII
INTERPRETING JESUS FOR TODAY

The first part of this outline for a contemporary Christology dealt with the historical data on which such a theological enterprise is based. This second part will consist in the religious interpretation of that data and of Jesus as the Christ. This interpretation is made in the light of, within the context or horizon of, the problem of human existence.

Every interpretation arises out of a focusing concern. But in a systematic theology such a concern should be made explicit. Moreover this problem should be more than just my personal question if it is to generate a Christology that illumines human existence as such. What then is the crisis of our time? I have suggested that that crisis can be identified, and that it is implicit in liberation theology. Stated very broadly it consists in the crisis of the meaning of historical existence as such which is raised by the degree and the sheer amount of human poverty and suffering that history displays. What does human existence mean, viewed now on a corporate level as social existence which we share as a race, when that human existence is so meaningless for so many? This is not simply the question of suffering, but of the massive suffering that characterizes global human existence today. There is no need to document this here; all are aware of it. The significant aspect of the situation, however, does need underlining, and that is the fact that it is a universal problem. It concerns everyone. Individuals or groups cannot ultimately claim that their lives have meaning while masses of others live out a seemingly senseless human existence. Because of the unity and solidarity of the race, apparent to us now more than ever before, it is logically and, if one is sensitive, emotionally impossible to claim that my personal human existence is meaningful and fulfilled while that of a third or a half of the race is not. What is called into question, then, is the meaningfulness of human existence as such in this world, in history. What is the *humanum*—what does it mean to be human and to live humanly in this situation? More precisely, what is put into question is the meaning of the symbol of salvation. The tradition holds that Jesus Christ is Savior and that salvation gives meaning to human existence. The question today is this: What does this mean in our current situation? Who is Jesus Christ and what is the salvation that he wrought?

In what follows I will discuss a possible response to these questions and thereby develop an interpretation of Jesus as the saving Christ. This will be done in several steps, but once again it has to be insisted that so brief a discussion can only constitute the barest outline that merely points the direction for a possible Christology. I shall begin by reflection upon what is going on in such an interpretation in order to clarify further some issues concerning method. Then I will deal with the work of Jesus, what has been traditionally called objective salvation or a theory of redemption. But this reflection will keep close to what we know of Jesus himself.[1] The third part will deal with the person of Jesus Christ, the Christological question narrowly so called. Then I shall return to the point of Christology, the question of the actual salvation that Jesus Christ mediates to human experience in history. The final point will be a summary or conclusion which will show how the themes of liberation theology are preserved in this interpretation of Jesus as the Christ, and how salvation addresses freedom in all three of its dimensions.

INTERPRETING JESUS AS THE CHRIST

An interpretation of Jesus as the Christ that goes into the formation of a Christology might fittingly begin with an account of what goes on in such an interpretation. The Christian interpretation of Jesus Christ is based on faith, Christic faith, that is, a faith in God mediated through Jesus. While it may seem evident that a religious interpretation is based on faith, still the implications of this are not always fully drawn out. Since interpretation of Jesus as the Christ is based on a faith stance toward Jesus, indeed since such an interpretation is precisely an expression of this faith stance, it follows that this faith is the inner source and the inner criterion of what is being expressed. In one sense, interpretation is interpretation of Jesus. In another stricter sense, interpretation is a coming to expression of what is implied in one's faith stance toward God mediated through Jesus. Two things flow from this. The first is the fact that the ultimate criterion of correctness or orthodoxy in every Christology is faith itself and whether or not it is adequately expressed, explained or accounted for. In other words, the adequacy of Christology is not measured by the comparison of one interpretation with another, either biblical or traditional. Rather it is judged by the inner logic of faith itself and whether or not that faith is accounted for. Secondly, the ultimacy of faith in God mediated through Jesus is shared by the medium itself. Christic faith means that one takes Jesus as the concrete medium of God to oneself; he is the disclosure of God, the place where and through which the ultimate meaning of reality, the world, human existence, history and God are revealed. Jesus must be such as to enable that mediation. This revelation and faith stance, then, constitute a given; this is the position in which the first and the latest Christians find themselves.[2] This positive fact of human faith in God mediated through Jesus is thus the basis of Christology. Christology is an explanation of this faith. This faith is the ultimate criterion of orthodoxy and no other; this faith must be coherently explained. And a coherent explanation will always imply that Jesus is not merely Jesus but also the Christ.

A Christological interpretation of Jesus is an interpretation in the light of the experience that Jesus is risen. This experience, as was noted earlier, is a faith experience that Jesus is alive and lives in the sphere of God. This faith of Christians today, despite significant differences due to proximity to and knowledge of Jesus, is not totally dissimilar to the original and originating faith experience of the first disciples. The structure of Christian faith today is analogous to that initial and founding faith witnessed to in the New Testament. In other words, Christology flows from an actual faith, as that faith exists today, and is not simply grounded externally or extrinsically on an objective faith witness taken as an external authority, even though this handing down is the way that the content of faith is initially communicated to and through the Christian community.[3] Christology emerges out of the inner faith of the community and the interpreter; it is not primarily a manipulation of objective ideas, concepts and formulae into a coherent system. Conceptual coherence is of course a task in systematic theology, but much more fundamentally and structurally Christology is an account of the faith that is within, a faith in God centered in Jesus of Nazareth.

There is then an inner structural tension in every Christological interpretation of Jesus. This interpretation contains two aspects that actually pull against each other, namely the historicity or actuality of Jesus' life reconstructed and imagined, and the religious interpretation that faith sees in that life. A religious symbol always has an intrinsic and intelligible this-worldy appearance and meaning, an internal coherence of its own. But at the same time it points beyond itself to a transcendent power and meaning in which it participates. That is, this transcendent power is found within the symbol by the religious experience of it. These two aspects are true of Jesus as well and must be held together in closest tension as both pulling against each other and as positively informing each other. On the one hand, Jesus was a human being who led a human life. It is not possible that an historical reconstruction of his life will demonstrate his transcendent significance, even as it is unlikely that that transcendence was evident to those who from the beginning rejected him, or to those who lived with him but turned away in discouragement in the end. Yet on the other hand, this Jesus was remembered and, in the light of a religious or faith experience of God's ratification of his life, the one who was remembered became the focus of initial and continuing Christic faith. Thus on one side Jesus and the memory of Jesus shaped the New Testament witness to him and Jesus continues to shape Christian faith in God. The mediating symbol enters into the interpretation. And on the other side, the experience of God through Jesus' life and in it reflects back and informs human appreciation of him. Jesus is disclosed and seen in a new light. These two dimensions of Christian faith, represented by history and dogma, thus pull against each other. And yet they also inform each other as well. There must have been something about or in the actual life of Jesus that points to the faith that God raised him; otherwise the original faith experience (and the resurrection itself) would be totally arbitrary and completely unintelligible even as a possible religious consideration. There must be some ground in Jesus' life to make the resurrection of *this* man, that is, as opposed to some other or any other, credible even for faith. Thus our actual faith in Jesus alive *looks for* and finds by religious interpretation the historical grounds for itself. In other words, Christological interpretation today is not unlike the formation of the Christologies of the New Testament itself.

Let me try to re-express this unity in tension which is crucial in religious interpretation and which has its anthropological ground in the very structure of religious symbol, experience and language. I suppose and begin with the fact that Jesus mediates transcendence to the Christian believer and the whole Christian community. On the one hand, looking back to the New Testament and through it to Jesus, one has to say that that transcendence cannot be reduced to history. For example, it does not appear as a super-naturalistic history, and the transcendence cannot be reduced to miracles and wonders. Ironically, the more one tries to see the transcendence that Jesus mediates in terms of "supernatural historical events," the more one really empties that transcendence, immanentizes it, and in making Jesus a wonder-worker makes him incredible as a mediation of God. But on the other hand, Jesus mediates transcendence. The elemental structure of this mediation is the same as in any concrete religious symbol. The sacred mountain for the Mexican Indians on the Yucatan peninsula mediates transcendence precisely by being the solid, permanent, overpowering, forbidding and majestic mountain that it is in its concrete particularity and thereness. So too, with the obvious differences implied in the fact that Jesus is a human being, Jesus did and the historical Jesus still does radiate transcendence, mediate it, disclose it, manifest it, to people who consider his life religiously. In other words, there is something about his life that was not like others and that enabled and enables him to have the religious impact that he has had. This transcendent dimension is not "added on" to but is found within his genuinely human career. But at the same time that person and human life constitute a medium of what is strictly transcendent. Thus one *does* find in one's analysis of the Christian religious experience of Jesus *historical grounds* for this experience of God in Jesus.[4]

We must insist again that Christological interpretation is interpretation of Jesus of Nazareth. The human person Jesus is no longer on earth and is not available to human experience in the same way as he was to his contemporaries. Earliest Christic faith and hence Christological interpretation included and was structured by a living memory of the man, since the resurrection experience is not to be considered as a *direct* experience or encounter with a supra-historical reality. Analogously the human being Jesus is no longer available to our direct experience except through historical research, reconstruction and representation. It follows that this historical reconstruction, Jesus as he is known through historical reconstruction, provides the concrete or earthly symbol that structures Christological interpretation just as in the past it was the memory of Jesus that served as the basis of this interpretation.

Moreover, what we know of Jesus by historical research, as little as this may be, operates in a special normative way in our interpretation. This is to be understood cautiously lest what can be said interpretatively of Jesus appear to be reduced to historical assertions. The principle is not to be taken to mean that one could not say more about God and about Jesus Christ than is revealed through Jesus' life and death, because the resurrection itself is a further datum of revelation. But what is said of Jesus Christ must be referred back to the Jesus who lived on earth and be correlated or verified in the historical contours and logic of his life as that is potentially known to everyone by historical research. Jesus then is the concrete referent and focusing point for Christian statements about God. His life, as reconstructed, is norm in the sense that one should not predicate of God or of Jesus as the Christ things that are contradicted by what is known of his life. Also, the account of his life is a focusing point in the positive sense that Christian assertions about God and about Jesus himself are to be seen as having some basis in the life of Jesus. Without such a norm or focus, there would be no protection against inauthentic images or experiences of Christ that are opened up by the pluralism of the New Testament itself. Epistemologically it seems necessary to interpret the Christian meaning of God and of Jesus in terms that have reference to the historical image provided by an historical reconstruction of the life of Jesus. Our statements should be referred back through Jesus as it were and from him into our own present and future. This is true even when these interpretations, which are made in the light of the resurrection, extend far beyond what the particularities of Jesus' life in itself may yield, that is, beyond any merely or strictly historical understanding of his life.

The interpretation of Jesus does not depend on our being able to say many things about his life. The binding of Christological interpretation to the historical Jesus is not be taken as a new fundamentalism. Such a mistake can be seen operating within or underlying two approaches to Christology that are radically opposed to each other. The one seeks to uncover as many details of Jesus' life as can be found to propose for our imitation. The other says that because these details cannot be uncovered, the structural basis of Christology is not Jesus at all but the New Testament kerygma or message about him. Rather the basis of Christology is both the sheer fact of Jesus' appearance and the fundamental structure or whole logic of his life taken precisely as a whole. Any particular detail of Jesus' life, each of which can only be established with varying degrees of probability, only has relevance insofar as it fits into the general scheme of his whole life. Christological interpretation then does not rest on any detail of Jesus' life that may be isolated and taken singly as the determining factor. It is rather the whole of his life that makes up the historical symbol on which Christian faith is based, and a portrait of that life can be reconstructed with authenticity.

Finally, it remains to underline the importance and significance of this last point. Jesus was a human being who lived a human life, the last years of which were given over to a public career in service of the Kingdom of God. As a concrete symbol, then, he is not simply an idea or a composite of qualities and virtues. Rather it is the whole of his life that defines who he was. In existential language he was what he became by the way he lived. How is one to grasp such a life as a whole? One way is to look for the most fundamental intention or direction of Jesus' life. This may be done by narrating the story of Jesus or stories about him as is done in the Synoptic Gospels. These stories, whether or not they are historically authentic or accurate in their detail, seek to disclose the transcendent dimension spoken of earlier that lies precisely within Jesus' earthly career. They may be read as seeking to disclose the transcendence that was present or was perceived within his concrete human life. More analytically, but with the same existential intention, Jon Sobrino speaks of the faith of Jesus.[5] Sobrino's use of this category does not represent an attempt to reconstruct Jesus' self-consciousness, which cannot be done directly since we have no historical sources. Rather, faith is a transcendental anthropological category. It may be assumed that Jesus as a human being lived by faith as all human beings do. The point of the category of faith, then, is that, when it is understood existentially, it operates as a hermeneutic device enabling one to ask about the fundamental option or the intrinsic logic of a human life. In Jesus' case, this is contained in his teaching and in the events of his life. The analysis of Jesus' faith then is really an analysis of the whole human life of Jesus as that is revealed in the stories of the New Testament about him. In sum, the stories about Jesus communicate the teaching and actions of Jesus, and in them the logic of Jesus' life as a whole is indirectly described and communicated. And, inversely, the historical statement that Jesus lived for the cause of God and other human beings in terms of the Kingdom of God is displayed in stories about him. Christology is interpretation of the work and person of this Jesus on the basis of this data.

THE WORK OF JESUS

Jesus' whole life is a revelation of God and of God's Kingdom. This revelation is not to be read in particular aspects of his life taken singly, as for example his cures or his confrontation with religious authority. As was said, we do not know enough about single elements in his life, except that they are elements of a coherent whole. That whole life is marked by the consistency of the message of the Kingdom of God that he preached and the manner of life he led, one which was itself conducted under God's rule. As it is frequently said, Jesus did not just preach the Kingdom of God, but he lived it and mediated it to the people with whom he associated. If this were not the case it is doubtful that he would have been remembered as significant at all. The picture drawn by historical research is of a person in whom the intention and power of the God he preached was realized; it became real and actual in his life. In other words, the inner logic and coherence of the actual life of Jesus, even as we know it, was set or constituted by God's cause, and this cause was symbolized by the Kingdom of God which was for human existence.

Jesus' life taken as a whole, then, is a symbol mediating a revelation or disclosure of the nature of God in relation to human existence and the nature of human existence in relation to God. What shines through Jesus' life, his message and conduct, is God's meaning or intention for human history and the intrinsic God-given logic and direction of human living.[6] This core of the revelation contained in Jesus' life is not complicated; it is utterly simple. One must get beyond the idea that for revelation to be significant it must be a revelation of a whole lot of things, answers to all sorts of human questions taken singly. The revelation mediated through Jesus' life is ultimately one and is able to be appreciated by every human being and thus transculturally. It is expressed well in the phrase of Hans Küng that God's cause is the cause of human existence.[7] And the other side of this, since every revelation of God is also a revelation of human existence, is that the meaning of human existence lies in surrender and commitment to God's cause. God is the power of life in the world, and human life is meant to reflect and to actualize God's general intention for it. It is not that this transcends at this level the message of the Old Testament; it simply ratifies and for the Christian definitively confirms it.

The death of Jesus also contains revelatory power. Positively it reveals the depth of Jesus' conviction. Dying is part of one's life. We can be quite sure that Jesus approached his death with fidelity.[8] Even the text that has been taken by some as a cry of despair is really one of hope since it is addressed to God. The way Jesus approached death discloses that the Kingdom of God, the rule of God's general will, is more important than his or my life taken singly. Jesus surrendered his life to the Kingdom he stood for; it was more important than his survival. This death then is the supreme confirmation of Jesus' life; his very life and the *whole* of it was handed over for the Kingdom of God.

But Jesus' death, again seen as a dynamic process, has another and more negative revelatory dimension. Jesus' death cannot be understood as simply an arbitrary incident, like being hit by a falling tree, or even as a decision of a few to eliminate him. Jesus' message and person were roundly rejected. The actual historical causality here thus takes on a deeper meaning when seen as the coherent result of the logic of Jesus' whole life and as in this way revelatory. And this historical logic too is terrifyingly simple. As far as we know, Jesus went around doing good and he was put to death for precisely that. He preached God as totally good, forgiving and *for* human life, and this amounted to a confrontation with the given religious and political culture. It was not only the leaders who rejected him. In a sense one can see a certain inevitability in this, and once one does, once one grasps this inevitability, one is standing nakedly before the radical sinfulness of human nature. The violent execution of Jesus is a revelation of the sinfulness of the human condition, and it appears strikingly in inverse proportion to the sheer goodness and love of God that is disclosed in or through Jesus' love and concern for his fellow human beings. Jesus died because of our sin.

The resurrection of Jesus is a further revelation of God through the life of Jesus in the sense that it is its ultimate transcendent culmination. It is Jesus who was raised and not someone else. The meaning disclosed in this resurrection is the final and absolute yes of God to the message and life of Jesus. Jesus' life, despite its apparent historical failure, is vindicated. What is disclosed in the resurrection, as experienced reality and as symbol, is that the message of the Kingdom of God of this Jesus is God's message. The resurrection also says that Jesus is God's messenger, and that the logic of the way he lived his life is the meaning of human life itself. Moreover, above and beyond that, the symbol "resurrection" is also a revelation of the future of this kind of life.[9] The resurrection is a symbol of hope that says death itself is overcome by the loving and saving power of God. This faith is thus an extension of faith in God as Creator and provident, the confirmation of the pointed faith that God is the author and thus the finisher of human life.[10] In his life Jesus was the one who was totally dedicated to the Kingdom of God and faithful to it to the end. And in the resurrection that fidelity is met by God's own overcoming of the tragedy of human life and even death itself.[11]

Looking back at the work of Jesus, then, how is his salvific work to be viewed or defined? Jesus Christ is the revealer or the revelation of God. Jesus Christ is Savior by being the definitive revelation or disclosure of God to human beings and to history at large. This is the conclusion that flows from taking an existential, concrete and historical approach to the Christ event. When one begins by seeing Jesus as a human being, which one must if the apologetic structure of Christology is to be maintained, the work of salvation does not appear as a transaction between God and God, between God and a divine Logos, but between God and a human being and then between God and human beings through the mediation of the historical event of Jesus. In terms of the various classifications of different types or kinds of salvation theories, the view of Jesus Christ as revealer might be called an exemplary theory of redemption: Jesus Christ is the teacher and model of salvation as the first saved and in the sense of being the paradigm of salvation itself.[12] Jesus Christ appears relative to the world as normative but not constitutive of the salvation of all human beings.[13] For Christians Jesus Christ is indeed constitutive of their actual salvation, but relative to those who never come in contact with him in the world, Jesus Christ is potential Savior. The universal relevance of Jesus Christ is an open possibility for the whole of human existence because in him is God's decisive and unsurpassable revelation of God's own self and of the intrinsic meaning of human life in relation to God.

The problem, however, of characterizing the view presented here as an exemplary or revelational theory of redemption is that this is contrasted with views that presuppose cosmological or ontological explanations as the very basis for understanding Jesus Christ. The conclusion is then too quickly reached that Jesus is being presented as "merely a prophet" or as merely a man, even though with the highest religious consciousness, and thus fit to be our model. Indeed this characterization is generally projected back on the liberal Christologies of the nineteenth century because these theologians generally eschewed (wrongly) constructive metaphysical or ontological speculation in the sense of the Scholastics. It must be recognized that to say Jesus is a normative revelation for human beings is to make an enormous claim, and one that is clearly ontological in its implications.[14] To claim any revelation of God is to get involved with the metaphysical presuppositions of how God is related to the world, and especially to this particular human being. To say that Jesus is the decisive revelation of God and what it means to be human is infinitely to transcend the idea that Jesus was merely a "model" or an "example" for human existence. In what follows we shall see how any Christology that claims that the event of Jesus is a genuine revelation or disclosure of God implies that God was at work in Jesus.

THE PERSON OF JESUS CHRIST

The strictly and narrowly Christological question about Jesus Christ concerns the nature of this person, his status in history and before God. And the consistent confession of Christians has been that the human being Jesus is also divine. The question is: What does it mean to say that a human being is divine? How may this be interpreted and explained today?

Again, this question, which concerns the historical Jesus, cannot be answered without looking at the historical Jesus. One cannot begin speaking about Jesus as a kind of pre-existent being or divinity or about the resurrected Jesus raised to the status of God without considering the human being Jesus who is a personage in our history. The statements about Jesus' divinity must be bound or linked to the Jesus of history in some overt way; negatively, they cannot simply be asserted on the sole basis of the resurrected Jesus since we do not know the resurrected Jesus apart from the Jesus of history. They are the same person.

Looking at Jesus one can say that God was operative in his life. This can be seen at several points or in different ways. First, the way he addressed God as Abba indirectly points to a profound religious experience that was the psychological ground or experiential source for his message and manner of life.[15] Second, the fidelity and obedience that characterized his life manifests a deep union of wills with God or dedication to God. Third, Jesus' whole life appears to have been marked by a self-abnegation or self-negation in relation to God. He did not preach himself but God and God's Kingdom. And, beyond that, the self-emptying and life lived for God appeared as a power that was at work in and through him. This would account for the authority which he displayed and which was recognized by his followers. In other words, the power of love that was exercised by Jesus may be seen as the power of love that is God's power, which is present in him precisely in the measure that he surrendered himself to that power. At this point, all of this is to be understood in the categories or on the level of Jesus' consciousness, although we know nothing about this directly, and dedication, that is, in the historical terms of a moral union. Surely God was present and at work in him to this extent.

The Christian affirmation is that God was present to and at work in Jesus in a qualitatively unique and unsurpassable way. There are at least two grounds for this confession. The first is the resurrection. Insofar as Jesus' resurrection is unique, so too is the implication that Jesus is God's in a unique and qualitatively special way. The experience and affirmation that Jesus is risen is at the same time an implicit assertion that God was present to Jesus during his life in a definitive way. And, second, the affirmation of Jesus' uniquely divine status is implicit to Christian faith in him. Christian faith takes Jesus as the decisive symbol for the disclosure of and contact with God, and as the basis for understanding the meaning of reality. As was said, such a religious symbol both remains what it is finitely and also mediates or makes present God. The intrinsic logic of a faith that takes Jesus as the final or normative revelation and disclosure of God necessarily gives that symbol a unique status relative to God. God is present and immanent there as in no other place, event or person.

Still another step to be taken is to try to express the manner in which the power of God was in Jesus, God's union with and presence to him and, reciprocally, his union with God. Here the many different symbols used for this purpose in the New Testament become both disclosive and authoritative.[16] The most significant of these, because they imply the highest claims, are "Spirit of God," "Logos" and "Son of God." But once again it is important to see that these are religious symbols that point to the transcendent dimension of Jesus' life and person and are not to be understood as if they were giving an objective description or literal account of empirical this-worldly data, and much less an objective description of transcendent reality. The Spirit of God is God's life-giving presence and power which the New Testament sees operative in Jesus in a unique way. Logos is God's wisdom, God's rationality that pervades the created whole of things, God's ordering and meaning-giving disclosive power and presence. It is the same presence and power of God as indicated by God's Spirit, but it contains as well deep metaphysical overtones from both Jewish and Greek culture. A Son of God is one especially chosen and beloved of God, a person elected to become God's instrument. All of these are figures of speech and religious symbols. Even when they become personified in Scripture, this is not literal speech. These symbols are not to be understood as explanations of how God was present in Jesus and hence how Jesus was divine. They are symbols that express and open up to the experience of others that God was in Jesus.

Finally, a finished Christology should try to explain or describe on yet another level, beyond the historical and metaphorical language of Scripture, the union of God and Jesus Christ. This must be done because this question is inevitably raised: Just what is the status of Jesus Christ ontologically, that is, as a human being and thus a being, relative to God and other human beings? How was divine being and power within him relative to his human status? Some norms for this language would be the following. It should be a dynamic conceptualization to correspond with a union between God and the freedom that is human existence. It must correspond to and illumine what we know of Jesus' historical life. It should be ontological language, dealing with the being of Jesus Christ, but should not describe the union in merely physical or cosmological concepts. The union was a personal one. Language that is dynamic and representative of an intercourse between two freedoms can also be ontological. But finally this kind of explanation will always remain speculative and hence changeable; that which it must obey is the logic of Christian faith commitment itself. This, as was said earlier, is the final norm for orthodoxy. In other words, Christians find themselves, as the earliest Christians found themselves, in a relationship to God that is mediated absolutely by Jesus who is therefore the Christ. From this the inevitable Christological question arises: What manner of man is this? And its response demands an understanding of Jesus and of God at work within him in such a manner that accounts for one's standing before God through an absolute commitment to Jesus Christ. What has to be explained is not that Jesus was a human being; that is a given. What is to be explained is how God was so present to him and he so united to God as to be the definitive revealer of God for the human race. Jesus is not a substitute for God but the definitive way to God.[17] And Christian faith does not attach itself to the historical Jesus as it were in himself, but to God through him because God was at work in him.

To summarize, the tension between the historical and the dogmatic interpretations of Jesus as the Christ is magnified in the final systematic and ontological "explanation" of his person. This tension and the cautions it contains give us the parameters for this question in Christology. On the one hand, ontological language concerning Jesus' divinity must be understood as remaining symbolic.[18] Even when one is integrating one's understanding of Jesus Christ into a total view of the world, God and history, what is said of Jesus' divinity must not be read as literal or representative knowledge. We are dealing here with absolute mystery, or, more precisely, how the transcendent God was present to and operative in the person of Jesus in a unique way. If the symbolic nature of this Christological language is forgotten, one will inevitably see disastrous consequences. An example of such a distortion is seen in the "two nature" expression of this mystery in which Jesus' divinity is asserted on the same plane as his humanity, as if it were not symbolic expression, so that inevitably Jesus' being a human being, despite the assertion of humanity, is absorbed into the divine to constitute an implicit monophysitism or docetism.[19] On the other hand, one cannot simply leave off the description of Jesus by saying that he was united to God through his intimate God-consciousness and the absolute commitment of his life and will. This functional language by itself is not "explanatory" or even sufficient because it begs the whole question of how that could have been the case in any human being. *How* could Jesus have been sinless? All the historical explanations of Jesus' divine quality inevitably raise the question of how God was present to this man in a unique way; indeed, every historical explanation forces the affirmation of Nicea that this was the case because no less than God was operative in the whole of Jesus' person and life in a unique way.

This tension will probably be best preserved today by some form of a Spirit as opposed to a Logos Christology. The symbol of the Spirit of God is in itself a more dynamic concept than the other, one that can be adjusted to preserve the integrity of Jesus' being a human being. Moreover, the Spirit of God is also a symbol that corresponds to the experience that human beings have of God operative in their own lives. If this symbol of God's Spirit were combined with Aquinas' use of the concept of instrumental causality (or sacramental or symbolic causality) in Christology, a concept that distinguishes and yet preserves the total integrity of the instrument even while it is joined to its higher and principal cause, God, one might be able to present the divinity of Jesus in a convincing way for our historically conscious culture.[20]

SALVATION THROUGH JESUS CHRIST

Although Christology has frequently focused narrowly on the constitution of Jesus Christ, a necessary question, the point of Christology is the salvation wrought by Jesus in the world. We return then to the work of Jesus Christ viewed as salvation that is released into history and appropriated by human beings.

What is the salvation that Jesus mediated? A response to this question must be formulated in terms of the problem of human existence that has come to dominate our consciousness today. This is the problem of the meaninglessness of human history that was formulated in Chapter II, so that it was seen to become the focus for theology today as was developed in Chapter III. Salvation does not lie in an affirmation that there is a God, nor even in a promise of immortality. Philosophers have affirmed this. It does not lie either in Jesus' preaching or announcement of the Reign of God. Utopias in themselves appear incredible to us today. And as was said earlier, the mere postulate of another world or an after-life by itself may undermine the meaning of the actual history of this world. Rather salvation appears in the way Jesus lived his life. His life was not simply an affirmation of the Reign of God; it was rather a creation of the Reign of God. This was manifest not in a cosmic act that accomplished an already complete Kingdom of God. Rather it appears as a process that was exemplified and effected in Jesus' actual historical doings. Jesus is a revelation from God that says that the meaning of history is not simply there for human beings to discover; it is rather a possibility to be created by human freedom. History *may* be meaningful, or it may indeed be meaningless. Certainly much of human history is meaningless, and our perceptions about the profound ambiguity of it all do not deceive us here. But in Jesus one sees a human existence that *is* meaningful. And were it generalized or extended out into the social sphere of public history, the result would be a just social order, constituted by just social relationships, where the lives of the suffering and oppressed would be attended to through the institutions that human beings create. Jesus thus reveals that meaningful history is *possible*, that is, it has a possible and not an inherent or necessary meaning, through God's power to the extent that human beings are willing to accept and live in God's power.

This revelation of Jesus that human history can be meaningful can only be apprehended itself as meaningful and credible by a person who is actively engaged in creating that meaning. The principle underlying such a statement is really quite simple and applies to all existential realities. On the one hand, one cannot explain to another who has never experienced freedom or acted freely what freedom is. The phenomenon of human love is incomprehensible to those who have neither experienced love nor themselves loved. So, too, given our situation in which the massive degree of social injustice and oppression of the weak calls into question the meaning and value of corporate human existence itself and its history, the sheer assertion that human living ultimately makes sense and is of ultimate worth cannot make sense unless it has some experiential evidence on which to rest. Without that evidence such an assertion appears utterly gratuitous; it is in fact groundless, arbitrary and incredible. But on the other hand, when one actually works to build just human relationships, when one struggles to assist in the emancipation of the freedom of some human beings and actually succeeds in some small measure, there one has real grounds, however tenuous, for asserting not only a meaning but possibly *the* meaning of history. In this effort one comes in contact not merely with an abstract idea or notion of salvation; rather one experiences it from within, by participation, in one's being a subjective agent for the creation of such a possible meaning. Ultimately the salvific meaning released into history by Jesus is not some idea of a comprehensive just social order that we expect to come about. The Kingdom of God will not be realized in history; such a utopic concept, apart from its critical function in human consciousness, still remains incredible for us. Rather the salvific meaning that is mediated through Jesus lies in his way of life, the actual service to fellow human beings in need. The victory, the Kingdom of God, is simply not within the power of human freedom. It is only at this point that the symbol of resurrection, the faith that God is also the finisher of history, has meaning. The point is that just as in the objective and exemplary case of the crucified one, we too have to recognize that the resurrection of history lacks coherence and sense unless it is a resurrection of a history that itself makes some sense and has some corporate value. One can only legitimately hope for resurrection and ultimate salvation who somehow grasps the possibility of corporate salvation here and now by participating actively in it.

For the salvation revealed by Jesus Christ to become real it must be historically actualized. The historical salvation mediated by Jesus' life, death and resurrection, therefore, really consists in discipleship.[21] To put it negatively, salvation is not simply believing the message of Jesus Christ concerning resurrection and eternal life or *that* he is Savior. It consists rather in conversion, and this implies living a life after the pattern of Jesus' life under God and God's rule. This *imitatio Christi* is not a doing of things that he did as if there were no cultural difference between his world and ours. It has nothing to do with mimicking the behavior of a first century Jew. It consists rather in allowing the revelation or meaning disclosed in Jesus' life not only to illumine our own but also to transform the way we live. It is an historical entering into the logic of the life of Jesus and allowing it to shape as fully as possible the fundamental logic of one's own life. It is a being opened up to the world and to God in a new way, a being-in-relation-to-God-and-the-world that is played out in one's fundamental option and action. This salvation is first of all a personal salvation, for this is where conversion and the conscious direction of one's life is centered. But it is also marked by a social dimension because human freedom extends outward into society and history and is in turn constituted by and in its relation to society. Moreover this personal salvation becomes itself a social history of Christian salvation when groups take up corporately the structure of Jesus' life in the world. It is not that this salvation is an exclusive Christian possession. God's salvation has been universally available in history.[22] Rather this salvation becomes explicitly Christian when one experiences the clarifying and definitive manifestation of the dynamics of God's salvation in Jesus Christ.

But, finally, there is more to the dynamics of salvation that has to be accounted for here. It was said earlier that a revelatory disclosure of God is always also a manifestation of human existence in relation to God. The revelation of God in Jesus and of God's relation to human existence is also a disclosure of the condition of human existence itself. And this is really a double disclosure: Human existence is laid bare for what it should or could be, but also as it actually is. Especially in the movement of Jesus' whole life toward a seemingly necessary violent death the mystery of the inner sinfulness of human beings is opened up to us. Thus the reality of the salvation manifest in Jesus Christ is really an external and objective salvation relative to history and the actual human condition. The possible meaning of human life is embodied in Jesus and the message of God has become publicly and historically available through the preaching of this message. But because of the reality of sin deep within the human condition, it still remains an objective and external vision, a possibility to be realized, and one which requires an internal or interior principle of appropriation in each human life. This is the only way to explain why some seem to accept this salvation through conversion and others do not. Traditionally this internal principle has been named by the biblical symbol, the "Spirit of God," and it has been treated in the history of theology under the category of "grace."

These will be the subjects of our next discussion. At present the Christological themes outlined here might be summarized in terms of the symbol of liberation.

THE THEMES OF LIBERATION IN CHRISTOLOGY

To conclude, I wish to simply point out how the salvation of Jesus Christ responds to the question of human existence, in all its dimensions, but especially to the problem of human existence where it comes to a focus in the crisis of meaning for historical existence that was described at the outset. We will then be able to see how the themes of liberation Christology are preserved here.

First, in the message of Jesus Christ the intrinsic logic of personal human freedom is revealed. Personal freedom as it actually exists always lies in a polar tension between action and passion, between actual freedom and actual bondage, dependence and unfreedom. The message of God mediated through Jesus addresses both poles of this tension. The message of Jesus, that which is revealed through his life, concerns the possibility of a freed freedom in service to the world of others. But even for freedom in the bondage of inescapable oppression, be it physical, biological, psychological or social, the revelation of Jesus is an offer to trust in human life because of God. This is an acceptance of life, not as it is, but in what it will become as guaranteed by God's rule. One can still be a disciple of Christ in sickness, old age and utter dependence. This opening up of the self in confidence to life because of God and for no other apparent reason is still a freedom and a new kind of existence when measured over against fatalism and despair. But God's revelation is not addressed only to human dependence. When freedom is more self-possessed, strong and active, the logic of one's trust should move a person, to the extent that this is possible, toward a more dynamic freedom that strives to act in concert with God's general will for the Kingdom as that applies in one's immediate situation.[23]

Second, the message of the Kingdom of God's rule is a social image that correlates directly with social reality and addresses the social bondage of human freedom. As a disclosure of both God and human existence at the same time, Jesus' message and life practice is a divine judgment that social oppressions are both against God's personal love for all and a product or effect of human sinfulness. As a message of salvation Jesus' life and resurrection are first of all a promise that this situation is not the end; God's Kingdom will come. This revelation is also the announcement of the direction in which human history now *should* tend. The Kingdom is an ideal model or religious vision for human society. And, finally, Jesus' appearance is a challenge of love to the freed freedom of individual persons and to groups to care for each other in society and to work for this Kingdom of love and justice. As in the case of Jesus, such a thrust will inevitably come up against resistance and unfold in conflict.

Third, to the problem of freedom longing for transcendence but in bondage to finitude, the message of Jesus Christ offers the promise of resurrection and final salvation. And to the freedom held in the bondage of sin and self-concern, which prevents a life from opening up to this promise and acting consistently with it, Jesus is a saving challenge to conversion to the rule of God. This conversion will only be effected, however, through the power of God's Spirit.

The term "liberation" and the themes of liberation Christology are preserved in this view of Christ as the revelatory response of God to the problem of human existence.[24] This is not a neutral Christology. But at the same time it responds to the problem of human freedom in the world in all its dimensions. To grasp the connection of Jesus Christ to human existence as it actually is today, one must begin Christology with an attempt to understand the historical Jesus and his message precisely in historical terms.[25] There is a strict correlation between the center of Jesus' message of the rule and Kingdom of God and a religious perception of the direction and intention in which actual human history and society should move. Jesus' message concerns the possible inner meaning of the whole of human existence.[26] It is the actual life of Jesus that is the intrinsic ground and source of Christian revelation because it is here that the Christian message was begun and first actualized. The risen Christ is the Jesus of history about whom we do know something historically. But the norming Jesus is also the risen Christ, interpreted for us and open to new interpretations. It may appear that Christology, in its concern to overcome abuses in spirituality, does not give sufficient attention to Christ risen—our hope for an absolute future. But then the Christian cannot hope for the absolute future without following the historical Jesus. Given the suppositions of our culture today and the concrete existential threats to the meaning of historical life, liberation theology is correct in viewing the salvation of Christ in historical terms. Consistent with this, then, it is true that Christ's salvation becomes an actual reality in history in effective conversion and discipleship. The praxis and process of liberation in history is salvation for those *who participate in it* on the basis of conversion. It is true that the passive reception of emancipation, the receiving by a person or a people of a new freedom at the hands of others, may be perceived as an objective and saving gift from God.[27] But this only becomes an interiorly appropriated religious salvation in the conversion and response of love that actively turns toward the service of others. Salvation consists in the active participation in the process of liberation for others. Understood in this way, in terms of Jesus the Christ, the identification of salvation insofar as it occurs within history with the process of liberation is theologically correct.

Schillebeeckx begins and ends his Christology with a story, a parable of a crippled man.[28] So, too, Latin American Christology begins with a story, not fictional but one that is historically actual, literal and going on right now. It is the history of the suffering of thousands of people in every urban slum in every city, of hundreds of thousands of peasants exposed, undernourished, uneducated and dying before their time because of disease in every country, adding up to millions of people on that continent. This is also the story of oppression, that is, one of conflict, violence and persecution, one not only of inability but also of refusal to address the situation and calculated control of it.[29] Like a parable the Latin American story is generalizable, but as history; it is occurring all over the world. This situation is our situation, this suffering is everyone's suffering, this senselessness crushes meaning out of everyone's human existence. Within the Latin American situation liberation theologians are retelling the Christian story which is about an actual human being who in his situation identified with the poor, marginalized and persecuted and went around doing good. In so doing, he understood himself as championing God's cause for human life and against forces that suppress it. For this he was willing to die. And "because of this" God raised him up (Phil 2:9) to confirm a revelation of God's will for history, to be a source of religious inspiration and commitment, and to provide a sign of human hope. The lived logic of Jesus' life is God's revelation to the world; it is simple, transcultural and universal; no one can fail to undertant it, for it deals with the basic elements of human existence: with good and evil, freedom and unfreedom, life and death. This revelation bestows salvation, a liberation at every level of human existence, in the measure that people take up the message through discipleship, that is, by living a life after the pattern of Jesus.

Chapter VIII
THE SPIRIT AS GOD'S GRACIOUS LIBERATING PRESENCE AND POWER IN HUMAN EXISTENCE

In the last chapter, it was said that Jesus' saving work should be characterized as revelation. Systematically, the transition from Christology to the theology of the Spirit of God or pneumatology is the transition from the salvation that was revealed in Jesus to its actualization in history, in other concrete beings. What one sees in Jesus is an external and objective message of salvation. The further question thus arises as to how this objective salvation becomes realized existentially in other human beings in history. The classical theological distinction that expresses this new consideration is the difference between objective and subjective salvation.

This distinction is really very basic to Christian understanding and thus deserves to be clearly underscored. The last two chapters of Christology proposed a revelational theory of redemption or salvation, a salvation that has actually been going on from the beginning of human history. Jesus Christ is Savior by being the public revelation to history of God's salvation in history. Jesus is the paradigm, the definite and definitive manifestation of how God acts in history in a gracious and saving way. This means that the salvation that was actualized in Jesus Christ was precisely the salvation of Jesus; what one sees in Jesus Christ is Jesus being saved by God. Jesus displays, reveals, manifests, discloses, exemplifies God's salvation in history. God acted in Jesus, and Jesus responded; thus God's salvation was completed in Jesus. But it is patently evident that that salvation is not completed in the world or in history. In Jesus, God revealed God's intention for history and human life and the direction in which history should move. However, if one assumes a concrete, existential and historical point of view, it becomes apparent that the world is little different today in terms of salvation than it was

140

before the advent of Jesus Christ. It is true that on the topic of salvation, I described the life of the Christian disciple as one that participated in salvation. But at the same time, the life and death of Jesus are also a revelation of the sinfulness of the human condition. The stance of discipleship is not automatically assumed by anyone. The message of salvation, then, remains an objective or external one, one still to be realized in human persons and in history at large. The question of both the theology of the Spirit and the theology of grace, then, concerns how this message becomes internalized and appropriated by human beings.[1] How does the salvation revealed in Jesus become the reality of human life and of history? For this to occur there is the need of an internal or interior principle in human existence, one that overcomes sin and appropriates this salvation into human life. In Christian theological tradition, this is the role of the Spirit of God and the question is dealt with in the theology of grace.

In this chapter on the Holy Spirit, I will use the two terms, "the Spirit of God" and "grace," as synonymous and materially identical in their referents. The Spirit of God is grace; grace is and refers to the Spirit of God. The two symbols thus point to the same identical reality. This conflation of these two Christian symbols is not consistent in the Christian tradition. Indeed, after Augustine it is not the dominant usage. Since this is the case, something should be said to recommend this usage, even though it is not possible to offer a full justification here.

Ultimately the justification of this conflation lies in the basic meaning of these two religious symbols. The Spirit of God is the biblical symbol for God's power immanent in the universe. It is the power of life in the Old Testament and applies especially to God's power as it is manifest in human beings. In Christian tradition, the Spirit is the immanent power of God working in human beings, inspiring, turning one to God, providing the basic energy for one's faith and movement toward God. In the New Testament, the Spirit appears to be poured out anew in the light of the eschatological happening in Jesus, but it is the same Spirit of God who is always at work in history. Jesus is experienced not only as alive but also as present to the community in the Spirit. At times no distinction is made between Christ present and the Spirit. The Spirit then is God present and as power at work within human lives.

Grace too is God's power at work in the world for salvation. The special quality of grace is that it is absolutely gratuitous and free. The doctrine of grace asserts that grace or salvation is not owed to human existence, not won for ourselves, so that we have no claim upon it. God's grace and the salvation which it brings are totally free. This corresponds to the biblical saying that the Spirit of God blows where it wills.

Although the terms "grace" and "the Spirit of God" do not have a consistent meaning or usage in the New Testament, still one of the ways
that the experience of the actualization of salvation through Jesus is
expressed is in terms of grace that refers to the pouring out of the Spirit.
And certainly the Spirit of God is grace. In other words, among the myriad meanings and functions of these symbols, the New Testament also
uses them as synonymous. Grace is the Spirit which has been given us.[2]
But no systematic or consistent use of these religious terms can in turn
be consistent with each and all of the New Testament usages.

The same is true of the tradition of the theology of grace.[3] Augustine indeed did consistently see grace in terms of the Spirit and tended
to identify them. In Aquinas, however, metaphysical questions and ontological categories shifted the notion of grace to refer to a created modi-
fication of the human soul caused by God. During the Reformation both
Calvin's and Luther's insistence on justification by grace through faith
shifted the focus of the term grace to Christ, God's forgiving Word, and
away from the Spirit.[4] Even Rahner, who in a sense reclaims the Augustinian tradition and whose whole system is open to an identification of
grace with the Spirit, seems to refuse to do this. Grace is the presence,
power and indwelling of the whole Trinity.[5] There is no consistent meaning, usage or referent to the term "grace" in theological tradition.

The result of this inconsistency of theological language is simply
confusion. It is almost impossible to study the theology of grace apart
from the history of the doctrine that mediates to us its content and
meaning. Yet it is very difficult to communicate exactly what has been
learned, or even what the subject matter was, when such a study is finished. I believe that the differences in the languages of grace can be transcended by the identification of grace with the Spirit of God and without
thereby compromising in any way the genuine insights that are part of
the tradition and which were generated by any particular language. This
may be a way of getting behind especially Catholic and Protestant differences in this crucial area, differences which are in large measure
sheerly a function of different languages. There is a development in theology and doctrine such that new distinctions are made, new insights
gained, new themes isolated and opened for investigation, new doctrines
formulated. The problem is that these doctrines tend to take on a life of
their own separated from the whole of the Christian message seen
through its center. In a sense, I am proposing a reversal of the development of the theological branches by a return to the trunk of the theological tree. Doctrines should be seen in their interrelationships, unifying foundations and central symbols. From a concrete, existential,
anthropological point of view, both the symbols "grace" and "the Spirit"

point to the immanent presence and power of God within human experience. The theology of grace is the theology of God's Spirit at work in human life. Thus what follows will be a theology of the Spirit, or the work of God's Spirit, in terms of the theology of grace.

What are the issues involved in the theology of grace, the theology of the Spirit? It is most important to set the questions of the theology of grace since, as was just mentioned, the history of this doctrine and its theology can be hopelessly confusing. During the course of history, the theology of grace has engaged a great number of diverse problems so that it is often difficult to discern exactly what is at stake in the whole of this theological discussion. Once the central issues are clarified, however, it will appear that this area of theology is absolutely foundational relative to the whole of Christian doctrine.

As far as I can see, taken analytically, there are three issues or questions at stake in the theology of grace. First of all, the theology of grace is a return to the question of just how God relates to human beings and to history. But here one is not dealing with this question objectively from a notion of God or from a merely objective look at Jesus' revelation, although these are not excluded. The question here is how God is experienced concretely as acting in my life and in the lives of other human beings. The Spirit of God is the symbol reflecting the actual Christian experience of God in Christian life itself. For example, in the doctrine of God, one says that God is turned toward history and human life and is provident. In the doctrine of Jesus Christ, one says that God has acted in history and in a definitive way. But what does it actually mean to say that God is provident, that God acts in history? How was God present in Jesus Christ? Nothing can really be affirmed here apart from some experience of God actually acting in history, some religious experience of God's Spirit present and at work in human beings. In this sense, this theology represents a *reprise* of some of the issues seen in the doctrines of God and Jesus Christ but from the distinctive point of view of religious experience illumined by the appearance of Jesus.

The second basic issue that immediately flows from the former is how human existence is related to God. God is experienced as acting in a new and definitive way in human history in the life of Jesus, and this is also a revelation of ourselves to ourselves. But what exactly does Jesus Christ reveal about the nature of human existence? That is, in the light of Jesus, how do Christians actually experience themselves as human beings standing before God and in relation to God? This is the question of Christian anthropology, the understanding of the nature of being human in the light of Christian revelation. A large part of the theology of grace is nothing more than a theory of human existence from the standpoint of the Christian experience of God's Spirit in human life. What does it mean to be human from the standpoint of Christian religious experience that is mediated, structured and illumined by Jesus?

Third, putting the former two issues together, the final basic issue implied in the theology of grace is precisely that of the union between God and human beings. Just how are we united to God? How is this union fashioned and constituted? The questions of how God relates to human existence and the reciprocal question of how human existence stands before God come together in the basic religious issue of the relation between God and human existence and history.

From these three issues, one can understand why that which is at stake in the theology of grace and the Spirit is absolutely foundational to both Christian theology and to Christian life. In the theology of the Spirit, one moves explicitly to the existential order of how God is actually experienced in Christian life. This self-consciously concrete and existential viewpoint gives the conclusions reached here a certain priority even over the notion of God and the meaning of Jesus Christ. This is so because what is affirmed of God and Jesus Christ really emerges out of the experience of God working salvation within human existence now in the present. Almost inevitably, the fundamental structures and contours of the actual historical and contextual experience of God and God's salvation provide the hermeneutic focus for understanding the data for theology from the past, the objective record of Christian tradition. This is so since affirmations about God and Jesus Christ can only have meaning to the extent that they correspond to some aspect of current experience. The issues contained in the theology of grace are so basic that one can find within positions taken here the fundamental ideas that structure a whole theology and give it its distinctive point of view in its interpretation of all the other doctrines.[6]

Moreover because of the foundational character of these issues and the explicitly existential point of view of this theology, it is also foundational in the sense that it bridges doctrine and life. The theology of the Spirit and the response it provides to the issues it engages supply the very basis for Christian spirituality, when spirituality is understood as synonymous with the Christian life. In defining existentially and theologically the fundamental relationship that obtains between God and human existence, in effect the theology of grace is methodologically circular: it interprets the doctrines of tradition out of Christian experience of the Spirit, and at the same time it applies these doctrines to the interpretation of the Christian life. In this area, one finds the basis for the meaning of such ideas as religion itself, piety, conversion, religious life, being united with God. All spirituality, all views of the Christian life, either presuppose or implicitly affirm conceptions that are explicitly dealt with in the theology of grace.

Because of the a priori character and relevance of the theology of grace and its existential significance for spirituality and the Christian life, it is vitally important that the context for it be set in connection with the problem of our time, the crisis of the meaning of history. Once again, the seeming meaninglessness of human historical existence must form the focus for the theology of grace. And as in the case of the Christ, this focus can be stated in terms of a question or a problem that has apologetic import. People outside Christianity ask whether hope of an absolute salvation outside of history does not necessarily make Christianity dysfunctional relative to taking with absolute seriousness the problem of human suffering. And this elicits the following questions for ourselves. What *is* the signficance of grace and existential salvation for our lives *within* history? Is Christianity, as life in the Spirit of God and a corporate spirituality and way of life, ultimately an attachment to God that allows human beings to tolerate, cope with, and passively endure the meaninglessness of history in the hope of an absolute salvific future out of this world? Is Christian salvation a purely personal and individual event, a cure, a healing, a making whole that establishes a person with an absolute and eternal identity before God alone? Or does Christian salvation contribute to making meaningful our public, social and historical human existence? Is the grace of God's Spirit an impetus to commit human freedom to history and an empowerment to participate militantly in history against the causes of human suffering and the forces of oppression? These questions could be rephrased in a hundred different ways. The point of them is to situate and focus the theology of grace, existential salvation and the Christian life within the context of the crisis of our time.

Once again I propose to respond to these questions through an interpretation of liberation theology. I will begin by briefly enumerating a number of fundamental themes that characterize the liberationist theology of grace. And in a constructive response to these themes, the discussion will consider in succession the idea of sin to which grace is a response, the reality of grace, the effects of grace and the general consequences of this for spirituality. In all of this it will again be most apparent that what is presented here is merely a schematic structure for a theology of grace that would have to be developed further and at great length.

THEMES FROM LIBERATION THEOLOGY

All of the suppositions, principles and themes enumerated in Chapter I have a bearing especially on the theology of grace, since they characterize the experience and context of liberation theology itself. In isolating five specific elements of the liberationist theology of grace, I am drawing on two major studies that deal explicitly with that subject and define as it were the distinctive character of the liberationist interpretation of the doctrine.[7]

Grace or the action of the Spirit of God is viewed as functioning in relationship to human freedom. Human existence itself is defined in terms of freedom. "A human being without freedom would not be a human person."[8] Yet assuming that human freedom is held in bondage, the essential function of the grace of God's Spirit is to free freedom, to release this fundamental quality of human existence to actually be liberated and free. Thus, in Segundo especially, the action or effect of grace is essentially a process of humanization.

On the existential level of concrete historical existence, therefore, liberation and salvation from God are convertible. God and God alone is the principle of salvation. And most concretely this salvation consists in the Spirit of God at work within humans. In other words, it is not in the first instance the content that fills choices and the commitment of freedom to a specific object; rather salvation is the very liberation of freedom itself. God's Spirit overcomes passivity and engenders activity.

The grace which overcomes the determinisms and obstacles to freedom at the same time directs it toward its exercise in the world and history. Freedom *from* is also a freedom *for,* a commitment of love in the world. God's Spirit does not draw human freedom out of the world, as for example in the conception of the late medieval classic *The Imitation of Christ,* but draws freedom into history and society toward the liberation of others.[9]

Thus the history of salvation in the world is a process of liberation in the world. This general view is typical of the whole of liberation theology, but the grounds for it are most carefully laid by Segundo with his view of the effects of grace as liberation.[10] In other words, the effects of the liberating action of God's Spirit in human existence are outgoing and expansive in history, so that one can see the total effect of God's grace in history as a collective history of liberation.

The conclusion of all this is that the Marxist critique of religion, or more generally the secular humanist view, does not hold in the case of Christianity. Or, for those generally sympathetic to Marxist analysis of society, its view of religion must be completely re-evaluated. For in

Christianity, the whole dynamism of the movement of God's Spirit in Christian life is toward participation in the process of liberation.[11]

This is no more than a list of the bare assertions of the liberationist theology of grace, and yet the cumulative force of these statements reveals a dramatic reinterpretation of grace and the saving action of God's Spirit in history. The fundamental question that is raised by all of them, however, is the same: Why do Christians need the concept of God's Spirit acting in history, the idea of saving grace, in order to explain human freedom and love? At least in quite ordinary situations the ideas of human freedom and love are taken for granted so that one does not need to invoke an intervention of God or grace to explain them. Does one need grace to explain the love of a mother for her child or every instance of self-sacrifice? Do not atheists participate in the process of human liberation? In order to ground the very idea of grace, then, one must turn to the bondage of human freedom by sin.

THE REALITY OF SIN

It was said earlier in the reflections on revelation and Christology that revelation is always a manifestation of both God and human existence, and that in Jesus, especially in his death, the human condition is revealed as sinful. I shall briefly outline in what follows the datum and the mystery of sin. For sin is the reverse side of grace. In a sense, like grace, so too sin must be revealed to us. How else would human beings know that we should not be the way we actually are? In the very revelation of grace sin too is disclosed, for grace is the disclosure that the human situation does not have to be the way it actually is. This correlation and reciprocity between sin and grace is reflected in the entire history of the theology of grace; grace has always been understood in close relation to sin.[12] Thus sin is a datum of Christian anthropology and salvation is to be understood, although not exlusively at least in part, as salvation from sin.

The term "sin" pertains to human freedom. Sin is not the same as evil which is a more objective and neutral term. If people die in an earthquake, this is not usually looked upon as sin. For whom would sin be predicated of in this case? Sin rather pertains to human responsibility and implies guilt. This sin can be found on all three levels of human freedom.[13]

In its most radical sense, sin pertains to personal human freedom. It is the bondage of human freedom to itself within itself. No one understood this better than Augustine, no one pondered it more deeply, and no one has described it more profoundly, not even Luther. Human freedom is indeed spirit, that is, non-matter, and hence precisely unencumbered and dominant over matter. Human freedom transcends the self and one goes out of oneself into the world with knowledge and choices and action. And yet the human spirit is at the same time turned in on itself; it is bound by egoism. The "natural" tendency of freedom is to go out of itself toward the other in order to use the other for the self. Of ourselves and by ourselves we cannot leave ourselves and surrender in altruistic love to another; the weight of our free spirit, its existential drive, is to subordinate all else to ourselves. This is not the same dynamic as described by Segundo who tries to reduce freedom to activity and sin to passivity. It is precisely in the activity of freedom, when freedom is most free and powerful, that it can be most sinful. In both Augustine and Luther, this fundamental bondage is called concupiscence—at worst an utter inability to transcend the self in love, at best the inescapable egoism that inherently flaws all our seeming love. The effect or symptom of this deep-seated sin consists in sinful acts, acts that treat other people as things or objects, as having no value in themselves, and hence in acts that injure others. But sinful acts are the tip of the iceberg to use the Freudian metaphor. If one does not recognize this, it will be very difficult if not impossible to recognize the working of grace.

Human existence is also sinful socially; there is such a thing as social sin, even though it is more difficult to recognize as sin and not merely evil. What one sees on the surface and what is clearly recognizable are the social effects of sin. One sees social institutions that not only structure the human freedoms of people, but also crush them, oppress their very being, cause suffering and push many toward untimely and unnecessary death. These structures are more than the effect of sin; such social structures may be called rightfully sin, and not merely the effects of sin, since they are not merely evil and products of nature. Two suppositions are needed to see this. The first is the phenomenon of interdependence; all human beings depend on one another, so that human existence itself is strictly social. The result is that the structures of society become internalized in each member of society to forge the condition of the consciousness and freedom of each person. The way we are as persons is socially constituted. The second is the fact that social structures are not the products of nature or creation but of human beings; they rest on the stuff of human freedom and can be changed. Therefore human beings are responsible for social structures; we participate in them and in so doing sustain them and help produce their effects. In other words, the overt effects of sin lead back to sin itself, and this is also a social reality in which we all participate and cannot fully escape. This is not quite the same as personal sin, for we have not personal but rather social responsibility for social structures. It is precisely social sin, analogous to personal sin in which we have personal responsibility, but still sin in which we participate freely and socially. And this is formal sin to the extent that we become aware of our situation and do not take responsibility for changing the structures in which we participate.

Human freedom also has a transcendent dimension, and on this level it is also in bondage and this bondage is sin. We have already described the transcendental longing of freedom for that which is infinitely beyond our capacity—for what is absolutely true and good, for the ideal, for the infinite and the absolute. Yet here again, human freedom appears tied to history, to the this-worldly, to what is tangible and thus immediately satisfies. The bondage appears then as the inability of human freedom to surrender itself, to give or hand itself over to that which infinitely transcends the self and on which the self is absolutely dependent. It is on this level that sin is called disobedience; it appears as unfaith, an absolute clinging to the self, to one's absolute auto-nomy, in the face of an appeal from the absolute and transcendent.

This description of sin is a description of human freedom and human existence. It points to the intrinsic structure of human existence as we know it. This structure itself is original sin; all stories about some originating event are simply projections that try to account for this mystery. Original and originating sin is the structure of human existence itself, and it is a mystery, for one cannot quite understand why the Creator created human existence this way. It helps, of course, to say that God takes human freedom absolutely seriously, and the very condition of freedom is the ability and possibility that it try to absolutize itself over against the other and even God. Yet this sin is more than a neutral possibility of fall; it seems more like an inherent tendency and inescapable bondage. The only thing that can be said is that this sin would be an embarrassment to God, a question put to God, if we did not know that while sin abounds, grace abounds even more. And this too is the structure of human existence from the very beginning.

THE REALITY OF GRACE

Christianity has consistently held that there are two orders of God's immanent activity in the world. The one is the order of creation in or by which God is present and active to the whole of finite reality by God's sustaining power. The other is the order of salvation which points to an ever new and different presence, activity and power that is saving. On the one hand, God is Creator and the whole finite order, the world and its history, is related to God as absolutely dependent creature. On the other hand, over and above this, God is Savior in a way that is revealed by the new and unique activity of God in history through Jesus Christ. Thus human existence also relates to God as saved when under the influence of God's saving activity.

As all know, this distinction between the orders of creation and salvation has had disastrous results for Christian theology. The distinction came to be seen in this-worldly terms. Christians saw a separation between a history that was fallen and sinful and a history that was under the influence of God's saving grace. The created world was divided into two histories. In the medieval period one has a division between nature and the supernatural or gracious saving order of God's presence that was "built upon" or laid on top of nature. When the order of creation or nature is viewed as sinful, the sphere of grace and salvation, which tended to be identified with the Christian community, appears as over against the secular human world and its public and social history. In the modern period, when human culture sees itself as an autonomous sphere defined by its own science, laws, politics and morality, the sphere of God's saving initiative appears as authoritarian, extrinsicist, interventionist and even unnecessary relative to life in this world.[14]

Today it is difficult to decide whether this traditional distinction between the two orders of God's relation to the world is useful. On the one hand, without this distinction, it is difficult to understand why the Christ appeared or even what the need of such a Savior is. The distinction corresponds to the religious experience of God present and active in human life in the precisely dramatic new way that is exemplified in conversion but which, by extension, is implied in all religious experience. Without some sort of similar distinction there would really be no basis for speaking of the experience of the ever new initiative of God's Spirit in the world for salvation. On the other hand, the distinction does seem to lead almost inevitably to the harmful consequences just mentioned. However grace is explained, it should not be seen as extrinsicist or interventionist. At least this is certain: whenever the attempt is made to distinguish between the orders of creation and saving grace, they must be held together in a close and inseparable unity.

One of the clearest schemes for seeing both a unity and a distinction between the orders of creation and human nature on the one hand, and the order of God's salvation and grace on the other, is that of Karl Rahner.[15] Cosmologically and on the side of God, Rahner projects that the whole divine purpose and intention of creation is *for* salvation. Thus the orders of creation and salvation are absolutely united in God; created reality is intended for salvation. Negatively, salvation is not an afterthought, so to speak. Indeed the opposite is the case. God creates in order to save by grace, so that the whole created order is subordinated to and unfolds within God's plan of salvation.

Thus Rahner further postulates a double relationship of God to the world. God holds reality in existence by efficient creative power, the power of being itself. But over and above this, God is *personally* present to and within the human existence that God already sustains in existence.[16] Although Rahner explains this in terms of two different kinds of causality, the distinction ultimately makes sense in terms of an analogy from human experience. One can be physically or bodily present to another, and even enter into an exchange with the other, without really communicating the self to the other. A personal communication is always an added act of freedom, a self-gift or self-transcending surrender to the other. Inversely, one cannot wrest knowledge of or genuine self-presence or self-gift from another; it is always precisely a gift from a person's freedom. The order of salvation for Rahner, then, is God's gift of self, God's personal self-communication and self-presence to human existence beyond mere presence by the efficacy of creative and sustaining power.[17] Although because of this distinction one must conceive of God's grace as God's presence to human beings "above and beyond" God's creative presence, Rahner is quick to add that God is so present to *all* human existence, always and everywhere to every single human being, in grace. This is consistent with the very purpose of God's creating activity and presence; the two orders are bound together inseparably. This personal presence of God to all human beings is expressed by the symbol "grace," or, in this analysis, by the idea of the Spirit of God. The symbol, "the Spirit of God," thus refers to God, but to God under the following specifying formality: God's Spirit is God as personally self-giving and communicating, God as personally present to and dynamic and active within human subjects.

All of human existence is created into the sphere or order of God's grace, God being present to human beings personally through God's Spirit. How then does human existence relate to God? All human beings are related to God as creatures sustained in being by God's power. As such human beings are gifted with a relative autonomy and freedom. Human beings are not God but stand over against God. But beyond that, all human beings exist in the sphere or order of God's personal presence and saving power. Grace is universally available; all human beings and human nature itself exist within the sphere of God's Spirit, that is, God's being present to them and within them in a personal way. Of course one may by God's grace respond to this presence or not. But the point is that there can be no separation, no separation in time and no separation of different areas of life, between creation and God's personal saving presence and influence. The order of grace is an "existential," or a layer of actual existence, that never entirely eradicates the "existential" of sin; the two coexist in every person in one degree or another always. Moreover the existential of grace is not laid on top of the order of creation or nature; it is embedded in it as its deepest intention, dynamism and goal. Thus grace or the personal saving presence and working of God within the human person is a level of human existence itself; grace, although distinct from our created nature, is intrinsic to human existence itself as an always present gift or offer of God's self. God's Spirit is the constant personal presence of God within the human spirit. Given this schema or structure, one may now ask what the effects of grace are in human life, that is, how the Spirit of God effects human salvation.

THE SPIRIT OF GOD AND SALVATION

In this section I shall briefly point to the effects of grace, how God's Spirit is at work in human existence and what it accomplishes there. What is the evidence for a description of this kind? Ultimately the evidence for the operation of God's grace is religious experience. Although the Christian witness is by no means the only source for this data, I fall back on the testimony of Christian theology and Christian tradition. Thus, Scripture and the theology of grace supply us with these conceptions of how God is operative in human life. And in every case, the working of God's Spirit in human existence appears as a form of liberation.

First of all, it appears that the basic and the primary work of God's Spirit is in personal freedom. God's salvation is first of all an initiative of God in history that appears on the personal level. To put this in another way, God's saving grace, God's acting in history for salvation, is God's personal presence and initiative within persons taken individually. This conclusion seems inevitable. But it is not to be taken as a reversion to personalism and individualistic existentialism. Mere personalism must be transcended, but at the same time it cannot be bypassed. God acts first in persons taken discretely. If this were not the case, then religious faith itself would cease to be a personal and responsible affair. It would no longer consist in a personal relationship with God but rather in a social phenomenon, where "social religion" is understood in its pejorative sense. Religious salvation and the most immediate effect of God's grace or action in the world occurs in persons. If this be the case, one may be tempted to fault liberation theology for not attending sufficiently to personal conversion and the power of grace in the life of individuals. But liberation theology is correct in its criticism of a

Christianity that too often remains on this personalist level, a Christianity which in its institutional forms is dedicated to fostering individualistic piety.

The first effect of God's Spirit in human existence, then, is to free freedom; it is the liberation of the human spirit from itself. The effect of God's Spirit or grace is to overcome selfishness or egoism, the curvature of the human spirit in on itself, and to release it in loving self-transcendence. Grace is the presence and power of God drawing the self out of the self in love of the other in and for itself. This is not rare, and certainly this force of God's Spirit may remain anonymous; one need not be Christian or even religious to experience this power of God fostering love.

Why then does one need God's grace to explain the common phenomenon of love? Such an explanation only appears cogent over against the background of the experience of sin. If the power of sin is appreciated, then too will the need for some explanation of the power of love that overcomes it. Given sin, one must ask why there is any goodness or love at all in the world. This sin is experienced not in others but in the self. Thus when one really transcends oneself in genuine love, when one goes out of the self in love and service of the other that is really altruistic, it is accompanied by the experience, if not the confession, that the force for this love is not I but the Spirit or grace of God within me. It is not really within our own capacity to truly or authentically love. Thus God's grace appears as God's presence and power within human existence drawing freedom out of itself in love. And the effect of God's grace is the opening up not of new objects for choice but a whole new horizon of possibility within these choices of a loving response to others. Without this first and basic level of the operation of grace in human experience, there could be no liberation movement in history; there could be nothing but a spiral of competition and violence.

Second, grace and salvation can also be seen operating on the strictly social level. This is so because, first of all, a freed or loving freedom opens up out into relationships with others, in society and in history. But over and above this, the force of love can be institutionalized even as its opposite sin can be. There can be institutions and societal structures whose purpose and whose effects are loving and beneficial for people. Such for example would be the Church. But institutional grace may also be anonymous. One thinks here of a variety of voluntary organizations that exist only to serve others. Here the effects of grace, which are in every case some form of love, become strictly speaking social in institutions or societal structures that actually serve the freedom of other human beings. It should be noted that these categories of social sin and social grace are heuristic terms. There is no such thing as pure social sin or pure social grace. These categories give one a lens for appreciating and analyzing social structures and institutions.

Third, the effects of grace are also experienced within the transcendent dimension of human freedom. At this point, the experience of grace is explicitly religious, for it involves a surrender to the absolute or the infinite, to God. Here grace or God's Spirit moves the human person or a group to surrender to God, to obedience to God, to acceptance of God's forgiveness, to trust in an absolute future and hence in life itself as meaningfully leading there. This too is an experience of liberation, of liberation from the world and at the same for the world in the love and service mentioned earlier. It is a freedom or liberation from ultimate fear of the world so that one can participate in the world under God's rule. In this experience one realizes that one's own freedom and its history is leading toward God, and one participates in the history of the world as having absolute value because it too is leading toward God.

This whole view of how God acts in history by being present to human freedom and of the structure of human response to it is to be understood as strictly anti-Pelagian. Without discussing at length the many dilemmas and conflicts that have arisen in the theology of grace, some of which have divided Christians, I can at least allude to some of the crucial points. First of all, on the dilemma between God's salvific initiative and the reality and value of human freedom, it is now a commonplace to say that there is no competition between God and human beings, between grace and human freedom. *Within* the operation of God's Spirit, there is no either/or between grace and freedom. God's grace is the initiator and sustainer of all self-transcendence by human freedom. But God's presence and power in the human spirit is at work precisely within freedom.[18] God's creative power holds human freedom and activity in existence. And God's Spirit both pushes human freedom toward self-transcendence and lures it into the future, so that the whole of human response is absolutely and totally dependent on God's grace.[19] Freedom is totally sustained and supported by God's personal presence and initiative. But as was said in Chapter V, God does not determine the specific choices of freedom. The self-limitation of God thus allows for the reality, effectivity and hence value of human freedom. This adds up to a theory of cooperative grace, similar to that proposed by Augustine and Aquinas, but it does not allow for the neo-Pelagianism typical of later medieval theology. The operations of God's Spirit and human choice and decision occur on radically different levels; there is no cooperation here as between equal partners. Human freedom's movement toward salvation unfolds in a sphere that is totally supported by the influence of God's Spirit, both in its initiative and in the unfolding itself.

There is then no conflict between grace and works, for the works of the saved person are totally enveloped, insofar as they are salvific, in God's initiative and power.[20] This schema therefore preserves the fundamental value in Luther's theology at this point, namely his radical anti-Pelagianism, which I take to represent a view that cannot be bypassed in the theology of grace. God alone saves, and for that salvation God is totally responsible. The difference of the view of grace presented here, both from Luther and Calvin, is that, as was said earlier, it focuses attention on God's ongoing saving activity in the world through the symbol of the Spirit and not exclusively on Jesus Christ. Seen from a concrete, existential and historical point of view, Jesus is the revelation of God's saving Spirit. As such, he is genuinely the Savior by being the revealer of God's Spirit. But the Spirit of God is at work beyond the sphere of knowledge of Jesus. This shift, I believe, is therefore necessitated by the recognition of the universal saving activity of God, that is, apart from explicit historical recognition of Jesus, and the contemporary requirement that one approach Christology "from below."

THE THEOLOGICAL GROUNDS
OF CHRISTIAN SPIRITUALITY

Now if this analysis of the way God acts in history for salvation and how human freedom stands in relation to God through God's grace is correct, then one can make some rather clear statements about fundamental issues. First of all, religious salvation, which consists in some form of response to and union with God, is seen as constituted in the personal level of human freedom. One is united with God when one goes out of the self in love.[21] Union with God is primarily a union of freedoms, a union of wills. God's overcoming of radical sin in us and the human response of love sustained by God constitute union with God and human salvation here and now. And this can occur anonymously or "unconsciously," so that one's union with the God who is love remains implicit rather than explicitly conscious. But as was seen earlier, the human spirit is bound to the world and history. The field for the exercise of freedom, and the possibility for love, is thus everyday life. We are bound or united to God by the way we live our ordinary lives and the responses we make to the opportunities to love in the world. And if this be the case, then one can clearly define the purpose of religion itself; it is to foster this union with God, the one forged in love of neighbor. This and no other is the most fundamental purpose of religion and all religious practices, to nourish union with God through a life of love for others in the world. All of this corresponds with the salvation that is manifest in the life of Jesus.

This view of the operation of grace also provides the basis for Christian spirituality. Spirituality refers here to the way one leads one's life as a Christian; spirituality is the Christian life. The issue involved in spirituality is how one is united to God or how one participates in God's salvation. If the analysis of how God relates to human existence by grace or God's Spirit is correct, then it follows that love of neighbor defines the necessary and sufficient ground for the Christian view of saved human life. It is necessary because union with God is constituted here; thus no experience of liberation on the transcendent and explicitly religious level of surrender to God which does not also include a life of love of neighbor is ultimately saving. It is sufficient since a life of love of neighbor even without the third level of explicit religious experience is one that is united with God. This is not to devalue the need to foster explicit religious experience of God; it is rather simply to see how this is related to the more basic level of the operation of God's saving grace.

One can also see in this analysis of the effects of grace the basis for a spirituality of working for social justice. It was said, relative to the second dimension of the liberation of human freedom, that the effect of grace as a freedom from the power of sin within us is a freedom of love that extends outward in society. Collectively this force of love will tend to establish itself in loving institutions, institutions that serve the neighbor socially. The second level then presupposes the first. From this it follows that one who participates in or works to foster such institutions of grace is by that very fact united with God. This then is not a spirituality apart from work for social justice that impels one to participate in such work. It is rather one that sees the very participation in the movement of liberation as constituting one's union with God.[22]

THEOLOGY OF THE SPIRIT OF GOD

As a summary and conclusion to this outline for a systematic theology of the Spirit, it may be asked if this structure accounts for the themes underlying the liberationist interpretation of Christianity. It should also correspond to the focusing problem for Christian theology today and be coherent with the doctrines of God and Jesus Christ. The theology of the Spirit is the existential counterpart of the doctrine of God; it points to how God is experienced within the Christian life as God has been revealed in Jesus Christ. And, inversely, the symbol of the Spirit of God may be used to illumine our understanding of the way God acted in Jesus Christ by the analogy of that event with general Christian anthropology. In other words, the inherent capacity of essential human existence for self-transcendence as a possible openness and recipient of the power of the Spirit of God that lies beneath the existential estrangement of sin at the same time provides the structure for understanding how God was at work in Jesus and Jesus was united with God. In this concluding section, I will take up each of the liberationist themes in the theology of grace enumerated at the outset of this chapter and interpret them descriptively in a way that is consistent with what has been said of the other doctrines.

First of all, grace operates in the human spirit in the deepest regions of its being spirit. At this level, the human spirit may be defined as freedom in the sense that freedom characterizes the most elementary capacity of human self-consciousness, reflection and ability to go out of the self in knowledge of the other as other, awe, reverence, humility, self-surrender, dedication, commitment and love. It is both natural and necessary that the operation of grace, God's personal presence and activity in the world, be seen in terms of an interaction with human beings at the point where they are most deeply and characteristically human.

But this point of contact is not merely determined by an existentialist anthropology. All the classic statements concerning the movement of God's Spirit and grace for salvation, both in the New Testament and the history of the theology of grace, describe it as effecting a newly released and freed freedom. Salvation is freedom from sin, both by God's personal forgiving, healing and accepting presence and by the power of God's Spirit to pry open a freedom that is bound within itself by sin for faith and love. This faith and love is in its turn a freedom from law. Christianity is neither extrinsicist nor authoritarian; the Christian God appeals to our freedom from within. By the power of God's Spirit the Christian even experiences a freedom over death itself. At practically every point, the record of the Christian testimony to the power of God's gracious salvation is cast in terms of freedom. What is important today is that this power be seen as affecting the whole of human existence, infusing freedom at all its levels, personal, social and transcendent. When this is not consciously attended to, one inevitably has a distorted or truncated theology of grace.

It is thus appropriate and exact to use the symbol of liberation as a modern equivalent for salvation. Salvation and liberation by the power of grace are convertible. Salvation should not be thought of as an objective transformation of the world or of an abstracted and reified human nature that occurred all at once and was completed in a single past event. Rather salvation is an ongoing process that is existential and historical. Salvation is God's action in history, or God acting in history, as that is experienced and symbolized by God's gracious spirit.

Liberation theology tends to bind closely together salvation and objective liberation on a social level, that is, human social emancipation. An extreme statement of this would say that salvation and social liberation are identical. In the view expressed here, the primary meaning of Christian salvation occurs on the personal level of human freedom. Salvation is a mode of being in the truth, an existence that is in tune with or united with the grounding intention of God for human beings. This coincidence or union with God is effected at the most basic level of the turning of a sinful freedom into a self-transcending freedom. This may be experienced in an explicitly religious manner. It is also an event and a condition that may obtain even when one is not conscious of it in a religious way at all. This freedom which is informed by love naturally or spontaneously expands outward into society and the struggle to establish and preserve graced institutions and to change societal patterns of behavior that destroy human lives into structures that effect and nourish equality, justice and freedom. Not to recognize this direction of personal freed freedom is quite simply a failure to see the intrinsic structure of freedom itself as both constituted by society and constituting it, and a failure to recognize the direction in which the thrust of God's spirit as that has been revealed in Jesus moves human beings. At still another level, freedom under the impulse of grace is drawn to recognize the ultimate source of genuine freedom and love in the transcendent power of God. Here the power of grace generates explicitly religious experience.

In this scheme, it is difficult to identify social liberation with salvation *tout court*. Participation in the movement for social liberation is salvation for those who participate in it under the influence of God's spirit. But it would not be accurate to say that a situation of passively received emancipation, a social liberation, is salvation for those who benefit from it.[23] Nor would it necessarily follow that all who participate in the struggle for liberation operate with motives that reflect the influence of God's freeing Spirit. Increased freedom is salvation when it becomes liberated from sin, when it is freed from its inner bondage and entrapment, from selfishness and egoism. In its first and primary moment, salvation is existential and personal. But this should not imply an implicit return to mere personalism in a pejorative sense.[24] An authentic triumph of grace over the bondage of personal freedom opens personal freedom to a concern for the oppression of people in society. Thus a concern for and a commitment to social emancipation is in a certain sense a criterion measuring the real presence of God's Spirit and the actuality of personal salvation. Freedom that is closed to the struggle for liberation in public social history is still in the bondage of sin. Our freedom in the measure that it fails to respond to the social oppressions in which we participate is closed to the movement of the Spirit of God.

Liberation theology then is correct when it views the gracious saving power of God's Spirit relating human freedom to the world and to history. This insight or awareness has been mediated to us in a new way by many of the suppositions of contemporary consciousness outlined in Chapter I. But most significantly it flows from the current conviction that God's Spirit for salvation is universally available. God is not more universal in creative power than in the personal presence, offer and power of God's Spirit for salvation. And if this be the case, then God's grace must be effectively mediated or encountered in every aspect of human life in the world. In other words, encounter with God's Spirit cannot be relegated to any particular religious sphere in an exclusive way, from which many people today feel themselves excluded, but must be the substratum of human existence itself in its life in the world and history, if indeed it is to be universally available. The implication of this insight is radical. It follows that response to God, union with God, is constituted by the faith or fundamental option of a person as that is actualized concretely by the way a person consciously directs and actually leads the whole of his or her life in history. Every aspect of life, every occupation, decision and action, defines the field of our encounter with God and constitutes how human beings are united with God.

Although this is a new heightened consciousness, it is not alien to the tradition of the theology of grace and spirituality. Although frequently in the history of Christian thought and life the power of God's Spirit was thought to draw human beings out of history in either flight from the world or attraction to things transcendent, an opposite tradition has never been lacking. The power of Christian salvation has always been directed into the world, history and society. This is the firmest implicit logic deep within the Augustinian and Thomistic views of the theology of grace and the ideas of cooperative grace. We exist at present in history and are moving toward a goal which is attained by the way human life is lived. In this context, the very reason and logic of the salvific power of grace is precisely that human beings might live in the world authentically, in truth and in goodness, in a way that is both saved now and leads to a salvation that is final and ultimate. This absolutely elementary logic is still preserved in the Reformation, especially by Calvin in his interpretations of the doctrines of providence, the Spirit, sanctification, the calling of the Christian, and the Christian life.[25] Grace is not a private possession and does not withdraw the Christian from the world. The exact opposite is the case. God's election and the influence

of the Spirit transform the person and the community and flows outward through them into society transforming it. Christian responsibility
is social responsibility in the use of God's creatures, in human activity
and stewardship, in witness in the public sphere.[26]

Liberation theology generalizes the dynamics of God's saving grace
in history in order to characterize human history as a history of liberation. Yet along with this seemingly over-optimistic view, liberation theology has recaptured for the Catholic imagination the doctrine of sin. It
sees sin as embedded in the very structures of society. It has thus rightly
reclaimed the idea, from tradition and more recently from neo-orthodox
theology, of God's judgment on human culture which is the other side
of the experience and revelation of God's grace. It must be said that both
sin and grace characterize all of human existence and at every level of
human freedom. It is impossible to find pure grace within personal,
social or transcendent human freedom. Thus there is but one human
history and not two, but it is one single history that is characterized by
both sin and grace, bondage and liberation, at the same time.

This single history is always ambiguous. History should be a history
of ever new realizations of the Kingdom of God. The inner purpose and
direction of history flows from God's intention in creation revealed by
Jesus in the symbol of the Kingdom of God. But because of sin, and even
beyond sin because of the sheer finitude and limited quality of human
nature, this Kingdom of God is utterly beyond the capacity of human
freedom.[27] However over against finitude and the grip of sin, God does
work in history. God's action in history is God's active rule; it is the
power of love which attracts or draws human freedom out of itself and
in the direction given in the message of Jesus, the objective Kingdom of
God. This Kingdom of justice is to be realized to the extent that it can
in history and to be finally actualized by God's own power in the absolute future. Thus the intention of history is God's intention of liberation,
its power is the power of God's Spirit, and it is carried forward by human
agents in whom God acts. But this history of liberation is also embedded
in and coexists with a history of sin. The Christian hope of course is that
liberation will prevail over sin. But this Christian view of things also
takes human freedom very seriously. One can only hope for final salvation insofar as one experiences salvation in a partial way now. And
Christian salvation here and now, both for persons and for groups, is
experienced and constituted by their participation in the history of
grace, the history of liberation.

Finally, the liberationist interpretation of Christianity, and especially the Christian liberationist movement and spirituality in Latin
America, responds convincingly to the humanist critique of religion.

Indeed this alternative vision of the world provides deeper grounds for commitment to the process of liberation than, for example, a Marxist view of reality, in its idea of a solidarity with other human beings that is also a union with God. It also provides more reason within faith for a hope that can look to the future. It may be, as was suggested in Chapter IV, that the full life of the Church has not reflected this spirituality. But the Church is always a product of its historical context and shares in the history of sin. In the next chapter, I shall discuss the doctrine of the Church from a liberationist perspective and in the light of the crisis of our time.

Chapter IX
THE NATURE AND LIBERATING
MISSION OF THE CHURCH

Up to this point we have proposed a trinitarian view of how God relates to human existence, and how human existence in its turn is related to God. God is Creator and as creatures we are absolutely dependent on God's sustaining power of being. But beyond God's creative immanence to all that is, the symbol of God's Spirit points to and expresses the experience of God's being personally present to and within every human being and personally active within human existence as a constant offer of salvation. And God has been revealed externally in an unsurpassable way in the life and resurrection of Jesus of Nazareth. In Jesus Christ the saving power of God has been disclosed in a public way for human salvation.

In this chapter we turn to the topic of the Church and we shall deal with it at a very fundamental level; this chapter will be an essay in fundamental theology. The Roman Catholic fundamental theology which treated the Church in the manual tradition prior to Vatican II had a strongly apologetic cast. It sought to demonstrate to the extent possible the divine institution of the visible Church and hence the divine quality and authority of its institutional structures. The Church tended to become a surrogate object of faith. Since Vatican II the argument of the fundamental theology of the Church has changed sharply. It is recognized that the doctrine of the Church is derivative; religious faith is in God, Christian faith in God is mediated through Jesus Christ, and the Church is the community that bears witness to God as revealed in Jesus Christ. Thus the Church is not properly the object of faith but the medium or historical vehicle through which one comes in contact with God in Jesus Christ. A fundamental theology of the Church, then, appeals to implicit faith or a search for God; and it responds by reflections on the Church that indicate what it is, or, better, what it should be and must be if it is to be an authentic, credible and reliable witness to and medium of God as revealed in Jesus Christ. The argument of a fundamental theology of the Church, then, is still apologetic, but the purpose and object of the logic has shifted. While the direct focus is on the Church, still it deals with the Church as a medium relative to God as revealed in Jesus Christ. The purpose is to respond to very basic questions about the Church in such a way that the characterization of what the Church is invites free participation in it, a participation of faith and praxis that in turn illumines human existence in relation to God as revealed in Jesus Christ.[1]

As an essay in fundamental theology the purpose of this chapter is not and should not be taken as striving for a complete or adequate ecclesiology. The intention is rather limited and may be defined quite simply as an attempt to point to some elemental concepts or symbols that disclose at a basic level, but without any extended development, the nature of the Church and its role or function in human history. This will be done primarily in the third part of this chapter. But these symbols are proposed so as to be faithful to the fundamental insights of liberation theology while at the same time transposing them into a broader historical and cultural context. Thus in the first two parts of the chapter I will enumerate the most significant principles of liberationist ecclesiology and then correlate with them some suppositions and questions concerning the Church that arise in a more general transcultural and apologetic context. And in the concluding section I will point out how the three basic symbols for understanding the Church today that are proposed here can also be seen as a response to the problem of human existence in its three dimensions.

PRINCIPLES FROM LIBERATION THEOLOGY

Perhaps the dominant doctrinal theme in the earliest stages of the emergence of liberation theology in Latin America was ecclesiology. The reality of the Church and the doctrine of the Church were more than any other single issue its central focus. For example, Gustavo Gutiérrez's *A Theology of Liberation* can be considered as a work in ecclesiology, one that flowed from the great renewal of ecclesiology that flowed from the Second Vatican Council. It is evident that beneath this ecclesiology there are a whole host of suppositions of a general nature that have a bearing on understanding the Church. But the following three principles or theses seem to be especially characteristic of liberationist ecclesiology.

The first most significant and far reaching of all is the principle that the Church should be understood in relation to the world. To put it negatively, the Church should not be understood as a self-enclosed historical phenomenon that is somehow imagined as set off from or existing apart from the world. The Church is part of the world. Thus the attempt to understand the Church theologically should not proceed exclusively on the basis of Christian sources without consideration of the world and the history and the secular society within which it exists. Liberation theology thus takes its cue from the "Pastoral Constitution on the Church in the Modern World" of Vatican II.

The significance of this principle is fundamental and far-reaching. It dovetails with the historical consciousness that underlies liberation theology and thus opens up the possibility of a sociological analysis of how in fact the Church in Latin America is related to its society. And these analyses lay the groundwork both for a self-critical appraisal of the actual Church and a redefinition of how the Church should relate to the concrete world in which it exists. But still more important than these actual proposals is the basic idea and its implications for a theological method in ecclesiology. To put it most strongly, all attempts to understand the Church that do not take into account its relation to the world are inadequate, one-sided and faulty. The Church exists in a double relationship, to God and to human society or the world. The world here stands for the whole sphere of history and society that are not the Church. The Church must be defined by this double relationship, and its nature can only be adequately understood as some kind of medium between God and the world, as an instrument of the purposes of God for the world.

A second principle of liberationist ecclesiology is that the Church is not the center of the world; the Church is in Gutiérrez' phrase "uncentered" in human history.[2] Many factors generated this insight or led to this conclusion. A concrete historical point of view engenders the empirical perception that the Church has not and does not command this position. And from a theological perspective the recognition of the universally operative will of God for human salvation led to the conclusion that, if this be the case, the saving grace of God's Spirit must be mediated by other means than historic Christianity. This implies that the traditional symbol of the reign of God must extend beyond the sphere of the Church. And thus one is led to an ecclesiology that ironically is not ecclesiocentric. Its center is God and God's Spirit. The Church has a special relationship to and knowledge of the working of God's Spirit through the revelation of Jesus Christ.[3] But the Church also has a responsibility to witness to this Spirit of God and cooperate with it insofar as it is active in the world and history at large.

Third, the Church has a concrete role to play in the social emancipation of human beings in the world. Probably no other thesis in the liberationist understanding of the Church is more prominent, and no other is more generally misunderstood or contested. It is misunderstood when it is caricatured to mean that the Christian Church is supposed to replace other human agencies and organizations in this task of human liberation. It is contested on the basis of the misunderstanding that this is the sole or exclusive or even most prominent mission of the Church in every circumstance. The thesis is also rejected on the basis of a post-Enlightenment consciousness of religion in general and Christian faith in particular as a purely individual and private affair.[4] It is further resisted on the bias against any optimism in human affairs, or on the basis of a radical doctrine of sin,[5] or on the misunderstanding of an equation or identification of freedom-giving objective social relationships with a salvation that comes from union with God.[6] But the thesis of liberation theology still stands against these misconstruals. For it is not a negation of human secular autonomy, but an assertion of Christian responsibility. It is not an exclusivist claim, but an imperative to cooperate with others. It is not a negation of the personal quality of faith, but an assertion of its social implications. It is not necessarily an assertion of undue optimism, which is hard to conceive in Latin America, but of the direction the engagement of Christian reflection and freedom should take. It asserts simply that, negatively, Christian consciousness and thus the Church should be publicly critical of social injustice and positively engaged in ameliorating human life in society according to its nature and capacity and specific means. As simple as this is, it implies that an ecclesiology that lacks this dimension is inadequate, one-sided and faulty.

There are of course other principles at work in the ecclesiology of liberation theology. In the theologies of both Gutiérrez and Segundo the Church is understood in close connection systematically with Jesus Christ and the doctrine of salvation as that unfolds historically through God's Spirit or grace. In Segundo the Church is also understood in terms of revelation and faith as the community of faith. The liberationist view of the Church is also characterized in opposition to sin, especially social sin and dehumanization. There are also the much more traditional and standard themes of the Church as the mediator of grace through the sacraments. But the three principles concerning the Church's relation to the world, its uncenteredness and its role in human emancipation define as it were distinctive features of liberationist ecclesiology. Indeed they imply or include and color most of the others.

In what follows I will point to three suppositions for studying the Church today that arise out of a much more general context. Each of these three suppositions or principles raises certain critical questions regarding the Church that must be addressed in a fundamental theology. It will be seen that these three premises for ecclesiology, although framed within a broader context, are coherent with the three principles of liberationist ecclesiology so that these latter may be subsumed into them.

THE QUESTION OF THE CHURCH TODAY

The particular way in which any doctrine of Christian teaching is understood depends largely on the cultural and intellectual context in which it is understood. The principles characteristic of liberation theology's understanding of the Church are not directly provided by the New Testament but arise out of the particular life situation of Latin America in conjunction with the traditional sources of theology. The historical situation of any theology provides it with suppositions and pressing questions that arise out of those suppositions that fairly demand a response if the Church is to become intelligible and, in turn, provide or mediate meaning for life within that situation.

This section, therefore, is designed to set the context for understanding the Church today. To do this I will isolate and underline three of the general presuppositions that constitute as it were a point of departure for an investigation of the nature and role of the church in today's world. In each case I will focus these contextual considerations into questions to which an adequate ecclesiology must respond.

The first supposition for beginning to understand the Church today is the recognition that the Church is an historical phenomenon and a human institution. This assertion may be taken as a common sense perception which both Christians and those outside the Church may share. The Church is a social phenomenon that is fully historical in all that that implies. For example, the Church had a beginning in time; there was a time, a very long period of time, when the Church was not. And, as in the case of any historical phenomenon, one cannot grasp in any fundamental way what the Church is without some notion of how it came to appear in history. Obviously much more can be said about the Church than can be deduced from its origins; the Church has had a long history, and in any historical and developing reality all of its essential features are not necessarily manifest in its embryonic state. But the point of departure for understanding the fundamental reality of the Church must include some consideration of how it came to be in the first place. Thus just as in the case of Christology where the theological tendency is to return to the historical Jesus and to view him as a human person whose historical life is the basis for later Christological interpretation made in the light of the Easter experience, so too one should begin ecclesiology from the perspective of the genesis of the Church to understand it.

Since the Church is an historical phenomenon, it has been subjected to all the vicissitudes of historical existence. It has been determined by the situation in which it emerged; it has developed and changed in the course of its historical movement through time. In short, the Church is a particular, historically determined and relative institution. No one who studies the history of the Church, its changing forms and the various relations it has assumed in relation to the world and society in which it has existed would hesitate to characterize the Church as a thoroughly human phenomenon indeed.[7] Because of this human character, the Church can be analyzed from the point of view of the variety of viewpoints that are provided by the human sciences such as philosophy, sociology, the sociology of knowledge, social psychology and so on.[8] The subject of ecclesiology, that which is spoken about, is the empirical Church, the Church as a phenomenon of history, the Church that we see. Even though the Church cannot be adequately understood theologically as merely an empirical organization, the fact that the Church exists in the world and in relation to history forces one to keep the empirical Church as one's point of reference and to avoid doctrinal reductionism.[9]

This historical point of view on the Church, one that is shared by all including Church members, raises the first problem or question for a fundamental ecclesiology. And this question can be simply put: What is the relation of this human community or society to God? For anyone sharing in an historical consciousness today the Church has been demystified. One cannot easily speak any more of the holiness of the Church and its divine quality as some objective and mystical characteristics distinct from the members of the Church who are sinful and human. The Church is a movement of people organized in history. In this context the question of the divine nature of the Church really becomes a question of the specific relationship of this particular historical movement to God's initiative. The question of the nature of the Church becomes less a question of a static essential structure, and more a question of the dynamic relationship that this institution bears in relation to God. The divine nature of the Church must be seen in how this historical community is related to God's action in history, in its own origins and in its ongoing historical existence. The full and divine nature of the Church, consisting as it does in its relation to God, must be defined in functional symbols that relate it to God's ongoing salvific activity that is operative in history as a whole. In short, what is the relation of the Church to God's activity in the world?

A second cultural supposition for understanding the Church lies in the fact of the religious pluralism of the world and in some of our current attitudes toward this phenomenon. History is made up of a wide variety of vital religious traditions and Christianity is only one of them. The uncenteredness of the Church appears against the background of religious pluralism. The world has not yet become Christian, and as far as can be seen the whole world will not turn Christian in the future. The newness of this phenomenon, however, really lies in the kind of recognition or appreciation that it receives. This moves between accepting this religious pluralism as a kind of historical inevitability, to an affirmation of the right of other religions to exist, and further still to a conviction of the positive value of many different religions. There should be religious pluralism. The richness of the mystery of God and the variety of human cultures demand it. This adds up to a very profound and far-reaching conclusion which, even when it is assented to verbally, is frequently resisted by Christian consciousness. To what extent is the Church willing to accept the fact of religious pluralism? Just what should Christian attitudes be in this matter? The inner tendency of Christian consciousness is to insist on the truth of Christianity and to feel that everyone should become Christian. But ultimately the demand that all people accept the truth of Christianity rests on an abstraction from concrete history, a judgment of the way things should be that prescinds from the actual historical situation and tradition in which peoples and cultures exist. It is not clear that everyone is called to be a Christian, neither here and now, nor in the future. In fact the opposite seems more clear once one assumes an existential perspective on the matter, one which ultimately respects personal and corporate freedom in their particularity and historical specificity. This supposition, then, must have a profound influence on how the Church is to be conceived today in contrast to an earlier understanding that presupposed the opposite.[10]

In many ways the Church has adapted its self-understanding to the situation of religious pluralism. The Church has, for example, recognized the principle of religious freedom. One should not think of church membership as an external obligation, something that can be imposed by an outside this-worldly authority. And this has further reinforced an emphasis on the Church as a community of free persons rather than an institution merely defined in legal terms of objective rights and obligations; the Church is ultimately a voluntary association. Furthermore, ultimate salvation is not dependent upon one's being a member of the Church. The Church has recognized that God's saving power extends beyond the borders of Church membership and is equally available to all human beings whatever their historical situation and allegiances might be. God's saving grace is primarily encountered in one's life in the world. But this very adaptation to the situation of religious pluralism raises the question of the Church in a new way. In terms of personal freedom, why should any given person be a member of the Church today? What does the Church hold out to the idealism and freedom of any given person that is worthy of the surrender of that freedom in commitment? In other words, is the Church simply another group or institution promising people comfort and their eternal salvation, or does it offer as well a direction to life, concretely in this world, of universal proportions and validity, one to which a person might fully dedicate his or her whole self? The question, then, in terms of personal freedom and motivation, is: *Why* should one be a member of the Church?

A third element of general cultural consciousness that has an important bearing on the self-understanding of the Church today is what is generally referred to as historical consciousness. I take this to point to our heightened awareness of being in a long and unfathomable history, of being products of seemingly arbitrary events of the past, and of being open to an unknown and unpredictable future. Historical consciousness tends to relativize cherished absolutes because they now appear as only fully intelligible within a particular historical situation and not as abstract truths that are immediately relevant to every situation; basic values do not appear to be universal. The Church appears differently in this framework. The Christian Church appeared very late in human history, at least from our perspective. How can its claims of containing a universal message that is relevant to the final salvation of *all* human beings be understood in such a way as to make sense?[11] The doctrine of the universality of God's grace for salvation also responds to this issue. Salvation goes on within the human race at an equal pace before and after the event of Jesus Christ. But this assertion too is a major new supposition that has scarcely been taken fully into account in common consciousness and in the theology of the Church.

This consciousness of being in history, of both the importance of our human history and its arbitrary and chaotic character, forces on us the ultimate question, "Why the Church?" Historical consciousness provides a new context for formulating the fundamental question of what the Church is meant to be: Exactly why does the Church exist in human history especially if final salvation is an offer and a possibility that is inherent to actual human existence as such? What is the purpose, God's purpose and assigned role, for this institution as a whole in human history? The question absorbs into itself the two prior questions about the Church; it provides the basic focus in one's attempt to understand the Church today. In the light of human history as a projected whole, and in view of the crisis of meaning for human existence as a whole that this history presents us with, one cannot respond to the question of the nature of the Church or why individual people should belong to it without explaining its mission in human history. One has to reach down to the deepest teleological foundations of the Church at this point: What is the Church for? And as a kind of primary focus for today, because of our historical consciousness, this question will be responsible for a dramatic shift in the understanding of the Church today, at least relative to some periods of the past.

Before moving toward a constructive response to these questions, it may be useful to recall clearly the criteria for such a response to be an adequate one. On the one hand, in keeping with a method of correlation, a theological understanding of the Church must be faithful to Christian sources. And this faithfulness to sources ought to be considered at a variety of levels. A theology of the Church should faithfully represent the biblical understanding of the Church, as that is contained in the images and symbols of the New Testament. It should also take the long history of the Church's self-understanding into account. More importantly, relative to biblical resources, theology should attend to the historical genesis and early development of the Church which lies behind the biblical theology. A genetic approach, an understanding of the Church's coming-to-be, demands this. And, finally, a theology of the Church must be faithful to and coherent with the other more basic doctrines already seen, namely, the doctrines of God, God's immanent Spirit, and God's final self-disclosure in Jesus Christ.

On the other hand, the theology of the Church must also respond to the problem of human existence. If a theology of the Church is to be credible today, it has to illumine the experience that human beings have of themselves today. And to be integral and adequate to that experience, a theology of the Church too would have to address the three levels of human freedom. The Church must be seen as addressing the transcendent dimension of human freedom. As an historical institution it has to be seen as a mediation of God to human freedom, a freedom that is in bondage to sin and in search of an absolute or permanently fulfilled human freedom. The Church must be understood as well as a response to the question of personal freedom, as a place that directs and channels my freedom out of itself toward values and ideals that can be realized in my concrete life and particular sphere of existence. And, finally, the doctrine of the Church has to respond to the question of social human existence. At this time, no issue is ultimately more important than this for the credibility of the Church. The role or mission of the Church in human history has to be such that it speaks to today's crisis of meaning that stems from the massive poverty, oppression and human suffering with which history confronts us. This response has to be more than a theory about or a message for history. Rather the Church should be understood in such a way that it both responds directly to human oppression itself by its own proper action, and at the same time releases power and activity in other spheres for human emancipation on a social level. In short, to be credible today, the Church has to be understood in such a way that its nature and function respond to the focusing problem of theology today, the crisis of meaning in historical existence.

THREE BASIC SYMBOLS FOR
UNDERSTANDING THE CHURCH

The Church is an historical phenomenon, and for this reason any valid understanding of it has to take into account its genesis. Critical historical study of the New Testament shows that the Church did not come into being all at once, so to speak, on a given date. Rather it was the product of an historical development that moved through stages. From a sociological and developmental point of view one might be able to describe these stages more or less in the following manner.

The immediate prehistory of the Church might be described as a movement that centered around Jesus of Nazareth; this movement had its basis or center in the ministry of Jesus. This Jesus movement may be seen as spanning the time of Jesus' life, death and the experience of his being raised up and alive with God. Second, after the Easter experience, this movement became what might be called a sect within Judaism as it became more clear that Jesus was to be accepted as the eschatological prophet, and Jewish religious expectation, in the case of the disciples, became focused on his person. Third, this sect gradually evolved into Christian churches in the more formal sense in which the term "Church" would be understood today. These would be bodies of Christian believers that were distinct from Judaism and autonomous in themselves. We say "churches" at this point because it would seem that this development was uneven and happened earlier in some places and some communities than in others because of circumstances.[12] Perhaps the major factor in this development, more important even than the many historical factors that would have contributed to it, is Christological, the acceptance of Jesus Christ as the absolute and universally relevant Savior, over against the Judaism that rejected this interpretation. Fourth, from the churches, although already implicit in them, evolved what is called the Church in a more total and unified sense of a large body or corporation extended over a vast area, but unified in a common faith whose source was Jesus Christ as originally mediated by apostles. This meaning of the term "Church" is found in Colossians and Ephesians.[13] This oneness in faith and in Christ present within the Church continued to develop into a more solidified institutional phenomenon during the course of the succeeding century. The writings of the second century indicate the further gradual institutionalization of the whole Church, the establishment of objective criteria for belief and practice. And, finally, this Church has also continued to develop into churches right up until our own day, as various sectors have become more or less autonomous and independent of others within the Christian movement as a whole.

The point of this view of the genesis and early development of the Church is not to chart the stages of this growth with chronological and sociological exactitude, something which might be very difficult if the development was uneven in different communities and contexts and given the limited data that we possess. Rather the point is simply to underline the fact that the Church did develop, and that there were also different layers of self-understanding in the gradual formation of the Church as well. What follows is a theological interpretation of the Church as it emerged through these developmental stages, especially as sect, churches and Church. What is intended here is not biblical theology in the sense of merely representing the doctrinal self-understandings that prevailed in the early Church. Rather it is an interpretation of the Church for today, but one which at the same time corresponds with and is faithful to the development of the self-understanding of the Church that is witnessed to in the New Testament. This interpretation revolves around three basic symbols that emerge out of or correspond to the historical development of the Church. These symbols are "the community of the Spirit of Jesus," "mission," and "sacrament." The term "symbol" implies that these categories are not empirical or merely descriptive of the Church as an historical phenomenon, but are theological terms. They express a religious experience and are meant to disclose a transcendent dimension in faith's understanding of the Church. At the same time these symbols have as their referent the historical community as it evolved. It should be clear, once again, that the point of centering an understanding of the Church around these three symbols is not to develop a detailed ecclesiology. This presentation may raise as many questions as it answers. We are dealing here with a very fundamental response to the central questions concerning the nature and the purpose of the Christian Church.

The Community of the Spirit of Jesus

Under the impact of the Easter experience and in the light of it, the earliest disciples came together in the faith that Jesus was raised into the sphere of God and that he was, indeed is, the eschatological prophet. The sign of the coming of the Messiah was the outpouring of the Spirit of God manifested in religious enthusiasm. Thus the earliest self-understanding of this new band of disciples, still a sect of Judaism, was that they were the eschatological community, awaiting the end-time, and formed by the Spirit of God and their faith in Jesus as Lord.[14] A first symbol for understanding what the Church is, then, is contained in the statement that it is the community formed in the Spirit of Jesus. The significance of this symbol may be read in each of its terms.

The Church is a community, the coming together of persons or people in a common faith and vision of reality. What binds these people together is their common faith, which in turn is a free commitment, a commitment of freedom. This first characterization of the Church protects it from various misunderstandings. For example, no matter how necessary the institutionalization of this community is for its continued survival and existence, the institutional aspects are not themselves constitutive of the full reality of the Church. The Church is assembly, the coming together of people, people united in a common faith; institution is meant to serve the interest of the community and its faith; it is functional, a means to an end. Objective institutions within a community are essential and necessary parts of the Church, but the idea of the whole Church can never be equated with a part or aspect of it. The term "Church" can never really have the meaning that is often assigned to it as something over against and distinct from its members. More positively, the idea of "community" points to the "event" character of the Church, the fact that it is a free or voluntary association of people. The ultimate historical bond that holds the Church together and binds any given person to it is not external authority of any kind, but the free commitment of each person to the others and to the whole impelled by the authority of God. And this authority itself appeals to human freedom. The Church is a people of God come together in faith.

This community is the work of the Spirit of God. The idea of God's Spirit stems from the experience of God as immanent to and active within human life. The symbol of the Spirit points to both the transcendent and the depth dimension of the Church. Although a voluntary association, this community is the work of the initiative of the transcendent God. This is not a club or a movement in history dedicated merely to the attainment of finite goals; the Church is God's people which means that God has taken the initiative and caused this community to arise. At the origin of the community, then, is the moving power of God. The Spirit is also the bond that holds the Church together in a common faith. God's Spirit is within the Church; God's Spirit is in the depth dimension, the ground, on which the whole Church rests. This is not to be understood in any magical or objectified way, but precisely in the historical way in which the Spirit has been seen operative in human lives. The Spirit is the symbol that expresses the experience of God in one's life and points to the power of transcendence that leads one to overcome sin and turn toward transcendent value by faith. The Church, then, as a whole community is filled with the Spirit of God through the members that make up the community. No objectified or personified presence of the Spirit within the whole is imaginable independent of the people who constitute the whole. This community as a whole is filled with the one or common Spirit of God insofar as the members participate in God's Spirit.

The Spirit of God within the Church is not anonymous; it is the Spirit of God as manifested or disclosed in the life and resurrection of Jesus. The faith of the Church is in God and in God's salvation as that has been revealed and mediated through the life of Jesus, the final or eschatological prophet. It is Jesus' salvific message, and ultimately Jesus Christ himself as the bearer of this message, that makes this community of the Spirit distinctive. There may be other communities that are grace-filled and moved by God's transcendent Spirit, but they are not the Christian Church. The pluralism of context and historical situation in which the Spirit of God may be at work does not invalidate a priori in any way the truth and genuineness of any particular manifestation of that Spirit.[15] Segundo is correct, then, in defining the Church as constituted by those who are explicitly aware of God and God's salvific design for human existence through Jesus Christ. The specificity of the Christian Church lies in its faith in God as manifested in Jesus Christ. The nature of the Church, what it is, is therefore symbolized by the phrase, "the community formed in the Spirit of Jesus." And thus one has a first response to the question of the Church, at least as to its nature and its relation to God.

Avery Dulles has suggested another foundational image for the self-understanding of the Church that is most fitting for our period, namely, "the community of disciples of Jesus."[16] This is an excellent and most apt fundamental view of the Church and it could easily be substituted for what is presented here. The image of a community of disciples is more empirical and historical, less doctrinal, although theological dimensions are readily implied in it. It is thus an open and flexible description showing easily the continuity between the earliest Church and the Church today. This phrase links the Church with Jesus and brings out the continuity between the band of Jesus' disciples during his lifetime and the nascent Church of the New Testament period.[17] The only reason one might prefer the insertion of the symbol of the "Spirit" in this first image of the Church is to underline the connection of this community to God. Both in the New Testament and systematically the dogmatics of the Church are connected very closely both to Jesus Christ and to the Spirit. The symbol of "the community of the Spirit of Jesus" presumes this double basis for the theology of the Church.

Mission

The historical developments that gave rise to this symbol for the self-understanding of the Church in the New Testament period were the gradual awakening consciousness that the parousia would be delayed, the final break of the Christian Church from Judaism, and the realization that the Church had in front of it a more or less long historical existence. The original community that was formed in the Easter experience was not a Church in the sense that the word is understood today. As a movement and then a sect it was a part of Judaism and did not enjoy an autonomous existence or independent understanding of itself. But gradually this community's faith in Jesus Christ made it distinct from the Jewish community and it began to take on a separate existence. As the successor to God's promises to Israel, this new people of God had a mission to the rest of the world and history. Relative to the Mediterranean world that it knew, this mission became the *raison d'être* of the Church, its very reason for being.

The historical biblical content of this symbol for the Church as a mission may be seen in the New Testament. The community had its centering focus in Jesus remembered and now risen. At first the Church seemed to live in an expectation of an immediate parousia: "Thy Kingdom come!" But as future history was opened up to this community's ken, and the historical or physical presence of Jesus in the world became more distant in the past, the community realized that its purpose or role in history was to carry forward the purpose and intention of Jesus, now absent, in the world. This community, then, is the Church of Jesus Christ whose mission in the world is to carry forward in history what Jesus did during his lifetime. Once again Jesus Christ is the specifying and meaning-giving center of the Christian Church, but now in a dynamic historical sense. The Church exists *in order to* do in history or the world what Jesus did in his lifetime.

The term "mission" is a religious symbol pointing to a dimension of the Church that is once again below or transcendent to the empirical community. Using the metaphor of depth, this symbol points to something that is prior to the community itself.[18] Historically, Jesus himself, Jesus' own sending out of disciples,[19] and Jesus' basic intention in his own historical mission are all prior to the Church. But even more deeply, the symbol "mission" encompasses the whole nature and existence of the Church community in an overall meaning-giving purpose that stems from Jesus' life which is its source. Using the concept of transcendence, the purpose of this community is God's own purpose for it, namely, that it carry on in the world the divine intention perceived through the historical mission of Jesus. The idea of "being sent to the world" is the divine intention behind the Jesus event and the movement of God's Spirit that accompanied and followed it. The role of the Church in human history is not the Church's but God's plan and intention.

The significance of this development and this symbol and understanding is that it turns the Church inside out.[20] This community does not exist for itself or in order to wait for God's final salvation. Rather the Church exists in the world, in time and public world history, and it has a role to play there; it has a dynamic historical task to accomplish for the world and for history. It is sent to human society, to the broader community that is the human race. It is meant to communicate to ordinary everyday human secular life. Just as one cannot say that the Church is for its members, because the Church is its members, neither can one say that the Church is for itself. The symbol "mission" is meant to express the perception of faith that God's intention for this community is that it be for the world, for human history, as the extension of the message of Jesus Christ for the world. Thus, for example, the strategy of the missionary and apologetic theology of the second century, which interpreted the Church in terms of Hellenistic culture so that Hellenistic culture would understand itself in terms of Christ's message, is paradigmatic for the Church wherever it is in the world. The Church is always sent to and for the world. Here one has the basis for a response to the second question concerning the Church: Why be a member of this community? The response to this question is not simply to seek one's own personal and final salvation. For ultimately one does not need to participate in the Church for that. Rather membership in the Church also implies a living and active faith that wants to share in the Church's mission as well.

Sacrament

The third symbol for understanding the Church is the idea of sacrament. And this corresponds with another stage in the Church's historical development, although only by association since the symbol as it is understood here arose much later. As the churches became autonomous and adjusted to their continued existence in history, the communities themselves became more institutionalized and the whole Church gradually evolved into a more or less unified institution, the one Church. The Church evolved into a public, social institution with more or less routinized or objectified offices, forms of worship and credal statements of belief. Harnack and others pointed out many of the dangers and problems connected with this development. But even he recognized the necessity of this development for the Church's survival.

The notion of sacrament points to this external, objective, socially public face of the Church. A sacrament is a symbol, in this case an outward phenomenon or sign, that mediates an inward experience, realization and reality, something other and more than the symbol itself. As a public institution, then, the Church is meant to make present, visible and effective in the world the inward reality of God's salvation that is present within the Church, in the body of its members. As in the case of Jesus Christ, who is the primal symbol or sacrament of God for the Christian, the Church too is meant to make visible after the pattern of Jesus the message of God and God's salvation, and thus communicate or mediate the reality of the Spirit to human history. The Church mediates to the world what the community itself shares in, namely, an explicit disclosure and the power of God's Spirit as that has been identified through Jesus Christ.

This notion of the sacramentality of the Church is to be seen in close connection with the first two symbols for understanding the Church. The external structure of the Church is never the thing itself; the Church is a community of persons, and the institutional aspects are always a function of the inner life of the community and should always be adapted accordingly. The particular external institutional forms of the Church developed historically in relation to the needs of the community and should continually develop to meet changing needs. Moreover the institution does not exist for itself, but for the community's and God's mission. Therefore the institutions of the Church should also be turned outward, so to speak, toward the world in order to address it. If the sacramentality of the Church is not seen in the context of the Church's mission, the institution will become an end in itself, not only choking off the charismatic vitality of the life of the members of the community, but also isolating the Church from society and the public life of history to which it is sent by God.

With this notion of sacrament, then, one has a response to the question of how the Church should go about its mission. What is the mission of the Church? Although expressed in still very general theological terms, the Church's mission is to be the sacrament of the salvation that it received from Jesus Christ. And this mission is to be accomplished in a public and visible way in history and society. Thus one has here as well a response to the third question concerning the Church. Why the Church? The Church is meant to continue to mediate to society and history the salvation that was revealed to and released into history by Jesus Christ. Without a structured community to embody it sacramentally, the revelation of Jesus Christ would cease to exist as an existential reality in history.

In sum the Church is the community formed by the Spirit of God manifest in Jesus, missioned or sent to the world, to be itself the tangible expression or sacrament of how God relates to human existence and of the purposes of God for personal and collective freedom. This characterization of the Church corresponds to the New Testament data, not simply to biblical theology or doctrine, but also to the Church as it developed historically. Certainly there are many more symbols that are apt for the Church which may be drawn from Scripture or current experience. The symbols chosen here however are not meant to be exclusive but rather precisely as inclusive and comprehensive of others. Their selection has been governed both by the New Testament, the historical genesis of the Church, and the questions to which our current situation gives rise and which demand response. We pass now to a more explicit response to these questions.

THE CHURCH IN THE CONTEXT OF
THE PROBLEM OF HUMAN EXISTENCE

The Church itself is not the response to the problem of human existence. It is God who is the ground of the meaning of human existence and of salvation. The response to the crisis of meaning and freedom is to be found in revelation and the power of God's Spirit. It is formulated around the symbols and in the doctrines of God, of God's saving Spirit, as these are revealed in the life, death and resurrection of Jesus. The Church *per se* is not constitutive of that salvation.[21] The Church is rather the recipient of God's saving grace; it participates in God's salvific power and truth as revealed in Jesus, and its role in history is to continue to embody it for human life and to mediate it to human history. The doctrine of the Church, therefore, does not provide the Christian answer to the question of human life and history. Quite to the contrary, the message and the reality of salvation revealed in Jesus and effected by the Spirit of God constitute critical norms for the Church. The Church always stands under the judgment of the message and the reality that together constitute its source and grounding principle. The Church is meant to be the mediating community of these realities.

The point to be addressed now has to do with how the Church mediates the salvation it recognizes in Jesus Christ. It was said earlier that the two criteria for adequately understanding the Church are fidelity to Scripture and intelligibility within and to our contemporary historical context. How then do the symbols for understanding the Church proposed in the last section respond to the question posed by the problem of human existence as this was formulated at the outset of this book? The response to this question presented here will still remain on a very general theological level. In comparison with history or sociology which would attempt to describe what the Church actually is and does empirically, theology is somewhat more idealistic. To deal with the Church theologically usually means to characterize what the Church should be and should do in the light of the reality it is called to mediate sacramentally to the world. This is done here without suggesting that the Church does not in any measure actually embody or fulfill these ideals, and yet with the recognition that the Church does not live up to them entirely because it is finite, limited, human and sinful.[22]

In general the Church is meant to be the sacrament of God's salvation for human existence. It should therefore address human existence comprehensively and integrally on all three levels of human freedom. On each of the three levels of human freedom to which the Church should mediate the salvation it has received from Christ, one may distinguish two aspects or sides to the question: what the Church should be, that is, within itself as a community, and what the Church should do, that is, from the perspective of the human society outside to which the Church is sent. In order to mediate the salvation it has received to others, to the world, sacramentally, the Church itself has to embody or contain that reality. The double-edged question then must be consistently asked: What must the Church be in order to perform effectively its mission in the world today?

The Transcendent Dimension of Human Freedom

The Church is an historical community, one that is institutionalized in various degrees in different confessions. As such it is part of the world, a visible organization that bears a relation to the whole world and other organizations in it. The Church is inescapably part of and related to the world. And as such it can be analyzed according to sociological laws and is organized and moved by relationships of political power. But this historical community and institution bears an explicit relationship to God. It is not simply a movement whose whole meaning lies in the pursuit of inner-worldly ideals and finite goals. It arose in history in response to the religious message of Jesus Christ and through the experience of him resurrected and the power of God's Spirit. It is founded on and governed by religious faith. The theme of transcendence, of being bound to God and God's cause, therefore, is constitutive of the Church, and the Church cannot be understood adequately apart from this transcendent dimension.

Because of its relation to God by the message of Jesus and the power of the Spirit, the Church responds to the religious dynamism of the freedom of the human spirit toward transcendence. Boldly put, the Church mediates contact with God. As a community of faith in God the Church preserves the message of Jesus about God and the person of Jesus himself as the bearer of that message and the personal norm of its faithful praxis. Through its preaching the Church provides a reality that appeals to the exercise of transcendent freedom in faith, and by its sacraments it concretely mediates the power of God's Spirit to nourish the praxis of faith. By its corporate prayer and worship it publicly expresses and shares its faith. In sum, the transcendent dimension of human freedom is filled by the Church as a community fashioned by the Spirit of God manifested by Jesus by mediating the object and goal of that freedom. In the Church, the other dimensions of freedom, its personal and social aspects, are all infused with this mediated power to its transcendent dimension.

How should this transcendent dimension mediated to freedom within the Church manifest itself beyond itself in the world? The Church should embody the salvation that it has received in faith from God. The Church is to be existentially united with God, and to be characterized by a transcendence of culture and society. The Church, in its members and as an institution, is called to be free with the freedom of Jesus from sin and from the fear of death, because it exists within the context of the promise of resurrection. In more existential terms, because it is in contact with God, the Church should not fear the world or what the institutions of society can do to it. Rather the members of the Church and the whole institution should embody the transcendent and prophetic freedom that comes from being in contact with God. This freedom and its transcendent source should be displayed in the world and society. The Church ought to be free to relate to the world and society without the deadly concern that institutions normally have for themselves and their own survival. The paradox here is that the Church will be free from the world in God only when it is free for the world; it will only actually be free in God when it is free from itself and attached to God's cause in human history. In other words, the Church may preach God, it may proclaim the values of the Kingdom of God, but they will only be real within the Church and seen there as such when the Church embodies them by its service outside itself. This paradox adds up to a deep and powerful critical norm for the leadership of the Church and the direction the Church takes in the world today: the Church is only in real contact with the transcendent God it preaches to the extent that it embodies a freedom from the world that actually turns in service to the world.

Personal Freedom

Negatively, the problem of personal freedom is one of bondage, of a freedom turned in upon itself. It is the problem of freedom's immobility or inability to seek the good beyond the self. Positively, the question of personal freedom concerns the direction in which a person should live his or her life, the ideals to which a person should surrender, the ultimate goals a person should live for. To what should human beings dedicate their personal freedom today?

Looking at the Church from the point of view of the exigencies of personal freedom, the first question concerns what the Church is in itself so to speak. The Church has a mission to respond to and heal personal freedom. The Church has a mission to be after the pattern of Jesus a place where human freedom finds forgiveness and acceptance; all persons in the Church should be received with the absolute loving acceptance that comes from God. The Church is thus a community of reconciliation, one that mediates the love of God so that this is a milieu of mutual love. The structures and the discipline of this community should be based on love and respect and exercised in a loving way. Law and internal discipline should communicate within the community to individuals the ideals of Jesus for the acceptance and service of the others. Looking at the internal life of the Church, the whole instititution in its doctrine, devotion, sacramental structure, discipline and spirituality should be such that it promotes a freedom dedicated to loving service of the neighbor. This is another critical norm for Church institutions and leadership which naturally tend toward the exercise of spiritual power, the demonic domination of human freedom in the name of God. Contrary to this, ministry within the Church should have as its primary goal the mediation of God's Spirit which addresses freedom, accepts individual persons, and opens up their freedom in love from God, love for God and loving service within the community.

The other side of the issue concerns the positive motivation that the Church provides for the personal freedom of individuals for their life outside the Church and in the world. As part of its mission to the world the Church is a community which promotes a sign morality.[23] A sign morality or spirituality flows from the fact that the individual is not a member of the Church merely to find his or her personal and eternal salvation. Rather as a member of the Church one also participates in and shares a personal responsibility for the mission of the Church to the world. The community provides purpose, direction, values and goals, in short a *telos*, for the exercise of personal freedom in the world within the sphere of everyday life. The ministry of the Church ought to be such that it guides and supports the freedom of individuals in a way that their lives may witness to the values of the reign of God in the world. Individual members of the Church, each in his or her own way and in the sphere of his or her own life, work and various activities, ought to personally take up the mission of the Church to sign forth Christian values in the secular sphere. These more or less self-evident principles provide another set of criteria for the integrity of both ministry within the Church and an ecclesial spirituality of Church members that such ministry is designed to support.

Social Freedom

In an earlier chapter I maintained that the crisis of meaning today lies at the level of social freedom and involves historical existence, our common existence as a race. This crisis lies in the senselessness and absurdity of a human existence that seems inevitably to entail "progress" and development at the expense of enormous physical suffering and oppressive conditions for a majority of the race. Everyone participates in one way or another in this absurd process that belies intelligibility. Whereas the Church has always mediated meaning to transcendent and personal human existence, and must continue to do so, it has also to face this new crisis. At stake here existentially and in a new way is the credibility of the whole of the Christian message. If the Church cannot provide meaning to the social dimension of human existence, then it does not supply meaning for human existence itself. One cannot salvage meaning for one's personal history in this world in a promise of eternal life without deciphering our common existence here and now in society and as a race. The focus for understanding the Church today, then, must be on the criteria that come from its sacramental role as an institution in history at large.

Within itself, the Church should be an institution that is free from social oppression. To the extent possible, the Church should be critical of itself in the light of the message it has received. This principle seems so obvious and self-evident that the simple statement of it seems to trivialize its relevance. But the Church in adapting itself to culture inevitably tends to mirror the society in which it exists. And because of this symbiosis, or simply because of the difficulty of change, it is often most difficult to even see the oppressive structures and alliances that it shares with society. Quite often prophetic criticism from Gospel values originates not within the Church itself but from the outside where people enjoy the needed critical distance. To respond to the oppressive conditions of history the Church has to be able to listen to the Spirit working outside itself in the world, measure itself and what it hears by the standards of the transcendent, prophetic and critical values of the Gospel. In short, the Church has to be constantly open to and willing to change, to reform itself into the future. The Church has at least to strive to be a place of social freedom if it is to offer meaning to human existence.

Looking beyond its borders, the mission of the Church is to be a sacrament to or for the world of the liberation that it has received through Jesus Christ in God's Spirit. The idea of sacramentality applied to the Church takes on its full meaning precisely in the context of social oppression and meaninglessness. The sacramentality of the Church lies precisely in its visibility, in the fact that it is a public institution. The Church abdicates its sacramental mission to society if it pretends that it has an a-social character, that it is an invisible community whose members participate in the public and social sphere only as private individuals and apart from their responsibility as Church members. Rather the Church as a public social institution stands for something in society, and when it abdicates responsibility for saying what it stands for, it ratifies and reinforces the social situation as it is. The Church tends to prevent change in society by any stance of neutrality.

Ideally, then, the Church should stand out publicly in society as an announcement of the values of the Kingdom of God. Through its words and actions it should be a leaven of society. As a community it should be concerned with promoting a corporate behavior that directly challenges the political, economic, social and cultural structures of society that deal out human misery. As liberation theology has formulated it, the Church ought to announce a direction for history, try to live in that direction itself, and publicly criticize the flagrant abuses of these values and of human life wherever they are found. But great care should be taken in the way the Church issues its denunciations. The Church risks hypocrisy, vacuous moralism and the appearance of sheer ridiculousness if it does not respond to the social injustices within its own institution, and if it does not recognize that there are people of good will already trying to ameliorate society independently of the support of the Church. Finally, the Church should be an active agent for social emancipation. The community should sponsor agencies and groups which actively mobilize human energy and talent to address the specific concrete issues and places where human freedom is crushed by the weight of particular social structures and institutions. The credibility of the Church's message, indeed the very reality of the power of God's Spirit which it claims as its ground, will ultimately be manifested to the world by what the Church does in the social arena.

CONCLUSION

We can summarize the argument here very briefly because it has unfolded at the very general level of principle. The Church has to be understood today in the light of the general world culture in which we live. The Church is a finite product of history, so that its relationship to God must be clarified. A wide variety of religious experience today is accepted as authentic and salvific, even by Christian doctrine, so that a reason for membership in the Church must transcend that of personal salvation. Salvation history in the world extends far beyond the chronological and spatial limits of this particular Church history, so that the Church has to justify historically and socially its role in human history. And this can only be done adequately if the Church responds to the whole of human existence, not only relative to the transcendent and personal dimensions of freedom, but also relative to social human existence, its lack of freedom and the massive forces of oppression that crush it.

An understanding of the Church that adequately corresponds to the historical origins of the Church, its initial biblical self-understanding and its early development may be formulated in the following symbols. The Church is a community grounded in the Spirit of God and formed in its faith by Jesus of Nazareth, whose mission is one of service to the world and human history by being a sacrament, that is, by mediating publicly to history what it has received from God. These symbols mediate at a very fundamental level an understanding of the Church in such a way that it will be seen to respond to the problem of human existence integrally, that is, on all three levels of human freedom.

It should be realized that in all of this there has been no consideration of the many practical issues and difficulties that confront the Church in its actual carrying out of its mission to the world. This has been no more than an exploration into the fundamental symbols that disclose what the Church should be in the light of the central Christian doctrines, the biblical account of the historical origin of the Church and of its original self-understanding, when these in turn are confronted with our culture and the suppositions and problems of our time. Ideals in themselves do not solve problems, but they do serve as norms and guidelines. They provide a vision and context for a solution. The following chapters which will deal with sacraments, ministry and spirituality will approach a bit more closely, but still from a theological point of view, some of the specific areas of Church life.

Chapter X
SACRAMENTS IN A MISSION CHURCH

The Church in a liberationist interpretation of Christianity is the community fashioned by God's Spirit after the pattern and in the likeness of Jesus Christ to be an instrument of God's initiative in human history. In general theological terms this mission has been further specified as the Church's role to be a sacrament of God's liberating power in the world. In this chapter I take up the liberationist view of the Church's sacraments. It may be that the language that describes the whole Church as sacrament was borrowed from the theology of the Church's sacraments, but in reality individual sacraments flow from the prior sacramental character of the Church as a whole.

An initial comment on the very notions of sacrament and sacramentality is appropriate at the start of this discussion. In the first instance the notion of sacramentality is to be understood as a fundamental or foundational aspect of religion. Sacramentality refers to the mediated and symbolic character of all awareness and contact with God that human beings enjoy in history. Some form of sacramentality constitutes the necessary structure of all contact with God. Human existence is bound to the finite world so that there can be no direct or unmediated engagement with God. In actual fact the notions of sacramentality and sacraments are closely associated with the Catholic Church because the development of sacraments in the Church up to the sixteenth century was retained in that Church. In contrast, the hinge on which the Reformation turned was the Word of God as found in Scripture, so that in varying degrees the Protestant churches shifted the center of gravity of their spirituality and worship to the Word of God. But this association of sacramentality, as the idea is used here, with Roman Catholicism and other high church traditions is not *per se* necessary. In its deepest or most elemental meaning of a symbol mediating God, the idea of a sacrament is more basic than the contrast between word and sacrament and hence prior to and comprehensive of both. At this fundamental level a sacrament is the Word of God in event and ritual act, and the Word of God as found in Scripture or preaching is a verbal sacramental symbol. In fact the theologies of the mediation of God through the word preached and through sacrament administered are quite similar, that is, relative to the mode of mediation. Both are external finite objective realities that mediate an inward force and power from God. Therefore what is said here of sacrament and sacramental mediation includes as well evangelization even when that term is understood narrowly to mean preaching the Word of God as found in the Gospel.

Once again I shall begin this discussion of sacraments by recalling some of the fundamental themes that characterize the distinctive understanding of sacraments in liberation theology. I will then try to set the context for an appropriation of these liberationist themes in a more general or universal way by underscoring our current cultural consciousness of historicity. Finally, in the light of these anthropological considerations, the last two portions of this chapter will sketch a fundamental theology of sacraments by defining their nature and efficacy.

It may appear that the argument in all of this moves from the theoretical to the concrete by some sort of descending logic. In a certain sense it is correct to say that the appeal here is from the general order to the concrete issue of sacraments. But at the same time behind this whole development lies the hermeneutical question contained in the problem of human existence as it is felt today, especially in the crisis of meaning that arises from the massive amount of human oppression seen in the world today and the almost equally massive human unconcern or fatalistic tolerance relative to it. In other words the point of departure is not "from above" in terms of either abstract principles or theological positivism. The reflection begins as in liberation theology itself with the concrete dilemma of human existence as it confronts faith. Thus even though what is said about sacraments here will be fundamental and very general, it is meant to apply to every form of sacramental, cultic, liturgical and explicitly religious mediation. What is offered here is not more than, and no less than, a fundamental theology of sacrament.

THEMES FROM LIBERATION THEOLOGY

The topic of sacraments does not lie at the center of liberation theology in Latin America even though early on in the movement Juan Luis Segundo devoted a volume to it.[1] But at the same time, as far as Catholic authors are concerned, the nature and function of sacraments cannot be far from a consideration of the actual life of the Church. Of the many characteristics of sacraments found in liberation theology, I see the following four themes as particularly distinctive and important.

First, sacraments are to be understood as functions of the Church. This seemingly naive statement actually implies a significant methodological principle. In effect it means that sacraments are not to be understood from the point of view of "natural" religion or the history of religions.[2] Negatively, the significance of this principle lies in the fact that frequently the Christian sacraments have been understood in such a way, especially in fundamental and apologetic approaches. If the Eucharist were characterized as a sacrifice, one began a theological explanation by an examination of sacrifice in other religious traditions in a search for its fundamental religious structure. Or one sought the common anthropological basis of ritual cleansing and initiation in order to grasp the dynamics of baptism. In contrast to this, liberation theology views Christian sacraments exclusively in terms of their specific meaning which stems from their place within the historical Christian community. Sacraments are activities of the Church; they are functions of the Christian community. Thus what they are, their meaning and their function, is sheerly derivative from the nature and function of this community. The nature of Christian sacraments flows from and participates in the nature and function of the Church. To understand the sacraments in any other way would be to distort their specifically Christian dynamics.

Second, liberation theology emphasizes the prophetic dimension of the sacraments. Sacramental practice is a form of cultic or ritual worship; sacraments mediate God's Spirit; sacraments and sacramental practice engender explicit conscious contact with God and God's power. But in liberation theology the God who is mediated is not merely, not only, a God of solace, comfort and reconciliation. God is also the God of the prophets, disturbing and challenging. In liberation theology sacraments appeal not only to a contemplative mood of affective and unitive love, but also to conscience and moral responsibility; they mediate God's will. For example, Gutiérrez asks whether or not it is even appropriate or authentic to celebrate God's unifying and reconciling presence to the community if a community is in fact torn by injustice and division.[3] I take it that this questioning is not a denial of a power within the Eucharist to heal and effect unity where it does not exist. Human perfection has never been seen as the condition for God's initiative in grace. It is rather a stress on the sacrament's prophetic call to unity against human complacency, tolerance of injustice, and sin. Even the Eucharist is a word of judgment and cannot simply or exclusively be characterized in the soft personalist categories of forgiving acceptance and tender love.

Liberation theology thus retrieves the harder social aspects of God's will, judgment and call to action latent within sacramental mediation.

Third, and closely related to this prophetic dimension, liberation theology insists on the historical efficacy of the sacraments.[4] This principle is coherent with the liberationist understanding of faith. Sacraments above all are meant to nurture and sustain faith. But faith in liberation theology is not mere belief. Faith is a commitment of one's life which plays itself out in praxis, so that informed action or praxis is the deepest carrier of faith itself. Hence the sacraments which sustain faith have their primary efficacy in the way a person leads his or her life. This efficacy is thus historical; it consists in the praxis of each person's life and in the common public behavior of the whole community. Segundo makes this point forcefully by contrasting sacraments with magic, by which he means ritual behavior that seeks to exert some influence on God in an almost causal way.[5] Sacraments are not magical. While the causality of the sacraments is not merely empirical or historical, the reality of the effectivity of the sacraments is to be measured by their historical efficacy, the change that is wrought through them in the lives of the recipients and as that is displayed in the exercise of their freedom.

A final theme of liberation theology's view of the sacraments consists less in a clear principle than in a tension and a question. The tension lies in the relationship between worship of God and action in the world, or between religious faith and moral issues in the sense of human initiatives for good and desired values in this world. And the question concerns the function and use of sacraments or forms of worship within this tension. Does liberation theology subordinate sacramental practice to moral ends? Is worship of God subordinated, in effect used, for the attainment of this-worldly goals however valuable they may be?[6] Worship of God is generally considered an end in itself, or something that is an absolute or the highest human activity, because it is rooted in the most fundamental creature-Creator relationship and ordained to the final, highest and absolute object and end of human existence itself.[7] Worship of God cannot be subordinated to or used in relation to the attainment of human goals, since this would in effect be another way of cynically manipulating God. While this is in no way an intention of liberation theology, still the question as it is put here corresponds to a suspicion of some concerning the logic of liberation theology, and it comes to something of a concrete focus in the theology of the sacraments.

Before attempting a constructive view of the sacraments that corresponds to and incorporates these themes of liberation theology, I wish to comment on the historical context that should govern sacramental theology today.

SACRAMENTS IN THE CONTEXT OF HISTORY

With the notion of sacramentality we are driven back again to the most basic questions concerning God and religion. How is human existence in contact with God? How do we know of God in the world? And how does God make contact with human beings personally or corporately?

A first response to these questions is that a sacrament mediates the experience of God. A sacrament is a piece of the finite world which is at the same time a religious symbol, and hence it is that through which human existence comes in contact with God. I will not repeat here what was said earlier concerning religious symbols in the discussion of revelation. However it is important to recall the dialectical quality of religious symbols and hence of sacraments. A religious symbol is not God, but it mediates God. Sacramental symbols therefore are finite and so neither holy nor sacred in themselves. Yet at the same time, because the experience of God is mediated through them, symbols share in what is mediated, and this participation endows them with a sacred or holy character.[8]

The anthropological basis of this view is religious experience. But like all consciousness, religious experience too has an objective character; it deals with reality and has an object referent. Thus religious experience is such that God is rendered present to it. And a sacrament not only stimulates or occasions a subjective or existential experience of God but also makes God present. In sacramentally mediated experience of God, God becomes present. This objective character of religious experience accounts for doctrines that are objective statements which in their turn appear to account for religious experience.

Thus sacramentality finds its theological basis in the doctrines of creation and the Spirit of God. The transcendent God is immanent to creation by the very power of God's creative activity. Therefore the whole of finite reality, the whole world and each of its parts, are potentially sacramental. God is there, present within the sheer finitude of all that is, as the reason of its being and the power that sustains it. Theoretically at least the presence of God could be recognized in any part of creation. In its finitude creation itself is sacramental. The term, "the Spirit of God," points to God's initiative over and above God's objective presence within reality by creative power. The notion of God's Spirit discloses God's presence and activity within human subjectivity and attempts to account for why a person turns toward an external sacrament with a religious response. God takes an initiative toward human beings; the Spirit of God is God's personal presence to human beings,

God's address, God's active pushing and evocative summoning forth of human response. While the Spirit of God is at work within human existence, still the experience of God summoned forth by God's presence in the Spirit is always mediated externally.[9] There is no experience of God that is not at the same time caused by the symbolic mediation of an external objective this-world reality. The experience of God's presence to human existence is always sacramental. In sum, the doctrines of creation and of God's Spirit are the basis of sacramentality. But the inverse is also true; the experience of portions of this world as sacrament is also the basis of these doctrines. Sacramentality is simply a very fundamental way of conceptualizing the experience of how God is present to human beings and they are in contact with God.

Theological conceptions of how human beings come in contact with God are rooted in anthropology which in turn finds its source in general consciousness and common human experience. For example, the view of sacramentality just presented depends on the conviction that all human experience is bound in some degree to our being-in-the-world and to sense data. Because of this significance of general anthropology, conceptions of the nature of human existence are bound to influence the conception of sacraments. It is more or less accepted that there has been a rather fundamental shift in our understanding of human existence with the Enlightenment. Without entering into a criticism of the legacy of the eighteenth century, it is still accurate to say that the consciousness of being in history which began then and has deepened all through the nineteenth and twentieth centuries has had a profound impact on how one views human existence today. The question that is raised, then, concerns the manner in which this historical consciousness comes to bear on the understanding of the sacraments.

One dimension of religious experience is related to human existence as a part of the world understood as nature. This fairly constant theme is one that is ever more being validated by science. Human beings are part of nature. The rhythms, laws, patterns and order of nature find their analogous echo in human life and growth.[10] God the Creator is both immanent to the whole world of nature and to us, so that the world when it is contemplated religiously is found to be suffused with God's presence, and that presence is also within human beings. This presence may be discovered in an almost infinite variety of objective situations and a multiplicity of kinds of reactions to them. With this organic view of nature Schleiermacher reduced this variety to a common experience of being part of an infinite Whole, and later to an experience analytically characterized as being absolutely dependent in being.[11] God may be experienced in the tranquility and peace and sheer beauty of a sunset, or in the primal emergence of new life of a dawn or sunrise. Even more dramatically the Creator appears as the source of the new life that is witnessed with wonder in childbirth. These experiences have engendered a common religious vision; the world itself is sacral, it has its being in God, and life in the world is a participation in that which is of God. God is with us and we are in and of God's creation. Human beings are an *imago Dei* and are oriented by a metaphysical teleology to return to God who is the creative intelligent source of nature and the world. It may appear that we are both close and distant relative to God. But in either case, sacramental experience is the bridge between us. And the Spirit awakens this contemplative vision and solidifies it into affective union even now.

There is also a second dimension of religious human experience that has been awakened by modernity. It is characterized by the historical consciousness that makes human beings aware of themselves as not only beings in the world of space and nature but also in time. This does not cancel out the former dimension of experience, but it does modify it. The world is not just nature; it is also secularity. Being, especially human being, exists in time and across the ages. Reality is constantly changing through the forces of process and evolution. In this world human existence is not just contemplative spirit but also active freedom; it is not just a part of nature but stands above it; it does not just passively endure nature, it actively manipulates and changes it. We see ourselves now as not only what we are by the forces of chemistry, biology and nature, but also as the potentiality for what we shall become by what we do. Human beings fashion themselves; they change through decision and action, and so does human existence as a whole. We are not only related to God by a metaphysical teleology but also by a chronological eschatology.[12] God may be close in nature, but God has also left us "on our own" so to speak in history. Thus we have to move toward (or away from) God in the future through time and historical creativity (or destruction). God is still present, therefore, in creation and by the Spirit, but not in the same way. In fact at times God appears pointedly absent and human responsibility appears charged to make God's presence felt. God is still present in the sunrise, but also as a question: What are we going to do for God in history given this new day? God is still present in childbirth, but as potentiality and grounding source for creativity. God's presence is also a question: What is intended by God with this new life? Is this new freedom going to contribute to history according to God's will or take from it? Will it move toward or away from God in the future?

The point here is not to highlight a contrast between Greek and Hebrew views of cosmos and history. Actually in a post-Enlightenment culture we are equally distant from both of these. Nor should it be contended that one of these experiences is valid and the other invalid, but rather that historical consciousness implies a qualitative shift that does not cancel out the validity of the elements in the other dimension of experience, but sets them in a new context. One could use the language of a shift in a basic paradigm or worldview, or one could speak of a sublation that does not exclude but rather sets in a new context of meaning and point of view. The difference here is not just a difference of fact, however, but one of principle. For example, it may be true that people in rural areas understand themselves as being close to nature, while in the cities people do not see the sun set or rise but only a constant smog, sometimes brighter and sometimes darker, caused by human beings. That may remain true in fact. But what is at stake here is a different understanding of human existence itself, even relative to those who live in rural areas or traditional cultures, whether they are aware of it or not. And this is the basis for a different anthropology which in turn asks for more and new and different meanings from the sacrament. Because God is seen in a new way, and because human existence relative to God is understood differently, the sacramental mediation between God and human beings must be understood differently. In short, new questions are now being put to any traditional understanding of being in contact with God through the sacraments.

One could probably go further and say that the new context of historical consciousness has raised a suspicion concerning the sacraments, at least as they have been traditionally understood and practiced. At this point in the argument of this book, this is not the suspicion of whether or not sacraments unite human beings to God, at least not directly. Rather it is a questioning of how they unite Christians to God. The suspicion concerns both the kind of God to whom sacraments as they are traditionally practiced unite us, and the anthropological suppositions of the spirituality and the Christian life involved in sacramental practice.

We can summarize the issue raised by historical consciousness in the following way. Due to the shift involved in the emergence of human consciousness of being in history, sacraments must be understood in relation to human responsibility in this world and history. Sacraments should mediate God to human existence in such a way that they are relevant to the Christian mission for the world and history. Since the experience of human existence as historicity does not cancel out the other more mystical or mystagogic dimension of experience, our understanding of sacraments today will involve tensions, the tension between contemplation and action, between religious worship and morality, between the sacred and the secular. But all these tensions should be resolved in such a way that sacramental processes bring the Christian message and the reality they mediate to bear on the problem of human existence as it is experienced today according to the three dimensions of human freedom. On each of its three levels, human freedom today is searching for liberation and a direction for its exercise. To put these questions positively, sacraments and sacramental ministry must respond to these human dilemmas: First, what is my personal freedom for in history? Where should it be directed? Second, given the social oppression in the world and human destruction of nature, how does sacramental practice, and the union with God that it mediates, respond to this problem? What do the sacraments say to our corporate Christian freedom relative to society and the world? And, finally, how do sacraments mediate God to the transcendent dimension of our freedom over time? In what way do they direct us to God through history or life lived in history?

THE GENESIS AND STRUCTURE
OF CHRISTIAN SACRAMENT

Having considered the anthropological context for understanding sacramentality in general, we turn now to a more systematic account of specifically Christian sacraments. There are two issues here that command attention. The first has to do with the genesis of the Christian sacraments, while the second concerns a description of their nature or structure. In responding to these issues, I will at the same time try to incorporate into the account the first two themes raised by liberation theology.

Segundo's method for understanding Christian sacraments is quite clear. He stresses the essential distinctiveness of Christian sacraments; they are elements of the Christian Church and as such unlike the sacraments of any other religion. Thus a history of religions methodology is ruled out as a way of studying and understanding them. Such a method will distort the meaning of the Christian sacraments because they will be seen as forms of religious rite and cult whose primary purpose is to put human beings in contact and at right with God in the pejorative sense of "religion." Rather the sacraments should be understood as elements of the Church and as having a function within the Church of fostering its mission in the world. By giving the sacraments a status of functions for building up the Church for its mission in history, Segundo relates them intrinsically to human existence in history and for history.

As far as I can see the positive statement of Segundo's thesis is sound. Christian sacraments as such are historical phenomena and have their distinctive existence within the Christian Church. A reservation concerning his thesis, however, might be appropriate relative to its negations which are stated too firmly. Surely there is no total discontinuity between Christianity and other religions, and the historical symbolism of any sacrament does not negate its intrinsic or "natural" symbolic value. And just as surely the sacraments do mediate an experience and contact with God. But having said this, it seems even more important to insist that the specific meaning of Christian sacraments is to be explained historically, in their genesis, for they are phenomena that arose within and as a function of the historical Christian community.

Thus like our understanding of the Church itself our understanding of Christian sacrament must be related back to Jesus who is the ground, source and origin of both. The primary sacrament or symbol mediating God in history for Christians is Jesus of Nazareth. Jesus is the origin and source of Christian faith, and also the ground, origin and source of the Church of which the sacraments are a part. And just as the Church itself is the historical continuation of the mission of Jesus in the world, and so refers back to Jesus as to its source, so too the sacraments, as mediations of our contact with God in history and within the Church, relate back to Jesus as to their source.

But how is this relation back to Jesus to be understood in the light of the general agreement today that Jesus did not institute any sacraments in the formal sense in which they are understood today? The sacraments arose in the course of the historical development of the Church, some earlier and some much later. Moreover the development of each of the sacraments was unique in the sense that each has its peculiar course of development. But at the same time it may be said that every sacrament relates back in some way to Jesus. This may be understood in such a way that each sacrament as it developed within the Church took on the specific meaning that faith in God as mediated by Jesus Christ gave it. Or, to put this in another way, symbols or events that may not have been specifically Christian took on a new Christian meaning in the light of the person of Jesus Christ or the faith generated by him.

Such a development, for example, can be seen as operative in the genesis of the sacraments of Eucharist and baptism. In the ritual meal one can see a natural and quasi-universal symbolism in the sharing of food together; such a meal evokes and effects human unity and reconciliation. The natural symbolism of the water of baptism implies cleansing. Both of these sacraments also had an historical meaning prior to Jesus and their adoption as Christian sacrament. It is impossible to understand the Eucharist adequately without reference to the Jewish passover meal and the long memory of the liberation recalled in the story of the exodus. And Jesus himself was baptized by the baptism of John that had its own dynamics prior to Jesus' acceptance of it. But both of these levels of meaning are transformed again in the Christian setting when they are reinterpreted either by Jesus or by faith in Jesus as the Messiah of God. Henceforth these rituals have a meaning determined by Jesus, by the life and teaching of Jesus and especially by the Christian faith in his death and resurrection. Thus both inherent and past historical symbolic meanings are subsumed into the meaning given historically by the event of Jesus Christ. This genesis applies to all Christian sacraments; they arose with the Church itself, some earlier some later, in its long and continuous historical development.

There has been a tendency in Christian theology to see the sacraments almost exclusively as symbolic representations of the risen Christ. It is being recognized today, especially by liberation theology, that the primary referent for the sacraments is the historical Jesus of Nazareth. An exclusive fixing on the risen Christ may imply leaving in the shadows the concrete historical life of Jesus and consequently a neglect of this dimension in our own religious life. In an extreme form, another side of this would be a fixing on Jesus Christ in his present status of being with God and the tendency of turning him into simply and exclusively an object of cult and worship.[13] An exclusive identification with the risen Christ would of course serve to strengthen our own hope for resurrection, but perhaps on false grounds if it served as well to foster neglect of present responsibility for historical life here and now. In contrast to this, then, one should say that the primary referent of the sacraments is Jesus of Nazareth. We do not know anything about the risen Christ apart from the historical Jesus. The risen one is Jesus. The resurrection is less a revelation of new Christian truths than a revelation of the person of Jesus himself and his privileged relation to God as the medium of God's revelation. Moreover Jesus is risen because of the life that he led on earth. And as for ourselves, we are not yet resurrected; resurrection remains a promise and a hope for the future. And ultimately that hope is grounded not only on the power of God's love manifested through Jesus, but also on the way of life that each leads in faith, a life for God and God's cause that leads toward the ultimate and promised future. This is what was revealed in the Jesus event. The historical Jesus, of course, is not to be held over against the risen one now alive with God. The issue is a question of focus and emphasis. The sacraments are to be seen as primarily referring back to the concrete figure of history, Jesus of Nazareth.

To summarize this discussion of the sacraments from an historical and genetic point of view, it may be said that sacraments are those finite pieces of reality that symbolize and re-present Jesus and the gestures of Jesus in the Christian community. Beyond their natural symbolism, Christian sacraments have an historical meaning that derives from Christian faith in God that has its historical focus in the Jesus of history now risen. Perhaps the clearest example of a sacrament, the one that is most widely and universally accepted by all Christians, is the New Testament itself. As a finite object, a book of collected writings, one that took over a century to develop in its final form, it is the primary sacrament after Jesus himself. It mediates Christian faith in God through the Jesus that it re-presents to Christian imagination.

Turning now to a more systematic account of the structure of the sacraments, we may take the lead from medieval theology which viewed the sacraments as consisting in two elements, matter and form. In Aristotelian philosophy these two dimensions of reality make up any and every finite being. These two elements, however, might be better recast in a more descriptive and biblical language of symbol and word. Each sacrament has this double dimension. It is a symbol, that is, an event, an action, a thing, or a ritual behavior. And at the same time this event is interpreted through human concepts and words, words that come from the word of Scripture and relate it back to Jesus Christ.[14] The word then is the interpretation, the explanation of the symbol, that which carries its specific meaning and significance. These two dimensions are closely intertwined, and at points it may be difficult to distinguish between them clearly. For the symbol also bears meaning within itself, and the word is also a symbolic form of communication.

Both of these dimensions are extremely important in their own way. The importance of the symbolic aspect of the sacrament is the fact that it makes the meaning it bears concrete, present here and now, tangible and actual within the community. These are concrete physical gestures after the pattern of Jesus, and hence they render Jesus present symbolically to the community. At this first level of description there is no need for a mystical understanding of this representation of Jesus. The historical Jesus is recalled or remembered, and made present historically by or in these community actions that imitate him. Given this empirical and historical human activity, it is on a deeper level that, within and through these tangible symbols that recall the historical Jesus, the Spirit of God is evoked and made actively and pointedly present to Christian existence. In this sense, sacraments cause grace by their symbolic and signifying causality. Christ risen and alive is made present by the Spirit.[15]

Symbols are also important because they are polyvalent; they have a somewhat open meaning and significance. Symbols in effect open up many meanings to different people and in different situations they take on different significances; they also respond to different levels of human questioning and all three levels or dimensions of human freedom. For this reason they share in a kind of potential universality and as such are vital as a unifying factor within the community. The sacraments unify and bind the community together at various levels here and now by focusing faith in a concrete and tangible form, but one that is polyvalent and open to pluralism.

The "word" dimension is equally important, if not more important precisely because of the polyvalence of symbol. Symbolic actions in themselves can mean just about anything. But such actions after the pattern of Jesus cannot be construed to mean everything nor just anything at all. Their meaning must be specified according to the norm of Jesus himself and according to his meaning as interpreted for us in the New Testament. It is often noted that sacraments should be adapted to the concrete circumstances and needs of the community; to make sense they must be comprehensible to a given culture. It would appear that this task of adaptation applies less to the symbol itself and more to the word that interprets it. The key to the relevance of sacraments to the life of the community and culture in which they are practiced lies in the word that interprets them to that community and culture. In this way symbol and word collapse into each other and mesh into one symbolic action. Together they communicate concretely the whole meaning of faith through the whole liturgical rite or action in a way that addresses the exigencies of a concrete community.

Langdon Gilkey, speaking from a Protestant perspective and thus presumably presupposing the importance of the word, has reinforced the need of the sacramental or symbolic dimension in Christian life and worship. Concrete and tangible symbols mediate the substance of Christian faith with power by grounding it in the concrete and solidifying the community around tangible mediating realities that communicate divine presence.[16] Speaking as a Roman Catholic, and presupposing this Catholic substance, I would stress the need for a stronger emphasis on the prophetic interpreting word in sacramental and liturgical practice. If Christain faith has entered into a period of stress brought on by a new crisis of the very meaning of social existence, then the response of the Christian message must be reinterpreted to respond to this crisis. The symbolic actions of the community represent the gestures of Jesus in the community and thus make God present to it through these words and deeds. The interpreting words that inform this sacramental practice must present these gestures in the prophetic way that makes them relevant to our current situation. The whole meaning of all the sacraments should be informed by the new challenge that God makes to God's Christian people through the life of Jesus Christ. Without this prophetic word, not apart from sacraments but precisely as the word that informs them and gives them their meaning for today, sacraments run the intrinsic risk of drawing Christian responsibility out of history and the social realm, and making the Church a sphere apart from the world into which people can escape from the challenges of history.

To conclude what has been said here, sacraments have an historical origin. Even when their symbolism has universal dimensions, that meaning is not simply an abstract transcultural truth, but refers back to Jesus of Nazareth and the paschal mystery, for he is the ultimate source and ground of all Christian meaning. The sacraments are re-presentations of the saving actions of Jesus himself in history. Sacramental action is an action of memory and recall. In the first moment sacraments are repetitions of the gestures of Jesus while he was on earth, or at least gestures that recall him or are associated with him. But in themselves these symbolic gestures need interpretation, especially relative to the context in which they are placed. The ministry of the word, which may be extended here to mean the whole presentation of the sacrament and the actions and tonality that surround it, is vital for translating the genuine meaning of the historical Jesus to the present situation. This word today should be a prophetic and challenging one, for, as was said earlier in dealing with discipleship, it is only in responding to evil by resisting it in the pattern of Jesus that the meaning of God's salvation in him becomes real.

SACRAMENTS FOR THE COMMUNITY IN HISTORY: THE EFFICACY OF THE SACRAMENTS

Christian sacraments have a universal transcendent dimension of meaning which shares at least something in common with the cult of other religions. They are concrete symbols and rites that mediate contact with God. But in Christian faith the sacraments have an historically derived meaning; they relate back to Jesus. And they are a function of the Christian community which also has its meaning and purpose in history from Jesus. Given this data, the question to be addressed now concerns the efficacy of the sacraments. How is the operation of the sacraments to be understood theologically? And how are we to view the tensions involved in Christian cult when measured against the demands of everyday life and the problem of human existence?

The efficacy of the sacraments cannot be thought of independently of a more general view of the whole economy of salvation mediated by Christ. The Christian sacraments are not autonomous entities; they are as Segundo has rightly pointed out functions and actions of the Church. And the Church itself is a community of the Spirit of God focused in its faith in God through Jesus as the Christ. In the first place, then, the sacraments as derivative from Jesus Christ are to be seen as revelatory. They focus in a point of time, here and now, in this liturgy on this occasion, Christian faith in God as mediated through Jesus Christ. They bring to bear in a tangible and concrete way the revelatory significance of Jesus Christ. They lift the message of Jesus as contained in his person and the tradition of the community out of the past and apply it concretely to a specific occasion, be it birth and initiation into the community or the more routine gathering of the community to worship God as God is known to us through Jesus.

At the same time, as was said earlier, the message and revelation of Jesus in itself is external and objective and needs an internal principle of appropriation. Thus the sacraments are ultimately efficacious by the power of the Spirit of God. Medieval theology said that the sacraments caused grace, and they did so precisely by being a sign, by symbolic causality. The same thing may be said in terms of Jesus' external revelation and the actuation of this within the human spirit through God's Spirit or grace. The sacraments mediate the Spirit of God; they are an explicit and objective offer and cause of grace, that is, they cause the Spirit to be consciously appropriated in a specific and thematic or focused way. By re-presenting the revelation of Christ in a symbolic and hence concrete way, and in a focused and pointed way, sacraments mediate a reappropriation of the salvation of Christ, always through the Spirit of God.

The notion *ex opere operato* really points in this direction. The phrase indicates a doctrine that arose before Augustine and which was used by him in his controversy with the Donatist church. The sacrament, it says, is effective simply by the placement of the act or ritual itself. It indicates that the efficacy of the sacraments therefore is independent of the holiness or intention of the minister. Of course this could be rendered ridiculous by a *reductio ad absurdum*. But at the same time the doctrine points in the direction of the truth that the initiative of God is prior to and the cause of the effectiveness of the sacraments. A sacrament is not merely, and not most fundamentally, an action of the minister, but of the whole community of faith prior to any individual, and without which there would be no sacrament. Moreover the faith action of the community has an objectivity in the life of Jesus to which it refers. And finally as a religious symbol it mediates the presence and action of

God through it. God is prior to the Church and to Christian faith by God's action in the life of Jesus Christ, and God's Spirit is prior to every faith response in human existence itself. In short, then, the efficacy of the sacraments may be understood in the terms of the whole economy of Christian salvation. They are effective by or through the coming together of word, understood here as the whole external ritual or symbolic action, and the Spirit in or within a human life and community.

It is true that because of the doctrine of *ex opere operato* the sacraments in Roman Catholicism have tended to take on an objective, institutional and almost a-historical character. Segundo is correct in polemicizing against a quasi-magical understanding of the sacraments, for this not only has prevailed in popular imagination and consciousness but has also been approximated in some theological accounts. But there is no reason to think of the efficaciousness or effectivity of the sacraments in other than existential and historical terms. This is not to deny the personal presence and effective power of God's Spirit in human subjectivity which has just been explained. It is rather to assert that the power of God is rendered explicit, historical and real through the sacraments in an existential way. Through the sacraments there is mediated a conscious encounter with God which plays itself out in a person's life. The sacrament occurs here and now, in a specific context, involving concrete people. The effects of the sacrament occur in different degrees in the lives of different persons; these effects are existential. The effects of the sacraments, then, are historical, and the truth of the sacraments *is* the existential encounter with God that plays itself out in time. On the one hand, to explain the sacraments as acts of faith and genuinely religious, that is, not simply human grasping at salvation and attempts at manipulating God, it is necessary to appeal to the mystery of the transcendent God's personal and immanent presence to human beings mediated through the sacraments as God's gracious Spirit. But on the other hand, it is not necessary to explain the sacraments in any other way, that is, beyond this symbolic mediation of the Spirit of God in specific circumstances to a particular group of people. In this way the efficacy of the sacraments is translated into terms of the concrete faith experience of people, and this in turn becomes real in the exact measure in which it becomes played out in their lives in history. The sacraments, therefore, have an historical efficacy.

From this it follows that one will find deeply embedded within the sacraments, within ritual and cult, some very basic tensions. The first of these may by seen in objective terms as the tension between the sacred and the secular, or between what is considered holy and what is of the world. On the one hand, the terms "holy" and "sacred" apply to God and in their proper sense exclusively to God. Only God is holy, and in the light of God's transcendence and holiness the world is demythologized, desacralized and secular. Things are not holy. And as Luther said quite correctly, neither is the Church holy in itself.[17] To say that the Church is holy is to make a statement about God; the Church is holy only insofar as God is operative in it, in its members and in its institutions. Thus, on the other hand, symbols and sacraments do participate in God precisely insofar as they mediate God's revelation and Spirit to human existence. But this is to be seen as an historical, existential and human event in which God is at work. The sacraments are forms of human behavior, actions stemming from faith and animated by the Spirit of God. They have no objective holiness whatever in themselves outside of the reality of the assembled community's faith commitment. Sacraments are human actions in which the presence of God's Spirit is rendered explicit in symbol and word and whose effects are also actualized on the existential historical level. The holiness that is derived from the Spirit of God must be translated away from things, which of course remain objects of reverence insofar as they recall Jesus Christ, and into the personal and corporate participation in and cooperation with the Spirit of God. It is to be seen as an existential and historical mode of human life, one that ultimately participates in God by doing God's will through God's immanent power.

A second tension, reflecting the first, may be seen in the subjective terms of human attitudes and motivation and intention. What is the relation between worship or adoration of God that is exercised in sacramental practice and the rest of human life? This tension may be generalized to cover every aspect of formal religion. The tension is between religion and morality, between prayer, which William James called religion in act,[18] and behavior in the other spheres of one's life. Certainly there can be no dichotomy or contrast between these two aspects of human life. The question then is one of seeing how they interrelate. This may be approached from two points of view. The first is from that of God insofar as God appears disclosed in Christian revelatory symbols. The second is from an anthropological point of view.

Looking at the Christian God who is absolutely transcendent, Creator and infinite, as well as sheer goodness and love, it must be said that God is to be worshiped and adored. This is required by the recognition of God's status, of God's being God. But granting this, one must still ask the question: What kind of God do we worship? God is also personal and has a general will for human beings. Thus it may be asked even further whether, according to God's will, God wants to be adored and worshiped. Certainly God is jealous when human beings worship other and false gods. But the consistent revelation of Christianity is that God's real desire is that God's will be done "on earth" and in history, "as it is in heaven." The core of Jesus' life and message is that God's cause is the cause of human existence itself, the cause of human beings and human life. From what we "know" of God's point of view through Christian revelation, there is absolutely no tension between religion and morality understood as love of neighbor if they are conceived correctly. Love of neighbor is honor and worship of God because it is God's cause. And focused worship of the Christian God that does not unfold within the context of love of neighbor is at best deficient worship, and at worst it conveys a false view of the Christian God. From God's point of view according to Christian revelation, then, it must be said that actions of worship of God by themselves or in themselves are not absolute or ends in themselves.

From an anthropological point of view, however, the response to this question may be somewhat different. Because of human finitude and creatureliness, human existence would cease to be without being held by the creative hand of God. It follows that worship of God is an essential and intrinsic dimension of an authentic and adequate response to reality itself. We are absolutely dependent on God; gratitude and submission to God is thus essential even to an intelligible self-understanding. It is understandable then why the need to actually worship God may be absolutely central for supplying ultimate meaning, coherence and true freedom for any given person. So radical is existential human insecurity in being that it can turn religion and worship into the negative project of a human attempt to effect salvation by or for itself by works or merit or some other form of bartering with God.

In contrast, authentic Christian worship and prayer is first of all a total surrender to God, to God's forgiveness and God's totally gracious recreative power of resurrection. And, secondly, this conscious attitude or prayerful practice is only real and authentic if it is integrated into the whole of a person's life as a surrender to God's will. This is where it will show up as an authentically real conviction or, ironically, a Pelagian counterfeit. That is to say, religion as an effort to win salvation is Pelagian. And it is manifest in faith without any effort at the works of love. It is itself a work, in the pejorative sense, and a begging for cheap grace. In contrast, a faith that spontaneously flows over into the works of love is authentic surrender to God. This is why the authentic love of neighbor that is manifest in the works of love implies an authentic faith in God, God's will and God's cause.[19] Thus, once again, worship, prayer and gratitude make up the fundamental attitude that should characterize the whole of any Christian life and spirituality. But this worship becomes real and authentic in the works of love in this world. There must be a basic integration and consistency between worship and the whole of a person's life, otherwise any formal act of worship will not be genuine.

To summarize, sacraments should not be considered as ahistorical holy objects. They are signs placed by the community of faith in a faith that recalls the gestures of Jesus and thus re-presents him and his message in concrete, tangible forms. The sacraments are efficacious insofar as they symbolize and awaken a conscious response to the prior and already present Spirit of God in human life. Their meaning is thus historical because it arises out of the concrete life of Jesus, and their effectiveness is historical insofar as through the Spirit they open freedom and move people to respond to God and to the world around them in a Christian way. From this one may generalize on the meaning of cult, worship, prayer and religious devotion in the Christian vision of reality, God and human life. These actions always have a bearing on the moral substance of human life, the freedom and responsibility that are constitutive of human existence. Worship, in the sense of one's total surrender to God on the deepest level of human motivation, is most manifest, from the point of view of God whose cause is the human life that God created, in love of neighbor. This love is the beginning of the expansion of human freedom toward God that only God's Spirit can effect. This is the direction that is revealed to us in the message of Jesus' life. And from an anthropological point of view, the worship that appears so essential and necessary for our own self-understanding will only be authentic when it includes a desire and an effort to surrender oneself to the will and cause of God. Only in this desire does the counting on God's forgiveness for our inevitable failure make any sense.

CONCLUSION

The fundamental insights and principles of liberation theology concerning the sacraments, even when this theology is considered beyond the immediate context of the poverty and oppression of Latin America, are basically sound.

Sacraments are to be understood as functions of the Church. The meaning of the sacraments, what they are and what they do, flows from the nature and function of the Christian community which is itself derivative from Jesus. The sacraments therefore should not be understood independently or apart from the mission of the Church and its historical role in history. All that has been said of the Church in its mission to be sacrament to the world defines as well the context and the intentionality of Christian sacraments.

Just as the Church has an historical existence, so too do the sacraments. The missionary Church must adapt itself to successive epochs and periods of history and become inculturated into particular social situations in order to be an intelligible sign to the world it addresses. Similarly the sacraments ought to be made responsive to history. Given the constitution of the sacraments in symbol and word, the continuous and stable element of the sacraments lies in the symbol or symbolic actions which are concrete and tangible gestures relating back to Jesus in the past and re-presenting him in the present. The interpretative element lies in the word. In each historical situation the sacraments must be interpreted anew by a word that responds to the historical and cultural situation. If the context of faith today is such that this faith is deeply threatened by the meaninglessness of our global corporate and social history, then sacramental practice, preaching and liturgical practice require the address of a prophetic word. Christian faith itself is challenged by a religious imperative from God as mediated by Jesus to discern human oppression where it exists, especially on the social level, and to resist it along with others of good will.

Sacraments have to be understood within the context of history and historical process in terms of personal and corporate freedom exercised in time in the world. Sacraments are moments of contact with God through God's initiative and thus of prayerful worship. Their overall efficacy, however, is existential and historical. The true test of the authenticity of sacramental practice is the Christian life which it engenders. Thus participation in the resistance against evil and the struggle for justice in the world is an intrinsic dimension of the efficacy of the sacraments and not added on as a consequence. In our historical context social involvement is the very direction in which the sacraments point as concrete memories of Jesus in a mission Church.

The next chapter will look more directly at the concrete ways in which sacramental practice responds to all of the dimensions of human freedom as the discussion turns to the question of ministry.

Chapter XI
MINISTRY IN A MISSION CHURCH

The last chapters dealt with the nature and liberating function of the Church in the world and with sacrament within the context of such a Church. The Church, it was said, is the community of the Spirit of God formed in its faith by Jesus as the Christ. This community as a whole is sent to and for the world after the pattern of Jesus and in the light of his message; it is to be the sacrament for the world of that which it has received from God. The message of the Church was also further defined; it is a message of liberation, one that addresses human existence in all the dimensions of its freedom. The Church mediates freedom from sin through contact with a forgiving God, a God who promises resurrection in answer to human finitude and death. The Church mediates God's Spirit and power to personal freedom that open up that freedom in love and service to the neighbor. And finally the Church is to be a sign of social grace in response to the social repression that so characterizes the world, a community that moves people toward fashioning structures in society that are marked by justice.

The discussion which follows will consider the ministerial activity of the Church within the context of a mission ecclesiology and in the light of liberation theology. Since the concern for ministry is so great today and the literature dealing with it so vast, I shall begin by situating the discussion and defining the limits within which the topic will be treated here. Once again the point of this chapter is not to develop anything like a complete, adequate or systematic theology of ministry. The aim is simply to reinterpret the basic intention of Christian ministry through the general principles that emerge out of the liberationist interpretation of Christianity.

LOCATING THE THEOLOGY OF MINISTRY

I take ministry to refer to the activity of service for the freedom of other human beings that is performed by Christians, that is, explicitly as members of the Church and with Christian motivation. Ministry is service, a form of *diakonia,* an activity performed on behalf of other human beings. Ultimately all ministerial activity is directed toward the freedom of other persons because freedom is the essence of human existence itself, and the whole meaning and power of Christian revelation is directed toward the release and empowerment of human freedom. Christian ministry is activity that is inspired by this Christian revelation received through faith. Its distinctiveness lies here even when objectively similar forms of activity and service may be performed by other persons and groups.

In his extensive study of Christian ministry from an historical and theological perspective, Bernard Cooke maintains that one really should not speak of ministry as if it were a common generic reality which can then be subdivided into activities that share a common denominator and are derived from it. Cooke prefers to assume "an historical-descriptive method" in his approach to ministry, one which is demanded when one views the Church as a concrete existential and historical reality. He wants to maintain that the variety of ministries in the Church are autonomous and arise spontaneously out of the Church community itself, and thus they are not to be considered as derived from any single ministerial office or function.[1] I am sympathetic to Cooke's insistence on this point, but without contradicting it the discussion here must be limited to a very general consideration of the principles of ministry. It would be impossible in a short space to consider all of the various ministries of the Church. Thus while admitting that the only way to develop an adequate theology of ministry would be to look at the several ministries of the Church in their distinctiveness, still I believe that it is possible to lay down some principles that pertain to ministry in general when viewed from a liberationist point of view.

There are a variety of ministries in the Church and a large variety of different ministerial responsibilities. On a fundamental level, all Christians by the very fact of their Christian faith are called to witness to the Christian message in the world. Thus by their baptism, by their membership in the Church, all Christians have the right to fulfill this call publicly. In a variety of ways all Christians are ministers in a formal and real sense. At the other end of a spectrum, however, there are official ministers who exercise an official ministry. These are ministers who have been accepted by the community as public representatives in particular ministries. For example, they may have been designated or ordained to perform specific ministerial functions such as the celebration of the cult or liturgy of the community. Between these two extremes there are many different degrees of professional ministry; there are a variety of ministers who work part-time or full-time in a variety of different ministries. In these reflections, I will not deal with the various levels or degrees of commitment to ministry. I will not dwell on the distinctions between the ministry of all the faithful and official ministry.[2] And I will not consider in any detail why ministers of word and sacrament may require a special community ordination, the nature of this ordination, or why other professional ministers might not also require a specific ordination for their specialized ministries. Thus if one allows a distinction between ministry and ministers, that is, a distinction between a discussion of the general principles of ministry and one concerning the official levels and specific tasks of designated ministers, the discussion here will be of the former general nature. It is presumed, however, that what is said theologically about ministry in general applies to all ministers whether they be official or not. If ministry is an integral part of the whole community, so that the various ministries emerge out of the Christian community as such, it would seem that a possible starting point for a theology of ministry might lie in some general considerations of ministry as such in a mission Church.

I take the theology of ministry as a reflection that lies "between" systematic or doctrinal theology on the one hand and concrete or actual Christian living on the other. As a help in understanding this "location," one may recall what was said at the outset about theology. Systematic theology is a discipline that tries to understand the nature of reality in the light of the symbols of Christian revelation. It is a normative or prescriptive discipline in the sense that it attempts to get at the truth, at an understanding of reality that one judges to be true. Theology is not a merely descriptive discipline, one that describes, for example, the way Jesus is actually understood in the Church, which may at any given time be heretical, or the way the Church actually is. Rather theology seeks to provide an understanding of the way things should be understood. In many ways theology is an effort not to contemplate or describe the actuality of Christian faith but to change it. Despite the pluralism of theologies, the underlying intention that characterizes all of them is that they aim at what is true.

But Christian symbols and theological understanding do not just hang in space; they are themselves rooted in the actual existential life of the Christian community. Besides any normative doctrinal understanding of reality one finds the actual life of Christians themselves, the actual way in which the community or communities believe and lead their Christian lives. Thus there are as it were two dimensions to the Christian phenomenon, the Christian Church, which may be characterized as the ideal and the actual, or what should be and what is. These two levels are intimately connected since theology flows out of the experience and lived reality of the community. Christian experience and life is the source for theology, and theology, as reflection on that life through the media of the symbols of tradition, is meant to reflect back on it to illumine and shape it.

Given the polarity of these two dimensions of the Christian phenomenon, one can say first of all that ministry itself lies in the tension "between" them, between theology and actual everyday Christian life, that active aspect of Christian behavior that is directed in service of the freedom of other human beings, both inside and outside the community, and for both building up the community and extending its mission outward. Ministry is the actual service by Christians that is directed to nurturing and fostering the Christian life itself and carrying forward the Church's function in the world. Obviously enough this ministry is conscious and should be performed in the light of an understanding of the nature and purpose of Christianity and the Church. Thus ministry is directed by some normative understanding of the Church and of reality in the light of Christian symbols. Not only ministry itself but also the theology of ministry may be understood as "located between" systematic theology and the existential reality of the Christian community. The theology of ministry is an explicitly applied and practical discipline; it seeks to provide the general norms and guidelines for the practical exercise of ministry.[3] Just as theological understanding in general emerges out of and relates back to Christian life by providing it with critical principles, so too a theology of ministry seeks to supply principles and axioms for the ministerial activity, in all its forms, that is in service of the Christian life.

Like any discipline that deals with human behavior the theology of ministry can unfold at a variety of different levels. At one extreme the discussion could be very general and deal with principles; at the other it could be very specific and concrete and deal with actual problems that arise within corporate Christian life. In other words, while remaining a practical discipline, the theology of ministry ranges from a consideration of the general principles that illumine all ministerial situations to analysis of actual cases and how the minister should deal with them. On the one side an adequate theology of ministry would consider the theological justification of the specific ministries that are found in the Church. On the other side, it should also consider the various skills that are needed for effective ministerial activity in any given sphere of the Christian life. In keeping with the intention of this book, which is to reinterpret Christian symbols on a basic general level in terms of liberation theology, this essay into ministerial theology will not go beyond the general discussion of principles. Our aim here is not to deal with concrete issues, as important as many of them are, but to understand the nature, meaning and direction of the very notion of ministry in a mission Church.

As a final introductory remark I would stress the importance of the theology of ministry, which I believe cannot be exaggerated. It is correct to say that the essence of the Church is ministry, and correspondingly that ministry is the very substance of the Church. This is true not only in the theoretical sense that the purpose of the Church in history is its role of ministry to the world. It is also true in the existential sense that ministry makes the Church to be what it actually is as an historical reality. Whatever the Church should be in theological theory, what the Church actually is is determined by the kind of ministerial leadership and service that actually takes place within it. Once one shifts to an existential historical and concrete point of view, ministry and one's conception of it become supremely important as the point where the theological interpretation of the symbols of Christianity come to bear on the actuality of the Church. What the Church is is decided and determined by its ministry, and a theology of ministry brings the critical principles of theology to bear on the nature and direction of that ministry.

The thesis concerning ministry in the Christian Church that underlies the whole development of this chapter can be stated rather simply: All Christian ministry is service *of* human freedom, that is, springing out of the free human spirit, a service *to* human freedom, and a service *for* human freedom's development and fulfillment. And since human freedom has three dimensions or levels, one can look at Christian ministry within the context of each of the dimensions of human freedom to which it is directed. The result of this general discussion will be a kind of fundamental theology of ministry offering principles, axioms and guidelines within which the further historical and technical studies of specific ministries may be pursued.

This particular development of the theological interpretation of ministry will begin with noting some of the themes and data from liberation theology which deal with or have a bearing on ministry. Then in the next section of the chapter I will list some principles and some axiomatic tensions that govern the Church's ministry. These generalizations are inspired by liberation theology, and they correlate with the themes found there, but they are recast in a larger and more universal framework and culture. In the concluding section I will discuss ministry in terms of the three dimensions of human freedom that must be ministered to. We begin then with themes from the theology of liberation.

THEMES FROM LIBERATION THEOLOGY

Liberation theology began as a movement within the Church in Latin America. In fact and not just in theory its theology began with praxis simply because the movement itself was one defined by a new concern for and direction and application of ministry. Only after and out of this vital ministerial practice did the theology of liberation emerge as coherent and critical reflection. One way of approaching the Latin American liberation theology of ministry would be to simply describe the various new ministries that have emerged on that continent and in other parts of the world. However, after recognizing these practical origins, it will be simpler and more in keeping with the theological intention of this book to enumerate some of the major theological positions of this theology that in turn have critically reinforced its ministerial activity. Since many of these themes have already been mentioned, they do not have to be fully developed at this point.

First of all, liberation theology understands the Church as a whole as turned outward toward the world. This theme has been accommodated in this representation of liberation theology by means of the religious symbol "mission."[4] The very purpose of the Church is to be for the world; it has a role to play in general human history. In Gutiérrez, who speaks of the Church being uncentered in favor of the general advance of the reign of God, the Church is understood as a community in relation to society, especially society's oppressive structures.[5] In Juan Luis Segundo the principle is expressed in a world-historical or even cosmological principle. The Church appeared in history to be a vanguard movement in an evolutionary process of the general human development of freedom.[6] The implications of this understanding for Christian ministry are really very basic, because Christian ministry has usually been viewed, at least tacitly if not explicitly, as service within the Christian community and in behalf of fellow Christians in the community.[7] The ecclesiological principle announced here shifts the basic intention and direction of all Christian ministry in a very elementary way.

Closely connected with the former theme and perhaps an extension of it is the idea that the Church is a public sacrament to the world of the message and power received through Jesus Christ. The point that is emphasized here is the public aspect of sacramentality. From a concrete existential and historical viewpoint the sacrament is the actual institutional Church insofar as it is visible in society. This visible Church in liberation theology is meant to be a public critic of society both by its existence, by what it is, and by its visible social actions, by what it does in society. At this point liberation theology shares with political theology the view that the Church is called to publicly address the sin and evil of the institutions of society, to denounce them and to prophetically announce the values of the Gospel.[8] When this position is internalized, the implications both for public or official ministry and for personal ministry are profound. The intention of ministry is to fashion a community that overtly addresses society, a community that is based on a common personal spirituality and view of the Christian life that is regulated by a sign morality.[9]

The theme in liberation theology that most directly pertains to a theology of ministry is the principle that the quality of Christian life takes precedence over the quantity of Christians that make up the Church. This principle is one of the key ideas in the theology of Juan Luis Segundo,[10] it has been incorporated into the theology of missions,[11] and it has enormous direct bearing on ministry. The principle envisages the possibility that all may not have a vocation to be a Christian, that being a member of the Church may not be the best means of salvation for everyone. Being a Christian involves responsibility and an active spirituality. The point of Christian ministry, therefore, should not be a sustained effort either to multiply conversions or to maintain a large Church of the masses in a condition of passive reception of sacraments. This view affects every phase of ministry. It influences the choice of ministries, the allocation of personal and material ministerial resources, as well as the way one goes about any particular ministry. It determines ministerial strategy, expectations and even the way the Word of God is preached. In short Christian ideals take precedence over every form of accommodation in Christian ministry.

A ministerial development that is closely associated with liberation theology is the formation of basic communities.[12] Although there are many very different types of basic communities, so that at best the term applies only analogously to all sorts of different styles and intentions within them, still there are certain common and distinctive features. Basic communities by and large are small enough that all the members know each other. Thus a basic community is held together intentionally by some specific shared goals. Ministry in a basic community may or may not be clerically led. Often they are more centered through Scripture and the Word of God than by the Eucharist. Thus these communities enjoy a certain autonomy relative to the traditional diocesan and parochial institutional structure of the Church. Ministry is governed more by spiritual leadership than by office. The structure and style of basic communities have implications for a theology of ministry, for basic conceptions of authority in ministry and its exercise, and for questions of office and ordination in relation to the community that is being ministered to. To a certain extent, if one stepped back and looked at such a small intentional community objectively, it would not be an exaggeration to say that each member is actually a minister to the others and to the whole.

Finally, the Church in Latin America has officially and publicly declared its preferential option for the poor.[13] This implies that the ministry of this whole Church is to be directed primarily toward or in behalf of the poor and the oppressed in that continent.[14] While this makes sense insofar as the vast majority of people in Latin America are poor, still this declaration marks a definite shift of focus and change of direction in the Church's ministry. It has been demonstrated historically that the Church for centuries has been chiefly aligned with and has primarily ministered to the wealthy, educated and powerful portion of society in Latin America. To this extent, then, the explicit redirection of the public policy of the Church in its ministry should imply basic changes in the style and direction of the actual ministry of the Church as well as in the content of the Christian message that is mediated by ministry.[15]

Since liberation theology is striving for a comprehensive understanding of Christianity, one could multiply at great length positions within it that have a bearing on Christian ministry. But at least the five themes that have been isolated here have a pointed significance for a liberationist theology of ministry, although this should not be seen as an exhaustive or exclusive summary. In what follows I will try to generalize these themes by enumerating some basic principles and tensions governing ministry that incorporate the liberationist themes and preserve the truth and value that they represent in a wider context.

PRINCIPLES AND AXIOMATIC TENSIONS IN MINISTRY

We begin this reinterpretation of a liberationist theology of ministry with a discussion of a number of principles and axiomatic tensions that govern Christian ministry in general. These principles flow out of liberation theology and will be seen to include the themes just enumerated; they also presuppose the whole theological interpretation of the first ten chapters of this book. It is especially important to bear in mind the fundamental global problem of human suffering, an issue that calls in question the very meaningfulness of our historical existence, as central to this theological interpretation. But at the same time the principles developed here are stated in a broader historical and cultural framework. To ensure this I enlist the historical and theological work of Bernard Cooke as a dialogue partner.[16]

A first fundamental principle for a theology of ministry is this: The source of Christian ministry is the whole Christian community itself which leads back to Jesus, so that the direction of Christian ministry comes from the Gospel. Ministry springs spontaneously from the Christian community of the Spirit. But Christian ministry is precisely Christian; its distinctiveness is determined by the nature of the Church of which it is a function. And the Church is the community of the Spirit of God formed in its faith by Jesus of Nazareth. Specifically Christian ministry therefore has like the Church and Christian faith itself a Christological basis. It follows from this that the direction of Christian ministry is ultimately determined or normed by the Gospel and its ideals. And since the Gospel must be continually reinterpreted in every historical period and situation, Christian ministry has to be guided by constant theological reflection. Christian theology, which has its own basis in faith in God mediated through Jesus, is "an indispensable element" in determining the nature and direction of Christian ministry.[17]

A second principle for ministry is that the actual historical and existential situation of human existence or freedom is an immediate criterion for ministry. In other words, the kind of ministry that is performed, the actual strategy of ministry and its immediate goals, and practical ministerial judgment are determined by the condition of the person, group or whole people to whom ministry is directed. Ministry is directed to human freedom and so must take account of the actual condition of that freedom that is being addressed. This almost self-evident principle can be best illustrated in the sphere of direct ministry to individuals on a personal and psychological level. If one is to draw a person toward Christian ideals, one has to work according to or within the framework of the actual capacity of the person concerned. But what is so clear in this example may also be generalized; it applies to concrete historical, social and cultural situations as well. The appropriate ministerial strategy is governed by the concrete situation. This accounts, for example, for the option of the Church in Latin America to direct its ministry primarily in behalf of the poor. And even more generally this principle accounts historically for the actual ministries that have arisen in the Church. The traditional ministries of the Church, the institutions and offices of ministry, were generated in response to the actual situations and needs of the people to whom they were directed. This principle, then, which becomes evident with the assumption of a concrete existential and historical viewpoint, both explains the genesis of the historic ministries of the Church and serves as a criterion for the ongoing judgment of the kind of ministries and the ministerial strategy that are needed in the Church at any given time. Ministries are to be defined and determined and governed "by the evolving needs and opportunities of the Church."[18]

These two principles unite to create a tension that is present in all Christian ministry, a tension that is axiomatic and inescapable in all forms of ministry. This tension may be viewed in a variety of ways as existing between the ideals of the Gospel and the actual condition of the community and the humanity it serves, or between the Christian ideal expressed theologically and what is possible, or between the Christian exigency for active freedom on the one hand and human passivity, mediocrity, immobility and sin on the other. No Christian ministry can avoid this tension. For ministry stems from the Gospel and is inspired by its ideals. This corresponds with and explains the insight of liberation theology that Christian ministry must be guided by the quality of Christian life. But at the same time, ministry continually addresses concrete situations that necessarily fall short of ideals on the fundamental level of sheer capacity and possibility.[19] In sum this basic tension pervades all ministry at all times, and any ministry that avoids it, that collapses this tension by disregarding one of the poles, will have disastrous results.

Another principle for ministry is that there is no area of human life to which the Gospel is alien. The principle could be stated positively as well: the values of the Gospel come to bear on every phase or in every area of human existence. And since this is the case, there is no sphere of human life that does not call out for Christian ministry. Because the Gospel addresses human existence itself, and concerns absolutely fundamental beliefs and values that govern human existence and the exercise of freedom, Christian ministry is appropriately directed toward every dimension of life. Christian ministry cannot be limited to some exclusive "spiritual" sphere; indeed there is no exclusively spiritual or religious sphere because human existence is spirit in the world, spirit enfleshed in the physical reality of everyday life. One may speak of three distinct levels or dimensions of human freedom, but there is only one human existence or freedom within these dimensions. This basic principle, then, legitimates the liberationist themes of a Christian ministry that is turned toward the world. For "world" in this usage means the whole sphere of secular human existence, the whole realm of free human activity, on which the Gospel comes to bear as surely as on the specifically religious sphere of life.[20] Christian ministry should be directed to every sphere of human life.[21]

The principle of the universal applicability of the Christian Gospel and ministry undoubtedly sets up a second tension within ministry. This is the tension between transcendent values and this-worldly values, both of which must underlie Christian ministry. On the one hand, Christian ministry cannot be dedicated exclusively to this-worldly goals or ends. It is at the same time a service of God's Word and motivated by faith. On the other hand, Christian ministry cannot be dedicated exclusively to purely spiritual or other-worldly objectives. For so-called "strictly religious or spiritual" ministry always has implications for life in this world and for behavior in every sphere of it. Positively, then, the spiritual quality of one's life and one's religious relationship to God is a single dimension of the whole range of one's concrete life and existence. And the whole of one's life in the world constitutes the totality of one's relationship to God. This tension, then, can only be dealt with by constant disclosure and critique in ministry: disclosure of the religious dimension that underlies secular life in the world and criticism of those secular activities that run counter to the spiritual values of the Gospel; disclosure of the secular implications of narrowly conceived spiritual or religious activities and criticism of those spiritual activities that undermine secular and worldly human responsibility in history.

It is also true that in principle Christian ministry has a double or twofold direction: it is aimed toward both life inside the Church and life outside the Church. It is useful to distinguish "between the ministries that exist to provide for the Church's service to the world and the ministries that exist to nurture the Church's own internal well-being."[22] This distinction, or, better, this double dimension to all Church ministry, is also intrinsic and inescapable. It flows from the inner nature of the Church as a mission, as being sent to the world to continue to mediate God's initiative in the world through Jesus Christ. As Troeltsch has pointed out, the Church inextricably stands in a double relation, to God and to the secular world outside it.[23] Its ministry, therefore, must attend to both of these relationships, to fostering and nurturing its inner and constitutive relationship to God and to activity which promotes its intrinsic and constitutive relation of mission to the world. Actually the terms "inside" and "outside" are rather impressionistic and can be understood in different senses. "Outside" the Church may mean beyond the boundaries of Christian faith and membership in the Church, as in the case of traditional missionary theory. Or "outside" may refer to a sphere of life that is not explicitly religious, that is, the secular sphere. In this second sense the Church may minister to a society that is generally Christian but in areas that are not overtly religious. In this case the distinction is similar to what is involved in the tension just described. This principle thus subsumes the themes from liberation theology concerning the Church's ministry outside itself and to the world.[24]

This last principle of the double direction of Christian ministry obviously defines another tension within that ministry. On the one hand such a tension between building up the community and service to the world is easily resolved by a social division of labor. Some ministries are directed exclusively toward the inner life of the community, such as ministries of leadership in worship. And other ministries are directed outward toward people and spheres of life that are not explicitly religious or Christian. But on the other hand and more deeply the "inside-outside" polarity refers to a constant tension of values, a tension within the meaning, motivation, direction and purpose of ministry. A Church ministry that so turns in on itself so that it loses its sense of responsibility to the world is inauthentic Christian ministry, just as much as a ministry to the world that loses its inner motivation of faith and gets lost in the world ceases to be explicitly Christian ministry. One of the very purposes of ministry within the community is to "prepare the community for its mission of evangelization and service to the world."[25] And all Christian involvement in the secular sphere, insofar as it is Christian, is grounded in and motivated ultimately by faith in God as mediated by Jesus. In other words a mere division of labor does not resolve this tension. The tension must be present in the whole life of the Church and in every single ministry because both of these dimensions are constitutive of the Church itself.

Yet another principle for ministry is the following: While the Church necessarily has offices of ministry and official ministerial representatives, still the responsibility for ministry is shared by all Christians as members of the Church. The Church as the community fashioned by God's Spirit from the very beginning gradually took on institutional forms. It is not possible to imagine a community that perdures in history that does not assume some institutional forms, some representational offices of ministry. Thus the Church not only has but must have official representatives who perform certain ministries necessary for the survival and health of the community. Some of these offices are evident a priori: there must be oversight or administration of the community, leadership of worship, offices for functions that meet other internal needs of the community and its mission outside itself. But at the same time the Christian Church as a whole is a community of ministry for ministry. This means that all Christians simply by virtue of being members of the Church share a responsibility for ministry. Intrinsic to being a Christian is the responsibility to witness to one's faith, the responsibility of loving service to one's neighbor, both inside and outside the Church, and the responsibility for the whole mission of the Church.[26] The reason or logic of this is more important than the principle itself because it concerns an insight into the very nature of the Christian Church. Before all else and prior to its institutionalization, although this is not a matter of time or chronological development but of the relation of dimensions of the Church, the Church is a community of people who are animated by God's Spirit. This vital community is formed in its faith in God by Jesus of Nazareth, so that the most basic impulse of the common faith life of the community is one of ministerial service in Jesus' name. All official ministries are grounded in the community itself; they are historical functions of the primal exigency of the community itself to exist and to perform its function in the world. In other words no single ministry or no function within the community is the basis of the community itself; all ministries are functions of the community. In short the Church is a community of ministry and ministers so that being a member of the Church is in some fundamental way being a minister of the Church.[27]

Still another principle relevant to ministry concerns religious authority. It may be said that the authority of all ministers in the Church is mediated and disclosive. Once again, these two qualities of authority in the Church are elementary and concern the very nature of the Church. Because they are so essential and basic they can be explained simply, the first theologically and the second anthropologically. First of all, authority in the Church has to do with God; religious authority ultimately has its basis in transcendence; it is God's authority. But no person or office is God. No human person or office is or has claimed to be God. Even in the case of Jesus there is absolutely no evidence that he directly claimed to be God. The structure of religious authority is always mediated. This means that every claim to religious authority in this world really points away from itself and beyond itself to transcendent truth. Second, from an anthropological point of view, the transcendent truth of every religious authority must be disclosed. Religious authority cannot prove itself or justify itself objectively but must appeal to the religious insight and freedom of another human being. Since no one possesses religious authority in himself or herself, every medium of religious authority is dependent on the inner and responsible commitment of human beings to it. Religious authority is ultimately or at bottom an existential reality, based on the insight and free commitment of faith on the part of the one who accepts it and which it attracts from within.[28] And, once again, this quality is displayed in Jesus who is the ultimate this-wordly Christian authority. He spoke as one with authority, who appealed to freedom, which is known by the fact that many turned away. The essence of Jesus' ministry is that it was a ministry to freedom.

These last two principles define a fourth tension that is intrinsic to Christian life and ministry as well as the way in which this tension may be seen as salutary and not destructive. There is a constant tension in the Church between conflicting authorities, and between the authority of various offices and the authority of charism.[29] The history of the Christian Church is a history of conflicting authorities, and there is no reason to think that this will suddenly cease. But it is crucial to understand and to enter into the historical process constructively. For example, the tension between official authority and charism is not a conflict between two separate and different authorities. The idea of an early fall of the Church from true charismatic authority to inauthentic institutional forms that was current in nineteenth century historical theology ultimately must be rejected because of its suppositions. Both people in offices and those not in offices may exercise genuine religious authority. What is crucial is the recognition that the nature of religious authority is ultimately a form of spiritual leadership that appeals to thought and freedom with reasons and values. Both of these typical kinds or forms of authority, and they are merely two extreme types, spring out of the corporate community of the Spirit formed in its faith in God by Jesus. The religious authority they mediate and disclose is not secular authority; it is not extrinsicist or in any way externally imposed coercive spiritual power. In an age of pluralism, where there are so many claimants to religious authority, the possibility of an absolute religious authority in this world ceases. All Christian authority is fundamentally moral authority. It is a function not of any office *per se*, which are not for that reason illegitimate but commonly recognized forms of exercising ministry with spiritual leadership, but of the ability of persons who exercise ministry to mediate and disclose God's truth. The dynamics of a new kind of nonclerical spiritual leadership are being anticipated in some basic communities in Latin America.

A final principle for ministry in the Church today stems from our concrete global historical situation. The focus of Christian ministry should be turned toward the poor and suffering of this world. In other words, this theme from liberation theology has more than merely local import. Because of the unity of the race and of human interdependence and solidarity which are at the heart of the Gospel, a preferential option for the poor is intrinsic to Christian faith and essential to the credibility of that faith before the world today. If the actuality of the Church is not moved toward social involvement on behalf of the cause of those masses of human beings who merely subsist in conditions that belie human dignity because of oppression and overt social injustice, then the Church will not be a sign of God's saving power through liberating love.

This final principle sets up another basic tension within Christian Church ministry, that is, a tension between the rich and the poor as the preferred object, constituency and concern for this ministry. That there is a tension here, one that should govern Christian ministry today, is undeniable. But it is most important that the nature of this tension be understood. The tension is not, or should not be, a conflict of classes within the Church. Although there may be class conflict in any given society, which Christian ministry should address, Christians as Christians are precisely not divided by class. Nor is the tension a division based on any moral superiority or virtue. Poverty like wealth can corrupt. Nor finally is this a tension between those who should be ministered to. Every Christian Church has a right to ministers independently of its material advantages, even though it is the poor who are in fact usually those who are deprived of ministers. Nor does this mean redefining the obvious meaning of the words "poor" and "social injustice" so that suddenly, by some spiritual trick, all are victims. Rather the tension consists in a focus and direction of ministry and its underlying intention. All Christian ministry should be *on behalf of* the poor. Insofar as all Christians share in the ministry of the Church, and the ministry of the whole Church should turn its attention to the global problems of human suffering, the option for the poor should be precisely an option of the whole Church including the wealthy and affluent. The idea that a concern for the poor should be against the rich is sheer nonsense; the option for the poor should be for the most part precisely the option of the rich. The tension, consequently, does not represent conflict within the Church. Rather it represents a reading of history and social injustice in terms of its victims and a shift in the primary focus of all ministry in behalf of those human beings who are most in need in today's world. Without this all-pervasive concern for the incredible amount of deprivation of the basics needed for human life that exists in the world today Christian ministry for the affluent itself loses its saving power. Admittedly the overcoming of this tension is an expression of a theological ideal. But it is only within the context of this ideal that the actual tensions that will arise relative to the allocation of Christian resources of ministry should be dealt with.

Surely there are many other principles for Christian ministry that should be considered, and other tensions that are intrinsic to its exercise. One could consider the necessary tension and balance that is required between ministry to individual persons and ministry to objective social structures,[30] or the tension between an emphasis on sin and love, and the strategies of criticism and constructive input in ministry,[31] or the tension between clergy and laity which in some cases corresponds to the tension between official and charismatic authority, or the tension between ministers and those ministered to, although this distinction too must be softened relative to the past insofar as the Church as a whole is viewed as a ministering community. But the intention here has not been to present in any measure a full account of ministry. What is represented here are merely some useful principles and axiomatic tensions which may help to illumine the liberating intention of all Christian ministry. And this is the subject of the concluding portion of this chapter.

CHRISTIAN MINISTRY TO FREEDOM AND FOR FREEDOM

There are many Christian ministries. Besides the common responsibility for ministry shared by all the faithful, one that is fulfilled by their everyday witness to Christian faith and a common display of love of neighbor, there is a large variety of special ministries. Some of the kinds of ministry throughout the long history of the Church which are discussed by Cooke are the following: prophecy, teaching, Church administration, leadership at the celebrations of liturgy, preaching, spiritual direction, apostleship or the task of missions, various modes of helping the needy, healing. But even this list accounts for only generic kinds of ministry; they are broad types which indicate a plurality of ministers and ministries that could be divided or subdivided in other ways. Actually there are as many ministries, old and new, as there are ways of actual Christian service.

My intention here is not to survey different kinds of ministry. The discussion will continue to deal with ministry on the rather general level of the imperatives for all Christian ministry that flow from the theological account of the liberationist interpretation of Christianity. In general, according to this interpretation, ministry is all active service engaged in by members of the Christian community to human freedom and for the release of human freedom. Accordingly the reflections which follow will be in terms of the three dimensions of human freedom to which ministry is directed.

The Church is the ongoing community of persons whose function is to actively sacramentalize the power of God in human history. It witnesses to the presence of God's Spirit to human life as revealed in Jesus. And more than this the community mediates and actualizes the effects of God's Spiritual presence. Ministry is that activity which makes the effects of this presence actual. The fundamental ministry of the Church, then, is to mediate God's presence to the transcendent dimension of human freedom. There can be no question about this, for this is what religion is. As a social phenomenon religion binds together in explicit consciousness and behavior human existence and God.

In the past this ministry has been intimately and inescapably linked to the personal dimension of human freedom. The opening up of human freedom of individual persons to transcendence is, if that transcendence is not demonic, at the same time a release and expansion of personal freedom, a setting of a person free. Paul, Augustine, Aquinas, Luther and so on all link religious ministry to the personal dimension of human freedom. The connection between the transcendent and personal levels of freedom is so close that these two may be considered simultaneously.

The main concern of these reflections on ministry, however, is the crisis of social freedom and the demands that this places on current Church ministry. So great is this phenomenon of social suffering that it calls in question the very meaning of human existence in this world. And so unattended is this crisis on the part of Christian ministry that ministry in general has been regarded as encouraging individualism and a privatized faith.[32] Thus even though transcendence has its immediate conscious effects in personal freedom, there is a new exigency to connect the power of God's Spirit to the social dimension of human freedom. The emphasis of ministry today must change its focus, not in such a way that personal, indeed individual, freedom is neglected, but in such a way that the personal freedom of individuals is seen as part of the corporate freedom of the Church which is itself defined in relation to the social crisis of human existence. The point of these reflections then is to emphasize the *unity* of these dimensions of freedom out of which ministry emerges and to which it is directed, and to emphasize how this unity may be seen within the focus that the current situation demands of Christian ministry. The thesis proposed here is both that the ministry of transcendence to personal freedom demands attention to the social sphere of human existence and that ministry to social freedom entails a mediation of transcendence to personal freedom. To illustrate this thesis the discussion may be set within the framework of the five tensions in ministry that have been suggested by the rise of liberation theology.

Ministry to Transcendent and Personal Freedom

The liberationist interpretation of Christianity involves a marked shift of focus and concern for our common social existence in the world. It stresses the historical impact of the liberative work of Jesus, the mission of the Church to the world, and an active life of discipleship in the world. But the significance of this shift of interpretation and emphasis comes to bear chiefly on personal and transcendent freedom and ministry to it. The implication of this theology is not exhausted by the addition of new forms of ministry to the world. On the contrary, the liberationist interpretation of the Church implies a new and changed conception of the way personal freedom is grasped by transcendence and responds to it. In an effort to show this I shall point to how the crisis of meaning in social human existence and freedom enters intrinsically into consideration of personal and transcendent freedom.

To begin, and as a basis of further considerations, one must appreciate that, although one may speak of distinctions, personal and transcendent freedom cannot be separated from social freedom. Human existence is one, and the human person is socially constituted. Human existence is freedom in solidarity. Thus one cannot minister integrally to personal and transcendent freedom without concern for the social structure of freedom, without concern for the social condition in which it is what it actually is. Ironically an historical and social consideration of the human person is more concrete and existential than an existentialist psychological analysis because it uncovers the full constitutive context of freedom.[33] This insight alone has enormous significance for all forms of ministry to personal and transcendent freedom, for preaching the word, for leadership of worship, for spiritual direction of personal life, for the general meaningfulness of Christian teaching. This can be illustrated by considering ministry to transcendent and personal freedom in terms of the several tensions within ministry that have been outlined.

The one tension that governs all ministry and ministerial theology is that which exists between the Christian ideals of the Gospel and the actuality of human capacity and possibility relative to the Christian life. Christian theology in interpreting the Gospel message provides certain norms for Christian life, yet actual human beings are finite, limited and sinful. The ideal Christian life is a freedom released into the activity of love, but the great masses of Christian faithful are often passive in their faith, mere receivers of Christian ministry. Juan Luis Segundo has stressed the idealistic values of Christian life and ministry; Christian life is an active response to Christ that is played out in an active life structured by a sign morality. Passive Christianity is a contradiction in terms; the Church is not to be viewed quantitatively as a Church of the masses in which the Christian life is defined by passive reception of the sacraments. This has led to the charge of "Christian elitism" in Segundo's regard. Can this conflict of views which has everything to do with ministerial strategy be mediated?

More needs to be said on this issue than can be discussed here. But much can be clarified if this problem is seen not in terms of an either/or alternative, but as a permanent tension in Christian life and ministry. On the one hand, ministry should never compromise Christian values and ideals by accommodation to a particular audience. Segundo is correct in his complaint that Christian ministry has often done just that. It has proposed, engendered and ministered to a spirituality of passivity and dependence on clerical sacramental service. It has proposed a religious or clerical ideal of spirituality for the laity. It has failed to be critical of the cooption of Gospel values and the Church by society and culture. Christian ministry must examine its suppositions, ideals and goals to make sure that they are genuinely the values of the Gospel which are appropriate for the *laos* of God who live their lives in the world.

On the other hand all ministry must begin with and take account of the actual capacity of those ministered to and draw out human freedom according to its possibilities step by step. A theology of ministry establishes goals, but only concrete perception and prudential judgment, nurtured with training in the necessary skills of ministry, can determine concrete ministerial strategy. Moreover it must be recognized that in many cases, such as that of the old or the sick and dying where active Christian life is an impossiblity, these people still deserve Christian ministry.

But, finally, this tension itself may be exaggerated because of another factor. It may be suspected that this whole seeming dilemma of ministry to a passive and nominal Christianity versus an active Christian life of grace is caused by clericalism. In fact this tension in ministry is often linked to the huge amount of time and energy which ordained ministers must give to the dispensation of sacraments and attention to individual needs in large parochial communities. It is closely connected to the idea that there is a shortage of ministers in the Catholic Church because practically speaking the whole exercise of ministry is limited to those persons who are ordained. As Schillebeeckx says, a shortage of ministers, who are to respond to all the various needs of the community, is a theological impossibility because ministry emerges out of the community itself.[34] If official and ordained ministry were conceived as the service to freedom that empowered more ministry in the community at large, if the very thing ministered to was a Christian life of active love and service, the seeming dilemma would cease to exist; it would be a life-enhancing and creative tension.

It is within the tension between this-worldly and other-worldly or transcendent values that the impact of a liberationist interpretation of Christianity and ministry to personal and transcendent freedom is most strongly felt. And that impact can be precisely defined by two principles. First, there is no transcendent spirituality that does not also govern how one lives one's life in the world. And, second, no one's life in this world is personal in the sense of being merely private, individual or lacking in social implications. And beyond this consideration of the nature of human existence itself one must add that all specifically Christian life should be led in a solidarity of love with other human beings, especially those who are marginalized within society and deprived of the necessary conditions for an integral human life. Once these principles are accepted, it follows that all Christian life is or is determined by a lay spirituality. The Church is the laity. And no union with God can be imagined that is not also defined by living in accord with God's general will for the world, history and society. The Church is not a "religious" or clerical community but is strictly a lay community of people whose lives are lived in the world, and all ordained ministers are not set apart from this community but ordained or designated to service of this lay community.[35] All integral ministry to transcendent and personal freedom, therefore, entails drawing into its ideals and strategy a concern for Christian life in the world. In other words, explicit ministry to transcendent freedom, whether it be cultic worship, healing or spiritual direction, should consciously attend to the transcendent implications of life in the world and the this-worldly implications of contact with the transcendent Christian God.

By and large, although not exclusively, ministry to transcendent and personal freedom takes place within the community. And ministry to social freedom, especially when dealing with objective structures rather than simply an assembly of individuals, is ministry reaching outside the Church. These two concerns, despite the tensions between them, must be drawn together tightly in ministerial strategy and activity. Whether the terms "outside" or "the world" are understood to refer to those people who are not Christians or to spheres of life that are not specifically Christian but secular and autonomous, the outward reach of the Church is a common or shared responsibility of all the faithful. This religious dimension of God's mission for the whole Church appeals to transcendent freedom, and thus formation in the consciousness of this must be part of an integral ministry to transcendence. One cannot have a private personal spirituality in a Church that has a public missionary role in society and history. In other words this concern for the outward reach of Christianity is an intrinsic requirement of ministry precisely to personal and transcendent freedom.

The tension between the authority of persons in office and the authority of charism has already been touched on with the criticism of clericalism. But more can be said from a liberationist viewpoint. The function of office in the Church and the purpose and direction of the use of this authority is to serve and to mediate to personal freedom the Spirit of God, God's judgment, God's empowerment, God's truth, God's forgiveness, God's general will for life's direction. Another way of stating this is that the purpose of the authority of office is to stimulate the authority of charism,[36] that is, the same authority of God as witnessed to and acted upon in personal Christian testimony and life. On the understanding that ultimately all religious authority is a moral quality closely aligned with spiritual leadership, the whole Church, in all its members, is to be an authoritative witness to God's truth in the world. And within this context there is a large variety of authorities in ministry corresponding to various ministerial activities and personal expertise in them. With the Church, then, those who are designated as administrative overseers or *episkopoi* have a special responsibility to use their community-given authority to mediate, disclose, serve and stimulate the authority of God within the variety of other ministries. And looking outward from the Church, as public officials of the Church, these ministers have the special responsibility of publicly representing the Church to the world.

Finally, in the ministry to transcendent and personal freedom there will necessarily be differences of ministerial strategy when dealing with the rich and with the poor. It is true that all human beings are equally poor before God because of our finitude, mortality, sin and need of healing; and we are equally rich in God's love, forgiveness and restoration. But the imperatives of God's liberating grace may be quite different for individual persons and groups who live in radically different social conditions. Consider, for example, the very different connotations that the saying that God is on the side of the poor may have in different social situations. Among the wealthy it may legitimately echo God's word spoken through the prophets pointing to God's will for the direction of human concern; among the poor it may imply the terrifyingly dangerous impression that "God is on our side." The point then concerns the direction in which human freedom is channelled by ministry's mediation of God's message and power in different situations to the socially rich and the socially poor. In what direction does ministry lead the personal freedom that is released by God's forgiving love? In the case of the poor ministry should mediate God's love so that it empowers people, overcomes passivity, fatalism and dependence, and motivates people actively in the direction of their own corporate, as opposed to merely private and individual, liberation. In the case of the rich, Christian ministry will emphasize God's will for stewardship, for Christian responsibility in the use and disposition of worldly goods according to God's will and love for those who are in need.[37]

Certainly a great deal more has to be said about ministry to transcendent and personal freedom. These reflections do not aim at being adequate or complete. But taken together they are meant to show very clearly how the focus of the liberationist interpretation of Christianity radically influences the Christian meaning of personal and transcendent freedom and how ministry must attend to this. In the following discussion on ministry to social freedom the effort will be to show how this ministry must be integrated with a concern for personal and transcendent freedom.

Ministry to Social Freedom

By and large, but certainly not exclusively as will be seen below, the social ministry of the Church is turned outward toward the world. In the liberationist interpretation of Christianity the whole Church is a mission and thus turned outward from itself to be a sign and sacrament to and for the world. Although ministry to individuals on a large scale automatically constitutes a social ministry, the discussion here envisages ministry more in terms of service and engagement in the context of the objective structures of society. As Cooke writes: "When we turn our attention outward, to the question of preserving or changing the structures of human society, we discover one of the most exciting and potentially important areas of reflection about the future of Christian ministry.[38] In one sense such ministry is crystalized in the specific category of apostleship or missionary. But the argument here is that the missionary nature of the Church implies that every ministry of the Church should bear this dimension of mission to the world. In fact there are many new and different kinds of ministry that are being developed on the basis of the missionary dimension of the Church; such new ministries are determined by the ongoing perception of the concrete needs of human beings in society. But what will be stressed in these limited reflections is the way in which these ministries include a transcendent religious dimension and take up into themselves personal responsibility and freedom.

Obviously enough there is a wide gap between the Christian ideal for social human existence and the actuality of our world. In fact the difference constantly causes radical scandal to Christian faith itself. But the very difference between this idealistic and visionary religious perception of a reign of God such that human society would become a kingdom structured by the values of God on the one hand, and the actual situations in which radical and dehumanizing injustice actually reign on the other, causes a contrast experience that allows the Christian Church to protest against society.[39] Because of its religious vision the Church can be and should be a public critic of secular society. Despite the caution that should prevail in exercise of this ministry which will be mentioned further on, in situations of flagrant social abuse of human life the Church should publicly react through its official representatives, thus engaging the whole Church.

Besides this negative function, the Church also has a positive role to play, in cooperation with all other human beings, to construct a better and more humane world. It is true that the secular sphere is autonomous from a sociological or scientific point of view, and that Christian revelation and faith provide no information about planning and decision-making in the construction of a better future.[40] But the specifically religious vision of human existence provided by the Christian message produces both convictions about the nature of human life that provide a direction for such planning and a positive religious and human imperative that motivates participation in this work. Christianity is not a religion that simply leaves to non-Christians the running of human history according to non-Christian ideologies and values.[41]

As a practical consideration it is extremely important to recognize at this point that the radical difference between the ideals of the Kingdom of God and actual society means that there cannot be an immediate transposition of them to society in the exercise of ministry. The convictions held on the basis of religious ideas and ideals and the perception of the actuality or "reality" of history are two different modes of perception and kinds of experience. Therefore ministry in this sphere must also be guided by scientific expertise, by thorough social analysis,[42] and by a competent use of social ethical principles. Secular humanists are rightly worried by religious fanaticism when it comes to bear on political social issues. In a pluralist society social ministry dealing with public social structures must be objectively reasoned and publicly argued by means of middle axioms, that is, socio-economic, political and ethical principles, through which Christian values are brought to bear on society in a reasonable way.[43]

This leads to the second tension in ministry between the concerns of transcendence and those for human life in this world. It may be stated with absolute conviction that ministerial involvement in the autonomous realm of secular society may be motivated by transcendent convictions. In other words, the transcendent dimension of human freedom may be fully engaged in a ministry to society; the commitment to the service of human life as that life is structured by the objective institutions of history may be and should be for Christians a strictly religious engagement. There are tensions here. Because of their urgency and immediacy a concern for the life and death issues of society and politics in this world can become totally absorbing on a psychological plane to the neglect of explicit reference to transcendence, even though this commitment always involves implicitly the question of transcendent values of ultimacy. But what must be stated flatly is that for Christians ministry to every dimension of social life is a religious ministry, a ministry that tries to be in accord with God's general will as revealed in Jesus Christ. Christian social ministry flows from the love of neighbor implicit in Christian faith, a faith and love that are formed by a concern for justice.

Ministry to the structures of society may also go on within the Church. It is not unimaginable that the social institutions of the Church itself may be unjust. In fact the axiom of the tension between ministry inside the Church and outside the Church is very relevant at this point since it provides a caution in the way the Church should exercise its ministry of criticism of society. The Church is called to witness to the values of the reign of God in society also by incorporating these values in itself. The Church is sign and sacrament to God's reign in its being. The Church cannot very credibly or effectively criticize a society for suppressing religious freedom if it does not allow some measure of religious pluralism and freedom of expression in its own ranks. This issue is a very serious one if the Christian Church's ministry is to be in any way effective in its prophetic witness against systemic structures of human inequality and injustice such as sexism, totalitarianism, censorship, suppression of other forms of free religious expression, negation of human rights and dignity, systematic suppression of the due processes of law and just procedure.

The tension between the authority of official offices and of charism is also especially operative in ministry to the world, at least in the Roman Catholic Church. The issue has to do with all the autonomous realms of secular society, with systems of social order, education, science, law, and so on; but it is especially visible in the sphere of politics when this term is narrowly understood as dealing with the direction of civil society and government. It is agreed by many that authority in this ministry is charismatic authority, one that pertains specifically to the laity as opposed to those who hold official authority as liturgical leaders and administrators of the community, that is, the clerical class. The reason for this is twofold. Positively the laity have the specific expertise that gives them the authority for ministerial leadership in this sphere, for the life of the laity is precisely one that is led more fully in the world of secular society. This authority is therefore autonomous and should not be completely under clerical control. Negatively, the official administrative authority of the Church represents and publicly witnesses to the whole of the Church's message. But actual engagement in concrete political affairs always commits the Church to specific plans and policies.

Therefore in order not to publicly reduce the Church's witness to any specific political option, regime, policy or course of action, and in order to allow the public witness of the Church to be critical of every social strategy and arrangement in the light of the transcendent values of the Kingdom of God, the public and official administrators of the universal Church should not be directly involved in any particular political movement or concrete social option. The role of official authority in these specific instances is to support semi-autonomous charismatic groups and ministries in the Church without assuming the responsibility of endorsing their specific strategies publicly.[44]

From one point of view this reasoning is both theologically and sociologically sound. There is genuine and autonomous charismatic authority in ministry within the Church, and the laity are the most competent to exercise this ministerial authority and leadership. There is also theological wisdom in the insight that the whole Church should not be totally committed in its witness to social justice to the narrowly defined policies or strategies of sectarian groups or parties. There is a wide range of pluralism in political, social, economic and cultural affairs and the Church must be in a position to bring the criticism of the Gospel to bear on all of them, as well as support the values contained in each of them.

But at the same time the negative stricture that official representatives of the whole Church should not be engaged in concrete political or social issues gives rise to the suspicion that these distinctions may be made within the framework of a clericalism that is itself faulty. Some of the reasons for this suspicion are the following. First of all, there are many instances of social crime and demonically evil institutions that deserve total official censure by the Christian Church. Prudential judgment and strategy are of course called for in the way the Church becomes involved; but that the whole Church should be against institutions such as systematic torture of prisoners, to choose only one example, is clear. Secondly there is no area of social ministry to secular life in which official representatives of the Church should be a priori excluded from participation in some way. The decision for or against political involvement of official ministers is not an absolute standard but requires prudential judgment. After all, lay Christians are not more competent for social ministry by reason of their keeping their Christian identity and motivation a secret; nor is it impossible that an official minister of the Church may be quite competent in some realm of secular affairs. Thus it would again seem that too much emphasis has been given to ordained clergy or religious as bearers of the burden of the whole Christian witness. Something has to give. There must be either a more extensive use of official "ordination" or "designation" so that it authorizes official leaders for a greater variety of special ministries, or a more generalized view of ordination as it currently exists so that there is more participation by official representatives of the Church in political ministry and, more generally, social ministry to the secular sphere. There will be cases of conflict between Christian leaders, and between Christian leaders and the whole laity of the Church, over specific social strategies relative to the meaning of the whole Christian message. But these may stimulate a theological and moral discussion within the whole Christian community that could be educative and salutary.

Finally, when the tension between ministry for the affluent and wealthy and ministry for the poor is viewed in terms of the objective structures of society, one sees a real conflict of competing interests. By definition an unjust social system, that is, institutionalized behaviors that govern business, education, political power and decision making, work and the distribution of goods, and so on, involves benefits for some at the expense of others. At this point Christian ministry makes a choice. Christian faith and love impels an analysis of such situations from the point of view of the victims of society, and its ministry should be dedicated to a change that engenders equality. In this case the direction of Christian ministry is the same as that taken by the prophets, namely, against the material benefits and interests of those the social system favors at the expense of the economically poor, marginalized, politically oppressed and socially victimized. In other words, on this objective level Christian ministry should be genuinely counter-cultural insofar as the cultural is represented in unjust social structures. This is inevitable. No one can deny the prophetic dimension of the historic Christian faith and tradition. But if this prophetic dimension of Christian faith does not actualize itself in social ministry, it is hard to maintain that it actually exists or that Christian ministry is faithful.

CONCLUSION

The point of this chapter may be summarized very briefly. Christian ministry is the active service to human freedom and for human freedom from within the Christian community. As such it is in sum the actualization of the Church as sign and sacrament of God's message and power in history initiated by Jesus. To be adequate ministry must address all the dimensions of human freedom in an integrated way.

The liberationist interpretation of Christianity and its ministry has disclosed and responded to the new historical and social crisis of faith that arises out of the massive human and humanly caused suffering that characterizes our world today. Thus in the liberationist interpretation the integrating factor of Christian ministry is a focus on how Christian faith and ministry respond to this crisis by impelling human beings, motivated by their transcendent Christian faith, to resist it. An integrated corporate ministry of the Church means that no aspect or dimension of human freedom is left unaddressed or uncared for. This imperative involves several intrinsic and inescapable tensions or competing emphases in ministry. This has to be recognized. However the conclusion here is that Christian ministry can be understood in such a way that the values involved in either extreme of each of these tensions may be preserved in the liberationist view of ministry, even while at the same time it preserves the needed focus and center that our period of history requires. What is proposed here, then, is an integrated concept of Christian ministry.

Actually the place where this integration of the multiple dimensions of Christian freedom ultimately or finally occurs is in the existential life of the community itself which ministry is intended to reflect and to serve. The final chapter will be a discussion of the liberationist view of the Christian life or spirituality.

Chapter XII
LIBERATIONIST SPIRITUALITY

The preceding chapters have surveyed the principles, the method and the theological interpretation of some of the central Christian doctrines that make up the liberationist interpretation of Christianity. In this final chapter I shall try to draw out the implications of this theology for spirituality or the Christian life.

It was pointed out already that the liberation theology of Latin America arose out of a particular context and experience. Faced with the conditions of massive poverty and human suffering due to oppression, Christians began to participate in the liberationist movement. Gradually people within this movement began to reflect on the Christian values, meanings and understandings that were implicit in their participation in the movement, that is, in their own praxis specifically as Christians. And thus a theology was generated. Thus if it is true that ministry was prior to liberation theology, it is even truer to say that the whole of liberation theology is based on and emerged out of a liberationist spirituality. It must be said then that "the theology of liberation was born out of a spirituality of liberation."[1]

But intellectual reflection as the phrase itself indicates is a bending back of the human mind on experience and behavior. Theological reflection is a critical appraisal of life lived and functions in its behalf. Thus one may presume that the value of any Christian theology lies in its bearing on human existence and particularly how human life should be led in the Christian view of things. The ultimate significance and even the existential truth of theological conclusions may be tested by the kind of life which they postulate and to which they lead. This chapter, therefore, will be both a summary and a concluding look at the liberationist interpretation of Christianity. It will survey liberationist principles and interpretations of the various doctrines in terms of the kind of spirituality that at the same time grounds this theology and is demanded by it.

Once again this reinterpretation of liberationist positions should begin by taking into account the themes that are found in the literature of liberation theology. The second part of this chapter will be methodological and in it I shall try to define exactly what is meant by the term "spirituality" as it is used here and how it may be approached from a theological perspective. Then the concluding portion of this chapter will consist in an attempt at a description of liberationist spirituality as this is implied in the liberationist interpretation of Christian doctrine.

THEMES FROM LIBERATION THEOLOGY

When one turns to the theological account of Christian spirituality in liberation theology, it is interesting to note at the outset the variety of ways in which the subject matter is approached. As will be shown further on, all liberation theologians assume a concrete historical, existential and anthropological point of view, and their fundamental conclusions merge into certain common positions and, more importantly, themes and principles. But at the same time liberation theologians use a variety of arguments and approaches to a definition of the Christian life, and they bring different theological symbols and doctrines to bear on the phenomenon called spirituality. It may be useful to look at some of these different approaches and the varieties of definitions of what spirituality is that they lead to.

One approach to spirituality leads through the theology of faith. In effect the meaning of the term spirituality is identified with faith. For faith is a whole attitude toward life and reality, including God, and the living out of an internalized vision. Spirituality is the lived faith commitment of the Christian. Thus Leonardo Boff, for example, tends to identify spirituality with faith, or faith life, because as "a way of living, a living faith implies a contemplative attitude towards the world."[2]

Another approach to spirituality leads through the doctrine of God and the symbol of creation.[3] The notion of creation echoes the religious experience of all reality as flowing from God's hands. Creation and its history is of life and for life. But one must also recognize that in the actuality of history the majority of human beings do not share in this life, but only in suffering and death at the hands of other human beings. Impelled by the perception of God's will in creation and a realistic appraisal of history's actuality, Christian spirituality consists in a commitment to negate the negation of life and to foster and nourish life wherever possible. Spirituality is a dedication to God's truth and will as they are manifested most fundamentally in creation itself.

The most common approach to and definition of spirituality in liberation theology is through Christology. "Christians are defined by their following of Jesus" and spirituality is the "particular way of being Christian" that is constituted by the way one follows Jesus.[4] In short, Christian spirituality consists in the traditional imitation of Christ, but within the context of one's particular historical and cultural situation. Since Jesus Christ is the point of mediation of one's faith in and contact with God, Jesus is the prototype and paradigm of the Christian life; the Christian prays according to the pattern of Jesus and discerns the will of God according to the structure of the way Jesus followed the will of his Father.[5]

Still another theological entry into the topic of spirituality is the symbol and doctrine of the Spirit. Spirituality is living according to the Spirit of God, the Spirit which empowers Christian life. "The animating force of the Spirit, expressed in different historical and social contexts of Christianity, generates in Christians themselves that which we call 'sprituality.'"[6]

And finally spirituality may be defined ecclesiologically or in terms of the nature, function and historical situation of the Church. Since the discernment of how the Spirit moves Christians to follow Christ is determined by the concrete historical situation in which the Church finds itself, the adaptation and confrontation of the whole Church with its surrounding culture determines the general lines of Christian spirituality for members of the community. Spirituality is the evangelical motivation of the whole Church and one cannot have an ecclesiology without a resultant view of spirituality or the Christian life.[7]

Despite the variety of theological routes taken to define spirituality by liberation theologians, there is a clear consensus concerning the nature of spirituality. Spirituality is a comprehensive term that signifies the whole way of life of the Christian, the manner in which the Christian lives. And this mode of life is always viewed in the context of the surrounding world and the historical condition of society. "A spirituality implies an overall, comprehensive attitude. It must comprise all aspects of one's life."[8] A spirituality involves a synthesis of all one's actions; it "develops around the core of a central intuition, which is in turn linked to the challenges of the historical moment that produced it."[9] Spirituality "is the disposition of the subject, his or her form of being, which relates that person to the totality of reality, with special reference to the transcendent and historical dimensions which that reality contains."[10] The point of this definition is to show that a person's relation to God is intrinsically determined by a person's relation to the world, history and society. In sum, spirituality is the whole way of life of the Christian, in

the Church and in the world, so that Christian spirituality is synonymous with the Christian life.

There is a consensus not only in the nature of spirituality but also
in the concrete elements and themes that characterize it in liberation
theology. These have been summarily enumerated by several authors
but the following text is both succinct, fairly comprehensive and exact.
Referring to the portrayal of liberation spirituality by Segundo Galilea,
Hennelly writes:

> First of all, he stresses that a conversion to God and a commit-
> ment to Christ can take place only through a conversion to our
> neighbor and through a commitment to those who suffer
> oppression. A second intuition insists that there exists a pro-
> found relationship between "salvation history" and the genuine
> liberation of the poor in Latin America so that "to commit one-
> self to the latter is to work together with Christ the Redeemer
> and to enter into his saving work." Third, liberating tasks must
> be seen as an anticipation and advancement of the kingdom of
> God, a kingdom which is marked by justice, equality, frater-
> nity, and solidarity. The fourth basic intuition envisions liber-
> ating praxis, that is, the activity that transforms society on
> behalf of the oppressed, as one of the most important exercises
> of Christian charity, since Christian love has to be incarnated
> and made efficacious in reality. Lastly, he emphasizes the value
> of poverty, which is not only a sharing in the plight of the poor
> but also a sharing in their struggle for justice, and which
> implies accepting persecution as a form of poverty and of true
> identification with Christ.[11]

At this point I wish to step back from these specific points and
themes in liberation spirituality in order to look at it from a more analytical point of view. Most of the liberation theologians would say that
liberation spirituality itself and their conception of it is new, one which
requires a change on the part of Christians when compared with a certain kind of spirituality that has obtained up to the present.[12] In what
does this shift consist? If one looks at the structure of liberation spirituality analytically, one can see four tensions or polarities that govern
the Christian life. These tensions are very similar to the tensions that
govern Christian ministry, which is not surprising since spirituality or
the Christian life is precisely that to which ministry ministers. One of
the terms that determines or governs the structure of ministry is the
actuality of Christian life or spirituality. In the case of each of these

polarities or tensions liberation spirituality may be seen as a reaction against a one-sided view of the Christian life and more positively as a spirituality that holds the two poles of the various tensions together.

The first tension is one between transcendence and immanence. This tension applies to God insofar as God is experienced as being both transcendent or absolutely other relative to the created sphere and immanent within creation and the human spirit. The tension also applies to human consciousness, motivation and attention in the direction of one's Christian spiritual life. Spirituality, as that which characterizes the whole of one's life, governs both one's explicit relation to God and one's intentional relations with the world. This tension characterizes the whole of liberation theology. In the question of spirituality liberation theology judges that in the past much of Christian spirituality has been dominated by the theme of transcendence to the neglect of God's immanence. From a theological perspective, then, liberation spirituality insists that contact with the transcendent God in prayer and other cultic activity does not "leave the world behind" but rather bestows an absolute depth and seriousness precisely to our life in this world.[13] The transcendent God to whom the Christian life is directed is the God of the Kingdom of God that Jesus preached, and this God is found immanently, in this world, in and through those moments by which the Kingdom of God is being fashioned in history. From an anthropological perspective liberation spirituality simply takes seriously the fact that God cannot be encountered directly or immediately beyond this world but only in and through this world. And since an integral spirituality must govern the whole of one's life, that mediation should not be limited exclusively to cultic symbols and behavior. Rather God is encountered also and indeed principally in encounters with the neighbor. God is found primarily "in hearing God's will and doing it."[14]

Another tension governing Christian spirituality, one which in many respects is similar to the first, exists between the spiritual and the material or corporeal dimensions of human existence. There is no doubt that these are two different dimensions of human life which can at certain points be seen as distinct even though they are inseparable. The problem occurs when these two symbols begin to be regarded as pointing to two separable spheres of existence, or to two radically different areas of concern. Liberation spirituality is a strong protest against a spirituality that limits the understanding and practice of the specifically Christian life to the sphere of the human spirit and which does not concern itself with the corporeal and bodily aspects of human existence. Spirituality is reduced to those aspects of human life geared toward more or less direct and spiritual encounter with God within the human spirit. In this view life in the world and human concerns for things in and of this world lie outside the sphere of Christian spirituality. In reaction to this, liberation theology asserts that "spirituality, following Jesus Christ, does not mean living in a spiritual, as opposed to corporeal, dimension." On the contrary, "spirituality embraces the whole human being, body and soul."[15] Thus liberation spirituality holds these two dimensions of human existence together. Spirituality is living a corporeal and bodily existence in the world according to the Spirit of God.[16]

A third dominant theme in liberation spirituality is the tension between contemplation and action.[17] In a sense this tension is the psychological side of the first two polarities, and another form of it may be seen in a tension between passivity and activity in the spiritual life. Of course the tension does not lie in a complete distinction, since contemplation is a form of human activity and generally human action is not blind or unconscious but knowing and intentional. But spirituality in its ideal form has often been reduced to prayer in the form of contemplation, a kind of inactivity by which one is filled with God's presence. Indeed a whole way of life revolving around this contemplative behavior has been put forward as the highest Christian ideal. In this view spirituality is identified with interiority, the inner spiritual domain of elevated intentions and motives. Liberation spirituality corrects this distorted view of the Christian life. It insists on the formula of contemplation in action, that is, contemplation both within the context of Christian activity, stemming from it and leading back to it, and within activity itself. The active dimension of Christian life in the world is a reality principle in the sense that action makes human intentions real and hence our psychological contact with God an objective one. "In short, doing is the condition which makes possible and confirms that the attitude of the one praying is Christian."[18] One's relationship to God involves prayer and contemplation, but it is finally constituted in the concrete activity of love.

And finally the tension between the personal and social dimensions of human existence is another constant theme in liberation spirituality. And the concern here, once again, should be viewed as a reaction against a one-sided view of spirituality. There is no doubt that the ultimate basis of every spirituality is a fundamentally personal experience. The problem, however, is that the term personal often means "merely personal" so that spirituality is reduced to the sphere of the individual's responsibility for his or her own individual relationship to God. In other words the domain of spirituality is constricted so that it includes only the direct relationship between the self and God and excludes concern for one's socially constituted relations to other human beings and the general responsibility with which one directs his or her life in the world. It is true that the pluralism of religions and life styles in modern societies strongly encourages this view. But liberation spirituality rejects this privatization and individualism by stressing the social constitution of the person and the social dimension of human freedom. It highlights the historical condition of human existence and the Christian values that are captured with the term "solidarity"; all human beings exist in a situation of solidarity with each other; we share a common human existence.[19] Liberation spirituality presupposes that one's individual relationship to God intrinsically involves the way one responsibly exercises one's personal freedom in directing his or her individual life in a secular and social world. Thus in terms of the subject of the Christian life a spirituality, if it is to be integral, must govern all aspects of personal life, that is, the Christian's personal, transcendent and social freedom, and his or her relations to self, God and others in society. And in terms of the object of Christian love, which is the most basic ingredient of the Christian life, Christian spirituality directs that love integrally toward self, God and other human beings both as individual persons and as members of a commonly shared human society.

This analytic view of liberation spirituality allows one to see that in fact the view of the Christian life which it depicts is one that is integrated, unified and comprehensive. And this is significant since at no other point is liberation theology more misunderstood than on this existentially religious plane of spirituality. Because it is reacting against a limited and reductionist view of the spiritual life, it is often judged to be extremist in its own right. And because of the urgency of the social situation in Latin America, one which involves the life and untimely and inhuman death of so many, the rhetoric of liberationist spirituality is viewed as over-simplified and itself reductionist. But in fact this analytic scheme allows one to measure the balance and integrity with which liberation theology unites the many dimensions that make up Christian spiritual life. In sum liberation theology holds together in unity the several tensions that govern all Christian spirituality.

Given this data from liberation theology I shall in the next section interpret and re-present it in the form of a general definition and consideration of the nature of spirituality. And with that basis we shall be in a position to conclude with a more descriptive account of liberationist spirituality.

SPIRITUALITY

The most basic meaning of the term "spirituality" is the way a person leads his or her life.[20] Thus it may be said that every human person has a spirituality. Human existence is human spirit in matter. This is not to be understood in such a way that human freedom can exist or operate independently of bodily determinisms. Rather, the human person is one, human existence is enfleshed spirit, and the determinisms of the natural and physical side of human existence are both the limits of freedom and the structure within and through which the freedom of the human spirit is exercised. Human beings as opposed to animals are conscious, intelligent and free. Without measuring the degree of this freedom, still one has to admit that they direct their lives intentionally. I would take spirituality, then, in its most basic meaning to refer to the way that any given person consciously directs his or her life.

The point of this general anthropological view of spirituality, of making this the primary referent of the term, is to overcome from the very beginning any divisions that would separate spirituality off from life in the world. Christian life is life shared in the world with other human beings, and the religious dimension of human experience does not lift one out from ordinary human existence and experience. All attempts to escape from the world while we exist in the world are based on illusion.[21] All spirituality, and especially Christian spirituality, as a form of existence in the world, should not isolate or separate human beings from the world and other human beings but rather bind them to a common human existence in solidarity with others in the world. It is crucial that from the very start spirituality be seen as something that Christians share with all other human beings in the world. All human beings have a spirituality.

Specifically Christian spirituality, then, refers to how Christians lead their lives, or to the Christian view of how human life should be led. As was seen in the doctrine of grace, the Christian life is ordinarily conceived of as a life led in and by the Spirit of God. And since the doctrine of the universal availability of grace implies that God's Spirit is present to all of human existence, one may say that any authentic spirituality, be it Christian or not, is a life led under the influence of the Spirit of God. From this point of view, it may be proper to characterize authentic spirituality as having to do with life in the Spirit of God. But the primary general anthropological referent should not be lost; even an inauthentic spirituality is still a spirituality.[22]

From a religious and Christian point of view, the issue involved in the question of spirituality is union with God. Even though the discussion of spirituality is the discussion of authentic human life, there is a dimension at stake here that transcends a merely humanistic level. The ultimate issue in the religious discussion of authentic human life is whether or not this life is in accord with and united to the ultimate principle of all reality, God. Thus Gustavo Gutiérrez' definition of Christian spirituality, which presupposes the more general use of the term, seems appropriate: "A spirituality is a concrete manner, inspired by the Spirit, of living the Gospel; it is a definite way of living 'before the Lord,' in solidarity with all human beings, 'with the Lord,' and before humanity."[23]

It is helpful to distinguish at least two distinct levels of spirituality, even though one could provide several other distinctions as well. The first and most basic level of Christian spirituality is that of the actual life of Christians. Here spirituality is viewed existentially; it is the concrete life that Christians actually lead, now, in the Christian community throughout the world, and also the life that Christians have led across the history of the Church. From this point of view, one could say that Christianity *is* a spirituality. Christianity and the Church are not so much a body of doctrines as a concrete movement in history, one that is constituted by the Christian life itself lived corporately by all Christians.[24] And, inversely, the personal spirituality of each person is part of the Church and the Christian movement. Spirituality on the existential level of actuality is pluralistic; it is characterized by the great differences that stem from the variety and diversity of times, places, cultures and circumstances in which Christians live their lives. It is also marked by the differences in persons and personalities in any given community. Ultimately one would have to say that at this existential level there are as many different spiritualities as there are individual Christians. Existentially each person's spirituality is unique.[25]

A second level of spirituality, and hence meaning of the term, refers to an understanding of the Christian life. Life lived is not blind; implicit in any Christian life is a view of the meaning of such a life and an understanding of human existence itself in Christian terms. When such an understanding is rendered explicit, one has a formal spirituality in the sense of a theory of the Christian life. Thus the term spirituality often refers to an organized and thematized conception or understanding of the contours of authentic Christian existence. As such this would not be very far or distinct from theology itself, or a theology of the Christian life. There will also be a pluralism of spirituality at this level as well. But insofar as theology is a quest for the true and the normative, it would also look for certain norms and criteria which would be common to all Christian spirituality.

These two levels of spirituality are precisely that, namely, levels or dimensions that cannot be separated from each other. They should be seen as two aspects of a single phenomenon, Christian life itself. Christian life without reflective awareness would hardly be Christian at all, but merely external socially determined behavior. And an understanding of Christian life that floated away from the concrete practice of Christians would be vacuous theorizing. But at the same time there is a clear distinction between living and formally reflecting on Christian behavior and practice in a disciplined manner. The relation between these two dimensions of spirituality when they are formally distinguished, then, may be seen as identical with the circular interrelation between theology and life. Theological spirituality should always arise out of the context and situation of actual Christian life and relate back to it. But in the course of intelligent critical reflection on life, together with use of Christian sources, a theology of the Christian life looks for truth as distinct from error. It is therefore not merely descriptive but also critical of actual Christian life. The circle here is identical with the circular genesis of liberation theology itself and more generally with the method of correlation in theology. A theology of the spiritual life should emerge out of a concrete situation and experience, be thematized in the light of critical principles and Christian sources, and reflect back critically on Christian practice. In terms of systematic or doctrinal theology, this theology will be significant or relevant to the extent that it embodies the kind of life out of which the doctrines come and the kind of life to which the doctrines point.

In this chapter I shall not be dealing with existential spirituality, at least not directly. This will not be a description of the actual liberationist spirituality of any particular community or group. Rather I shall propose a spirituality on the basis of theology and in theological terms. It is supposed here that this theology has arisen out of a specific spirituality and praxis in a real life situation. What now has to be expressed is the way it has a bearing on Christian life in general terms. The question then is how the liberationist interpretation of Christian doctrine relates back to Christian life. What do these doctrines say about the way Christians are supposed to lead their lives?

As a first answer to this question it may be said that a theoretical understanding of the Christian meaning of life relates to actual Christian spirituality in two ways. First, theology provides norms for the Christian life. Theology in effect should be a normative spirituality. Theology plays a critical role relative to the Christian life. Both positively and negatively, theology provides the critical norms for Christian living. This does not mean that theology will, should or even can on a theoretical basis overcome pluralism in Christian life. But still it seems safe to say that not every form of behavior is compatible with Christian faith. Some forms of behavior are not authentically Christian nor appropriate to a Christian vision of truth; other forms of action are integral to and constitutive of all Christian life everywhere. Theology, then, does try to overcome relativism and to establish the fundamental principles within which all Christian life ought to be consistent in order to be authentically Christian.

Secondly, theological spirituality also relates back to actual Christian life evocatively. Theology appeals to life by providing reasons for intelligence and values for freedom, and it does this within the context of the religious imagination. It provides ideals for the will and for human commitment, decision and action. In effect, theological spirituality is an ideology, in a positive sense of that term, that is meant to become a vision for the imagination. Thus theological statements ought to be able to be transformed into performative statements that point the direction for Christian life. Theoretically such ideas would apply to everyone. But it is also obvious that one can only perform in accordance with one's capacity and limits, and within the context of one's historical situation. Yet an ideal should remain just that, and should not in itself be measured by the exceptional cases or the lowest common denominator of the Christian community's actual practice.

These two functions of theological spirituality relative to existential spirituality must be seen as concomitant, simultaneous and complementary. The normative quality of theological spirituality is to be understood within the context of its evocative power. The normative authority of Christian theology is not extrinsicist, and it may not be imagined today that the normativity of Christian theology can be formulated into an external law and discipline to which Christians become passively submissive. On the contrary, the normativity and authority of theological spirituality are internal; this authority appeals to human reflection and conscious freedom which it in turn releases and empowers into action. Only in the measure that theology mediates to human subjectivity and freedom the authority and empowerment of the Spirit of God that are contained within the basic Christian symbols is the normativity of theological spirituality effective. Only in this sense then is theological spirituality a normative spirituality.

In all of this it may appear that theology is approaching what may be called a fundamental Christian ethics or moral theology. In the recent history of Roman Catholic theology there was a fairly sharp distinction if not separation between doctrinal theology and moral theology. This was grounded in a narrowly conceived theology of faith that located the act and attitude of faith in the human intellect as an assent to truth, thus cutting off human will, freedom and action from their position of being intrinsic to faith itself.[26] This split was reinforced by the subdivisions of theological disciplines in which doctrinal theology was quite separate from moral theology and argued from revelation, whereas a largely autonomous moral theology argued extensively from natural law and a critical and rational appraisal of cases. But a more integral view would hold that it is impossible to separate these disciplines into self-contained and water-tight compartments. All theology is practical theology insofar as it bears some implications for human life and how it is to be lived. All theology is implicitly an ethics, at least in a foundational sense.

At the same time there is a distinction between theology or theological spirituality and the discipline of ethics, and this difference can be illustrated in two ways. First, one can have a fully developed ethics or theory of human behavior without religious faith or theology. A rational or humanistic ethics can be developed independently of theology. But one cannot have Christian faith or theology without an ethical component. It would seem then that, like religious piety itself, the theology of spirituality is distinct from a narrow conception of ethics but intrinsically includes ethics.[27] Second, the distinction between theological spirituality and ethics can be clarified by seeing what theology adds to ethics. This is precisely the appeal to transcendence, which in Christian theology is a God who is related to and concerned with human behavior. Relative to human subjectivity, then, theological spirituality adds to ethics an existential appeal from God for a personal response to a higher transcendent and personal norm that is contained within all objective prescriptions and may even exceed them. Over and above the objective normativity of ethics, theological spirituality includes a personal appeal from God, or God's will, which invites personal existential commitment of one's life.[28] Theological spirituality, therefore, is distinct from ethics, yet it is ethical; it includes rational ethics but suffuses it with an appeal to the religious imagination and faith which call for a personal response to a personal God.

The direction of the liberationist spirituality that will be presented here should be clear from the whole perspective of this book and the interpretations of doctrine that have already been put forward. I have assumed the basic validity of the experiences that underlie liberation theology and its theological interpretation. However the effort has been to abstract this local theology from its concrete historical conditions and to reinterpret it in a more general context of historical human existence as such. The purpose here has been to get behind the local theology to find its relevance for Christianity as a whole. Thus here too the point will be to make a general statement concerning the spiritual life of all Christians, an understanding that will be broad enough to cover the whole of Christianity. Needless to say, a spirituality that is so universal that it would apply to all Christians as they live their lives in the world would have to become practical and concrete in diverse ways according to the actual situation in which it must be lived out concretely. Presumably, therefore, the way that this spirituality would be localized in Latin America would look very much like the movement out of which liberation theology actually sprung. And when this spirituality is localized in other situations, it will have different concrete manifestations.

The spirituality that is presented here is a lay spirituality. It is presumed that on the most basic level of the Christian life there is no such thing as a double standard. Christian life in its fundamentals is one. Therefore the norms and the ideals articulated at this level apply to all Christians according to their capacity—to the laity in general as well as professional ministers and those who embrace a religious life. Obviously there will be many differences and perhaps even exceptions to some principles when different groups react to the actual conditions of a concrete situation or when specific roles, tasks or functions within the Church are at stake. But in general a lay spirituality is the norm for Christian life.

The description of a Christian and liberationist spirituality that follows will unfold on the level of generality. There will be no investigation of any concrete situation, nor will there be any consideration of the middle axioms that are needed to understand any particular ethical or moral dilemma of the Christian life. The point here is not to try to deal with existential spirituality where in each case ethical decisions are called for and where Christian morality and spirituality are finally decided. Theological spirituality by itself, without the necessary historical analysis and research required for concrete ethical decisions, provides only certain directions, principles, thematic guidelines, general norms and ideals for the Christian life. In every case these ideal principles must be acted out according to the situation and circumstances of one's actual Christian life.

Finally, we can pinpoint even more exactly what is going on in this transition from doctrinal theology to a theological spirituality. The transition is negotiated simply by determining the implications of theological understanding for individual Christians and groups as they live out their lives in the world. On the supposition that a theological statement of one's understanding of reality contains a moral implication for Christian life and spirituality, one may transform the objective statements of theology into performative statements for the Christian life. What will be described, therefore, are hypothetical Christians, any individual person or group of persons, and by extension the whole Church taken concretely and existentially. These Christians stand in and before the world, in their own particular history and in general human history, as they try to decipher the meaning of reality and themselves in relation to it, as they direct their lives in the light of Christian symbols. With this point of reference the theological statements of the preceding chapters will be transformed into general ideal descriptive statements concerning how any given Christian ought to experience reality and act in the light of Christian symbols. In all of this, however, it is presumed that these ideal descriptive statements remain general and abstract. These theological ideals will always be balanced in actual life by the local situation, by a person's capacity, and by ordinary human weakness, blindness, discouragement and failure.

LIBERATIONIST SPIRITUALITY

The following account of liberationist spirituality is in effect a summary of the Christian doctrines presented in the previous chapters but re-presented in the form of descriptive and performative language. The line of development is one that simply recapitulates the preceding chapters. The primary referent for any spirituality is the individual person, although he or she should not be seen as merely an individual isolated from others, society and the world. In the pages that follow this individual idealized Christian will be referred to in a variety of forms. He or she may be referred to as "we," or as "this person," or simply as "the Christian."

The Christian, like any other person, may be characterized as a center of freedom or potential freedom. On the personal level, the Christian is a center of self-consciousness; he or she is conscious of the self as a potentiality for creative action in the world which both determines the self and influences the world at the same time. This person is also aware of his or her relation to other people. Human existence is a being-with-others, and so the Christian ought to be aware that his or her existence is determined by others, both interpersonally and socially, even as one's personal actions have an effect on others, directly or indirectly. The self cannot be conceived as isolated but only as in solidarity with other people in a common social human existence. Moreover, like all human beings, the Christian too has a transcendent dimension to his or her freedom. He or she thus experiences a longing for permanent and stable being, both for the self and for others; this is the longing for the fulfillment of human existence that is called salvation. As a first norm, one may say that an integral spirituality must respond to and take into account these three levels of human freedom that make up anyone's personal existence.

Life in the world, as that world is interpreted for us today by contemporary culture, is the context and the supposition for Christian spirituality. Christians are part of the human race and so exist in total solidarity or oneness with other human beings. If a Christian is mature, he or she ought to feel some responsibility for the world, the world close at hand to everyday life, and the wider world in which we all participate together. This Christian takes this world with a close to absolute seriousness; while one is alive there is absolutely no escape from the world; it is all we have in the sense that God, who is totally other than the world, cannot be experienced apart from the world but only through the world and in relation to the world. Thus the Christian ought to feel or experience absolutely no split or division between this world and the religious longing for final salvation, between religious commitment and secular life. If there is any final salvation, the hint of it must be experienced within historical life; and there is no ground for hoping for such a thing, if it is not to be experienced somehow now in the world by way of anticipation, and if it is not to be worked out in and through one's life in this world. Secular life therefore is the place where this person's religiosity will be lived out because the Christian should feel at home in history and in the world. One must presume that God's creative activity is purposeful and that we exist in the world for a reason.

Because of his or her broad horizon of consciousness and sense of historicity, this person has an open attitude toward human freedom and creative human possibilities. Newness and change are not surprises; the very nature of human existence is to be a project of creativity and change. But in honest moments the Christian also has to feel some disorientation and even insecurity because of historicity. Moreover when the Christian looks at the history of human suffering and the sin that causes it, just as prevalent after Christ as before, just as widespread in Christian culture as beyond it, he or she has to admit that ultimately there is no answer to this. Christian spirituality is not exempt from the doubt and crisis of meaning that history presents to everyone. The underside of history, its measureless amount of suffering and life lived in inhuman conditions, make it appear chaotic and meaningless. But the Christian is one who is convinced that he or she is called to create or make meaning within history by the use of his or her own freedom.

The Christian knows that the salvific meaning of history that is revealed in the life of Jesus Christ, namely, God's will that God reign in a kingdom of justice and reconciliation, can be experienced as authentic or even true only in the measure that one participates in an historical movement that makes this salvific liberation real and actual. The meaningfulness of history is necessarily a function of corporate human freedom; the Kingdom of evil, suffering and suppression of human freedom can only become positive insofar as it is actively opposed by love and resisted by a struggle for emancipation. The Christian, therefore, has a concern for and a commitment to the emancipation of those who are in bondage and who suffer the most, and a desire to contribute to their release whenever, wherever and however it is possible. In short, for Christian consciousness, the active dedication of one's own freedom to such work is profoundly and decisively religious.

Along with the realization that the human person is part of and bound to the world and history, the Christian also knows that God cannot be experienced or known directly. Indeed even to a perceptive and religiously conscious person, it frequently appears that God is absent from the world. Sometimes this person may feel abandoned in a purely secular environment. Moreover whatever we as a race do know of God is always through a faith that is directed to some form of historical revelation. The Christian has become used to the fact that these revelations are many and various; there are a great number of different and contradictory revelations and religions, all seeming to compete with each other and thus seeming to relativize the whole religious domain. But while this may sometimes be a deeply uncomfortable realization, still this person knows that as a Christian, he or she stands in a long tradition. This Christian is a member of a community of common symbols that extend back to Jesus Christ and beyond that back into Jewish history, and they have provided, and they continue to provide, religious meaning for countless hosts of different peoples. The particularity of that tradition of revelation and the specific identity of being a Christian do not separate this person from other peoples or religions. Being a Christian for this person is not exclusivistic; it does not serve to isolate the Christian but rather unites him or her in solidarity with all other human beings. The revelation in Jesus Christ is precisely that God is the Father of all and hence being a Christian is precisely a being in solidarity with all other people.

The Christian realizes that the symbols of Christian self-understanding themselves have constantly shifted in their meaning over history. But this causes no anxiety because this person knows that these symbols must be reinterpreted in every age to illumine human existence in each specific culture. And as for the present, these symbols mediate a vital religious experience for this person, for him or her here and now, and they seem to be potentially revelatory and relevant for others as well. This Christian, therefore, has a desire to share this meaning with others, but not to impose it, since that strategy would contradict the symbols themselves which guarantee human freedom on the basis of God's love which is universal.

The Christian described here has deep faith. Faith for a Christian is primarily a way of life. My faith is the logic of my whole life; faith is the root of one's spirituality. Faith is not the same as simply believing in doctrines or a theological system, but is the sum and total coherence of a person's life as he or she stands before God in the world now and toward the future. The life of Jesus Christ is the focus of this faith; God is mediated to this Christian's faith by the whole life of Jesus of Nazareth. And after the pattern of Jesus' own life, this Christian is aware that his or her faith has a moral substance because human existence itself is freedom. One's faith includes one's decisions and actions. One's faith in God implies and intrinsically demands a loving attitude toward all human beings because they are God's own and share in God's love. And thus, reciprocally, the way this Christian has actually responded to God is constituted by the way he or she has responded to other people in the constant encounters that make up daily and historical life.

This is the Christian's faith response to God. And if there is worry and anxiety within faith itself, it is a concern about infidelity, lack of courage, sin. The question here is not orthodoxy, but how this Christian allows the symbols of faith to move his or her freedom. Faith is commitment; the question is whether and how I give myself to God and God's truth and will, and to other human beings and their future in history. Faith is the core of spirituality, and existentially this faith in God is inseparable from love of neighbor and hope for the future.

We turn now to the content of faith and the direction in which the major symbols of Christian faith point Christian spirituality. How is God present to the Christian, and how does he or she respond to God? This is a difficult relationship to describe because it is paradoxical. On the one hand, the Christian is aware of his or her total and absolute dependence on God. God is God and therefore totally infinite, absolute, awesome, holy. The temptation is to stop one's life activity, to look up and simply to worship God. On the other hand, one has an experience of one's own relative autonomy, of one's freedom, and of the conviction that there is a reason behind one's being created thus. There is a feeling of purpose in the Christian's experience of freedom; he or she was created to do something with human life and has been left more 'or less alone to do it, although in solidarity with others and not without the external guidance of Jesus Christ and the internal empowerment of God's Spirit. These two experiences seem to pull against each other.

Interestingly, in the symbols of Scripture the Christian sees a God who is far more concerned with what one does with his or her freedom in the world than with God being worshiped. There one sees a God who has given us a share in God's own creative power. God is worshiped or not in what one does or fails to do with one's freedom. God intends the world to be shaped by our freedom and intelligence, but in line with God's truth, with God's general but still open and not determining will. The Christian knows the contours of God's general will for human existence through the Jewish and Christian Scriptures, and especially through the life of Jesus of Nazareth as portrayed in the New Testament. This will of God is general in the sense that it does not specify every human decision. Within the context of God's general intention for human existence human beings are left to their own responsibility in concrete situations to discern the possibilities of human action that reasonably correspond to and fulfill God's general will.

Obviously the Christian should not abdicate his or her responsibility for history and hand it over to others who share less than godly values and goals. For the Christian, then, to worship God is ultimately to surrender the whole of one's life, to the extent possible, to the will of God. And that will as far as we know is totally and absolutely for or in favor of human life, for people who are God's own people. God's will for human existence in this world is for justice being extended to all of God's people. And thus God's will extends especially out toward those people who have nothing, or nothing but God, insofar as they are the victims of various forms of oppression, fated existence, suffering, poverty, misfortune and violence in this world. If to know God is to do justice, as the prophets said, then to worship God is to surrender to God's will by service to the neighbor who is most in need, or who crosses one's path at any time.

So the Christian's stance before God is complicated. At one level, this Christian stands apart from God, free, and he or she may even protest to God because of the immensity and seeming futility of the task that has been imposed on human beings, and the limited knowledge, the finitude, the weakness and powerlessness that are the only tools we have to accomplish it. In a way the Christian knows that the historical task that is ours as human beings is doomed to failure while we are in this world. Yet on a deeper level this is all encompassed in the Christian consciousness by a sense of total dependence, gratitude and acceptance of what is. Human beings need God totally, because God is the only hope of the possibility of an ultimate meaning for human suffering, and hence for human history itself, in the future. And yet in order to possibly share in that meaning, one has now to commit oneself to the seemingly impossible will of God and be of service to those who suffer, and to dedicate oneself to work against the causes of the suffering itself. This is experienced by the Christian as a sacred and religious obligation that is written into historical human existence itself by the creating will of God.

It is ultimately in the light of Jesus who is the Christ that Christian spirituality takes its stand before God. We may ask, therefore, how the Christian relates to Jesus himself and then how he or she relates to God according to the disclosure or revelation of God mediated by the Christ.

The Christian relates to Jesus on one level the way everyone else does to another human being. But over and above this, the person we are typifying here marvels at the utter simplicity and depth of Jesus' message and knows that it is universally relevant and existentially of inexhaustible richness religiously. God, it says, is ultimately pure love and totally bent on the cause of human life and human beings, especially those who are neglected in this world. This is of course an extraordinary claim because there is a great deal of evidence in human history and nature that militates against it. So great is the confusion of evidence that the only possible way to come to any conclusion about the ultimate nature of God and reality is by basing one's claim on some particular historical revelation. For the Christian Jesus Christ is this decisive revelation.

But for the Christian, the person of Jesus is also identified with this message; Jesus mediated it by *living* it through the power of God that was *within him*, and God further confirmed both the message and the person of Jesus by raising him up. In other words, this Christian realizes that if the human being Jesus himself, the Jesus of history, did not live out his message, the very substance of the message would be questionable.

The Christian's special relation to Jesus Christ can therefore be seen at three points. First, for the Christian Jesus is *the* mediator or mediation of God in history. Thus the Christian allows this person Jesus to be God's revelation and communication to human beings in history. Jesus thus shares in the power of God; the power of God is in him, and he is the ultimate criterion or norm, the standard, for determining who God is. Jesus is an absolute norm in the sense that all others, all other revelations, are subordinate in relation to him. Second, the Christian allows Jesus to determine his or her view of human existence and what it means to be human. This applies not so much to Jesus' words or actions taken singly as to the person of Jesus as a whole and the total meaning of his life as that is communicated to us in the New Testament. Once again, then, Jesus is norm and standard. And, third, the Christian believes that Jesus is alive and with God and therefore he or she relates to him as still alive and spiritually present or relevant to the whole world. This is so even though all we know of this risen Jesus is that he is risen and that he is the same Jesus of Nazareth, the Jesus of history.

The relation of the Christian to Jesus is therefore unique. But for such a relationship to be authentic or even real, it must inform the whole of a person's life and be played out in action. The Christian, therefore, is conscious that his or her relationship to Jesus and to God through Jesus consists ultimately in discipleship. Discipleship is not imitating Jesus' actions or words; this would be impossible two thousand years later. Rather this Christian's discipleship consists in informing his or her own life with the basic pattern, logic or form of Jesus' own faith and life. This was a life totally given to the cause of God which was the cause of human beings. In the measure that Jesus really is a disclosure of the intrinsic meaning of God and human life to this Christian, in the same measure will this Christian internalize the pattern of Jesus' life in his or her own. Jesus himself was united historically to his Father by his experience of God which unfolded in his public mission to his world, serving those who were neglected and wanting because this was God's will and cause. This becomes the inner core of this Christian's life on earth as well.

We may now ask how in the end the Christian experiences that he or she is united with God in the light of Jesus' revelation. Another way of putting this question would be the following: How does this particular Christian experience salvation existentially? This is not enormously complicated. But at the same time this experience does have various dimensions that should be distinguished.

First of all, when the Christian looks back at the Jesus affair, there is a negative aspect to his or her identification with it. In one way or another, in some certain degree or measure, I stand over against Jesus as did the people who rejected his message and his person. His life of sheer goodness convicts the Christian of sin. We all have to live with this inescapable truth about ourselves. Yet despite this deep layer of sin within us, both personally experienced by us and pointed out for us by Jesus, one can also accept God's acceptance of us and God's forgiveness. In this revelation the Christian experiences an enormous religious liberation, an entirely new freedom from all existential anxiety. One experiences as well a freedom to consider, to decide and to act without having to prove oneself before God. If one is really accepted by God, what does one have ultimately to fear? This Christian, then, is an ontically free person, freed by the revelation of God in Jesus Christ and God's acceptance of human beings as they actually are.

Second, this freedom, which is experienced as a release, becomes a reality in the actual life of love and service for others that marks this person's Christian existence. And when in any given case the hold of sin or egoism actually seems to be overcome in the Christian's life, he or she recognizes that this occurs through the immanent power of God within whom is the source of all love in the world. "Not I but the grace of God within me." At the same time one does not have any sense of personal holiness, and yet one knows that his or her life is positively united with God in the exact measure that one responds to the needs of other people after the pattern of Jesus. Here love joins faith concretely; one's faith is one's love, and one's love is one's faith. The center of this experience is the merging together of the religious and the moral spheres of human existence, as well as the sacred and the secular, without any confusion between them or reduction of one to the other. The Christian's life in the world is religious insofar as it is based on a conscious surrender to the general will of God for the world and is cognizant of being supported by God's Spirit of love present within. One is both at home in the world and in history and united with God there.

Third, however, this spirituality extends still further. The Christian is very conscious that he or she has more than an individual personal existence. All human beings live their lives within social structures and public institutions. Thus the Christian is aware of his or her social existence and social responsibility. This results in a religious and moral imperative that directs the Christian's life in two ways. First of all such a person is outraged and almost scandalized by the amount of suffering, especially unnecessary and humanly caused suffering, that attacks human lives and in the end threatens the meaningfulness of human existence itself. Besides the victims themselves, all human beings and all Christians are implicated and threatened by these patterns of human behavior and structures of society that suppress elemental human freedom and crush human life itself in the world. The reflex reaction of Christian faith is a critical attitude toward all the structures of society that suppress the freedom of the many in favor of a few and the desire to attack them in return. Secondly and more positively, within the context of the experience of the suffering of fellow human beings, the Christian is impelled by love to constructively cooperate in changing unjust institutions. The Christian actively supports those groups or movements that are engaged at the pressure points of society in trying to alter death-dealing social institutions and refashion more humane and liberating ones in the direction of a generally more just society and meaningful history.

Even more concretely, the Christian will choose a career or life vocation in an institutional form of work that itself contributes something positive to society. Whatever his or her career or form of work may be, this person participates in it, or tries to change, transform or shape it, in such a way that that form of life serves others in the direction of human emancipation. This may really be the core of a Christian's spirituality because it consumes the greatest part of his or her time and much of his or her psychic energy. In this way, this person lives as well a corporate spirituality by participating in an institution that in some measure also corresponds with the general will of God for human liberation in history.

We now must ask what membership in the Church contributes to this person's spirituality, for up to now we have described a fairly integral Christian spirituality with no mention of the Church. It would seem that the Christian life just described could be led outside of the Church. This is true, but on the one condition that the Christian Church continued to exist. In other words, Christian spirituality cannot exist independently of the Church; without the existence of this community as a plausibility structure, Christian spirituality itself would cease to exist. The Church is ultimately a voluntary association and institution of Christians whose purpose is to support Christian life in history. Therefore even free Christians who choose to live their Christian lives outside the Church need the Church in an indirect way.

This Christian, therefore, is an active participant in the life of his or her local Church. The reason for this participation is very clear in this person's mind. The Church is an organization in which Jesus Christ is continually represented to the members so that they may be continually nourished in their own mission spirituality after the pattern of Jesus. The Church is for the support of a mission spirituality, so that personally this Christian participates in it to help support others in their spirituality and to draw support from them in his or her own Christian life.

A major element of this support consists in the preaching, sacramental, ritual and worshiping dimension of the Church's life. The Christian realizes that prayer is an enormously important dimension of his or her Christian life because one has to keep in constant contact with life's ultimate grounding source, namely God as revealed in and by Jesus and as experienced and affected by God's Spirit. There is a need for this even as there is a need in life for reflection, for taking stock, for explicitly recognizing what often remains only implicitly at work in one's consciousness. But even while recognizing this importance, this Christian knows that this is not itself of final, absolute or ultimate importance; it is not in itself the heart of the matter. For example, it is certain that the Eucharist is indeed the heart of Christian cultic worship, at least in Roman Catholicism, but the Eucharist is not itself the heart of Christian spiritual life. That lies in being existentially united with God in or through or by the whole of one's life. Cultic participation, therefore, is not a matter of external obligation for this person; rather it fits into his or her life according to the existential demands of this person's whole life of Christian love.

Added to this, as a member of this institutional Church, this person assumes responsibility for it, in the measure possible, that it too be a public sacrament, sign and witness before society of the offer of God's message and grace that it claims to represent. To put it crudely, the Christian envisioned here does not merely "live off" the Church but contributes something to it. Thus this person tries to promote and participate in the formation of group activities that actually address social problems, on all levels of the Church's structure.

We must also ask what the themes from eschatology add to this view of Christian spirituality. Eschatology, one's view of the end time, has a completely encompassing role in theology; it is another view of the whole from the perspective of history's end. To see the role of this for spirituality, then, we must go back to the beginning and reassert some of our suppositions to show how eschatology determines Christian hope.

The Christian we have been describing has a sense of reality as it is. He or she knows that human existence is bound to his imperfect world and especially to time. Time inevitably leads to diminishment and to death, and human finitude is itself a series of unfulfilled ideals and daily deaths. Moreover sin within oneself can be even more discouraging. Therefore no Christian can live the Christian life without hope. Hope is directed toward permanent or eternal meaning and life; it is hope in God; it is hope on the basis of the resurrection, God's raising of Jesus into God's own sphere of being. In this perspective of realism, of time and of the future, therefore, this Christian's faith merges with hope. The ultimate object of faith and hope lies both in the present and in the future. It cannot lie only in the future, for then it would have no ground at all on which to base itself. It cannot lie only in the past and present, since life is not complete and there is not sufficient evidence to believe that the forces of sin and ultimately death might not dominate.

The Christian therefore is really sustained by hope in a promise, the promise of the resurrection, that the Kingdom of God will be for all persons and for all of history. Given the doctrine of the universality of sin and the experience of it deep within the self, one cannot logically simply have hope only for oneself. Moreover the Christian also recognizes that one cannot have hope logically if one does not participate in the fashioning or the realizing of the values of the reign of God here and now in this world. Presumably Jesus was raised because of the life that he lived. The resurrection was the culmination of his life. Thus Christian eschatology must be a continuous eschatology, that is, one that affirms some continuity between life in history and an absolute end time. That which is of positive value in history when measured by the religious symbol of the Kingdom of God will be preserved. This must be so by a negative reasoning process, for, if it were not the case, Christian theology would also surrender the possibility of establishing any meaningfulness of actual human history at all.

The only possible basis of both faith in and hope for the Kingdom of God, therefore, is that one participate in the movement toward it as an agent of its being brought about through life in this world. Here the Christian's hope thus joins with an active love of neighbor. One can only authentically hope for meaning in the end time if one actively shares in that meaning here and now in history by a faith informed by an active love. And that which one hopes in is an absolute future which is continuous with the values of the Kingdom of God that are established in this world, for only this continuity allows historical human existence to actually be meaningful.

To conclude, there is an intimate and inseparable connection between theology and spirituality, and between liberationist theology and the integral spirituality described here. And this relationship might be captured in the idea or notion of contemplation. Theology, as an interpretation of reality in terms of the symbols of Christian revelation, provides a vision of reality, a way of seeing the world and history in relation to God. For Christians this faith vision evokes the contemplative attitude out of which they fashion the whole of their lives in the world. This contemplation does not escape from the world and history in an ascending vertical direction. Rather it is a contemplation rooted in hope, faith and love that experiences God within the world and, as transcendent as God is, nowhere else. The contemplative attitude of this spirituality hopes that God will forge the Kingdom of God in the end time out of what we actually see and experience in history. This spirituality has a faith that sees the Kingdom of God in the little bits and pieces of history where people are being served and cared for by other people. This faith sees God's hand working through human agency in this; these little victories in the struggle for the emancipation and liberation of other human beings are the ultimate experiential ground of faith that justifies hope. And, finally, the faith and hope of this spirituality is informed by love, because only through participating in this movement of history can faith and hope continue to survive. One thus contemplates God within history; and one is a contemplative in and by one's action in history.

Epilogue
INTERPRETING THE INSTRUCTION OF THE SACRED CONGREGATION FOR THE DOCTRINE OF THE FAITH ON LIBERATION THEOLOGY

In September of 1984 the Sacred Congregation for the Doctrine of the Faith of the Roman Catholic Church published the document on liberation theology entitled "Instruction on Certain Aspects of the 'Theology of Liberation'" (Appendix). While recognizing that there is a pluralism of liberation theologies, and that liberation theologies are current in many different parts of the world, by and large the focus of the document is on the liberation theologies that have emerged in Latin America. There are of course ecclesial documents that carry more authority than this relative to Latin American liberation theology, such as the statements of the Episcopal Conference of the whole of Latin America formulated at Medellín in 1968 and Puebla in 1979. But because this is a statement on doctrine from a congregation of the Roman Church, a statement from the center so to speak, it has implications for the periphery. Thus even though the intention of this book has not been to simply reproduce historically Latin American liberation theology, but rather to construct the outlines for a liberation theology beyond the confines of that continent, still this document has a bearing on all liberation theologies and it deserves comment.

When the Instruction appeared in 1984 it immediately became the subject of wide discussion, and this discussion continues today. Because of its nuances and ambiguities this document deserves more extensive study, including a history of its genesis, a summary of the discussion about it and a detailed commentary on all its aspects and every assertion contained in it. The purpose of these remarks is not to provide such extended commentary. I cannot at this point provide the historical background of the progress of liberation theology in Latin America which helps make up the political context for this document. Nor can I give a thorough exegesis of all of its statements. Rather I simply wish to characterize the fundamental structure of the document in order to provide a context for the reading and further study of it. Despite the ways it has often been portrayed and used an analysis of the text will show that it is not a condemnation of the liberationist movement and spirituality. The opposite is the case; in it the Roman Catholic Church reasserts its social commitment to and preferential option for the poor which is the basis of liberation theology. It is not a condemnation of any liberation theologian. On the contrary it provides a hypothetical system of thought constructed by its authors in order to point out dangers in this particular kind of theology. Nor finally is it a condemnation of liberation theology as a whole. On the contrary, as the title indicates, it deals with only certain aspects of this hypothetically constructed system.

In all such disciplinary communications by the teaching authority of the Church there are two distinct dimensions of this document. The first concerns its theological content; the second concerns the political import of it. This seems to be a convenient division for organizing the following all too brief remarks.

THEOLOGICAL CONTENT

Roughly speaking the Instruction contains two main parts. The first part, after the introduction lays down precisely the limits of its purpose and intention, deals with the genesis of liberation theology (Chapters I–V). The second part, after a transition (VI), presents a deductive theoretical account of some errors in some theologies of liberation (VII–X). Chapter XI contains a summary review and an exhortation, and the document concludes with a quotation from Pope Paul VI.

The reader will immediately notice the difference between the two main parts of the Instruction. In general the first is very sympathetic to the perceptions and values that underlie liberation theology. The second is equally strong against perceived contradictions to Christian faith in some aspects of some liberation theologies. So great is this difference that it has been suggested that the document was prepared by at least two different authors of very different persuasions. And yet there is a clear logic to this transition. Prior to its publication a group of liberation theologians in Latin America wrote to the Congregation as it prepared the document, warning against the possible misunderstanding of a document critical of liberation theology as a retraction of the Church's commitment to social justice and its preferential option for the poor.

Whether explicitly intended or not, the first part of the Instruction is a response to this fear. "This warning should in no way be interpreted as a disavowal of all those who want to respond generously and with authentic evangelical spirit to the 'preferential option for the poor.' It should not at all serve as an excuse for those who maintain an attitude of neutrality and indifference in the face of the tragic and pressing problems of human misery and injustice" (Introduction; cf. also XI, 1).

The first element of the theological content of the Instruction, then, is a clear and forceful endorsement of the values that underlie all liberation theologies. Even though the first section is carefully nuanced, containing as it does numerous cautions, reservations and foreshadowings of the criticisms that will be made later, still there is no qualification whatsoever in this document of the Church's commitment on behalf of the poor and the oppressed, and against the political and structural violence from which they suffer. "The scandal of the shocking inequality between the rich and poor—whether between rich and poor countries, or between social classes in a single nation—is no longer tolerated" (I, 6). It is supportive of the men and women who are engaged in liberationist movements, that is, of their motives and their pastoral action in behalf of the poor. The Instruction states declaratively that it stands behind the recent social teachings of the Church from which liberation theologians frequently argue support, especially the documents issued by the whole Latin American hierarchy at their conferences at Medellín in 1968 and Puebla in 1979. These documents have been the principal ecclesiastical support for the development of liberation theology during the past two decades.

I use the term values here in distinction from the more conceptually formulated principles which the Instruction goes on to criticize in its second major part. By values I mean general and only vaguely formulated ideals and responses to them that serve as the underlying driving force that leads to the pursuit of critical knowledge and actions stemming from it. The second part of the Instruction criticizes certain specific conceptions that concretize these values insofar as they may be found in some aspects of some theologies of liberation. And this criticism, although carefully constructed, is marked by both precise limits and certain ambiguities that require some attempt to formulate a framework for understanding and reception.

The fundamental criticism of some aspects of some liberation theologies is contained in Chapters VII–X. It consists in a wholistic presentation of Marxist analysis which is presented as the basis of some forms of liberation theology (VII); a conception of how the application of Marxist concepts to Christian values occurs in the thinking of some theologies of liberation (VIII); and finally the results or conclusions that flow from this use of Marxism in the interpretations of Christian faith and doctrine by some liberation theologies (IX–X). Some comments on the underlying logic and internal intentionality of these three steps are crucial for understanding the document in both its explicit and implicit teaching.

First of all, the clearly and explicitly stated intention of the Instruction, its "precise purpose," is that it is directed to "certain forms of liberation theology" (Introduction). This narrowness of focus is underlined by its endorsement of the intention, motivation and dynamism of liberation theology for the poor and against social evils. And it is important enough to be repeated in a later chapter. There are many different theologies of liberation and theologians of liberation, and the proposed criticism is only directed to deviations from the faith within this whole body of literature (VI, 8–9).

At the same time, given this limitation and reserve, the Instruction in several places makes unqualified statements concerning either the theology of liberation or the theologies of liberation which thus depict the whole of liberation theology as under criticism against the stated intention of the document. I am at a loss as to how to explain this inconsistency and ambiguity the importance of which should not be overlooked. Ordinarily significant documents are prepared with great care, and certainly the authors were aware that any portion of this Instruction could and would be quoted verbatim, so that any particular reference to the theologies of liberation in an unqualified way would be misleading. In any case, according to the explicit intention of the document its criticisms apply only to some aspects of some liberation theologies.

As a help to understand the criticism of some aspects of some theologies of liberation presented in these four chapters it may be useful to state in schematic form its logic. Marxism, insofar as it is authentic Marxism, is an objective body of doctrine. Second, it is a systematic whole from which no part, no level of thinking nor fundamental category or concept, can be isolated without implying the whole system. Third, the basic feature of the whole system of Marxist thought is its atheism and its denial of the spiritual autonomy and destiny of the human person. But special emphasis is laid on the negative and deterministic elements of the ideology of class-struggle in Marxism. Therefore, fourth, the use of Marxist categories or language implicitly and inevitably, even when it is not intended, leads to an acceptance or endorsement of a Marxist world-view that is contradictory to and negates Christian faith (VII). But, fifth, this is what some theologies of liberation have done, so that the logic and content of Marxism determines the content of their so-called Christian affirmations. And, reciprocally, one should understand these particular theologies in terms of Marxism (VIII). Thus, finally, one can list the objective errors of some theologies of liberation by understanding them in terms of Marxism and not in terms of authentic Christian principles and doctrines (IX–X).

While this analysis appears to be quite clear and straightforward, it also contains some ambiguities and restrictions that do not appear on the surface. Attention to these will show that the criticism not only must be applied only to some aspects of some theologies of liberation, but also only under certain well-defined conditions. There are three such reservations.

First, the term "Marxist analysis" can be understood in two quite different ways or senses. "Marxist analysis" can be understood objectively, that is, as an objective body of doctrine or a closed system of understanding the whole of reality, one part of which is an objective theory of human existence and the dynamics of history and society. Stemming from the nineteenth century figure Karl Marx and others, the significant point here is that Marxism in this sense is an objective system of understanding which, to the extent that they are authentically and integrally Marxists, current thinkers simply accept and adhere to as an objectively given wholistic system. Without explicitly saying so, the Instruction uses the phrase "Marxist analysis" in this objective sense.

But the term "Marxist analysis" can also be understood in a subjective and existential sense. In this usage a Marxist analysis may refer to an actual description of cultural realities and the existential attempt to understand the structure and dynamics of this or that particular social situation through the use of Marxist concepts, categories and distinctions. In this sense the term "Marxist analysis" does not refer to a finished or wholistic doctrine concerning all reality, all history or every society, but to a current interpretation of a specific aspect of a twentieth century situation which is Marxist only insofar as some of the objective distinctions used by Marx or Marxists are actually used or employed in this description of actual data. This existential use of Marxist analysis, however, is not a simple appropriation and application of objective doctrines as a response or solution to questions asked today; rather it is an actual hermeneutical exercise that remains open to the complex reality that is being described and interprets it in the light of certain categories of Marxism that may illumine any given situation and are only useful to the extent that they do.

Perhaps a better way of expressing the distinction that is being described here is through a contrast between the phrases "the Marxist analysis" and the now common and more neutral expression "a Marxian analysis." The former indicates a fundamental option in favor of a complete objective system of thought; the latter indicates a use of Marxist distinctions in an actual analysis of a given situation where the concrete phenomena govern the conclusions.

Once this distinction is made and the Instruction's objectivist understanding of "Marxist analysis" is recognized, another of the ambiguities and implicit reservations of the document follows. The Instruction exclusively intends to warn against those aspects of some theologies or theologians of liberation that have primarily opted for a specific wholistic body of doctrine called Marxist. And by contrast any liberation theologian or theology that does not rest on this fundamental option is not intended as the object of the Instruction's discussion.

Second, this rather important distinction and reservation in the meaning of the Instruction is confirmed by what may be taken as its key or central methodological premise. In Chapter VIII the Instruction insists that one cannot borrow a basic category or concept from "Marxist analysis" without including as well the whole system. In other words, even when one thinks one can employ only certain aspects of Marxism to be used as instruments for analysis and expression, implicitly and by a necessary logic the whole system is implicated so that in the long run its integral world-view becomes operative and comes to bear to determine the resultant theological position. But this makes sense only on the prior premise of conceiving Marxist analysis as an objective and closed system of thought to which one surrenders oneself completely. In other words, the logic of the transition is purely conditional; it only makes sense insofar as a commitment to Marxism as an objective and wholistic frame of reference determines the fundamental option of the theologies in question. The logic does not apply to theologies or theologians which have not made this fundamental commitment.

That the systems of thought that are generated in history need not be taken and used exclusively as objective complete wholes can be demonstrated by innumerable cases in the history of ideas simply because the historicity of consciousness makes this the norm rather than the exception. But one case is extremely noteworthy in the history of Christian theology. At the beginning of the thirteenth century Aristotle's philosophy of nature and metaphysics were just becoming known in the newly forming universities of Western Europe. And during the course of that century Christian theology underwent a revolution in which Aristotelian analysis of nature, in the sense of the intrinsic structure and principles of operation of all that is including human nature, gradually became the substratum of theology. In a word, Aristotle's language, his concepts and categories, became the vehicles of Christian self-understanding and expression.

However, during the course of the thirteenth century the thought of Aristotle and the use of Aristotle in Christian theology were condemned by the Church, either regionally or universally, at least five times. And the reason for this condemnation, we may assume, was legitimate when viewed from a certain point of view. The basis for the condemnation was the consideration of Aristotle's thought from a wholistic and objective point of view. Aristotle was an empiricist; nothing could be understood without first appealing to the senses. Aristotle was a naturalist; he had no doctrine of the supernatural or grace. The ultimate principles of intelligibility were intrinsic to a closed system of reality; he had no doctrine of creation or radical transcendence. When his philosophy was accepted objectively *en bloc,* as indeed it was by some in Paris, it contradicted Christian faith and was rightly condemned. In general the use of Aristotle's thought scandalized many who accepted an Augustinian world-view.

Yet a subjective and existential use of Aristotle's categories was ultimately successful in transforming theology in an acceptable and salutary way. One does not have to dwell on the achievement of Aquinas to show that one can use categories of even a tight system of thought such as Aristotle's without embracing the whole doctrine if it is taken existentially as a medium for expressing a prior and deeper faith and a commitment to analyze reality as it is revealed through actual data.

The theoretical distinction we have made, therefore, is also a very real and practical one. On this basis it seems reasonable to call attention to and to underline what is being warned against by the intrinsic logic and intention of the Instruction. It is addressed against deviations from Christian faith by some theologians, specifically those theologians of liberation who, although they call themselves theologians, have made their primary commitment to the objective system of Marxism and to the whole of it. But this does not refer to all liberation theologians nor the whole of liberation theology, on the assumption there were such a systematic whole, nor to any particular theologians who retain a Christian faith commitment. Presumably there are theologians of liberation who, like Aquinas, are using Marxist analysis in an existential and subjective way. One can presume that most of these theologians who betray a good deal of historical consciousness are also aware that one cannot simply apply a nineteenth century doctrine from a particular cultural environment to twentieth century reality in another environment without changing its conceptions rather basically. Marxist language can take on new meaning in Christian Latin America even as Aristotle took on new meaning in Christian Western Europe safely when its users remain totally "open to the reality to be described" (VII, 13), that is, "the scandal of the shocking inequality between the rich and the poor" (I, 6) to which the social concern of the whole Church is committed.

Third, having commented on the major and minor premises of the critical argument against some aspects of some theologies of liberation, it is important to situate the status of the conclusion. What is criticized is a wholistic system of thought: "We are facing, therefore, a real system, even if some hesitate to follow the logic to its conclusion" (IX, 1). This system of thought is viewed as flowing principally from the concept of class-struggle in Marxism, but in such a way that this implies the whole objective system of Marxism. It is characterized by an enumeration of a whole series of positions relative to various aspects of Christian faith that are really contradictory to Christian faith and Catholic teaching.

Two things must be kept in mind in reading these two sections which constitute the primary object and conclusion of the whole Instruction. The first is that these positions are put forward in these chapters as inimical to Christian faith. In one case or other one might question whether the position as it is stated might not be understood in a more benign fashion. But in general the Instruction intends to present these positions precisely as errors. In other words they should be understood precisely as in opposition to Christian faith. They are such because they are presented as interpreted in an integral Marxist as opposed to a Christian sense.

A second issue and question, however, is whether or not liberation theologians generally or any particular liberation theologian actually holds any of these positions. These assertions in fact and in the intention of the authors of the Instruction do not come from any single liberation theology or any liberation theologian. They are positions that have been constructed by the authors of the document in a very methodical way. It is exactly because of this that they are to be construed as errors, for they have been fashioned on the premise that their meaning is determined not by Christian faith but on the basis of Marxist premises to be read in a Marxist sense. By the internal logic of the Instruction, then, these positions are purely hypothetical relative to any particular theology or theologian of liberation. They apply to the actuality of any liberation theology only on the basis and to the extent that that theology is Marxist in a very narrow sense.

The structure of the Instruction in this regard is quite similar to that of the encyclical letter of Pius X of 1907, *Pascendi Dominici gregis*, which condemned modernism. The method of that encyclical was the following: From the movement of thought and writings of some Catholic theologians in the beginning of this century, the encyclical abstracted some ideas out of context, reinterpreted them, and fashioned them into a system of thought that was and is heretical and contradictory to faith. Even though this system of thought represented no single theologian involved in the movement, the encyclical represented clearly and forcefully errors, deviations from Christian faith and dangers in theology. But current scholarship has shown historically that the positions defined by the encyclical did not exist in the thought of the majority of the significant writers in the period in question.

So too in this case. This Instruction presents a whole list of positions contrary to Christian faith that may serve as a touchstone for extremes to which liberation theology should not go. But another and different question concerns whether or not in fact any liberation theologian actually holds the system that is outlined here or indeed any of the assertions that make it up. It is theoretically possible that some participants in the liberationist movement as in any other movement may be motivated by less than Christian faith. But every liberation theologian who is a Christian theologian can join the Sacred Congregation for the Doctrine of the Faith in condemning these positions as they are stated here.

We may summarize our interpretation of the theological content of this Instruction at this point. Although this document appears to be straightforward on the surface, it is like all such communications actually a carefully constructed and, with some notable exceptions, qualified statement that must be interpreted. Positively, it endorses the values of commitment to the poor and reaction against the unjust social structures that exist in Latin America and which underlie all liberation theologies. And this is done with repeated insistence and very strong language. Negatively, it is a rejection of an objective and systematically understood Marxist world-view as inimical and incompatible with a Christian world-view. It is not a condemnation of or even a criticism of liberation theology as a movement or of any liberation theology, but of some aspects of some unnamed theologies of liberation. And these theologies are unnamed because in this document the aspects defined and criticized are very narrowly defined and hypothetically created on the premise that they are not Christian at all but are determined in their meaning by a complete and prior acceptance of the logic of a Marxist system of thought. Thus all liberation theologians who are truly theologians, that is, those who are dedicated to the cause of the poor against social oppression and injustice on the basis of the vision of things mediated by Christian faith, even those who employ useful concepts and categories that stem from the thought of Karl Marx in an existential or heuristic way that is open to the reality of the situation described in this document and in Medellín and Puebla, can join with this Instruction in condemning the errors and dangers to which it points.

POLITICAL USE

I said at the outset that the point of these comments was very limited; I have not attempted a detailed commentary on all of the assertions of this Instruction. And far less have I tried to situate it among the very complicated historical and political forces, both inside and outside the Church, that have surrounded the genesis and development of liberation theology and hence this document. But at the same time one cannot prescind completely from the fact that this Instruction was not only a theological document warning against the possibility of theological errors; it was also a political act and a political event. And this fact deserves at least some very general observations.

By calling the Instruction a political act and event I mean the following: This Instruction is a function of the whole history of the social interactions between liberation theologians and those people who have responded to both them and to the movements represented by liberation theology. The term "political" is used very generally here to mean the interactions of positions, decisions and actions in the running of human affairs on the social and public levels. The rise and development of liberation theology has had and continues to have political implications, and this document is now part of the history of liberation theology. This means that the Instruction is not merely a theological tract that bears study. Rather it has been used and will continue to be used by people to shape consciousnesses, as a basis for decisions and actions, as a symbol of support or as a weapon against persons, groups, ideological positions and planned courses of action. Along with the use of such an instrument is the possibility of its abuse. And it seems to me that the possible misuses of it are no less dangerous than the errors and abuses against which the document warns. And these abuses can occur both outside the Church and inside the Church as well.

The dangers of the abuse of this document by forces outside the Church are so evident that the Instruction itself took special care to warn against them more than once. Basically they consist in using this document against the interests of the poor which are those of the whole Church itself in Latin America, or against the Church's characterization of and militant stance against the social injustice and oppression that marks Latin American societies. This could be done by various agents or sectors of the social-political spectrum which are only vaguely and often inaccurately described as the rich, the oppressors, established governments, the right, conservatives and so on. And it can be done in innumerable ways, by propaganda, by misquotation or half quotation in newspaper and pamphlet, by any attempt to discredit liberation theology as a whole against the intention of this document and thus undermine the forces that militate against the unjust social structures in place. Indeed, given the way newspaper accounts and more generally mass political discussion necessarily deal with such documents concerning public issues, that is, on a rhetorical level that scarcely transcends slogans, the careless use in this document of such phrases as "the 'theologies of liberation'" in an unqualified sense and against the explicit intention of its authors is astonishing and lamentable. It fairly invites public distortion and political misuse of the Instruction.

This occasional lack of caution in the Instruction itself should alert the reader to the fact that there are also dangers of its abuse within the Church itself. No one has to be told that liberation theology not only has critics within the Church but also enemies. The enemies may be vaguely and often wrongly simply grouped together and labeled as the extreme right, conservatives, traditionalists, reactionaries, pre-Vatican II mentalities, affluent and self-concerned Christians and so on. Such characterization cuts off legitimate critical discussion of what is at stake in liberation theology and pillories those who have sincere questions about it. But at the same time it does point to some groups in the Church who have absued and do abuse this document against the intrinsic logic of its assertions. The way in which such an abuse occurs is immediately evident: It is a use of this document as a principle of interpretation for what actual liberation theologians are actually saying. It would not only be incorrect but also dishonest not to attend to the intrinsic genesis and logic of any theologian's thought in order to understand the meaning of his or her assertions, but rather to apply an external and hypothetically constructed criterion as a principle of interpretation. This would also contradict the logic of this Instruction. Such an abuse, while directed in its first instance against particular theologians and in general against the whole movement of liberation theology, would also indirectly and inescapably compromise the commitment of the Church for the poor and against social oppression.

These comments on the political use of this Instruction are actually intimately connected with how its content is understood theologically. And they may be concluded with what can only be characterized as a plea. It seems that the general public discussion of liberation theology, unlike the discussion inside the theological community, is often carried on in the crudest and most over simplified context imaginable. Liberation theology is placed in the middle between competing exclusive and monolithic alternatives that are represented by abstract block-thinking and expressed in slogans. It must be either the materialist West or the atheistic East; either a rapacious capitalism or an idolatrous communism; either Christianity or Marxism in which no person of one part could possibly enter into dialogue or communicate with a person of the other; either a conservative-traditionalist or a liberal-progressivist where each is stereotyped. Unfortunately the outward style of the 1984 Instruction regarding certain aspects of some liberation theologies seems on the surface to fall into this pattern, and for this reason it seemed necessary to interpret the logic of its assertions. The plea is that it not be understood either by those outside the Church or by those inside the Church in the crude unnuanced and uncritical terms of the popular discussion and that liberation theology as a theology be interpreted critically in the context of historical consciousness.

In such a context it is possible, for example, that a traditional hierarchically organized peasant Church can be a powerful symbol and force for resistance against an officially atheistic and totalitarian repression of individual and social freedom in Eastern Europe, even while the same kind of Church may be a symbol and an agency reinforcing social injustice in another continent and culture such as Latin America. It is not impossible that any given communist person or party might cynically use Christian language while concealing real political intentions and goals and a totally Marxist view of reality. But neither is it impossible for an authentic Christian with the critical awareness of someone like Aquinas to use concepts from another world-view heuristically to illumine reality and at the same time express the Christian vision of it. In a context of historical consciousness critical thinking on all levels, coupled with openness to data and an honest spirit of dialogue, is needed to prevent political uses of this document which would in turn negate the spirit of Christianity.

Appendix
SACRED CONGREGATION FOR THE DOCTRINE OF THE FAITH: INSTRUCTION ON CERTAIN ASPECTS OF THE "THEOLOGY OF LIBERATION" (VATICAN CITY, 1984)

The Gospel of Jesus Christ is a message of freedom and a force for liberation. In recent years this essential truth has become the object of reflection for theologians, with a new kind of attention which is itself full of promise.

Liberation is first and foremost liberation from the radical slavery of sin. Its end and its goal is the freedom of the children of God, which is the gift of grace. As a logical consequence, it calls for freedom from many different kinds of slavery in the cultural, economic, social and political spheres, all of which derive ultimately from sin and so often prevent people from living in a manner befitting their dignity. To discern clearly what is fundamental to this issue and what is a byproduct of it is an indispensable condition for any theological reflection on liberation.

Faced with the urgency of certain problems, some are tempted to emphasize, unilaterally, the liberation from servitude of an earthly and temporal kind. They do so in such a way that they seem to put liberation from sin in second place and so fail to give it the primary importance it is due. Thus, their very presentation of the problems is confused and ambiguous. Others, in an effort to learn more precisely what are the causes of the slavery which they want to end, make use of different concepts without sufficient critical caution. It is difficult, and perhaps impossible, to purify these borrowed concepts of an ideological inspiration which is incompatible with Christian faith and the ethical requirements which flow from it.

The Sacred Congregation for the Doctrine of the Faith does not intend to deal here with the vast theme of Christian freedom and liberation in its own right. This it intends to do in a subsequent document which will detail in a positive fashion the great richness of this theme for the doctrine and life of the church.

The present instruction has a much more limited and precise purpose: to draw the attention of pastors, theologians and all the faithful to the deviations and risks of deviation, damaging to the faith and to Christian living, that are brought about by certain forms of liberation theology which use, in an insufficiently critical manner, concepts borrowed from various currents of Marxist thought.

This warning should in no way be interpreted as a disavowal of all those who want to respond generously and with an authentic evangelical spirit to the "preferential option for the poor." It should not at all serve as an excuse for those who maintain an attitude of neutrality and indifference in the face of the tragic and pressing problems of human misery and injustice. It is, on the contrary, dictated by the certitude that the serious ideological deviations which it points out tend inevitably to betray the cause of the poor. More than ever, it is important that numerous Christians, whose faith is clear and who are committed to live the Christian life in its fullness, become involved in the struggle for justice, freedom and human dignity because of their love for their disinherited, oppressed and persecuted brothers and sisters. More than ever, the church intends to condemn abuses, injustices and attacks against freedom, wherever they occur and whoever commits them. She intends to struggle, by her own means, for the defense and advancement of the rights of mankind, especially of the poor.

I. AN ASPIRATION

1. The powerful and almost irresistible aspiration that people have for liberation constitutes one of the principal signs of the times which the church has to examine and interpret in the light of the Gospel.[1] This major phenomenon of our time is universally widespread, though it takes on different forms and exists in different degrees according to the particular people involved. It is, above all, among those people who bear the burdens of misery and in the heart of the disinherited classes that this aspiration expresses itself with the greatest force.

2. This yearning shows the authentic, if obscure, perception of the dignity of the human person, created "in the image and likeness of God" (Gn. 1:26–27), ridiculed and scorned in the midst of a variety of different oppressions: cultural, political, racial, social and economic, often in conjunction with one another.

3. In revealing to them their vocation as children of God, the Gospel has elicited in the hearts of mankind a demand and a positive will for a peaceful and just fraternal life in which everyone will find respect and the conditions for spiritual as well as material development. This requirement is no doubt at the very basis of the aspiration we are talking about here.

4. Consequently mankind will no longer passively submit to crushing poverty with its effects of death, disease and decline. He resents this misery as an intolerable violation of his native dignity. Many factors, and among them certainly the leaven of the Gospel, have contributed to an awakening of the consciousness of the oppressed.

5. It is widely known even in still illiterate sections of the world that, thanks to the amazing advances in science and technology, mankind, still growing in numbers, is capable of assuring each human being the minimum of goods required by his dignity as a person.

6. The scandal of the shocking inequality between the rich and the poor—whether between rich and poor countries, or between social classes in a single nation—is no longer tolerated. On one hand, people have attained an unheard-of abundance which is given to waste, while on the other hand so many live in such poverty, deprived of the basic necessities, that one is hardly able even to count the victims of malnutrition.

7. The lack of equity and of a sense of solidarity in international transactions works to the advantage of the industrialized nations so that the gulf between the rich and the poor is ever widening. Hence derives the feeling of frustration among Third World countries and the accusations of exploitation and economic colonialism brought against the industrialized nations.

8. The memory of crimes of a certain type of colonialism and of its effects often aggravates these injuries and wounds.

9. The Apostolic See, in accord with the Second Vatican Council and together with the episcopal conferences, has not ceased to denounce the scandal involved in the gigantic arms race which, in addition to the threat which it poses to peace, squanders amounts of money so large that even a fraction of it would be sufficient to respond to the needs of those people who want for the basic essentials of life.

II. EXPRESSIONS OF THIS ASPIRATION

1. The yearning for justice and for the effective recognition of the dignity of every human being needs, like every deep aspiration, to be clarified and guided.

2. In effect, a discernment process is necessary which takes into account both the theoretical and the practical manifestations of this aspiration. For there are many political and social movements which present themselves as authentic spokesmen for the aspiration of the poor and claim to be able, though by recourse to violent means, to bring about the radical changes which will put an end to the oppression and misery of people.

3. So the aspiration for justice often finds itself the captive of ideologies which hide or pervert its meaning and which propose to people struggling for their liberation goals which are contrary to the true purpose of human life. They propose ways of action which imply the systematic recourse to violence, contrary to any ethic which is respectful of persons.

4. The interpretation of the signs of the times in the light of the Gospel requires, then, that we examine the meaning of this deep yearning of people for justice, but also that we study with critical discernment the theoretical and practical expressions which this aspiration has taken on.

III. LIBERATION, A CHRISTIAN THEME

1. Taken by itself, the desire for liberation finds a strong and fraternal echo in the heart and spirit of Christians.

2. Thus, in accord with this aspiration, the theological and pastoral movement known as "liberation theology" was born, first in the countries of Latin America, which are marked by the religious and cultural heritage of Christianity, and then in other countries of the Third World, as well as in certain circles in the industrialized countries.

3. The expression "theology of liberation" refers first of all to a special concern for the poor and the victims of oppression, which in turn begets a commitment to justice. Starting with this approach, we can distinguish several often contradictory ways of understanding the Christian meaning of poverty and the type of commitment to justice which it requires. As with all movements of ideas, the "theologies of liberation" present diverse theological positions. Their doctrinal frontiers are badly defined.

4. The aspiration for liberation, as the term suggests, repeats a theme which is fundamental to the Old and New Testaments. In itself, the expression "theology of liberation" is a thoroughly valid term: It designates a theological reflection centered on the biblical theme of liberation and freedom, and on the urgency of its practical realization.

The meeting, then, of the aspiration for liberation and the theologies of liberation is not one of mere chance. The significance of this encounter between the two can be understood only in light of the specific message of revelation, authentically interpreted by the magisterium of the church.[2]

IV. BIBLICAL FOUNDATIONS

1. Thus a theology of liberation correctly understood constitutes an invitation to theologians to deepen certain essential biblical themes with a concern for the grave and urgent questions which the contemporary yearning for liberation and those movements which more or less faithfully echo it pose for the church. We dare not forget for a single instant the situations of acute distress which issue such a dramatic call to theologians.

2. The radical experience of Christian liberty[3] is our first point of reference. Christ, our liberator, has freed us from sin and from slavery to the law and to the flesh, which is the mark of the condition of sinful mankind. Thus it is the new life of grace, fruit of justification, which makes us free. This means that the most radical form of slavery is slavery to sin. Other forms of slavery find their deepest root in slavery to sin. That is why freedom in the full Christian sense, characterized by the life in the Spirit, cannot be confused with a license to give in to the desires of the flesh. Freedom is a new life in love.

3. The "theologies of liberation" make wide use of readings from the Book of Exodus. The exodus, in fact, is the fundamental event in the formation of the chosen people. It represents freedom from foreign domination and from slavery. One will note that the specific significance of the event comes from its purpose, for this liberation is ordered to the foundation of the people of God and the covenant cult celebrated on Mt. Sinai.[4] That is why the liberation of the exodus cannot be reduced to a liberation which is principally or exclusively political in nature. Moreover, it is significant that the term freedom is often replaced in scripture by the very closely related term *redemption*.

4. The foundational episode of the Exodus will never be effaced from the memory of Israel. Reference is made to it when, after the destruction of Jerusalem and the exile to Babylon, the Jewish people lived in the hope of a new liberation and, beyond that, awaited a definitive liberation. In this experience God is recognized as the liberator. He will enter into a new covenant with his people. It will be marked by the gift of his Spirit and the conversion of hearts.[5]

5. The anxieties and multiple sufferings sustained by those who are faithful to the God of the covenant provide the theme of several Psalms: laments, appeals for help and thanksgivings all make mention of religious salvation and liberation. In this context, suffering is not purely and simply equated with the social condition of poverty or with the condition of the one who is undergoing political oppression. It also includes the hostility of one's enemies, injustice, failure and death. The Psalms call us back to an essential religious experience: It is from God alone that one can expect salvation and healing. God, and not man, has the power to change the situations of suffering. Thus the "poor of the Lord" live in a total and confident reliance upon the loving providence of God.[6] Moreover, throughout the whole crossing of the desert, the Lord did not fail to provide for the spiritual liberation and purification of his people.

6. In the Old Testament, the prophets after Amos keep affirming with particular vigor the requirements of justice and solidarity and the need to pronounce a very severe judgment on the rich who oppress the poor. They come to the defense of the widow and the orphan. They threaten the powerful: The accumulation of evils can only lead to terrible punishments.

Faithfulness to the covenant cannot be conceived of without the practice of justice. Justice as regards God and justice as regards mankind are inseparable. God is the defender and the liberator of the poor.

7. These requirements are found once again in the New Testament. They are even more radicalized as can be shown in the discourse on the Beatitudes. Conversion and renewal have to occur in the depths of the heart.

8. Already proclaimed in the Old Testament, the commandment of fraternal love extended to all mankind thus provides the supreme rule of social life.[7] There are no discriminations or limitations which can counter the recognition of everyone as neighbor.[8]

9. Poverty for the sake of the kingdom is praised. And in the figure of the poor, we are led to recognize the mysterious presence of the Son of Man, who became poor himself for love of us.[9] This is the foundation of the inexhaustible words of Jesus on the judgment in Matthew 25:31–46. Our Lord is one with all in distress; every distress is marked by his presence.

10. At the same time, the requirements of justice and mercy, already proclaimed in the Old Testament, are deepened to assume a new significance in the New Testament. Those who suffer or who are persecuted are identified with Christ.[10] The perfection that Jesus demands of his disciples (Mt. 5:18) consists in the obligation to be merciful "as your heavenly Father is merciful" (Lk. 6:36).

11. It is in light of the Christian vocation to fraternal love and mercy that the rich are severely reminded of their duty.[11] St. Paul, faced with the disorders of the church of Corinth, forcefully emphasizes the bond which exists between participation in the sacrament of love and sharing with the brother in need.[12]

12. New Testament revelation teaches us that sin is the greatest evil, since it strikes man in the heart of his personality. The first liberation, to which all others must make reference, is that from sin.

13. Unquestionably, it is to stress the radical character of the deliverance brought by Christ and offered to all, be they politically free or slaves, that the New Testament does not require some change in the political or social condition as a prerequisite for entrance into this freedom. However, the Letter to Philemon shows that the new freedom procured by the grace of Christ should necessarily have effects on the social level.

14. Consequently, the full ambit of sin, whose first effect is to introduce disorder into the relationship between God and man, cannot be restricted to "social sin." The truth is that only a correct doctrine of sin will permit us to insist on the gravity of its social effects.

15. Nor can one localize evil principally or uniquely in bad social, political or economic "structures" as though all other evils came from them so that the creation of the "new man" would depend on the establishment of different economic and socio-political structures. To be sure, there are structures which are evil and which cause evil and which we must have the courage to change. Structures, whether they are good or bad, are the result of man's actions and so are consequences more than causes. The root of evil, then, lies in free and responsible persons who have to be converted by the grace of Jesus Christ in order to live and act as new creatures in the love of neighbor and in the effective search for justice, self-control and the exercise of virtue.[13]

To demand first of all a radical revolution in social relations and then to criticize the search for personal perfection is to set out on a road which leads to the denial of the meaning of the person and his transcendence, and to destroy ethics and its foundation, which is the absolute character of the distinction between good and evil. Moreover, since charity is the principle of authentic perfection, that perfection cannot be conceived without an openness to others and a spirit of service.

V. THE VOICE OF THE MAGISTERIUM

1. In order to answer the challenge leveled at our times by oppression and hunger, the church's magisterium has frequently expressed her

desire to awaken Christian consciences to a sense of justice, social responsibility and solidarity with the poor and the oppressed, and to highlight the present urgency of the doctrine and imperatives contained in Revelation.

2. We would like to mention some of these interventions here: the papal documents *Mater et Magistra, Pacem in Terris, Populorum Progressio* and *Evangelii Nuntiandi.* We should likewise mention the letter to Cardinal Roy, *Octogesima Adveniens.*

3. The Second Vatican Council in turn confronted the questions of justice and liberty in the pastoral constitution *Gaudium et Spes.*

4. On a number of occasions the Holy Father has emphasized these themes, in particular in the encyclicals *Redemptor Hominis, Dives in Misericordia* and *Laborem Exercens.* These numerous addresses recall the doctrine of the rights of man and touch directly on the problems of the liberation of the human person in the face of the diverse kinds of oppression of which he is the victim. It is especially important to mention in this connection the address given before the 26th General Assembly of the United Nations in New York, Oct. 2, 1979.[14] On Jan. 28 of that same year, while opening the Third Conference of CELAM in Puebla, John Paul II affirmed that the complete truth about man is the basis for any real liberation.[15] This text is a document which bears directly upon the theology of liberation.

5. Twice the Synod of Bishops treated subjects which are directly related to a Christian conception of liberation: in 1971, justice in the world, and in 1974, the relationship between freedom from oppression and full freedom, or the salvation of mankind. The work of the synods of 1971 and 1974 led Paul VI in his apostolic exhortation *Evangelii Nuntiandi* to clarify the connection between evangelization and human liberation or advancement.[16]

6. The concern of the church for liberation and for human advancement was also expressed in the establishment of the Pontifical Commission Justice and Peace.

7. Numerous national episcopal conferences have joined the Holy See in recalling the urgency of authentic human liberation and the routes by which to achieve it. In this context, special mention should be made of the documents of the general conferences of the Latin American episcopate at Medellin in 1968 and at Puebla in 1979.

Paul VI was present at the Medellin conference and John Paul II was at Puebla. Both dealt with the themes of conversion and liberation.

8. Following Paul VI, who had insisted on the distinctive character of the gospel message,[17] a character which is of divine origin, John Paul II, in his address at Puebla, recalled the three pillars upon which any

authentic theology of liberation will rest: truth about Jesus Christ, truth about the church and truth about mankind.[18]

VI. A NEW INTERPRETATION OF CHRISTIANITY

1. It is impossible to overlook the immense amount of selfless work done by Christians, pastors, priests, religious or laypersons, who, driven by a love for their brothers and sisters living in inhuman conditions, have endeavored to bring help and comfort to countless people in the distress brought about by poverty. Among these, some have tried to find the most effective means to put a quick end to the intolerable situation.

2. The zeal and the compassion which should dwell in the hearts of all pastors nevertheless run the risk of being led astray and diverted to works which are just as damaging to man and his dignity as is the poverty which is being fought, if one is not sufficiently attentive to certain temptations.

3. The feeling of anguish at the urgency of the problems cannot make us lose sight of what is essential nor forget the reply of Jesus to the Tempter: "It is not on bread alone that man lives, but on every word that comes from the mouth of God" (Mt. 4:4; cf. Dt. 8:3).

Faced with the urgency of sharing bread, some are tempted to put evangelization into parentheses, as it were, and postpone it until tomorrow: first the bread, then the word of the Lord. It is a fatal error to separate these two and even worse to oppose the one to the other. In fact, the Christian perspective naturally shows they have a great deal to do with one another.[19]

4. To some it even seems that the necessary struggle for human justice and freedom in the economic and political sense constitutes the whole essence of salvation. For them, the Gospel is reduced to a purely earthly gospel.

5. The different theologies of liberation are situated between the preferential option for the poor forcefully reaffirmed without ambiguity after Medellin at the conference of Puebla[20] on the one hand, and the temptation to reduce the Gospel to an earthly gospel on the other.

6. We should recall that the preferential option described at Puebla is twofold: for the poor and for the young.[21] It is significant that the option for the young has in general been passed over in total silence.

7. We noted above (cf. 3) that an authentic theology of liberation will be one which is rooted in the word of God, correctly interpreted.

8. But from a descriptive standpoint, it helps to speak of theologies of liberation, since the expression embraces a number of theological

positions or even sometimes ideological ones, which are not simply different but more often incompatible with one another.

9. In this present document, we will only be discussing developments of that current of thought which, under the name "theology of liberation," proposes a novel interpretation of both the content of faith and of Christian existence which seriously departs from the faith of the church and, in fact, actually constitutes a practical negation.

10. Concepts uncritically borrowed from Marxist ideology and recourse to theses of a biblical hermeneutic marked by rationalism are at the basis of the new interpretation which is corrupting whatever was authentic in the general initial commitment on behalf of the poor.

VII. MARXIST ANALYSIS

1. Impatience and a desire for results has led certain Christians, despairing of every other method, to turn to what they call "Marxist analysis."

2. Their reasoning is this: An intolerable and explosive situation requires effective action which cannot be put off. Effective action presupposes a scientific analysis of the structural causes of poverty. Marxism now provides us with the means to make such an analysis, they say. Then one simply has to apply the analysis to the Third-World situation, especially in Latin America.

3. It is clear that scientific knowledge of the situation and of the possible strategies for the transformation of society is a presupposition for any plan capable of attaining the ends proposed. It is also a proof of the seriousness of the effort.

4. But the term *scientific* exerts an almost mythical fascination even though everything called "scientific" is not necessarily scientific at all. That is why the borrowing of a method of approach to reality should be preceded by a careful epistemological critique. This preliminary critical study is missing from more than one "theology of liberation."

5. In the human and social sciences it is well to be aware above all of the plurality of methods and viewpoints, each of which reveals only one aspect of reality, which is so complex that it defies simple and univocal explanation.

6. In the case of Marxism, in the particular sense given to it in this context, a preliminary critique is all the more necessary since the thought of Marx is such a global vision of reality that all data received from observation and analysis are brought together in a philosophical and ideological structure, which predetermines the significance and importance to be attached to them. The ideological principles come

prior to the study of the social reality and are presupposed in it. Thus no separation of the parts of this epistemologically unique complex is possible. If one tries to take only one part, say, the analysis, one ends up having to accept the entire ideology. That is why it is not uncommon for the ideological aspect to be predominant among the things which the "theologians of liberation" borrow from Marxist authors.

7. The warning of Paul VI remains fully valid today: Marxism as it is actually lived out poses many distinct aspects and questions for Christians to reflect upon and act on. However, it would be "illusory and dangerous to ignore the intimate bond which radically unites them, and to accept elements of the Marxist analysis without recognizing its connections with the ideology, or to enter into the practice of class struggle and of its Marxist interpretation while failing to see the kind of totalitarian society to which this process slowly leads."[22]

8. It is true that Marxist thought ever since its origins, and even more so lately, has become divided and has given birth to various currents which diverge significantly from one another. To the extent that they remain fully Marxist, these currents continue to be based on certain fundamental tenets which are not compatible with the Christian conception of humanity and society. In this context certain formulas are not neutral, but keep the meaning they had in the original Marxist doctrine. This is the case with the "class struggle." This expression remains pregnant with the interpretation that Marx gave it, so it cannot be taken as the equivalent of "severe social conflict," in an empirical sense. Those who use similar formulas, while claiming to keep only certain elements of the Marxist analysis and yet to reject this analysis taken as a whole, maintain at the very least a serious confusion in the minds of their readers.

9. Let us recall the fact that atheism and the denial of the human person, his liberty and his rights, are at the core of Marxist theory. This theory, then, contains errors which directly threaten the truths of the faith regarding the eternal destiny of individual persons. Moreover, to attempt to integrate into theology an analysis whose criterion of interpretation depends on this atheistic conception is to involve oneself in terrible contradictions. What is more, this misunderstanding of the spiritual nature of the person leads to a total subordination of the person to the collectivity and thus to the denial of the principles of a social and political life which is in keeping with human dignity.

10. A critical examination of the analytical methods borrowed from other disciplines must be carried out in a special way by theologians. It is the light of faith which provides theology with its principles. That is why the use of philosophical positions or of human sciences by the the-

ologian has a value which might be called instrumental, but yet must undergo a critical study from a theological perspective. In other words, the ultimate and decisive criterion for truth can only be a criterion which is itself theological. It is only in the light of faith and what faith teaches us about the truth of man and the ultimate meaning of his destiny, that one can judge the validity or degree of validity of what other disciplines propose, often rather conjecturally, as being the truth about man, his history and his destiny.

11. When modes of interpretation are applied to the economic, social and political reality of today, which are themselves borrowed from Marxist thought, they can give the initial impression of a certain plausibility to the degree that the present-day situation in certain countries is similar to what Marx described and interpreted in the middle of the last century. On the basis of these similarities, certain simplifications are made which, abstracting from specific essential factors, prevent any really rigorous examination of the causes of poverty and prolong the confusion.

12. In certain parts of Latin America the seizure of the vast majority of the wealth by an oligarchy of owners bereft of social consciousness, the practical absence or the shortcomings of a rule of law, military dictators making a mockery of elementary human rights, the corruption of certain powerful officials, the savage practices of some foreign capital interests constitute factors which nourish a passion for revolt among those who thus consider themselves the powerless victims of a new colonialism in the technological, financial, monetary or economic order. The recognition of injustice is accompanied by a pathos which borrows its language from Marxism, wrongly presented as though it were scientific language.

13. The first condition for any analysis is total openness to the reality to be described. That is why a critical consciousness has to accompany the use of any working hypotheses that are being adopted. One has to realize that these hypotheses correspond to a particular viewpoint which will inevitably highlight certain aspects of the reality while leaving others in the shade. This limitation, which derives from the nature of human science, is ignored by those who, under the guise of hypotheses recognized as such, have recourse to such an all-embracing conception of reality as the thought of Karl Marx.

VIII. SUBVERSION OF THE MEANING OF TRUTH AND VIOLENCE

1. This all-embracing conception thus imposes its logic and leads the "theologies of liberation" to accept a series of positions which are

incompatible with the Christian vision of humanity. In fact, the ideological core borrowed from Marxism which we are referring to exercises the function of a determining principle. It has this role in virtue of its being described as "scientific," that is to say, true of necessity.

In this core we can distinguish several components.

2. According to the logic of Marxist thought, the "analysis" is inseparable from the praxis and from the conception of history to which this praxis is linked. The analysis is for the Marxist an instrument of criticism, and criticism is only one stage in the revolutionary struggle. This struggle is that of the proletarian class, invested with its mission in history.

3. Consequently, for the Marxist, only those who engage in the struggle can work out the analysis correctly.

4. The only true consciousness, then, is the partisan consciousness.

It is clear that the concept of truth itself is in question here, and it is totally subverted: There is no truth, they pretend, except in and through the partisan praxis.

5. For the Marxist, the praxis and the truth that comes from it are partisan praxis and truth because the fundamental structure of history is characterized by class struggle. There follows, then, the objective necessity to enter into the class struggle, which is the dialectical opposite of the relationship of exploitation, which is being condemned. For the Marxist, the truth is a truth of class: There is no truth but the truth in the struggle of the revolutionary class.

6. The fundamental law of history, which is the law of the class struggle, implies that society is founded on violence. To the violence which constitutes the relationship of the domination of the rich over the poor, there corresponds the counterviolence of the revolution, by means of which this domination will be reversed.

7. The class struggle is presented as an objective, necessary law. Upon entering this process on behalf of the oppressed, one "makes" truth, one acts "scientifically." Consequently, the conception of the truth goes hand in hand with the affirmation of necessary violence, and so, of a political amorality. Within this perspective, any reference to ethical requirements calling for courageous and radical institutional and structural reforms makes no sense.

8. The fundamental law of class struggle has a global and universal character. It is reflected in all the spheres of existence: religious, ethical, cultural and institutional. As far as this law is concerned, one of these spheres is autonomous. In each of them this law constitutes the determining element.

9. In particular, the very nature of ethics is radically called into question because of the borrowing of these theses from Marxism. In fact, it is the transcendent character of the distinction between good and evil, the principle of morality, which is implicitly denied in the perspective of the class struggle.

IX. THE THEOLOGICAL APPLICATION OF THIS CORE

1. The positions here in question are often brought out explicitly in certain of the writings of "theologians of liberation." In others, they follow logically from their premises. In addition, they are presupposed in certain liturgical practices, as for example a "eucharist" transformed into a celebration of the people in struggle, even though the persons who participate in these practices may not be fully conscious of it. We are facing, therefore, a real system, even if some hesitate to follow the logic to its conclusion. As such, this system is a perversion of the Christian message as God entrusted it to his church. This message in its entirety finds itself then called into question by the "theologies of liberation."

2. It is not the fact of social stratification with all its inequity and injustice, but the theory of class struggle as the fundamental law of history which has been accepted by these "theologies of liberation" as a principle. The conclusion is drawn that the class struggle thus understood divides the church herself, and that in light of this struggle even ecclesial realities must be judged.

The claim is even made that it would maintain an illusion with bad faith to propose that love in its universality can conquer what is the primary structural law of capitalism.

3. According to this conception, the class struggle is the driving force of history. History thus becomes a central notion. It will be affirmed that God himself makes history. It will be added that there is only one history, one in which the distinction between the history of salvation and profane history is no longer necessary. To maintain the distinction would be to fall into "dualism." Affirmations such as these reflect historicist immanentism. Thus there is a tendency to identify the kingdom of God and its growth with the human liberation movement and to make history itself the subject of its own development, as a process of the self-redemption of man by means of the class struggle.

This identification is in opposition to the faith of the church as it has been reaffirmed by the Second Vatican Council.[23]

4. Along these lines, some go so far as to identify God himself with history and to define faith as "fidelity to history," which means adhering

to a political policy which is suited to the growth of humanity, conceived of as a purely temporal messianism.

5. As a consequence, faith, hope and charity are given a new content: They become "fidelity to history," "confidence in the future" and "option for the poor." This is tantamount to saying they have been emptied of their theological reality.

6. A radical politicization of faith's affirmations and of theological judgments follows inevitably from this new conception. The question no longer has to do with simply drawing attention to the consequences and political implications of the truths of faith, which are respected beforehand for their transcendent value. In this new system every affirmation of faith or of theology is subordinated to a political criterion which in turn depends on the class struggle, the driving force of history.

7. As a result, participation in the class struggle is presented as a requirement of charity itself. The desire to love everyone here and now, despite his class, and to go out to meet him with the non-violent means of dialogue and persuasion, is denounced as counterproductive and opposed to love.

If one holds that a person should not be the object of hate, it is claimed nevertheless that if he belongs to the objective class of the rich he is primarily a class enemy to be fought. Thus the universality of love of neighbor and brotherhood become an eschatological principle, which will only have meaning for the "new man" who arises out of the victorious revolution.

8. As far as the church is concerned, this system would see her only as a reality interior to history, herself subject to those laws which are supposed to govern the development of history in its immanence. The church, the gift of God and mystery of faith, is emptied of any specific reality by this reductionism. At the same time it is disputed that the participation of Christians who belong to opposing classes at the same eucharistic table still makes any sense.

9. In its positive meaning the "church of the poor" signifies the preference given to the poor, without exclusion, whatever the form of their poverty, because they are preferred by God. The expression also refers to the church of our time, as communion and institution and on the part of her members, becoming more fully conscious of the requirement of evangelical poverty.

10. But the "theologies of liberation," which deserve credit for restoring to a place of honor the great texts of the prophets and of the Gospel in defense of the poor, go on to a disastrous confusion between the poor of the scripture and the proletariat of Marx. In this way they pervert the Christian meaning of the poor, and they transform the fight

for the rights of the poor into a class fight within the ideological perspective of the class struggle. For them, the "church of the poor" signifies the church of the class which has become aware of the requirements of the revolutionary struggle as a step toward liberation and which celebrates this liberation in its liturgy.

11. A further remark regarding the expression "church of the people" will not be out of place here. From the pastoral point of view, this expression might mean the favored recipients of evangelization to whom, because of their condition, the church extends her pastoral love first of all. One might also refer to the church as people of God, that is, people of the new covenant established in Christ.[24]

12. But the "theologies of liberation" of which we are speaking mean by church of the people a church of the class, a church of the oppressed people whom it is necessary to "conscientize" in the light of the organized struggle for freedom. For some, the people, thus understood, even become the object of faith.

13. Building on such a conception of the church of the people, a critique of the very structures of the church is developed. It is not simply the case of fraternal correction of pastors of the church whose behavior does not reflect the evangelical spirit of service and is linked to old-fashioned signs of authority which scandalize the poor. It has to do with a challenge to the sacramental and hierarchical structure of the church, which was willed by the Lord himself. There is a denunciation of members of the hierarchy and the magisterium as objective representatives of the ruling class which has to be opposed. Theologically, this position means that ministers take their origin from the people, who therefore designate ministers of their own choice in accord with the needs of their historic revolutionary mission.

X. A NEW HERMENEUTIC

1. The partisan conception of truth, which can be seen in the revolutionary praxis of the class, corroborates this position. Theologians who do not share the theses of the "theology of liberation," the hierarchy and especially the Roman magisterium are thus discredited in advance as belonging to the class of the oppressors. Their theology is a theology of class. Arguments and teachings thus do not have to be examined in themselves since they are only reflections of class interests. Thus the instruction of others is decreed to be, in principle, false.

2. Here is where the global and all-embracing character of the theology of liberation appears. As a result, it must be criticized not just on the basis of this or that affirmation, but on the basis of its classist view-

point, which it has adopted *a priori* and which has come to function in it as a determining principle.

3. Because of this classist presupposition, it becomes very difficult, not to say impossible, to engage in a real dialogue with some "theologians of liberation" in such a way that the other participant is listened to and his arguments are discussed with objectivity and attention. For these theologians start out with the idea, more or less consciously, that the viewpoint of the oppressed and revolutionary class, which is their own, is the single true point of view. Theological criteria for truth are thus relativized and subordinated to the imperatives of the class struggle. In this perspective, orthodoxy, or the right rule of faith, is substituted by the notion of orthopraxy as the criterion of the truth. In this connection it is important not to confuse practical orientation, which is proper to traditional theology in the same way that speculative orientation is, with the recognized and privileged priority given to a certain type of praxis. For them, this praxis is the revolutionary praxis, which thus becomes the supreme criterion for theological truth. A healthy theological method no doubt will always take the praxis of the church into account and will find there one of its foundations, but that is because that praxis comes from the faith and is a lived expression of it.

4. For the "theologies of liberation" however, the social doctrine of the church is rejected with disdain. It is said that it comes from the illusion of a possible compromise, typical of the middle class, which has no historic destiny.

5. The new hermeneutic inherent in the "theologies of liberation" leads to an essentially political rereading of the scriptures. Thus a major importance is given to the exodus event inasmuch as it is a liberation from political servitude. Likewise, a political reading of the Magnificat is proposed. The mistake here is not in bringing attention to a political dimension of the readings of scripture, but in making of this one dimension the principal or exclusive component. This leads to a reductionist reading of the Bible.

6. Likewise, one places oneself within the perspective of a temporal messianism, which is one of the most radical of the expressions of secularization of the kingdom of God and of its absorption into the immanence of human history.

7. In giving such priority to the political dimension, one is led to deny the radical newness of the New Testament and above all to misunderstand the person of our Lord Jesus Christ, true God and true man, and thus the specific character of the salvation he gave us, that is above all liberation from sin, which is the source of all evils.

8. Moreover in setting aside the authoritative interpretation of the church, denounced as classist, one is at the same time departing from tradition. In that way one is robbed of an essential theological criterion of interpretation and, in the vacuum thus created, one welcomes the most radical theses of rationalist exegesis. Without a critical eye, one returns to the opposition of the "Jesus of history" vs. the "Jesus of faith."

9. Of course the creeds of the faith are literally preserved, especially the Chalcedonian creed, but a new meaning is given to them which is a negation of the faith of the church. On one hand, the Christological doctrine of tradition is rejected in the name of class; on the other hand, one claims to meet again the "Jesus of history" coming from the revolutionary experience of the struggle of the poor for their liberation.

10. One claims to be reliving an experience similar to that of Jesus. The experience of the poor struggling for their liberation, which was Jesus' experience, would thus reveal, and it alone, the knowledge of the true God and of the kingdom.

11. Faith in the incarnate word, dead and risen for all men, and whom "God made Lord and Christ"[25] is denied. In its place is substituted a figure of Jesus who is a kind of symbol who sums up in himself the requirements of the struggle of the oppressed.

12. An exclusively political interpretation is thus given to the death of Christ. In this way its value for salvation and the whole economy of redemption is denied.

13. This new interpretation thus touches the whole of the Christian mystery.

14. In a general way this brings about what can be called an inversion of symbols. Thus instead of seeing, with St. Paul, a figure of baptism in the exodus,[26] some end up making of it a symbol of the political liberation of the people.

15. When the same hermeneutical criterion is applied to the life and to the hierarchical constitution of the church, the relationship between the hierarchy and the "base" becomes the relationship of obedient domination to the law of the struggle of the classes. Sacramentality, which is at the root of the ecclesial ministries and which makes of the church a spiritual reality which cannot be reduced to a purely sociological analysis, is quite simply ignored.

16. This inversion of symbols is likewise verified in the area of the sacraments. The eucharist is no longer to be understood as the real sacramental presence of the reconciling sacrifice and as the gift of the body and blood of Christ. It becomes a celebration of the people in their struggle. As a consequence, the unity of the church is radically denied.

Unity, reconciliation and communion in love are no longer seen as a gift we receive from Christ.[27] It is the historical class of the poor who by means of their struggle will build unity. For them, the struggle of the classes is the way to unity. The eucharist thus becomes the eucharist of the class. At the same time they deny the triumphant force of the love of God which has been given to us.

XI. ORIENTATIONS

1. The warning against the serious deviations of some "theologies of liberation" must not at all be taken as some kind of approval, even indirect, of those who keep the poor in misery, who profit from that misery, who notice it while doing nothing about it or who remain indifferent to it. The church, guided by the Gospel of mercy and by the love for mankind, hears the cry for justice[28] and intends to respond to it with all her might.

2. Thus a great call goes out to all the church: With boldness and courage, with farsightedness and prudence, with zeal and strength of spirit, with a love for the poor which demands sacrifice, pastors will consider the response to this call a matter of the highest priority, as many already do.

3. All priests, religious and lay people who hear this call for justice and who want to work for evangelization and the advancement of mankind will do so in communion with their bishop and with the church, each in accord with his or her own specific ecclesial vocation.

4. Aware of the ecclesial character of their vocation, theologians will collaborate loyally and with a spirit of dialogue with the magisterium of the church. They will be able to recognize in the magisterium a gift of Christ to his church[29] and will welcome its word and its directives with filial respect.

5. It is only when one begins with the task of evangelization understood in its entirety that the authentic requirements of human progress and liberation are appreciated. This liberation has as its indispensable pillars: the truth about Jesus the savior, the truth about the church and the truth about man and his dignity.[30]

It is in light of the Beatitudes, and especially the Beatitude of the poor of heart, that the church, which wants to be the church of the poor throughout the world, intends to come to the aid of the noble struggle for truth and justice. She addresses each person, and for that reason, every person. She is the "universal church. The church of the incarnation. She is not the church of one class or another. And she speaks in the name of truth itself. This truth is realistic." It leads to a recognition "of every human reality, every injustice, every tension and every struggle."[31]

6. An effective defense of justice needs to be based on the truth of mankind, created in the image of God and called to the grace of divine sonship. The recognition of the true relationship of human beings to God constitutes the foundation of justice to the extent that it rules the relationships between people. That is why the fight for the rights of man, which the church does not cease to reaffirm, constitutes the authentic fight for justice.

7. The truth of mankind requires that this battle be fought in ways consistent with human dignity. That is why the systematic and deliberate recourse to blind violence, no matter from which side it comes, must be condemned.[32] To put one's trust in violent means in the hope of restoring more justice is to become the victim of a fatal illusion: Violence begets violence and degrades man. It mocks the dignity of man in the person of the victims, and it debases that same dignity among those who practice it.

8. The acute need for radical reforms of the structures which conceal poverty and which are themselves forms of violence should not let us lose sight of the fact that the source of injustice is in the hearts of men. Therefore it is only by making an appeal to the moral potential of the person and to the constant need for interior conversion that social change will be brought about which will truly be in the service of man.[33] For it will only be in the measure that they collaborate freely in these necessary changes through their own initiative and in solidarity, that people, awakened to a sense of their responsibility, will grow in humanity.

The inversion of morality and structures is steeped in a materialist anthropology which is incompatible with the dignity of mankind.

9. It is therefore an equally fatal illusion to believe that these new structures will of themselves give birth to a "new man" in the sense of the truth of man. The Christian cannot forget that it is only the Holy Spirit, who has been given to us, who is the source of every true renewal and that God is the Lord of history.

10. By the same token, the overthrow by means of revolutionary violence of structures which generate violence is not *ipso facto* the beginning of a just regime. A major fact of our time ought to evoke the reflection of all those who would sincerely work for the true liberation of their brothers: Millions of our own contemporaries legitimately yearn to recover those basic freedoms of which they were deprived by totalitarian and atheistic regimes which came to power by violent and revolutionary means, precisely in the name of the liberation of the people.

This shame of our time cannot be ignored: While claiming to bring them freedom, these regimes keep whole nations in conditions of servitude which are unworthy of mankind. Those who, perhaps inadvertently, make themselves accomplices of similar enslavements betray the very poor they mean to help.

11. The class struggle as a road toward a classless society is a myth which slows reform and aggravates poverty and injustice. Those who allow themselves to be caught up in fascination with this myth should reflect on the bitter examples history has to offer about where it leads. They would then understand that we are not talking here about abandoning an effective means of struggle on behalf of the poor for an ideal which has no practical effects. On the contrary, we are talking about freeing oneself from a delusion in order to base oneself squarely on the Gospel and its power of realization.

12. One of the conditions for necessary theological correction is giving proper value to the social teaching of the church. This teaching is by no means closed. It is, on the contrary, open to all the new questions which are so numerous today. In this perspective, the contribution of theologians and other thinkers in all parts of the world to the reflection of the church is indispensable today.

13. Likewise the experience of those who work directly for evangelization and for the advancement of the poor and the oppressed is necessary for the doctrinal and pastoral reflection of the church. In this sense it is necessary to affirm that one becomes more aware of certain aspects of truth by starting with praxis, if by that one means pastoral praxis and social work which keeps its evangelical inspiration.

14. The teaching of the church on social issues indicates the main lines of ethical orientation. But in order that it be able to guide action directly, the church needs competent people from a scientific and technological viewpoint, as well as in the human and political sciences. Pastors should be attentive to the formation of persons of such capability who live the Gospel deeply. Lay persons, whose proper mission is to build society, are involved here to the highest degree.

15. Theses of the "theologies of liberation" are widely popularized under a simplified form in formation sessions or in what are called "base groups" which lack the necessary catechetical and theological preparation as well as the capacity for discernment. Thus these theses are accepted by generous men and women without any critical judgment being made.

16. That is why pastors must look after the quality and the content of catechesis and formation, which should always present the whole mes-

sage of salvation and the imperatives of true liberation within the framework of this whole message.

17. In this full presentation of Christianity, it is proper to emphasize those essential aspects which the "theologies of liberation" especially tend to misunderstand or to eliminate, namely: the transcendence and gratuity of liberation in Jesus Christ, true God and true man; the sovereignty of grace; and the true nature of the means of salvation, especially of the church and the sacraments. One should also keep in mind the true meaning of ethics, in which the distinction between good and evil is not relativized, the real meaning of sin, the necessity for conversion and the universality of the law of fraternal love.

One needs to be on guard against the politicization of existence, which, misunderstanding the entire meaning of the kingdom of God and the transcendence of the person, begins to sacralize politics and betray the religion of the people in favor of the projects of the revolution.

18. The defenders of orthodoxy are sometimes accused of passivity, indulgence or culpable complicity regarding the intolerable situations of injustice and the political regimes which prolong them. Spiritual conversion, the intensity of the love of God and neighbor, zeal for justice and peace, the gospel meaning of the poor and of poverty, are required of everyone and especially of pastors and those in positions of responsibility. The concern for the purity of the faith demands giving the answer of effective witness in the service of one's neighbor, the poor and the oppressed in particular, in an integral theological fashion. By the witness of their dynamic and constructive power to love, Christians will thus lay the foundations of this "civilization of love" of which the conference of Puebla spoke, following Paul VI.[34] Moreover there are already many priests, religious and lay people who are consecrated in a truly evangelical way for the creation of a just society.

CONCLUSION

The words of Paul VI in his "Profession of Faith," express with full clarity the faith of the church, from which one cannot deviate without provoking, besides spiritual disaster, new miseries and new types of slavery.

"We profess our faith that the kingdom of God, begun here below in the church of Christ, is not of this world, whose form is passing away, and that its own growth cannot be confused with the progress of civilization, of science, of human technology, but that it consists in knowing ever more deeply the unfathomable riches of Christ, to hope ever more strongly in things eternal, to respond ever more ardently to the love of

God, to spread ever more widely grace and holiness among men. But it is this very same love which makes the church constantly concerned for the true temporal good of mankind as well. Never ceasing to recall to her children that they have no lasting dwelling here on earth, she urges them also to contribute, each according to his own vocation and means, to the welfare of their earthly city, to promote justice, peace and brotherhood among men, to lavish their assistance on their brothers, especially on the poor and the most dispirited. The intense concern of the church, the bride of Christ, for the needs of mankind, their joys and their hopes, their pains and their struggles, is nothing other than the great desire to be present to them in order to enlighten them with the light of Christ and join them all to him, their only Savior. It can never mean that the church is conforming to the things of this world nor that she is lessening the earnestness with which she awaits her Lord and the eternal kingdom."[35]

This instruction was adopted at an ordinary meeting of the Sacred Congregation for the Doctrine of the Faith and was approved at an audience granted to the undersigned cardinal prefect by His Holiness Pope John Paul II, who ordered its publication.

Given at Rome, at the Sacred Congregation for the Doctrine of the Faith, Aug. 6, 1984, the feast of the Transfiguration of Our Lord.

Cardinal Joseph Ratzinger
Prefect

Archbishop Alberto Bovone
Secretary

NOTES

PREFACE

1. Other examples of such a work are Walter Rauschenbusch's *A Theology for the Social Gospel* (New York/Nashville: Abingdon Press, 1945) which, growing out of four lectures he gave at Yale in 1917, views the whole of Christian faith from the point of view of a contemporary interpretation of the Kingdom of God; or Gregory Baum's *Man Becoming: God in Secular Language* (New York: Herder and Herder, 1970) which reinterprets the doctrines of Christian faith from the point of view of the shift, mediated by Blondel in Roman Catholicism, to human experience as the place where these doctrines find meaning; or Langdon Gilkey's *Message and Existence: An Introduction to Christian Theology* (New York: The Seabury Press, 1979) in which this same concern for human experience as a mediator of meaning is combined with a skillful and perceptive application of Tillich's method of correlation to deliver a reinterpretation of the basic doctrines of the creed.

INTRODUCTION

1. "Faith," writes William Lynch, "has a similar (to that of expectation, hypothesis or theory in perceiving data) relationship to the world; it provides a structure or a context. It is a way of experiencing and imagining the world; or it is a world within which we experience or imagine. It composes it or, if you will, it recomposes the world according to its terms." William F. Lynch, *Images of Faith: An Exploration of the Ironic Imagination* (Notre Dame: University of Notre Dame Press, 1973), p. 17.

2. As Tillich and Rahner have aptly expressed it, human existence is spirit in matter and in the world which is structured by an ontological polarity of freedom and destiny, or nature and "person," so that the limiting structures of spiritual knowing and willing are also the platform for freedom and self-transcendence. See Karl Rahner, "The Theological Concept of Concupiscentia," *Theological Investigations,* I (Baltimore: Helicon Press, 1961), pp. 347–

382, esp. pp. 359–366, and Paul Tillich, *Systematic Theology,* I (Chicago: University of Chicago Press, 1967), pp. 198–201; II, p. 42.

3. At this point, however, it is important to distinguish the substantive and the existential meanings of the term "freedom." In its basic substantive sense freedom may exist without any apparent manifestation of its exercise, as in the case of a comatose individual. Thus it is still useful to speak of the human spirit.

4. Thus in Schleiermacher's phenomenological analysis of human existence self-consciousness is always simultaneously world-consciousness and God-consciousness, because human freedom stands in this triple relationship. Cf. Friedrich Schleiermacher, *The Christian Faith,* I (New York: Harper Torchbooks, 1963), #30, pp. 125–126. It seems to me that this fundamental structure of human freedom or consciousness is picked up by David Tracy where it serves as the intrinsic basis for his differentiation of three distinct subdisciplines in the one theological enterprise. See David Tracy, *The Analogical Imagination: Christian Theology and the Culture of Pluralism* (New York: Crossroad, 1981), pp. 55–56, 85 n. 29. Cf. also Peter C. Hodgson, *New Birth of Freedom: A Theology of Bondage and Liberation* (Philadelphia: Fortress Press, 1976), pp. 114–165.

5. The idea of a method of correlation is common property today and is employed in one form or another by all theologians, other than fundamentalists, even when they seem to be reacting against it. For a variety of accounts of this elementary structure of theological reflection see Paul Tillich, *Systematic Theology,* I, pp. 59–66; Langdon Gilkey, *Naming the Whirlwind: The Renewal of God-Language* (Indianapolis and New York: The Bobbs-Merrill Co., 1969), pp. 415–470; Schubert Ogden, "What Is Theology?" *Journal of Religion* 52 (1972), 22–40; David Tracy, *Blessed Rage for Order: The New Pluralism in Theology* (New York: Seabury Press, 1975), pp. 3–21, 43–87; Hans Küng, "Toward a New Consensus in Catholic (and Ecumenical) Theology," *Consensus in Theology?* ed. by Leonard Swidler (Philadelphia: The Westminster Press, 1980), pp. 1–17; Edward Farley, *Theologia: The Fragmentation and Unity of Theological Education* (Philadelphia: Fortress Press, 1983), pp. 151–173.

6. Bultmann has succinctly summarized this law of interpretation: "This is, then, the basic presupposition for every form of exegesis: that your own relation to the subject-matter prompts the question you bring to the text and elicits the answers you obtain from the text." Rudolf Bultmann, *Jesus Christ and Mythology* (New York: Charles Scribner's Sons, 1958), p. 51.

7. As far as I can see it is impossible to *prove* either that this or any other area or dimension of human existence is attacked by a radical crisis that is central and all-encompassing. One can point to the data that feed such a common experience; one can describe the experience itself and at best make an intuitive generalization. But at this level of generalized analysis there is no demonstration beyond the appeal to experience itself. As an external support for such an appeal, however, one can point to more and more theologians, beyond political and liberation theologians, who are gradually coming to rec-

ognize the social existential dilemma that faces our common human existence as a race. The crisis concerns the meaningfulness of precisely our common history.

8. For the theory of symbol of Tillich see Paul Tillich, *Systematic Theology*, I, pp. 238–247; "Theology and Symbolism," *Religious Symbolism*, ed. by F. Ernest Johnson (New York: Harper & Brothers, 1955), pp. 107–116; *Dynamics of Faith* (New York: Harper & Row, 1957), pp. 41–54; "The Religious Symbol," *Myth and Symbol*, ed. by F. W. Dillistone (London: S.P.C.K., 1966), pp. 15–34. Although expressed in more objective ontological categories, Karl Rahner's theory of religious symbols is structurally similar to Tillich's. See Karl Rahner, "The Theology of Symbol," *Theological Investigations*, IV (Baltimore: Helicon Press, 1966), pp. 221–252.

9. See John E. Smith, *Experience and God* (New York: Oxford University Press, 1968), pp. 68–98, where he discusses the epistemology and structure of symbol in the context of revelation and knowledge of God and applies this to the case of Jesus Christ.

10. The following confession of faith of Edward Schillebeeckx illustrates the structure of Christian faith and the role of Jesus in it as the symbol and objective focus for that faith: "I can understand Jesus only as one who in his human form brings us an understanding of God which is salvation, which brings liberation to men and women. In Christ we are given an answer to the question of God, and at the same time an answer to humankind's quest for salvation." Edward Schillebeeckx in his preface to John Bowden, *Edward Schillebeeckx: Portrait of a Theologian* (London: SCM Press, 1983), p. x.

11. Such an apologetic approach to both the meaning and reality of God is of course essential for the modern period. For a sound statement of this need and a method of going about it, one which combines the insights of several theological traditions, see David Tracy, *Blessed Rage for Order: The New Pluralism in Theology* (New York: The Seabury Press, 1975).

I. THE SUPPOSITIONS OF LIBERATION THEOLOGY

1. For a study of the analogous similarities and differences between liberation theology and the social gospel movement through a comparative analysis of Gustavo Gutiérrez and Walter Rauschenbusch, see T. Howland Sanks, "Liberation Theology and the Social Gospel: Variations on a Theme," *Theological Studies*, 41 (December 1980), 668–682. A good overview of the themes of liberation theology in Latin America is found in José Miguez-Bonino, *Doing Theology in a Revolutionary Situation* (Philadelphia: Fortress Press, 1975).

2. This experience of and concern for the poor is a leading theme throughout Gustavo Gutiérrez' *A Theology of Liberation: History, Politics and Salvation*, trans. and ed. by Caridad Inda and John Eagleson, (Maryknoll, N.Y.: Orbis Books, 1973) which comes to a climax in the last chapter, "Poverty: Solidarity and Protest," pp. 287–306. And in Gutiérrez' writings after this book, a representation of which are found in his *La Fuerza Histórica de los Pobres: Selección de Trabajos* (Lima: Centro de Estudios y Publicaciónes, 1979), this

experience becomes even more explicitly the primary methodological focus in his theology. Finally, in 1979 the Catholic Church as a whole in Latin America, through its episcopal conference, expressed its "preferential option for the poor." *Puebla: III Conferencia General del Episcopado Latino-americano* (Lima: Labrusa, S.A., 1979), no. 1134, p. 238.

3. Historical consciousness is not a theme that liberation theology has reflected on directly and at great length as has been the case in northern theologies since the nineteenth century. Rather it is a supposition which is simply taken for granted in the whole of liberation theology and is implied in its basic intention and major themes.

4. This theme of autonomy and the value of human freedom, while common to all liberation theologians, is most pronounced in the work of Juan Luis Segundo. It is illustrated on the collective level in this dramatic text from Teilhard de Chardin which he cites more than once: "Hitherto men have been living at once dispersed and closed in on themselves, like passengers who have met by chance in the hold of a ship without the least idea of its mobile nature or the fact that it is moving. Living, therefore, on the earth that grouped them together, they could think of nothing better to do than quarrel among themselves or try to amuse themselves. And now, by chance, or rather by the normal effect of the passage of time, our eyes have just been opened. The boldest of us have made their way to the deck, and seen the ship that carried us. They have noted the creaming of the bow-waves. They have realized that there are boilers to be fed and a wheel to be manned. Above all, they have seen the clouds above them and smelt the fragrance of the islands over the circle of the horizon. The picture of men ceaselessly in agitation over the same spot has gone; this is no longer an aimless drifting, it is a *passage to be made good*. It is inevitable that some *other* sort of Mankind must emerge from that vision." Cited by Segundo in *Evolution and Guilt*, trans. by John Drury (Maryknoll, N.Y.: Orbis Books, 1974), p. 124, from Rideau, *The Thought of Teilhard de Chardin* (New York: Harper and Row, 1967), p. 302.

5. That freedom is the highest human value is a supposition throughout the writings of Juan Luis Segundo, and it reaches explicit formulation in a number of places. For example, Segundo maintains: "A man without freedom would not be a human person." *Grace and the Human Condition*, trans. by John Drury (Maryknoll, N.Y.: Orbis Books, 1973), p. 44.

6. See John Coleman, "The Situations for Modern Faith," *Theological Studies*, 39 (December 1978), 601–632, for a clear review of the religious sociological literature on secularization. Coleman shows the many different interpretations of this term and the data to which it refers. There is still no clear consensus on the very meaning of secularization.

7. David Tracy, in *The Analogical Imagination: Christian Theology and the Culture of Pluralism* (New York: Crossroad, 1981), Chapter 8, esp. pp. 355–364, gives a vivid description of the contemporary situation which is typified by the experience of "homelessness," or "not-at-homeness." His characterization of our period certainly rings true. However, with the phrase "being at home in the world," I am, I think, pointing to a different level or aspect of the

same experience Tracy captures so well. In a sense it is our tendency to define ourselves exclusively as historical and part of this world, and the current identification of human existence as no other than this-worldly, that are the supposition and perhaps the cause of contemporary disorientation and alienation. The chaos of history and the shocking injustices of our world leave us reeling precisely to the degree that, on another level, we define ourselves as at home in this world.

8. It is a fact that many or most of the internationally known liberation theologians were educated in Europe, and they carry with them the North Atlantic theological and conceptual tradition. But while Latin Americans share this wider theological language, their theological reflection is being brought to bear on the concrete situation of Latin America. The aim and direction of this thought is to create an indigenous theology and it already bears a distinctive accent. Thus I believe that Schillebeeckx's appraisal of Latin American theology is not entirely just. He writes: "[F]rom a theological point of view I have not found anything very different in all this literature from what has been said more precisely by J.-B. Metz and J. Moltmann. . . . Despite all the promise, I have to say that there is not yet a specifically Latin American theology in contrast to the other non-European theologies, like for example Black theology, which in fact has a stamp of its own." (Edward Schillebeeckx, Christ: The Experience of Jesus As Lord, trans. by John Bowden [New York: Crossroad, 1980], p. 762.) His judgment, although carefully qualified, is made entirely on the basis of theoretical and constructive concepts. Yet Latin American theology is distinctive as a practical theology because of its constant concern for a spirituality or Christian life that is consonant with a particular and critically urgent situation. At this level rhetoric and language, the symbols chosen and metaphors employed, have great theological significance. Yet Schillebeeckx is correct in insisting that distinctions between them supply no grounds for polemics between liberation and political theology.

9. While once again this is a quality of all liberation theology, pertaining as it does to its fundamental logic, this historical viewpoint is highlighted and insisted upon by Ignacio Ellacuría. See for example his Freedom Made Flesh: The Mission of Christ and His Church, trans. by John Drury (Maryknoll, N.Y.: Orbis Books, 1976) where the title announces this theme. See also Ignacio Ellacuría, "La Iglesia de los Pobres: Sacramento histórico de Liberación," ECA (Centro de Estudios Centro-americanos), 32 (1977), 707–722. From the Protestant tradition this historical point of view is emphasized by Rubem A. Alves, in A Theology of Human Hope (New York: Corpus Books, 1969) and José Miguez-Bonino, "Historical Praxis and Christian Identity," in Frontiers of Theology in Latin America, ed. by Rosino Gibellini and trans. by John Drury (Maryknoll, N.Y.: Orbis Books, 1979), pp. 260–283.

10. One of the clearest illustrations of this general statement of the methodology of liberation theology is found in Leonardo Boff, Teología del Cautiverio y de la Liberación (Madrid: Ediciones Paulinas, 1978). Cf. also Raúl Vidales, "Methodological Issues in Liberation Theology," Frontiers, op. cit., pp. 34–57.

11. Thus liberation theology presupposes and joins the movement in Roman Catholic theology begun in the modernist period by Maurice Blondel and continued by existentially conscious theologians before the Second Vatican Council and especially afterward by socially conscious theologians. The principle announced by Blondel was that for Christian doctrine to make sense, it had to somehow be experienced by people in their actual life situation. For a most clear and concise statement of this "Blondelian shift," see Gregory Baum's account of it in *Man Becoming: God in Secular Language* (New York: Herder and Herder, 1970), pp. 1–36.

12. This presupposition is clearly announced by Juan Luis Segundo in the first chapter of his *The Community Called Church,* trans. by John Drury (Maryknoll, N.Y.: Orbis Books, 1973), pp. 3–12. The significance of this presupposition is that it defines a shift of perspective from which everything looks different. See also Jon Sobrino, "Evangelización y Iglesia en América Latina," ECA (Centro de Estudios Centroamericanos) 32 (1977), 723–748.

13. Gutiérrez, *A Theology of Liberation,* pp. 258–262. See also Joseph Comblin, *The Meaning of Mission: Jesus, Christians, and the Wayfaring Church,* trans. by John Drury (Maryknoll, N.Y.: Orbis Books, 1977), pp. 1–25.

14. Gutiérrez, Segundo and other liberation theologians make explicit reference to Marx and other neo-Marxist social analysts throughout their work.

15. Michael C. Reilly, "Cross-Cultural Evangelization," *America,* 141 (December 22, 1979), 409.

16. The use of social analysis in theology is explicitly required by Gustavo Gutiérrez in the opening pages on method in theology in his *A Theology of Liberation.* The theme is explored at greater length in Juan Luis Segundo's *The Liberation of Theology,* trans. by John Drury (Maryknoll, N.Y.: Orbis Books, 1976).

17. The term "solidarity" is not only a constant in Latin American theological writing, it plays an even greater role in the common language of religious groups committed to the ideals of liberation. Like the religious symbol, "the people," it contains deep spiritual and theological resonances.

18. Both Segundo and Gutiérrez are theologically dependent on Karl Rahner here. See Gutiérrez, *A Theology of Liberation,* p. 70, and Segundo, *Grace and the Human Condition,* pp. 21–29 and *The Community Called Church, passim.* See John Langan, "Liberation Theology in a Northern Context," *America,* 140 (January 27, 1979), 46–49, where he correctly identifies the theology of grace as a major premise in Latin American liberation theology. The significance of the supposition becomes apparent when compared with Catholic attitudes toward the availability of grace and salvation outside the Church prior to Vatican II's doctrine, and with positions of the non-availability of salvation outside the Church held currently by some evangelical groups.

19. See especially Gutiérrez, *A Theology of Liberation,* pp. 36–37 175–178. This does not imply a reduction or emptying of a presupposed objective content of one symbol into that of the other. Rather it means that each symbol is filled and informed with the resonances of the other. What this means in terms of content is the subject matter of this book.

20. *Ibid.*, pp. 198–203. A fuller account is that of Segundo in the whole of his *Grace and the Human Condition* where he adopts an Augustinian view of Christian salvation through a grace that opens a sinful will up to freedom and active love.

21. See José Miguez-Bonino, *Christians and Marxists* (Grand Rapids, Michigan: Eerdmans, 1976), pp. 133–142.

22. This thesis is being developed from an anthropological point of view and without prejudicing the reality of grace. Liberation theology is not Pelagian and explicitly, although dialectically, surrenders the entire work of salvation to God's utterly gratuitous initiative through grace.

II. THE PROBLEM OF HISTORY AND THE FUNDAMENTAL STRUCTURE OF THEOLOGY

1. Gustavo Gutiérrez, *A Theology of Liberation: History, Politics and Salvation,* trans. and ed. by Caridad Inda and John Eagleson (Maryknoll, N.Y.: Orbis Books, 1973), pp. 45–50.

2. For example, Rosemary Ruether, who is certainly sympathetic to the movement of liberation theology, has warned against particularizing and absolutizing one form of oppression through which one interprets God and Christianity. She counsels self-criticism in face of the too easy decision that God is on our side. These remarks are made relative to black liberation theology but they are relevant here. See Rosemary Radford Ruether, *Liberation Theology: Human Hope Confronts Christian History and American Power* (New York: Paulist Press, 1972), pp. 127–144.

3. The genesis of liberation theology is generally well known and understood since it is a main theme in the theology itself. Liberation theologians frequently explain their theology precisely in terms of how it arose, what the factors were and are that force a shift from previous and more traditional theology. See the standard account of Gutiérrez, *A Theology of Liberation,* pp. 1–131. A full account of the rise of liberation theology, especially with the circle of Gutiérrez, is given by Roberto Oliveros, in *Liberación y Teología: Génesis y Crecimiento de una Reflexión, 1966–1976* (Mexico City: CRT, 1977).

4. Once again, this is a consistent insistence on the part of Gutiérrez. As he gradually stripped away various false interpretations of the center or starting point to his own theology, such as the exodus account, other scriptural incidents, or a particular economic and market analysis, he was left with the basis for the whole movement consisting in concern for the poor. See Gustavo Gutiérrez, *La Fuerza Histórica de los Pobres: Selección de Trabajos* (Lima: Centro de Estudios y Publicaciónes, 1979), pp. 106–107.

5. This negative perception is described by Edward Schillebeeckx in *God The Future of Man,* trans. by N. D. Smith (New York: Sheed and Ward, 1968), pp. 136, 153–154, 164. He takes up the experience again and develops it further in *Jesus: An Experiment in Christology,* trans. by Hubert Hoskins (New York: Crossroad, The Seabury Press, 1979), pp. 621–622.

6. Gutiérrez, *A Theology of Liberation,* p. 103.

7. Jon Sobrino, *Christology at the Crossroads: A Latin American Approach,* trans. by John Drury (Maryknoll, N.Y.: Orbis Books, 1978). pp. 17–21, 33–37. Something of the same thesis is implicit in Juan Luis Segundo's *The Liberation of Theology,* trans. by John Drury (Maryknoll, N.Y.: Orbis Books, 1976) where he polemicizes against what he calls "academic theology" and defends the priority and primacy of praxis in theology.

8. Gutiérrez, *La Fuerza Histórica de los Pobres,* pp. 102–107.

9. As Schillebeeckx surveys the problem, no mode of human thinking or any religious revelation or system has in any sense solved this existential problem. See Edward Schillebeeckx, *Christ: The Experience of Jesus as Lord,* trans. by John Bowden (New York: Crossroad, Seabury Press, 1980), pp. 670–723.

10. See Paulo Freire, *Education for Critical Consciousness* (New York: The Seabury Press, 1973), esp. pp. 41–45. Also his *Pedagogy of the Oppressed,* trans. by Myra Bergman Ramos (New York: Herder and Herder, 1970), discusses the condition and consciousness of the poor and oppressed at length.

11. One has to be very careful here not to project on to other cultures, especially cultures that are not western and are less technological and industrial, ideas and values concerning freedom that are proper to the west. This is a fallacy easily fallen into. I do not mean to suggest either that the ways in which freedom is conceived or the ways in which its ideals are materialized in the west are a norm for human freedom. Nor do I suggest that any group of poor people does not have valid ideals in this regard. The restrictions of freedom that are described here are very close to the physical and biological level where oppression attacks life itself. The poverty supposed here is really destitution, not noble simplicity. Moreover, the complaint registered here is simply a report and an echo of one that is coming from the poor, the oppressed and those who suffer themselves, and from around the whole world.

12. The issue for theology is not simply the existence of God but much more importantly the question of the concept or image of God. It is not simply the question of whether or not God is, but what kind of God is further disclosed in our new historical situation. Actually these two questions cannot be separated. But the emphasis today should be on the very meaning of the term "God" and the image that that term conveys.

13. Sigmund Freud, *The Future of an Illusion,* trans. by W. D. Robson-Scott and revised by James Strachey (Garden City, N.Y.: Anchor Books, Doubleday, 1964), pp. 75–92.

14. This idea of the need of the release of evil from all religious mystification so that it may be duly fought against is a requirement of William James. See his "Is Life Worth Living?" *Essays on Faith and Morals,* ed. by Ralph Barton Perry (New York: Meridian Books, 1962), pp. 1–31, esp. 15–16. James of course did not concur in Freud's atheism even though he did share some of his humanistic values.

15. Paul Tillich, *The Courage To Be* (New Haven: Yale University Press, 1952), pp. 40–63. These problems or crises are not exclusive; they are all oper-

ative all the time. It is a question of a particular type of existential anxiety coming to predominance at the end of specific eras because of historical circumstances.

16. This does not imply that the problem of human existence is a merely intellectual one. The suggestion that the sheer existence of human poverty, suffering and evil of our contemporary history raises an intellectual problem or dilemma would be a total misunderstanding of what is being said here. The problem *is* the existence of vast amounts of suffering; the crisis is constituted by human victimization. The problem is also existential, that is, this suffering involves a crisis of meaning, a profound question and anxiety about the sense and purposefulness of human historical existence. At this *existential* level, *all* share in the actual suffering of the poor and oppressed; it is a universal problem. That this involves no intellectualization of the human problem of actual suffering will become clear when it is seen that the *only possible* solution to it lies in praxis.

17. Schillebeeckx, in his book *Christ,* does not find the distinction between objective and subjective salvation helpful, at least not as the Scholastics employed it. Cf. p. 514. The reason for this, I believe, is that he is afraid that the idea of salvation will become abstract and objectified and thus spoken about apart from actual lives within human history. This is a legitimate concern. Yet I find the distinction still useful, so long as one realizes that the objectification, the abstract generalization about an historical reality, is meaningless apart from its concrete referent.

18. The term "praxis" has been discussed a great deal, especially in the context of the relation of praxis to *theoria* or theory. The meaning of the term "praxis" varies greatly in different theologies and authors. A general descriptive definition will suffice here: "Praxis regards human action as what we actually do, and probably or possibly can do. Minimally, it can be a mere technical or mechanical repetition of movements, assembly-line routines with slight subjective engagement. More adequately, praxis is involvement and commitment; by our actions we become who we are." Matthew Lamb, "The Theory-Praxis Relationship in Contemporary Christian Theologies," *Proceedings of the Catholic Theological Society of America,* 31 (1976), p. 150. The more distinctive meaning of praxis in liberation theology will appear in what follows.

19. The absolutely essential role of grace in this process will be taken up in a later chapter.

20. This strong statement presumes the logic of the problem of human existence described earlier. The presumption is the unity and solidarity of corporate human existence. The terms "social" and "historical" are almost synonymous here since they refer to the whole of our public corporate history that includes the personal history of each one. This history is marked by grave injustices that cause untold human suffering. To find personal salvation apart from and despite this situation is to implicitly reaffirm that our public corporate existence *is* irremediably negative and meaningless.

21. Gutiérrez, *A Theology of Liberation,* pp. 27–33, esp. p. 32.

22. This does not imply that the past history of suffering is suddenly rendered meaningful. The history of oppressed freedom is a perpetual scandal to all human faith and hope. At best faith can hope for a redress of this scandal by God beyond history. But this faith itself is logically impossible without some participation in a movement of historical liberation. And once entered into such a faith will also grant some minimal and dialectical this-worldly meaning for the history of suffering precisely insofar as it actually motivates human freedom to resist, minimize and overturn it. This existential-historical interpretation of the this-worldly meaning of salvation will be developed in Chapter VII.

III. METHOD IN THEOLOGY IN THE LIGHT OF LIBERATION THEOLOGY

1. Raúl Vidales, "Methodological Issues in Liberation Theology," in *Frontiers of Theology in Latin America*, ed. by Rosino Gibellini, trans by John Drury (Maryknoll, N.Y.: Orbis Books, 1979), p. 42.

2. Practically all the early works in liberation theology deal at some length with the particular and specific generative method employed in this theology. See especially the volume of papers from the conference explicitly discussing theological method: *Liberación y Cautiverio: Debates en torno al Método de la Teología en América Latina* (Mexico City: Comité Organizador, 1975).

3. Gustavo Gutiérrez, *A Theology of Liberation* (Maryknoll, N.Y.: Orbis Books, 1973), p. 45.

4. For example, Leonardo Boff, *Teología del Cautiverio y de la Liberación* (Madrid: Ediciones Paulinas, 1978).

5. An early example of this methodological principle is seen in the collection of Juan Luis Segundo, *De la Sociedad a la Teología* (Buenos Aires: Carlos Lohlé, 1970).

6. Gutiérrez, *A Theology of Liberation*, pp. 36–37; also pp. 149–178.

7. Gustavo Gutiérrez, "Liberation Praxis and Christian Faith," in *Frontiers of Theology in Latin America, op. cit.*, p. 24.

8. Juan Luis Segundo, *Liberation of Theology*, trans. by John Drury (Maryknoll, N.Y.: Orbis Books, 1976).

9. Vidales, "Methodological Issues in Liberation Theology," p. 46.

10. Paul Tillich, *Systematic Theology*, I (Chicago: The University of Chicago Press, 1951), pp. 34–68, esp. 59–66.

11. Needless to say there has been an enormous amount of discussion on the question of method in theology, and Tillich's formulation has been criticized and nuanced from every point of view. But after the discussion is over, the general consensus still stands that contemporary experience enters into the structure of theological method and understanding, and in such a way that allows for ongoing reinterpretation of the Christian symbols and message. Two recent examples of Roman Catholic reformulations of the method of correla-

tion that preserve its basic structure are David Tracy, *Blessed Rage for Order: The New Pluralism in Theology* (New York: Crossroad, The Seabury Press, 1975), pp. 43–56; Hans Küng, "Toward a New Consensus in Catholic (and Ecumenical) Theology," in *Consensus in Theology?* ed. by Leonard Swidler (Philadelphia: The Westminster Press, 1980), pp. 1–17.

12. A very clear statement of this is that of Vidales. The structure of theology consists in exegesis and then hermeneutics, the second step being a reinterpretation of the past relative to the present concrete situation. Theology "must constantly reformulate its views at each concrete historical moment, for it must serve faith as it is lived by people in the concrete circumstances of history." "Methodological Issues in Liberation Theology," p. 37. The same structure is laid down by Segundo: "Here is a preliminary definition of the hermeneutic circle: it is the continuing change in our interpretation of the Bible which is dictated by the continuing changes in our present-day reality, both individual and societal. . . . The circular nature of this interpretation stems from the fact that each new reality obliges us to interpret the word of God afresh, to change reality accordingly, and then to go back and reinterpret the word of God again, and so on." *Liberation of Theology,* p. 8.

13. The organization of this anthropological schema is dependent on Peter C. Hodgson, *New Birth of Freedom: A Theology of Bondage and Liberation* (Philadelphia: Fortress Press, 1976), pp. 114–165.

14. Edward Schillebeeckx in his essay to determine the meaning of Christian salvation also follows a method of correlation in which the meaning of that salvation must fall within the general parameters of what is human, since it is precisely a salvation of human beings. There must therefore be some correlation with a general anthropology. Yet since human nature is a history, he despairs of establishing anything that might be called a detailed account of humanity that is also universal. But at the same time he believes that one can lay down a number of anthropological constants; there is a certain unity of the human race and one can determine transcendental principles which are both universal and open to endless historical determinations. The general anthropological schema outlined here is meant in the same spirit as the "anthropological constants" of Schillebeeckx and in fact it includes at least implicitly all the elements that he finds. See Edward Schillebeeckx, *Christ: The Experience of Jesus as Lord,* trans. by John Bowden (New York: Crossroad, The Seabury Press, 1980), pp. 731–743.

15. For a short but lucid correlation of the Christian message, as seen in its fundamental symbols, with our contemporary human experience, see Langdon Gilkey's *Message and Existence: An Introduction to Christian Theology* (New York: Crossroad, The Seabury Press, 1979).

16. David Tracy, throughout the second part of his *The Analogical Imagination: Christian Theology and the Culture of Pluralism* (New York: Crossroad, 1981), has a great deal of very pertinent reflection on focus, or what he sometimes calls "focal meaning," even though this category is not raised to explicit prominence in his methodological apparatus. In general, focus has a double meaning in his usage: it can be objective, as in the objective centering

point of Christian faith, namely, Jesus Christ. Or it can be subjective, as in the centering concern of the theologian arising out of the contemporary historical situation. I am using the term "focus" in the second sense in this context.

17. The theme of revelation will be developed further in Chapter V.

18. Hans Küng, "Toward a New Consensus in Catholic (and Ecumenical) Theology," p. 5.

19. This position has been operative in modern theology since the beginning of the nineteenth century. It was put forward in Roman Catholicism by the modernist movement but rejected by the Church at the beginning of this century. But finally it has gained general acceptance in Catholic theology since the Second Vatican Council. Once one assumes a concrete, existential and historical point of view, this position becomes self-evident.

20. The point here is also quite fundamental and should not be understood in such a way that Christian theology is seen as resting exclusively on a revelation that occurred in the past and whose meaning is completely fixed in the past. Fundamentalism and historical critical method are not the only alternatives in dealing with the earliest sources of Christian theology. The supposition here is that Christian revelation is an ongoing existential phenomenon within the community, and that besides historical criticism other methods of interpretation, such as literary and existential hermeneutics, can help bring the meaning of the Christian sources of the past to bear on our present situation. Thus the thesis here is really quite basic and it simply stands in opposition to a fundamentalism that is more common than is generally presumed. Unless Christian theology is conditioned by historical consciousness through an historical critical method, it will not be truly released for its task of interpreting original revelation in a way adequate to the present situation.

21. I say "appears to be" because in its fundamental intention it is not. There is actually a complex hermeneutic at work in liberation theology which this and the last chapter have tried to explain. But because much of liberation theology is written on behalf of and for a popular audience, namely the poor, it often makes a simple and direct appeal to Scripture and thus gives the impression of fundamentalism.

22. See Schubert M. Ogden, *The Point of Christology* (San Francisco: Harper & Row, 1982), pp. 86–96, 148–168, for a discussion of a liberationist interpretation of Jesus Christ which is demanded today because of the specific requirements of our current historical situation.

IV. THE THEOLOGY OF FAITH AND ULTIMATE CONCERN FOR JUSTICE

1. Gustavo Gutiérrez, "Liberation Praxis and Christian Faith," in *Frontiers of Theology in Latin America,* ed. by Rosino Gibellini, trans. by John Drury (Maryknoll, N.Y.: Orbis Books, 1979), pp. 19–22.

2. Gustavo Gutiérrez, *A Theology of Liberation: History, Politics and Salvation,* trans. and edited by Caridad Inda and John Eagleson (Maryknoll, N.Y.: Orbis Books, 1973), pp. 198–203.

3. "More and more, then, faith surfaces as a liberation praxis." Gutiérrez, "Liberation Praxis and Christian Faith," p. 20.

4. See Jon Sobrino, *Christology at the Crossroads: A Latin American Approach*, trans. by John Drury (Maryknoll, N.Y.: Orbis Books, 1978), pp. 79–108, where he analyzes the faith of Jesus as the paradigm for Christian faith, which is defined most generally as simply discipleship or following Jesus.

5. The Kingdom of God is a major theme in Sobrino's Christology because it is the central category capturing Jesus' preaching. So too in the Christology of Leonardo Boff, *Jesus Christ Liberator: A Critical Christology for Our Time*, trans. by Patrick Hughes (Maryknoll, N.Y.: Orbis Books, 1978). In general the symbol of the Kingdom of God is a very important term in the popular rhetoric of liberation theology and the movement it represents.

6. See Paul Tillich, *The Courage To Be* (New Haven: Yale University Press, 1952), pp. 57–63.

7. See for example H. Richard Niebuhr, *Christ and Culture* (New York: Harper and Row, 1951). Even more specifically pertinent is the programmatic survey by Avery Dulles, "The Changing Forms of Faith," in *The Survival of Dogma* (Garden City, N.Y.: Doubleday, 1971), pp. 17–31.

8. Paul Tillich, *Dynamics of Faith* (New York: Harper and Row, 1957), pp. 4–8, 105–111. In general, the analysis presented here accepts Tillich's description of the existential quality of faith.

9. William James, *The Varieties of Religious Experience* (New York: Collier Books, 1961), pp. 163–165.

10. Gordon W. Allport, *The Individual and His Religion: A Psychological Interpretation* (New York: The Macmillan Co., 1950), pp. 131–132.

11. Reference could be made here to any one of a number of classical phenomenological accounts of the anthropological grounds of faith that have been written in the modern period. Such names, for example, as Schleiermacher, Kierkegaard, Newman, Blondel, Otto, James, Tillich, Rahner, and Ramsey immediately come to mind. In all of these accounts, each one of which has its own method and distinctiveness, there are certain common elements or themes.

12. Tillich, *Dynamics of Faith*, pp. 1–4. Tillich's view of faith as ultimate concern is not far from Kierkegaard's characterization of it as infinite passion. For Kierkegaard faith is the antithesis of objective knowledge of things finite. Faith, like all truth, is dynamically subjective, which is not to be seen as opposed to objectivity but as transcending it. The subjectivity of faith and of all significant truth is an assertion of its sheer existential quality. Faith is interest, engagement, passion, concern, commitment. One can see that religious and Christian faith are given an existential seriousness that utterly transcends faith as mere belief or acceptance of truths. One is in a different thought scheme at this point. And from this viewpoint, to consider faith as synonymous with belief is practically to deny it as faith. See Soren Kierkegaard, *Fear and Trembling* in *Fear and Trembling and The Sickness Unto Death*, trans. by Walter Lowrie (Garden City, N.Y.: Doubleday Anchor Books, 1954), pp. 6–132, and especially Soren Kierkegaard, *Concluding Unscientific Postscript*, trans. by David F. Swenson (Princeton: Princeton University Press, 1941).

13. Maurice Blondel, *L'Action: Essai d'une critique de la vie et d'une science de la pratique* (Paris: Alcan, 1893), pp. 1–16.

14. James, *The Varieties of Religious Experience*, p. 377.

15. Paul Tillich, *Systematic Theology*, III (Chicago: University of Chicago Press, 1963), pp. 129–134. In this treatment of faith in the *Systematic Theology* the passive voice is more prevalent than in *Dynamics*.

16. In the following analysis of the various dimensions or structure of faith I am borrowing from Friedrich Schleiermacher's phenomenology of religious consciousness as found in *On Religion: Speeches to Its Cultural Despisers*, trans. by John Oman (New York: Harper and Row, 1958), especially the second speech, pp. 26–118, and in *The Christian Faith* (New York: Harper and Row, 1963), pp. 5–18. But I am not consciously attempting to reproduce his thought. The same position on the existential character of faith, the distinction but inter-relation between faith, knowing and doing, and between faith and its expression in beliefs, can be culled from other modern theologians as well. Schleiermacher is useful because of his straightforward and clear phenomenological analysis.

17. Schleiermacher, *The Christian Faith*, pp. 125–127; *On Religion*, p. 47.

18. "We may ask which element has the greatest density of reality: the indirect and 'orthopractical' expression of God in ethical action or the indirect symbolic expression of the source of this practice in explicit nomenclature: 'my God,' 'our God.' Both seem to me to be indispensable, but in view of the experiential structure of revelation, the symbolic-religious talk of God owes its density of reality to the *mediation* of *ethical existence. . . .* We do not find salvation primarily by means of a correct interpretation of reality, but by acting in accordance with the demands of reality." Edward Schillebeeckx, *Christ: The Experience of Jesus as Lord*, trans. by John Bowden (New York: Crossroad, The Seabury Press, 1980), p. 61. This same insight and conviction is seen in a whole host of modern thinkers. In Blondel, especially, faith as a real appropriation of its transcendent object is climaxed in the forms of decision and action.

19. For Blondel, it would not quite be true to say that faith is action. Faith is rather the logic of one's action, and action is the materiality, actuality and reality of one's faith, because faith which is merely notional, and possibly dead, is no faith at all unless it becomes real in action. Once again, faith is an existential reality that is actualized not simply by prayer but also in ethics or the whole conduct of a person.

20. In the Thomistic sense of a habit. See Aquinas, *Summa Theologiae*, II-II, q. 4, aa. 1–5. But not in such a way that its objective ontological quality or character is seen in contrast to its conscious and existential character.

21. Dietrich von Hildebrand, *Christian Ethics* (New York: David McKay Company, 1953), pp. 241–243.

22. This tendency is consistently noted by philosophers and theologians across the Christian tradition. In Augustine, human existence is characterized by an openness and a drive toward Truth and the Good. But beneath these faculties of knowing and willing, there is the deeper orientation of the free human spirit for being itself. "If you begin by wishing to exist, and add a desire

for fuller and fuller existence, you rise in the scale, and are furnished for life that supremely is. . . . If you wish more and more to exist, you will draw near to him who exists supremely." Augustine, *On Free Will,* in Augustine, *Earlier Writings,* ed. and trans. by John H. S. Burleigh (Philadelphia: Westminster Press, 1953), III, vii, 21, p. 183.

23. In Rahner, the human spirit, although transcendent, is bound ontologically to matter, the physical, appearance, the world, and history by a transcendental relation. Therefore its encounter with the transcendent is always and inevitably mediated through history. This idea occurs throughout his writings, but see for example Karl Rahner, *Hearers of the Word,* trans. by Michael Richards (New York: Herder and Herder, 1969), pp. 130–149. Schleiermacher expresses the same thing more simply in phenomenological terms of consciousness: There can be no consciousness of transcendence apart from consciousness of this world. Schleiermacher, *The Christian Faith,* I, pp. 125–127. The point of these statements is that they undercut all natural religion or unadulterated transcendental or universal faith mediated through reason as an abstraction. Every faith is bound to the world and history, and thus will take on a particular historical shape.

24. For an account of the myriad ways in which historical symbols may structure religious faith see Mircea Eliade, *Patterns in Comparative Religion,* trans. by Rosemary Sheed (New York: Sheed and Ward, 1958).

25. These general forms, determined by social, historical and cultural factors, and thus influencing and structuring the faith of the community as a whole, are the forms investigated by Dulles in "The Changing Forms of Faith."

26. Study on various progressive psychological forms of faith, which are called types and stages, have been investigated by James Fowler. See James Fowler, "Toward a Developmental Perspective on Faith," *Religious Education,* XIX (1974), 207–219, for a preliminary report. A later and fuller account can be found in Jim Fowler and Sam Keen, *Life Maps: Conversations on the Journey of Faith* (Waco, Texas: Word Books, 1978), pp. 14–101. And, finally, Fowler's fullest statement appears in James W. Fowler, *Stages of Faith: The Psychology of Human Development and the Quest for Meaning* (New York: Harper and Row, 1981).

27. This is the whole point of Hans Küng's, *On Being a Christian,* trans. by Edward Quinn (Garden City, N.Y.: Doubleday, 1976). Being a Christian, the essence of Christian faith, is determined historically by the event of Jesus and he himself becoming the Christian message.

28. The argument here is the same as that of Sobrino in *Christology at the Crossroads.*

29. In Tillich, faith is being grasped by ultimate concern. And love is the force that binds and unites persons separated. Thus being in faith and being united to God by love are materially the same. Faith necessarily implies love. "The concern of faith is identical with the desire of love." *Dynamics of Faith,* p. 112. Hope, on the other hand, is the expectation of the future and is a quality of both faith and love. In Rahner, however, hope is human openness and abandonment to the unfathomable mystery of God, especially as absolute future.

Both faith in God and love of God are united and rooted in hope as in an a priori ground, namely, this openness and surrender of the human spirit. Karl Rahner, "The Theology of Hope," *Theology Digest,* Sesquicentennial Issue (February 1968), pp. 78–87.

30. This analysis is dependent on Karl Rahner's in "Reflections on the Unity of the Love of Neighbor and the Love of God," *Theological Investigations,* VI (Baltimore: Helicon Press, 1968), pp. 231–249. See also Rahner's, "The Mission of the Church and the Humanizing of the World," *Doctrine and Life,* XXI (April and May 1971), pp. 171–178, 231–242.

31. It is not enough to say that love of God is inseparable from the love of one's neighbor. It must be added that love for God is unavoidably expressed *through* love of one's neighbor. "We find the Lord in our encounters with human beings, especially the poor, marginated, and exploited ones. An act of love towards them is an act of love towards God." Gutiérrez, *A Theology of Liberation,* pp. 200–201.

32. This brief analysis is taken from Paul Tillich, *Love, Power and Justice: Ontological Analyses and Ethical Applications* (New York: A Galaxy Book, Oxford University Press, 1960), pp. 54ff.

33. Von Hildebrand, *Christian Ethics,* pp. 236–239. See the whole of Chapter 17 which deals with "Value Response."

34. This is expressed sharply and succinctly by Tillich: "The immediate expression of love is action. Theologians have discussed the question of how faith can result in action. The answer is: because it implies love and because the expression of love is action. The mediating link between faith and works is love." *Dynamics of Faith,* p. 115.

V. THE IMAGE OF GOD AND THE PROBLEM OF HUMAN EXISTENCE

1. Juan Luis Segundo, *Our Idea of God,* trans. by John Drury (Maryknoll, N.Y.: Orbis Books, 1974), p. 12.

2. I take this as a further and necessary task for an adequate theological account, but one that cannot be performed here within the limits of this chapter. It is important that one realize that the modest proportions of this chapter will inevitably leave many issues unaddressed.

3. Segundo, *Our Idea of God,* p. 22.

4. Segundo, *Our Idea of God,* p. 23.

5. Segundo, *Our Idea of God,* p. 44.

6. Gustavo Gutiérrez, *A Theology of Liberation: History, Politics and Salvation,* trans. and ed. by Caridad Inda and John Eagleson (Maryknoll, N.Y.: Orbis Books, 1973), pp. 149–168.

7. Segundo, *Our Idea of God,* p. 37. Essentially Segundo and Gutiérrez are in complete agreement on the conflation of the two symbols of salvation and liberation and the seeing of this whole as an historical process. Jon Sobrino too sees salvation as an historical process. See *Christology at the Crossroads:*

A Latin American Approach, trans by John Drury (Maryknoll, N.Y.: Orbis Books, 1978), p. 227. But at the same time the category of salvation plays a very small and even negligible role in his Christological method and language.

8. José Miguez-Bonino, "Historical Praxis and Christian Identity," in *Frontiers of Theology in Latin America,* ed. by Rosino Gibellini and trans. by John Drury (Maryknoll, N.Y.: Orbis Books, 1979), pp. 277–278.

9. Juan Luis Segundo, "Capitalism Versus Socialism: Crux Theologica," in *Frontiers of Theology in Latin America,* pp. 245–249.

10. Segundo, "Capitalism Versus Socialism," p. 247.

11. Gutiérrez, *A Theology of Liberation,* pp. 272–279.

12. Segundo, *Our Idea of God,* p. 153.

13. Segundo, *Our Idea of God,* p. 37.

14. For the distinctions between the "natural" transcendental and categorical or historical aspects of revelation, see Karl Rahner, *Foundations of Christian Faith: An Introduction to the Idea of Christianity,* trans by William V. Dych (New York: A Crossroad Book, The Seabury Press, 1978), pp. 170–174.

15. This corresponds to Gregory Baum's first principle for reinterpreting our idea of God, which states that God cannot be conceived as simply over-against human existence, because God is related to and enters into the reality of what human beings are. See Gregory Baum, *Man Becoming: God in Secular Language* (New York: Herder and Herder, 1970), pp. 170–180. Baum explains that in this formulation he is placing a greater stress on the traditional theme of God's immanence than has been the case in the past in order to avoid extrinsicist theology. In the view of God that is presented here I wish *also* to keep the transcendence of God in clear view, but this transcendence of God is something that can be experienced and is when one experiences God.

16. It is most important to continually insist on this point. For example, Gordon Kaufman holds that because God is not an object of perception, the symbol "God" does not refer to God directly. Rather the symbol which points to God represents the attempt of the human imagination to somehow grasp the whole of reality by means of a central and centering symbol which provides meaning for the whole precisely by unifying, synthesizing and organizing all of reality in and around itself. Thus the theology of God is a work of construction by the imagination, but one which must be consistently critical of itself in the light of new experience and data. See Gordon D. Kaufman, *The Theological Imagination: Constructing the Concept of God* (Philadelphia: The Westminster Press, 1981), pp. 25–30. I have no fundamental disagreement with Kaufman's view. However, what follows will rely more on the religious experience of the religious imagination, and does not really engage sufficiently in the necessary further step of the more systematic effort of critical construction. This would be, however, a necessary step because practically anything can be justified on the basis of someone's religious experience.

17. What is said here corresponds to Baum's second principle for reinterpreting our concept of God, namely, that every statement about God is also a statement about human life, because God enters into the definition of the

human. Baum, *Man Becoming,* pp. 181–189. Although Baum's statement is more ontological, whereas I am speaking of revelation and awareness of God, the two positions are isomorphic.

18. Although for the Christian the central and normative symbol that mediates our idea of God is Jesus the Christ, still this chapter on God fixes mainly on Christian symbols that emerged out of the Jewish tradition and Scriptures prior to Jesus. Thus there is something of the same fiction at work here as in Calvin's *Institutes* where, for the sake of systematic order, he speaks of God before dealing with Christ, even though for him there is no true knowledge of God apart from Christ. Although I do not hold this latter position, still a Christian view of God is incomplete outside of a consideration of the revelation mediated by Jesus. But, finally, as with Calvin, insights from Jesus and the whole Christian tradition are tacitly at work in this chapter.

19. Rudolf Otto, *The Idea of the Holy,* trans. by John W. Harvey (New York: A Galaxy Book, Oxford University Press, 1958), pp. 12–40. As *mysterium* God appears in our consciousness as totally other; as *tremendum,* God appears in our consciousness as awe-inspiring, overpowering, total energy; as *fascinans,* God is attractive and draws forth human desire. It seems to me that one cannot bypass the manifold of data that one finds through a phenomenology of the various not strictly rational consciousnesses human beings have of God. Religious experience in terms of imagination, feeling and emotive response also communicates something of God to us.

20. For Gilkey, we know God by what God does; each doctrine corresponds to some activity of God relative to us and our world. And creation is the most Godly of activities revealing the most characteristic of God's qualities. See Langdon Gilkey, "God the Creator," in *Maker of Heaven and Earth: A Study of the Christian Doctrine of Creation* (Garden City, N.Y.: Doubleday, 1959), pp. 77–105, esp. 78–79.

21. Effectively what is being described here may be called cosmologically a panentheistic position, distinguishing it from pantheism which denies creation its relative autonomy and from some form of deism that postulates God as being totally outside and extrinsic to the finite world. Both of these latter positions are contradicted by the common religious experience that is described here.

22. For an extended survey of the history of the doctrine of providence and a discussion of its relevance for a contemporary interpretation of history, see Langdon Gilkey's *Reaping the Whirlwind: A Christian Interpretation of History* (New York: A Crossroad Book, The Seabury Press, 1976). I shall return to Gilkey's reinterpretation of providence further on in order to qualify the last point made here.

23. "He who does not love does not know God; for God is love." 1 Jn 4:8.

24. Thus I see the prophetic imagination and ministry as based on an experience of God as both transcendent and as immanent love. In the section that follows I will show how this view of God comes to bear on human existence, especially in its historical and societal forms.

25. The theme of God as absolute and incomprehensible mystery is a major one in the theology of Karl Rahner. See, for example, his brief discussion in *Foundations of Christian Faith,* pp. 57–66.

26. See Edward Schillebeeckx, *Christ: The Experience of Jesus as Lord,* trans. by John Bowden (New York: A Crossroad Book, The Seabury Press, 1980), pp. 672–715, for a survey of the ways in which the various religions try to deal with the problem of human suffering.

27. It is a given in elementary sociology that religion is the "substance of society" in such a way that it is perhaps the main force that guarantees the order of any society, giving it sanction in symbols of ultimacy and encouraging internalized attitudes of acceptance of the way things are. See the standard works of Peter Berger and Thomas Luckmann, *The Social Construction of Reality: A Treatise in the Sociology of Knowledge* (Garden City, N.Y.: Doubleday, 1966) and Peter Berger, *The Sacred Canopy* (Garden City, N.Y.: Doubleday, 1967). The phrase that religion is the substance of society is Paul Tillich's, in *Theology of Culture,* ed. by Robert C. Kimball (New York: A Galaxy Book, Oxford University Press, 1964), p. 42.

28. This calls for a prophetic attitude and ministry based on an experience of God's transcendence and yet universal love. The transcendence of God relative to human existence serves a double function. On the one hand it stands over against the "curved-in character of human existence" that absolutizes ourselves as individual persons, our families, our communities, our nations, our species, and thus destroys the themes of solidarity, mutuality, cooperation, collegiality and constructive collaboration in our interdependence. On the other hand, God's transcendence as a focus of fascination and devotion draws out or evokes human self-transcendence in the direction just indicated. Thus Kaufman, *The Theological Imagination,* p. 36. Corresponding to this God evokes a prophetic attitude and ministry. "The task of prophetic ministry is to nurture, nourish, and evoke a consciousness and perception alternative to the consciousness and perception of the dominant culture around us." Walter Brueggemann, *The Prophetic Imagination* (Philadelphia: Fortress Press, 1978), p. 13. This task of empowering "people to engage in history" has two elements or functions. It consists of criticizing the cultural consciousness of the past or present, and of energizing or drawing forth a new vision, an alternative perception of how things should and could be. In effect God does this, and the ministry consists in mediating the symbol of God in such a way that one sees one's particular history in the light of God's transcendent freedom and will for justice. *Ibid.,* p. 14. This corresponds to the strategy of liberation theology expressed as "denunciation" and "annunciation." Gutiérrez, *A Theology of Liberation,* pp. 265–272.

29. See Schillebeeckx, *Christ,* pp. 776–779, for a balanced discussion of the eschatological proviso that stems from the experience of God's proviso. He writes: The Christian "has the obligation, in faith, to further what is good and true for a realization of humanity; to fight energetically against everything which vitiates human physical life, burdens human psychological life, humiliates one as a person, enslaves one through social structures, drives a person

into an irresponsible adventure through irrationality, makes the free exercise of a person's religious feeling impossible; and finally, to oppose everything that infringes human rights and reifies human beings as a result of their working conditions and the bureaucracy which shapes them. This productive and critical impulse, stemming from Christian belief in God, directed towards both activity which contributes to human salvation and a well-determined political course of action for a better future for mankind, does not in fact neutralize the eschatological proviso." *Ibid.,* p. 779.

30. In a later chapter the discussion will turn to the existential aspect of this problem which is seen in the tension between sin, grace and freedom.

31. Gilkey, *Reaping the Whirlwind,* pp. 246–253, 279–280.

32. God's creative power sustains all in history by overcoming non-being; it sustains duration itself. God's providence is this same continued creative power insofar as it not only sustains continued existence in being but also provides possibilities for the future. But at the same time the relative autonomy of human existence is real, and human freedom is really creativity. God is not the sole actor of history. "God has not ordained the shape of the destiny that comes to effectiveness as the given from the past: the freedom involved in past events has done that in relation to the possibilities then presented by providence." Gilkey, *Reaping the Whirlwind,* p. 249. The self-limitation of God, already involved in creating human beings as other than God's self, preserves the reality, the creativity and the importance of human freedom, and it corresponds to our experience of the openness of history.

33. Bonino, "Historical Praxis and Christian Identity," pp. 260–283, and Segundo, "Capitalism versus Socialism," pp. 240–259.

34. Bonino proposes the resurrection of Jesus "in the flesh" as a paradigm for understanding this problem. There is both continuity and discontinuity between historical praxis and the Kingdom of God. "Historical Praxis and Christian Identity," pp. 272–276.

35. Thus, returning to the issue of the eschatological proviso, Segundo writes: "Far from *relativizing* any given present, the eschatological aspect of any Christian theology *links the present to the absolute.* Absolutization is necessary for all effective human mobilization. What the Christian eschatological aspect does, then, is prevent that mobilization from degenerating into human rigidity, petrification, and a sacralization of the existing situation merely because it does exist." "Capitalism Versus Socialism," p. 256.

36. The strongest expression of this Christian belief is found in Luther's formula of justification by grace through faith which means that human beings are accepted precisely as sinners, "no matter what," if one has faith.

37. David Tracy's description of the strategies of disclosure assumed by contemporary theologians, especially the third with its focusing concern for history and praxis, although not excluding the routes of manifestation and proclamation, is an accurate description of what I have attempted in this chapter. However, instead of focusing on Jesus Christ, I have centered the analysis on other classic symbols for God. See David Tracy, *The Analogical Imagina-*

tion: Christian Theology and the Culture of Pluralism (New York: Crossroad, 1981), pp. 371–404.

38. How God acts in history on behalf of the poor will be dealt with in a later chapter.

VI. THE STRUCTURE AND DATA OF CHRISTOLOGY

1. Throughout this work and especially this chapter the term "symbol" refers to religious symbols which are any piece of finite reality, any thing, event, concept, situation, text, narrative or person which mediates contact with God. This term is thus very broad but is meant to bring home the fact that all human contact with God is indirect and mediated. Human experience of God is always had through the world and one's historical situation in it. The point being made here is that in the case of Christianity, the central symbol is the concrete historical person, Jesus of Nazareth. See Chapter IV on the Christic form of Christian faith, and the Introduction and Chapter V for a brief discussion of the notion of symbol.

2. Two major works in Latin American liberation Christology are Jon Sobrino, *Christology at the Crossroads: A Latin American Approach,* trans. by John Drury (Maryknoll, N.Y.: Orbis Books, 1978) and Leonardo Boff, *Jesus Christ Liberator: A Critical Christology for Our Time,* trans. by Patrick Hughes (Maryknoll, N.Y.: Orbis Books, 1978). Sobrino has clarified some of his thinking in *Crossroads* in a collection of articles entitled *Jesús en América Latina: Su Significado para la Fe y la Cristología* (San Salvador: UCA/Editores, 1982). Both these authors share this emphasis on the historical Jesus, although Sobrino is more insistent than Boff, with other recent Catholic Christologies such as Hans Küng, *On Being a Christian,* trans. by Edward Quinn (Garden City, N.Y.: Doubleday & Co., 1976) and Edward Schillebeeckx, *Jesus: An Experiment in Christology,* trans. by Hubert Hoskins (New York: A Crossroad Book, The Seabury Press, 1979).

3. David Tracy, in his *The Analogical Imagination: Christian Theology and the Culture of Pluralism* (New York: Crossroad, 1981), pp. 322–347 (with special attention to the notes) is critical of an approach to Christology which lays too much emphasis on a recovery of the Jesus of history through historical-critical method and the making of Jesus a "norm" for Christology. It is clear that the term "norm" is used too loosely both in liberation Christology and in the work of Küng and Schillebeeckx and that the terms needs further examination. My hunch is that the term really refers to the fundamental (in the sense of "fundamental theology") *structure* of Christological understanding. Jesus is the ground of the New Testament message about *him.* In one's fundamental understanding of Jesus Christ one must be able to say *something* significant about that man, if one is not to fall back into the absolute paradoxes of Kierkegaard.

4. Important as this symbol, the Kingdom of God, is for theological reflection, it also plays a major role in the more common language of preaching and general spirituality in Latin America. In the ordinary understanding of Chris-

tians caught up in liberation spirituality, the "Kingdom of God" points to what society under God should be and provides religious motivation and direction for everyday commitment.

5. Jon Sobrino's Christology, which borrows extensively from Jürgen Moltmann's theology of the cross, may be cited to call this generalization into question. And more generally, there is a tendency in Latin America to correlate the suffering of Jesus with the general condition of suffering and oppression which characterizes the situation of the majority of people on that continent. Yet I would still maintain that the dominant theme in Sobrino's Christology is the imitation of the life of the historical Jesus. It may be argued that we cannot know the "actual life and history of Jesus" in any detail. In fact liberation Christology is based on the *pattern* of Jesus' life as that is portrayed in the Synoptic Gospels especially. But the point is that the imagination underlying liberation Christology has its focus on the life lived by an actual human being in history.

6. See especially Sobrino, *Christology at the Crossroads,* pp. 299–307, 388–395.

7. On the missionary purpose and structure of the theology of the early apologists see Jean Daniélou, *Gospel Message and Hellenistic Culture,* trans. and ed. by John Austin Baker (Philadelphia: The Westminster Press, 1973), pp. 7–15.

8. Wilfred Cantwell Smith proposes that all theology be done in the context of the unity of the race and the unity of religious experience and history, and not primarily on the basis of the suppositions of a particularist and confessional standpoint. Although much more work needs to be done simply on the definition of such a perspective, the suggestions that he offers so persuasively amount to a paradigm shift for Christian theology and are especially a profound challenge to traditional Christology. See his *Toward a World Theology: Faith and the Comparative History of Religion* (London: Macmillan Press, 1981). See also Paul F. Knitter, "Theocentric Christology," *Theology Today,* 40 (July 1983), 130–149.

9. I take this to be a seminal idea, one that causes a change in one's basic perspective. It is reflected in much of contemporary theology precisely insofar as theology employs a method of correlation. A fine expression of this view is Langdon Gilkey's *Naming the Whirlwind: The Renewal of God-Language* (New York: The Bobbs-Merrill Company, 1969), in which he argues that the very meaning, as opposed to the truth, of Christian language is called into question by post-modern culture. This has occurred not only outside but also inside the Church. Thus apologetics is required for theology itself, not just to mediate an understanding of Jesus Christ to outsiders, but also to ourselves.

10. That Jesus was a human being is a datum for faith in the special sense that since we do not really know fully what it means to be human, faith allows Jesus to define that for us. Faith accepts Jesus' true humanity as not only real humanity but also as the archetype or definition of what humanity is. See Schillebeeckx, *Jesus,* pp. 599–601.

11. The phrase, "the historical Jesus," refers to the actual, concrete, this-worldly person Jesus of Nazareth as he can be retrieved, reconstructed and known through critical historical research. This is understood as distinct from Jesus resurrected and alive but out of empirical history and no longer an actor in history like ourselves. It is also distinct from the full reality, historical and existential, that constituted the actual person of Jesus. No historically reconstructed portrait of an historical person is equivalent or adequate to his or her concrete reality. But these distinctions for the sake of clarity should not be blown up into separations and oppositions. I understand that it is Jesus who was raised, and that what little can be known of Jesus is true to his historical actuality.

12. The term "substantial" here means something about the substance of Jesus' life that is reflected in the message that he preached and the overall conduct of the way he led his life. From the sources and in that data one can perceive and even know with a very high degree of historical probability something of the "logic of Jesus' life." The logic of a person's life is its overall governing intention which, like a fundamental option, is lived out in practical and concrete detail until one's death. It is captured by narrative forms, stories about a person, as for example in the Synoptic Gospels, because the logic of one's life is constituted by one's action, behavior and whole course of life. "Substantial" therefore is not used quantitatively here and does not refer to a large amount of historical detail about Jesus.

13. "Sufficient" here does not mean that knowledge of the historical Jesus is all one needs for Christology. Rather it means that one does not need more historical knowledge. What we know of Jesus historically is enough historical knowledge.

14. Often the terms "Jesuology" or "Jesusology" are used pejoratively because they suggest a reduction of the significance of Jesus Christ to what can be determined on immanent grounds by an historical method. If this is what is meant, then it is certainly a pejorative implication. Yet the idea represented by these terms has a positive side of recalling what I am calling here the structure of Christology. This becomes immediately apparent when one assumes an apologetic point of view. Christians are those persons in the world who have a faith in God that is mediated by, focused on, and structured by a person who lived in history. The specifically Christological questions revolve around who this person is and what he did.

15. The religious epistemological theory behind this position is one that requires a this-worldly symbol within history as the basis of all religious knowledge and revelation. For an account of this in terms of an historical "medium," where the structure of a medium is identical with what I have called "symbol," see John E. Smith, *Experience and God* (New York: Oxford University Press, 1968), pp. 68–98. From this theoretical basis it is difficult to accept the position of Schubert M. Ogden as expressed most recently in his *The Point of Christology* (San Francisco: Harper & Row, 1982). For him the objective focus or subject matter of Christology is not the "empirical-historical Jesus" but rather the "existential-historical Jesus" who is presented in the kerygma of the New

Testament. But despite his desire to be clear about what is meant by the existential-historical Jesus, the category is still ambiguous. In some places it seems that the existential faith portrait of Jesus is precisely of and about Jesus; the existential includes the actual person of Jesus so that reductively Jesus would still be the focus of Christology, the kerygma would be founded on *memoria Jesu,* and there would be no subject-object dichotomy. Far more often the impression given is that the existential-historical Jesus is a datum within itself, occasioned by Jesus but an isolatable existential reality expressed in the kerygmatic terms of the New Testament, which is as such the objective mediating symbol of our faith in God. In other worlds, there is a break or gap between the existential subjectivity of the framers of the kerygma and Jesus of Nazareth, so that, by a *reductio ad extremum,* were one to use incarnational language, the incarnation occurred in the first disciples or in the New Testament texts. This interpretation is strengthened by Ogden's total concern for soteriology, one that requires no speculation concerning the status of Jesus. Thus I see Ogden presenting a structure of Christology and Christian faith that is radically different than the one presented here. In his theocentric view the objective focus of Christian imagination is the kerygma of the New Testament which mediates God; in our theocentric view the objective focus of the Christian imagination moves through the New Testament to the person of Jesus who mediates God.

16. In terms of David Tracy's characterization of systematic theology as the interpretation of Christian classics, Christology is the interpretation of a classic person. And today such a systematic account should also include an apologetic dimension. In general, Tracy dissociates himself from the procedure of trying to use the historical Jesus as a norm for interpreting Jesus Christ and the Christian message. (See note 3.) I would agree that the historical Jesus cannot be the exclusive norm for Christology. But I still cannot see why what we can and do know about Jesus would not be *a* norm and *a* criterion for Christology since it exerts a continually corrective influence on images that contradict that knowledge and serves as a concrete positive and realistic historical image for inspiration in the Christian life. "The significance of the historical Jesus for Christian faith is that knowledge of this Jesus may be used as a means of testing the claims of the Christs presented in competing kerygmata to be Jesus Christ." Norman Perrin, *Rediscovering the Teaching of Jesus* (New York: Harper & Row, 1967), p. 244. My question relative to Tracy's suggestions is whether in *The Analogical Imagination* he moves Christology from being a study of a classic person to the study of classic texts, and thereby loses the fundamental apologetic edge that he established in his earlier work, *Blessed Rage for Order: The New Pluralism in Theology* (New York: A Crossroad Book, The Seabury Press, 1975). This is still a genuine question on my part, since as far as I can see Christology involves keeping several norms in balance so that the issue is one of emphasis. But as far as Schillebeeckx, Küng and liberation theology are concerned, with their approach through the historical Jesus, they are combining an apologetic (fundamental) and systematic method

and not dissociating them. I shall return to the question of norms in the next chapter in the discussion of interpreting Jesus.

17. Küng, *On Being a Christian*, p. 352.

18. "There is not such a big difference between the way we are able, after Jesus' death, to come to faith in the crucified-and-risen One and the way in which the disciples of Jesus arrived at the same faith." Schillebeeckx, *Jesus*, p. 346. I assume that Schillebeeckx means that there is a fundamental structure of the faith experience that is the same in spite of the obvious differences, as for example the closeness to Jesus and the disciples' concrete memory of him.

19. There is also a certain similarity between our period and the thrust of Chalcedon. We too are moving from a docetic kind of Christological consciousness toward a new stress on the humanity of Jesus. The point that is being made here, however, is that the structure of Christology today is the reverse of that which is exemplified in Chalcedon and the whole movement of Christology in the patristic age that became defined as orthodoxy. That Christology moved from the presupposition and assertion of Jesus' pre-existence and divinity to the full recognition that he was *human*, that is, not unambiguously that Jesus was a human being, but that he had a true human nature. The structure of Christology for today must presuppose that Jesus was a human being and this needs no argument or definition. From this point of departure one must explain what one means by Jesus' divinity.

20. The idea that Jesus himself is the normative symbol for Christology refers back first of all to the argument that defines the structure of Christology. The actual this-worldly person, Jesus, is the basis and referent of Christology. It is for this reason that the historical Jesus, Jesus as uncovered by historical research, enters into Christology as a critical norm, although not as an exclusive norm.

21. The basis of this assertion is the structure of all religious statements as expressions of religious experience. Christian doctrine arises out of Christian faith experience and life commitment. The ultimate norm for doctrine, then, is commitment to God as revealed in Jesus, and any expression of, rendering account of, or statement that is faithful to and coherent with that commitment and its implications is orthodox. Rahner expresses this position relative to Christological orthodoxy in "The Quest for Approaches Leading to an Understanding of the Mystery of the God-Man Jesus," *Theological Investigations*, XIII, trans. by David Bourke (London: Darton, Longman & Todd, 1975), pp. 195–200, esp. p. 198. Or see the reprise of this in *Foundations of Christian Faith: An Introduction to the Idea of Christianity*, trans. by William V. Dych (New York: A Crossroad Book, The Seabury Press, 1978), pp. 293–298. This same idea is found in Küng, Schillebeeckx, Boff, Sobrino and still others. The point, however, is that both in the beginning and today, attachment to God through Jesus, or commitment to Jesus as the point of contact with God, characterizes the genesis of Christology, indeed of Christianity itself, and thus this existential commitment is its basis and its ultimate norm and criterion. Negatively, the norm does not consist in statements about Jesus in their literal historical sense.

22. I realize that the term "norm" is in itself very ambiguous and perhaps should not even be used without an adequate account of how norms function. In fact there are several norms in theology and Christology and not just a single one. I have mentioned faith commitment itself as a norm for orthodoxy as opposed to propositions. Fidelity to common experience today is also a norm since we cannot affirm as theologically true what we take on other grounds to be untrue. But no matter how it is employed, the norming quality of our historical knowledge of Jesus does not refer to a process that can be applied mechanically or in an exact mathematical way. Ultimately, the normative function of our historical knowledge of Jesus for Christology refers back to the structure of revelation and faith and the boundedness to this world of human imagination and knowledge even in religious experience.

23. See Küng, *On Being a Christian,* p. 383.

24. Both Schillebeeckx and Küng speak of the historical Jesus, that is, Jesus as he can be retrieved through the discipline of history, as a norm for Christology. But it is important to distinguish a positive and a negative function of such a norm. The historical Jesus is a negative norm insofar as one should not predicate of Jesus and his significance for Christian faith what is contradicted by historical evidence. An example of how one can see this negative norm functioning today is seen in Roman Catholic theology's reinterpreting what may have been the consciousness of Jesus in contrast to medieval Scholastic views. Relative to nineteenth century Protestant theology, a concern for a truly historical appreciation of Jesus allows one to see that statements such as those common in liberal theology that Jesus had the highest or perfect God-consciousness are not really historical statements but rather speculative attempts to coherently ground Christian faith in Jesus. This negative function is important for a critical interpretation of the meaning of the titles and images given to Jesus in the New Testament and in the course of Christian tradition such as, for example, "Christ the King" or its antithesis "Christ the Revolutionary." Positively the historical Jesus is not strictly a norm; one cannot maintain that one can only assert of Jesus what the discipline of history can establish about him. But while not strictly a positive norm the historical Jesus is a presentation of the person who is the subject matter of Christology, and this focus positively guides and directs Christian imagination. An example of this function may be seen in the manner in which the notion of the Kingdom of God which was central in Jesus' life and teaching is being incorporated into current Christology.

VII. INTERPRETING JESUS FOR TODAY

1. Despite Schillebeeckx's dismissal of this distinction between objective and subjective salvation, at least as it was handled in Scholastic theology, I believe it still makes sense to distinguish, but not to separate, the objective question of how Jesus is Savior and how that salvation is appropriated by other human beings in history, even though existentially Jesus Christ is really Savior only insofar as people are actually saved through him. See Chapter II, note 17,

and Edward Schillebeeckx, *Christ: The Experience of Jesus as Lord,* trans. by John Bowden (New York: A Crossroad Book, The Seabury Press, 1980), p. 514.

2. See Chapter VI, note 20. On the most basic level in which this faith is constituted, namely, faith in God mediated and focused through the person of Jesus, this faith does not change. The elementary, specific and defining structure of Christian faith is its Christic form, that is, as faith in God, the object of all religious faith, the person of Jesus is its determining concrete historical symbol. But the psychological form of this faith, and the social historical form of it as well, must change in the course of personal and social history. See Chapter IV on the changing forms of faith.

3. These statements do not imply a denial of the authority and normativity of Scripture and the New Testament witness. Nor do they minimize the fact that faith in God through Jesus is further mediated through the witness of Scripture. Therefore, the witness of the New Testament is also a norm for current theology. What is being asserted here, however, is that religious experience of Jesus in any age also has a relative autonomy above and beyond its sources. Faith in God through Jesus, once engendered, is not simply a function of its mediation through the New Testament witness and interpretation. If this were the case, one could not reinterpret the New Testament apostolic witness, one would be bound to repeating the words of Scripture fundamentalistically. Christology, therefore, inevitably requires a holding together in balance, in mutual and self-critical tension, a variety of norms: the historical Jesus who is being interpreted, the original, originating and constituting interpretations of Jesus that are found in the New Testament, interpretations of Jesus from Christian history and tradition, and our own historical situation which provides the context and language for our own interpretation of Jesus and the particular focus for it.

4. The best chronicle of this tension in New Testament interpretation that I know is still the debate between Alfred Loisy in *The Gospel and the Church,* trans by Christopher Home, intro. by Bernard B. Scott (Philadelphia: Fortress Press, 1976) and Maurice Blondel, "History and Dogma," *The Letter on Apologetics and History and Dogma,* ed., trans. and intro. by Alexander Dru and Illtyd Trethowan (New York: Holt, Rinehart and Winston, 1964), pp. 219–287. Both of these men were right in what they defended; both were wrong in not appreciating what the other had to say. The debate is a good example of two differentiated consciousnesses, the one through the discipline of history, the other through the discipline of philosophy, that could not really understand or appreciate the point of view of the other. A good expression of the mediating position I am expressing here, I think, is found in Schillebeeckx's meditation on how transcendence must be found within the *human* career of Jesus. Edward Schillebeeckx, *Jesus: An Experiment in Christology,* trans. by Hubert Hoskins (New York: A Crossroad Book, The Seabury Press, 1979), pp. 626–636.

5. Jon Sobrino, *Christology at the Crossroads: A Latin American Approach,* trans. by John Drury (Maryknoll, N.Y.: Orbis Books, 1978), pp. 79–145.

6. Leonardo Boff, "Salvation in Jesus Christ and the Process of Liberation," *Concilium,* 96 (1974), 80–85.

7. Hans Küng, *On Being a Christian,* trans. by Edward Quinn (Garden City, N.Y.: Doubleday & Co., 1976), p. 251. Küng uses this refrain to structure the center portion of his Christology dealing with the life of Jesus, pp. 214–277. Schillebeeckx too uses the formula describing Jesus as the "champion of man's cause as God's cause." Edward Schillebeeckx, *Interim Report on the Books* JESUS & CHRIST, trans. by John Bowden (New York: Crossroad Books, 1981), p. 54.

8. According to Norman Perrin, this is not a hard fact of historical knowledge, but it is one that can be defended vigorously. I suppose that he means that all the evidence points toward it, while none of the evidence contradicts it. See Norman Perrin, *Rediscovering the Teaching of Jesus* (New York: Harper & Row, 1967), p. 236.

9. As far as I can see, Jesus' resurrection does not in itself disclose a general resurrection. Rather it reveals the resurrection of Jesus' kind of life. One can, and the New Testament does arrive at the notion of general resurrection and universal salvation. But at the same time one is also confronted there with the mystery of sin and the idea of judgment that must always be taken into account. Although there is no consensus on this in theology today, more and more theologians speak with Origen of universal salvation. But this can only be done cautiously with attention to the other data.

10. Küng, *On Being a Christian,* p. 360.

11. That is, in Jesus' case and, more generally, for his kind of life. One must be careful here not to reify abstract language. Death is not an entity; it is a concrete event in each person's life.

12. See, for example, Gustaf Aulén, *Christus Victor: An Historical Study of the Three Main Types of the Idea of the Atonement,* trans. by A. G. Hebert (London: SPCK, 1950), pp. 139–176. I refer to the type as contrasted with classical objective theories and not to the content that Aulén ascribes to the subjective theory, which he draws largely from nineteenth century theology. Boff asks what the meaning of salvation and liberation wrought by Jesus Christ is. The question, he says, should be asked in such a way that it "uncovers and establishes the concrete means which incarnate in history the liberation of Jesus Christ. Discussion on the universal level is not sufficient; it must be verified in the course of human life. Without this mediation universal explanations remain unreal and ideological. . . ." Leonardo Boff, *Teología del Cautiverio y de la Liberación* (Madrid: Ediciones Paulinas, 1978), p. 206. Boff reinterprets salvation existentially and historically in this work and in contrast to classical objective conceptions.

13. See J. Peter Schineller, "Christ and Church: A Spectrum of Views," *Theological Studies,* 37 (December 1976), 545–566 for the typology in reference to which this statement is made. A constitutive Christology is one that maintains that Jesus causes the salvation of all human beings. A non-constitutive and normative Christology, as is maintained here, asserts that while Jesus may cause the salvation of those who have some historical connection

with him, he is not the cause of the salvation of all, because not the cause of an experience of revelation through him. Rather Jesus is the normative revelation of the God who saves also apart from Jesus' historical influence, and he is the revelation of the pattern of saved and ultimately meaningful authentic human existence. The meaning of the word "normative" is precisely determined by its use in opposition to absolute historical relativism. A normative revelation of God is one that is decisive and unsurpassable. Without some such norm in history no absolute commitment to God and the benevolent nature of reality, no really final commitment to history, is possible. Such a normative view of Jesus Christ, however, does not positively reveal a sum of data about God or negate all other positive revelations of God. It does however negate any claim to authenticity of a revelation of God that depicts God as demonic or malevolent. The normativity of Jesus and his revelation is attached precisely to the benevolence of God that he mediates; God is a God of boundless love. There have been and there may be further authentic revelations of God, but they will not portray God as other than the God of Jesus Christ in this respect.

14. In the context of our culture, with its historical consciousness and pluralism, and given the variety of revelations of God that we encounter, the claim that there is a definitive, unsurpassed or normative revelation of God and human existence is a far more exacting claim than that a Savior figure descended from the heavens, became an incarnate God and ascended again to the heights was to the culture of the eastern Mediterranean in Jesus' time.

15. Schillebeeckx makes much of this, considering it central to an explanation of Jesus' life. *Jesus,* pp. 256–271, 652–661. Whether or not New Testament data confirms it, one may assume that Jesus had an experience of God.

16. They are normative in the sense that they must be accounted for. They are not normative in the sense of external conceptual prescriptions. Since these conceptual symbols do not all mean the same thing on the level of conception, since indeed at some points they are in opposition, if taken literally they would contradict and cancel each other out.

17. This view is insisted upon by Jon Sobrino throughout his *Christology at the Crossroads.*

18. Religious language is always symbolic language, but it may also be explicitly ontological language. The term "religious symbol" *per se* implies that we do not know transcendent reality directly. Thus all religious language has both a finite intelligibility and also points the mind toward transcendent reality allowing it to participate in or become aware of absolute mystery. But when a finite piece of reality is itself a religious symbol, this has implications for the nature of that reality. For example, the doctrine of creation lies behind the function of religious symbols, for it implies that all reality participates in God's creative power and thus is able to mediate God through its very finitude. In the case of a human person being God's symbolic mediator, and being so in a unique way, the participation of that symbol, namely Jesus himself, in the presence and power of God is also unique. The point here, however, is that the human "explanation" of this in ontological terms remains symbolic language. It is not really explanation but a rendering of this religious experience in terms

conceptually coherent with one's overview of the world and of being itself. The construction of these explanations is not subjectivist or sheer projection, however, for the project must correspond to what religious experience tells us to be the case.

19. Karl Rahner, *Foundations of Christian Faith: An Introduction to the Idea of Christianity,* trans. by William V. Dych (New York: A Crossroad Book, The Seabury Press, 1978), pp. 290–291. The reference here is not to the Chalcedonian formula itself which may be interpreted as precisely against monophysitism and as preserving the paradoxical unity of the finite integrity of Jesus' being a human being and the real presence of no less than God to and within his life as symbolic and real mediator of God. It is rather neo-Chalcedonian theological development that bears this criticism.

20. For example, Thomas Aquinas, *Summa Theologiae,* III, q. 48, a. 6. The limits of space and the intention of these chapters forbid an essay into speculative Christology at this point. However the lines along which such a speculative constructive effort would proceed would follow the Spirit Christologies of the New Testament.

21. These reflections, made from an existential and historical point of view, are interpretations of major themes underlying the whole of Sobrino's Christology in *Christology at the Crossroads.* There discipleship is taken as the primary response to Jesus on the further premise that Jesus is portrayed primarily as "the way" to God and that one cannot know who Jesus is unless one is a follower of Jesus. All of this presupposes an existential view of religious knowledge and a certain view of the priority of praxis to theory in effective or "real" religious knowledge. This is consistent with the view of faith proposed in Chapter IV. The basis of this position extends well beyond Sobrino to a whole tradition in modern philosophy and theology both Catholic and Protestant.

22. The grounds for this lie in the theology of grace and the doctrine of the Spirit of God. The symbol of the Spirit of God was of course operative in the whole Old Testament tradition and is associated with creation itself. Chapter VIII will deal with the doctrine of the Spirit which is the always contemporaneous principle of salvation.

23. In its attention to social oppression and the death it dispenses on a wide scale, liberation theology does not deal carefully or at length with the forms of passivity, bondage and dependence on the personal level of human freedom that cannot be overcome. But this theme is not totally overlooked either. For example, Sobrino sees conversion to Jesus Christ in terms of the possibility of each person, and thus he distinguishes between the conversion of those who will inevitably remain more passive and those who are released for some active discipleship. *Christology at the Crossroads,* pp. 55–61.

24. See the six themes characteristic of liberation Christology outlined at the beginning of Chapter VI.

25. These two chapters on Christology have justified the stress of liberation Christology on the historical Jesus, but they have not tried to recapture and represent the power and rhetorical persuasiveness of that Christology. Beyond that, I have tried also to justify the use of Scripture by liberation theo-

logians against what sometimes appears as an uncritical and naive representation of Jesus. In fact, because liberation theology in Latin America is a theology not only in behalf of the poor but also directed to the poor and uneducated (in terms of formal education), its rhetoric is often uncluttered with critical distinctions. But within its presentation I see four norms or criteria at work. The first is the focus on Jesus as an actual human being and the use of the historical Jesus as a critical norm for Christ projections. Our new apologetic context demands this. Second, there are the New Testament stories about Jesus that represent his life in a narrative form and thus appeal to human imagination in order to disclose and release possibilities for our human life today. For a parallel in North American theology see David Tracy's self-consciously methodological and rhetorically powerful representations of Jesus through an interpretation of New Testament genre in the second half of his *The Analogical Imagination: Christian Theology and the Culture of Pluralism* (New York: Crossroad, 1981). This is where the religious power of Christology lies, in retelling the story of this man in a way that tries to disclose his transcendent claim upon us. What is important here, however, is that these narratives be bound both critically and through the human imagination to the human being Jesus. Third, attention is given to the various normative statements and interpretations concerning the person and work of Jesus in the New Testament, conciliar and theological tradition, all of which, however, need reinterpretation for today. And, fourth, our contemporary situation and context is a norm because it sets forth the particular demand for the intelligibility that is needed today. This crisis of the meaning of history sets the focus for our theology.

26. Liberation Christology, I believe, does not stress enough a distinction between salvation as an objective historical process, which can be described through abstraction and generalization, and subjective salvation, which ultimately has its basis in personal, but precisely not individualistic, conversion. This is altogether understandable given the current situation in Latin America and the merely personalist, private and existential interpretations that it seeks to overcome. But a movement for liberation on the social level *may* be motivated by *mere* self-interest and not the service of others. One needs a religiously self-critical principle that is also written into theology. Emancipation and amelioration of one's social condition in no way ensures religious salvation or union with God; in fact the opposite is often the case. This self-critical statement is present in liberation theology as a whole. But the distinction between a general social process of liberation and personal participation in it on the basis of religious and Christian grounds preserves this critical dimension within the more general identification of salvation and liberation.

27. I use the term "emancipation" here in distinction from liberation to mean a freedom on any level bestowed on a person or a people but toward which they remain entirely passive, without responding to or participating in the liberating process. Schubert Ogden too sees need for clarifying distinctions within the ambiguously general notion of liberation. Although I do not reproduce his distinctions here, I borrow the term emancipation from him. See Schu-

bert M. Ogden, *Faith and Freedom: Toward a Theology of Liberation* (Nashville: Abingdon, 1979), p. 95.

28. Schillebeeckx, *Jesus,* pp. 17–18, 673–674.

29. One of the best and most accurate, and hence depressing and disorienting, retellings of the Latin American story is by Penny Lernoux, *Cry of the People* (Garden City, N.Y.: Doubleday & Co., 1980).

VIII. THE SPIRIT OF GOD'S GRACIOUS LIBERATING PRESENCE AND POWER IN HUMAN EXISTENCE

1. Although this position is consistent in the whole of Christian tradition, few theologians in the history of theology have expressed this systematic linkage between the doctrines of Christ and the Spirit, between faith in Christ that generates salvation and the role of the Spirit, more clearly than John Calvin. The Spirit is the interior principle of the appropriation, of real or actual illumination, love and acceptance, of the external Word of God addressed to us through Jesus. See John Calvin, *Institutes of the Christian Religion,* ed. by John T. McNeill and trans. by Ford Lewis Battles (Philadelphia: The Westminster Press, 1960), Bk III, Ch 1, pp. 537–542.

2. See Edward Schillebeeckx, *Christ: The Experience of Jesus as Lord,* trans. by John Bowden (New York: A Crossroad Book, The Seabury Press, 1980), pp. 463–535. Here, after surveying the whole New Testament corpus from the point of view of the themes of grace and salvation, Schillebeeckx tries to synthesize the great pluralism and variety of data found there into a few of its most elementary usages, meanings and ideas.

3. I have surveyed some of the principal contributions to a theology of grace from Christian tradition in Roger Haight, *The Experience and Language of Grace* (New York: Paulist Press, 1979).

4. In spite of Calvin's clarification of the idea of justification by his view that salvation consists in both justification and sanctification, he still agrees with Luther in holding that saving grace is essentially justification through accepting Christ by faith. And he faults Augustine for identifying the idea of grace with sanctification and the Holy Spirit. "Augustine's view, or at any rate his manner of stating it, we must not entirely accept. For even though he admirably deprives the human person of all credit for righteousness and transfers it to God's grace, he still subsumes grace under sanctification, by which we are reborn in newness of life through the Spirit." *Institutes,* Bk III, Ch 11, *op. cit.,* p. 746.

5. Karl Rahner, "Some Implications of the Scholastic Concept of Uncreated Grace," *Theological Investigations,* I, trans. by Cornelius Ernst (Baltimore: Helicon Press, 1961), pp. 343–346. Rahner is however open to the scriptural language of grace referring to the indwelling of the Spirit. It should be noted further that this is an early article of Rahner in which he is arguing with Scholastic theology and thus presupposing both that tradition and an objective doctrine of the immanent Trinity. I am proposing a theology of grace

and the Spirit "from below," from religious experience, so that these symbols are in their first moment expressions of Christian experience. I would argue that if this method or point of view were applied to Rahner's theology consistently, his system would lead toward the identification of the symbol "grace" with that of the "Spirit of God." As far as I can see, the whole first part of Rahner's *Foundations of Christian Faith: An Introduction to the Idea of Christianity,* trans. by William Dych (New York: A Crossroad Book, The Seabury Press, 1978), on grace *is* Rahner's doctrine of the Holy Spirit. In other words, although the equation is not always verbalized, it is actually being made. But occasionally Rahner does make this equation explicitly. Cf. p. 317.

6. This can be verified in the major landmarks in the history of the theology of grace, for example, in the theologies of Augustine, Aquinas, Erasmus, Luther, Calvin, Schleiermacher, Rahner and liberation theology. In the case of Aquinas, however, who is less experiential in his theology than the others, the concept of experience merely has to be broadened to include a consciousness that was shaped and differentiated by Aristotelianism in order to see that the point obtains in his case as well.

7. These works are: Juan Luis Segundo, *Grace and the Human Condition,* trans. by John Drury (Maryknoll, N.Y.: Orbis Books, 1973), and Leonardo Boff, *Liberating Grace,* trans. by John Drury (Maryknoll, N.Y.: Orbis Books, 1979).

8. Segundo, *Grace and the Human Condition,* p. 44.

9. *Ibid.,* pp. 86–94.

10. See for example the general description of history as a history of liberation-salvation in Gustavo Gutiérrez, *A Theology of Liberation: History, Politics and Salvation,* ed. and trans. by Caridad Inda and John Eagleson (Maryknoll, N.Y.: Orbis Books, 1973), pp. 149–187. Here Gutiérrez views history in general by interpreting it in terms of the objective symbols of scriptural theology. The existential basis for the position, however, lies in an interpretation of the experience of saving grace.

11. Juan Hernández Pico, "The Experience of Nicaragua's Revolutionary Christians," *The Challenge of Basic Christian Communities,* ed. by Sergio Torres and John Eagleson, trans. by John Drury (Maryknoll, N.Y.: Orbis Books, 1981), pp. 70–73.

12. Augustine is the father of the dogma of grace in western theology. He also fathered the view of the radical sinfulness of human nature which nowhere appears with such thoroughgoing profundity before him. At bottom he was not arguing with Pelagius simply over a doctrine of grace, which Pelagius held and in a manner more traditional than Augustine, but over sin. Augustine's basic argument, namely that if human freedom was sound, Christ came in vain, is a statement about the bondage of human freedom. All that we do of positive salvific value, then, is initiated by God's Spirit released by Christ.

13. The best treatment of the doctrine of sin in a very short space to appear in recent years is that of Langdon Gilkey, *Message and Existence: An Introduction to Christian Theology* (New York: A Crossroad Book, The Seabury Press, 1979), pp. 111–157. See also Reinhold Niebuhr, *The Nature and Destiny*

of Man, Vol. I, *Human Nature* (New York: Charles Scribner's Sons, 1964), pp. 178–264.

14. Thus liberal theology in the nineteenth century denied the supernatural sphere and with this tended to blur or eradicate a distinction between two orders of reality, that of creation and that of redemption or salvation. Christianity was viewed as a particular religion within the general context of natural religion or religion as such. For liberal theology, the distinction of these two orders leads to an interventionism which is unintelligible. But liberal theology also lacked a radical doctrine of sin which to us today also appears unintelligible.

15. Karl Rahner, "The Order of Redemption within the Order of Creation," *The Christian Commitment,* trans. by Cecily Hastings (New York: Sheed and Ward, 1963), pp. 38–74.

16. This theory is proposed in Rahner, "Some Implications of the Scholastic Concept of Uncreated Grace," pp. 319–346.

17. Rahner takes this to indicate a real distinction of manner of being present. The purpose of this distinction is to preserve intact the tradition of double gratuity; both creation and grace are totally gratuitous. God does not "have to" be present to us by grace or save human existence. For my part, I am not prepared to affirm this real distinction because of the ambiguity of the results to which it often leads. I take this as a useful thought scheme to express the experience of the new initiative of God and the gratuity of grace whether this is a double or a single gratuity and initiative.

18. The idea of Aquinas is constructive: God works in creatures according to their natures. Since human beings are free, God works in human existence from within freedom and not against it through coercion or force. Aquinas, *Summa Theologiae,* I–II, Q. 113, a. 3.

19. Or, in the language of Langdon Gilkey, the Spirit is the symbol pointing to God's presence within human existence and active in the human community, and the Kingdom of God is an eschatological symbol pointing to the future and telos of that presence of the Spirit, and thus drawing people toward it. Langdon Gilkey, *Message and Existence,* pp. 219–221. A response to the Spirit of God is a surrender to God's rule (subjective or existential) so that one directs one's freedom toward the Kingdom of God (objective).

20. Luther, in order to make the contrast between faith and works, defined works precisely in contrast to the grace that, in the view expressed here, sustains faith and works together. "But works, being inanimate things, cannot glorify God, although they can, if faith is present, be done to the glory of God." Martin Luther, "The Freedom of a Christian," *Luther's Works,* 31, ed. by Harold J. Grimm (Philadelphia: Fortress Press, 1957), p. 353. I believe that this very limited sense of works as "inanimate things" is what allows Luther to make such sharp and paradoxical negations of the value of human freedom relative to salvation. Once the idea of "works" is seen as a more general and less pejorative term, as including also the whole of a person's response to reality, and as possibly being sustained by God and the justifying and sanctifying power of God's Spirit, much of the antithesis and paradox is removed from

Luther's view. In his positive account of the justified person grace through faith spontaneously flows over into the works of love. "Therefore, if we recognize the great and precious things which are given us, as Paul says (Rom 5:5), our hearts will be filled by the Holy Spirit with the love that makes us free, joyful, almightly workers and conquerors over all tribulations, servants of our neighbors, and yet lords of all." *Ibid.*, p. 367.

21. The ideas of justification by faith and justification by love are convertible. As far as I can see, it makes no sense to separate faith and love when one is speaking of a radical response to God. Faith includes love, love implies faith; at a deeper level, below a phenomenology that can make distinctions between these two as consciously motivated acts, faith and love are both characterizations of a fundamental self-transcending openness to God. See Paul Tillich, *Dynamics of Faith* (New York: Harper & Row, 1957), pp. 112–117, and Karl Rahner, "The Theology of Hope," *Theology Digest,* Sesquicentennial Issue (February 1968), pp. 78–87.

22. I have developed this theme of participation in the construction and maintenance of institutions of social liberation as an authentic spirituality in "Institutional Grace and Corporate Spirituality," *Spirituality Today,* 31 (September-December 1979), pp. 209–220, 324–334.

23. In Chapter VII this same point was made in the context of the salvific work of Christ.

24. I have just suggested that the poor in this struggle for liberation may be just as much a victim of sin and egoism as anyone else. But the cause of liberation pursued by the poor and by all people in behalf of the victims of society is not a response to the moral goodness or virtue of the poor. The struggle for justice in society is a response to objective oppression and injustice. Liberation theology is thus correct in insisting on the distinction between subjective virtue and objective justice. The victims of injustice are especially loved by God because of their victimization, not because they are morally good. And the Spirit of God moves human freedom to respond to the victimization of people which is objectively unjust and sinful, a sinfulness in which we all participate, and not to some idealized notion of the virtue of poor people.

25. See especially Calvin's short treatise on the Christian life in the *Institutes,* Bk III, Ch 6–10, *op. cit.,* pp. 684–725.

26. Ernst Troeltsch, in *The Social Teaching of the Christian Churches,* II, trans. by Olive Wyon (New York: Harper Torchbooks, 1960), pp. 576–655, interprets the specific contribution of Calvin and Calvinism to the theology of the relation of the Church and Christian spirituality to the world and society.

27. There is some basis and reason in Aquinas' refocusing the issue of grace in relation not only to sin but also to the finitude of human nature. See Haight, *The Experience and Language of Grace,* pp. 58–61. The salvific impulse and initiative of God's Spirit not only restores sinful human freedom but also enhances human finitude. This dimension of the workings of grace becomes apparent when grace is seen in the context of death and the enormous complexity of the task of building the Kingdom in the world even apart from the problem of sin.

IX. THE NATURE AND LIBERATING MISSION OF THE CHURCH

1. For an account of this shift in the fundamental theology of the Church see Avery Dulles, "The Church: Witness and Sacrament of Faith," in *A Church To Believe In: Discipleship and the Dynamics of Freedom* (New York: Crossroad, 1982), pp. 41–52. The same article appears in René Latourelle and Gerald O'Collins, ed., *Problems and Perspective of Fundamental Theology* (New York: Paulist Press, 1982), pp. 259–273, under the title "The Church: Sacrament and Ground of Faith."

2. Gustavo Gutiérrez, *A Theology of Liberation: History, Politics and Salvation*, trans. & ed. by Caridad Inda and John Eagleson (Maryknoll, N.Y.: Orbis Books, 1973), p. 256.

3. Thus Juan Luis Segundo in defining the specifying characteristic of Christians and the Church calls them those "who know" that which has been going on in history from the beginning. See Juan Luis Segundo, *The Community Called Church*, trans. by John Drury (Maryknoll, N.Y.: Orbis Books, 1973), pp. 10–11, 24–25.

4. Johannes Metz in his early characterizations of political theology defines one of its primary characteristics as an effort to overcome this individualistic and privatizing bias. See Metz, *Theology of the World*, trans. by William Glen-Doepel (New York: Herder and Herder, 1969), pp. 108–111.

5. In general one can credit a retrieval of a radical doctrine of sin for a general abandonment of the theology of the social gospel reflected for example in the work of Walter Rauschenbusch. It is not that Rauschenbusch lacked a "firm" doctrine of sin, for the concept of sin is a major theme in his classic work *A Theology for the Social Gospel* (New York-Nashville: Abingdon Press, 1945). But a radical doctrine of sin, both personal and collective, in the tradition of Augustine and the Reformers, and represented by the neo-orthodox theologians, tended to view with suspicion all ideas of progress and social amelioration and their connection with Christian faith.

6. The Church in every Christian theology is viewed in one way or another as the mediator of liberation, the liberation that comes from Christ through faith by grace. Salvation is a form of liberation. The distinctive element of liberation theology, as indeed of the theology of the social gospel, is that this liberation is also related to human, secular and social emancipation. The term "emancipation" is used here to state this principle clearly. See Schubert Ogden, *Faith and Freedom: Toward a Theology of Liberation* (Nashville: Abingdon, 1979), pp. 69–95.

7. A classic study of the relationship of the Church to the world and the influence of the world and history on the Church is that of Ernst Troeltsch, *The Social Teachings of the Christian Churches*, 2 vols., trans. by Olive Wyon (New York: Harper Torchbooks, 1960).

8. For example, James Gustafson, *Treasure in Earthen Vessels: The Church as a Human Community* (New York: Harper and Row, 1961). See also the methodological essays of Joseph A. Komonchak, "Ecclesiology and Social

Theory: A Methodological Essay," *The Thomist* 45 (1981), pp. 262–283; "Lonergan and the Tasks of Ecclesiology," in *Creativity and Method: Essays in Honor of Bernard Lonergan, S.J.*, ed. by Matthew L. Lamb (Milwaukee: Marquette University Press, 1981), pp. 265–273.

9. The phrase, "doctrinal reductionism," is Gustafson's in *Treasure*. It refers to a language about the Church that is purely biblical, doctrinal or theological. "A doctrinal reductionism refuses to take seriously the human elements in the Church's life, or if it acknowledges them it does not explore or explicate them except in doctrinal language" (p. 105).

10. Wilfred Cantwell Smith, in his *Toward a World Theology: Faith and the Comparative History of Religion* (Philadelphia: The Westminster Press, 1981), deals with the significance of the world religions for Christian faith and theology.

11. Segundo, *A Community Called Church*, pp. 3–11.

12. Another interpretation of the development of the Church during the first century would stress the element of unity in the consciousness of all the churches among themselves. In this view the development was not so much one in which the apostolic movement created distinct churches, but a movement by which the one Church took up residence in different places. Thus the Church remained the one Church of God, or of Jesus Christ, because each remained close to its common source; there was one Church but it existed in Corinth, in Rome, in Antioch, and so on. For example, see the salutation of *Clement's First Letter* (ca. 96) in *Early Christian Fathers*, trans. and ed. by Cyril C. Richardson (New York: Macmillan Publishing Co., 1970), p. 43. It is difficult to adjudicate these positions, on either historical or theological grounds, because of the lack of clear data and because pluralism always involves both unity and differences within that unity. The point that I am emphasizing here is simply that the various churches inevitably took on something of their own character due to their specific historical circumstances.

13. See Hans Küng, *The Church*, trans. by Ray and Rosaleen Ockenden (New York: Sheed and Ward, 1967), pp. 230–231.

14. Rudolf Bultmann, *Theology of the New Testament*, Vol. I, trans. by Kendrick Grobel (New York: Charles Scribner's Sons, 1951), pp. 37–42.

15. See H. Richard Niebuhr, *The Meaning of Revelation* (New York: The Macmillan Co., 1960), pp. 38–42.

16. Avery Dulles, "Imaging the Church for the 1980s," in *A Church To Believe In*, pp. 1–18. The same article was also published in *Thought* 56 (1981), pp. 121–138 and *Catholic Mind* 79 (1981).

17. This continuity should be insisted upon. But Dulles passes over too rapidly the issue of Jesus' intention of founding a Church, as opposed to a band of disciples, and the formal characteristics which would make such a band specifically the Christian Church, as opposed to another kind of religious community, for example, a Jewish community.

18. In the words of Moltmann: "What we have to learn . . . is not that the church 'has' a mission, but the very reverse: that the mission of Christ creates its own church. Mission does not come from the church; it is from mission and

in the light of mission that the church has to be understood." Jürgen Molt-mann, *The Church in the Power of the Spirit: A Contribution to Messianic Ecclesiology*, trans. by Margaret Kohl (New York: Harper & Row, 1977), p. 10.

19. Jon Sobrino, who also insists on the prior nature or quality of the reality of mission to the formation of the Church itself, sees this dimension of mission rooted historically in Jesus' life and his sending out of the disciples on mission as recorded in the Synoptic Gospels. Jon Sobrino, "'Evangelización e Iglesia en América Latina,'" *Encuentro 80* 1 (Enero-Febrero 1980), pp. 151–153. This article is also found in *ECA* (Centro de Estudios Centroaméricanos) 32 (1977), 723–748.

20. J. C. Hoekendijk, *The Church Inside Out*, trans. by Isaac C. Rottenberg (Philadelphia: The Westminster Press, 1966).

21. The point here is that salvation is the work of God, one that extends beyond the borders of the Church. In another sense, as the medium of saving grace to Christians, one could say that the Church is constitutive of the salvation of Christians.

22. The following idealistic description of the Church is meant to mediate a contrast experience. The Church is not fully what is described here, and this will be immediately apparent to the reader. There is no need to single out and enumerate the failings of the Church at this point. As David Tracy has said: "Who but a fool would attempt to refute this charge of corruption to the historical reality of the Christian church? ... And yet, for the Christian self-understanding the church remains an authentic object of faith." *The Analogical Imagination: Christian Theology and the Culture of Pluralism* (New York: Crossroad, 1981), p. 50. This utopic account is thus both an implied internal self-criticism of the Church on the basis of the message of Jesus Christ and a stimulus for constant reform.

23. Segundo, *The Community Called Church*, pp. 78–86.

X. SACRAMENTS IN A MISSION CHURCH

1. Juan Luis Segundo, *The Sacraments Today*, trans. by John Drury (Maryknoll, N.Y.: Orbis Books, 1974). This volume was originally published in 1971.

2. Cf. Segundo, *Sacraments*, pp. 12–15. This principle is really fundamental to the whole logic and thesis of Segundo concerning the sacraments and is a supposition running throughout the book.

3. Gustavo Gutiérrez, *A Theology of Liberation: History, Politics and Salvation*, trans. and ed. by Caridad Inda and John Eagleson (Maryknoll, N.Y.: Orbis Books, 1973), pp. 262–265. Segundo treats the prophetic function of sacraments in terms of their power to signify, raise consciousness and challenge Christian responsibility. "A community gathered around a liberative paschal message needs signs which fashion it and question it, which imbue it with a sense of responsiblity and enable it to create its own word about human history. This is precisely what the sacraments are—and nothing else but that." Segundo, *Sacraments*, p. 99. Cf. also pp. 50–51.

4. Segundo, *Sacraments,* pp. 53–59. "[The efficacy of the sacraments] demands that the sacraments be historically 'true': that is, efficacious with respect to human liberation in real-life history. In other words, the sacraments will be valid and efficacious, as Christ intended, to the extent that they are a consciousness-raising and motivating celebration of human liberative action in history. That does not reduce them to a merely human gesture. God is operative in them, but God's activity consists in working through the praxis of human beings. Hence it condenses in the sacramental celebration where human beings intensify their conscious awareness of the import and liberative force of their action. Where that does not happen, there efficacious truth and true efficacy will be missing—no matter how perfect the rite is. And hence, we would not be dealing with the Christian sacrament" (p. 55). This theme is also prominent in Sobrino, at least implicitly, in terms of a contrast between cultic worship and historical discipleship. See Jon Sobrino, *Christology at the Crossroads, A Latin American Approach,* trans. by John Drury (Maryknoll, N.Y.: Orbis Books, 1978), pp. 299–304.

5. Segundo, *Sacraments,* pp. 55–59 and *passim.* Segundo's definition of magic is the following: "Magical actions are different from ordinary actions in two respects, insofar as their outcome is concerned. Firstly, in terms of expected efficacy, there is no normal relationship between the means employed and the outcome. Secondly, the outcome is not dependent on whim; it is tied by a superhuman power to certain fixed ritual gestures or words." *Sacraments,* p. 6.

6. A strong criticism of liberation theology at this point, not precisely in terms of worship, but of a lack of subordination of human piety and ethics to God and God's purposes, is found in James Gustafson, *Ethics from a Theocentric Perspective,* I, *Theology and Ethics* (Chicago: The University of Chicago Press, 1981), pp. 22–25. Of course Gustafson criticizes a great deal of Christian theology for the same thing, of making human existence the measure of the content of religious piety. But his extreme theocentric point of view in this book allows the question to be put with utmost clarity in terms of a contrast of basic visions of reality. Other vaguer articulations of the same suspicion are couched in terms of a reduction of the vertical dimension of Christian faith to the horizontal. This objection will be met in the course of this chapter. The framework for a response consists in seeing the Christian message as appealing integrally to all three dimensions of human freedom.

7. See Juan Luis Segundo, "Capitalism versus Socialism: Crux Theologica," in *Frontiers of Theology in Latin America,* ed. by Rosino Gibellini and trans. by John Drury (Maryknoll, N.Y.: Orbis Books, 1979), pp. 240–259, where he explores the qualifications "absolute" and "relative" as applied to human activity in relation to its historical and ultimate goals.

8. Virtually the same theology of symbol, one sharing this paradoxical or dialectical quality, is found in both Karl Rahner and Paul Tillich. See Karl Rahner, "The Theology of Symbol," *Theological Investigations,* IV, trans. by Kevin Smyth (Baltimore: Helicon Press, 1966), pp. 221–252; Paul Tillich, "Theology and Symbolism," in *Religious Symbolism,* ed. by F. Ernest Johnson

(New York: Harper and Brothers, 1955), pp. 107–116; "The Religious Symbol," in *Myth and Symbol*, ed. by F. W. Dillistone (London: S.P.C.K., 1966), pp. 15–34. Cf. also John E. Smith, *Experience and God* (New York: Oxford University Press, 1968), pp. 68–98.

9. In this schema I am following the tradition of double gratuity in the theology of grace formulated by Augustine and preserved in the theology of Rahner. See Karl Rahner, "The Order of Redemption within the Order of Creation," in *The Christian Commitment*, trans. by Cecily Hastings (New York: Sheed and Ward, 1963), pp. 38–74.

10. See Gustafson, *Theology and Ethics*, pp. 195–325, where he exploits the datum of human existence as a part of nature and uses the data of science in a unique way for theological understanding.

11. "What is all science, if not the existence of things in you, in your reason? What is all art and culture if not your existence in the things to which you give measure, form and order? And how can both come to life in you except in so far as there lives immediately in you the eternal unity of Reason and Nature, the universal existence of all finite things in the Infinite?" Friedrich Schleiermacher, *On Religion: Speeches to Its Cultural Despisers*, trans. by John Oman (New York: Harper & Row, 1958), p. 39. Cf. *The Christian Faith*, I (New York: Harper & Row, 1963), pp. 5–26, for a transcendental phenomenological account of God-consciousness as an experience of absolute dependence.

12. For the impact of the consciousness of being in history on theology see Johannes B. Metz, *Theology of the World*, trans. by William Glen-Doepel (New York: Herder and Herder, 1969).

13. Sobrino, *Christology at the Crossroads*, pp. 278–286.

14. In medieval theology the distinction between matter and form, the symbol and its informing interpretative word, applies analogously in each sacrament. The symbol may be a thing, or an action, or a combination of both. In the case of Scripture, which may also be conceived as a sacrament, it would be necessary to look at the writings empirically, as a book with marks on a page, in order to distinguish, although not separate, the symbolic dimension from the levels of meaning that inform the book.

15. The efficacy of the sacraments will be discussed further on in this chapter.

16. Langdon Gilkey, "Symbols, Meaning, and the Divine Presence," *Theological Studies*, 35 (1974), pp. 249–267.

17. Martin Luther, *Lectures on Galatians 1535, Luther's Works*, 26, ed. and trans. by Jaroslav Pelikan (St. Louis: Concordia Publishing House, 1963), p. 285.

18. William James, *The Varieties of Religious Experience* (New York: Collier Books, 1961), p. 361, quoting Auguste Sabatier.

19. For mediations between false oppositions set up on the basis of the distinction between faith and works see Schubert Ogden, *Faith and Freedom: Toward a Theology of Liberation* (Nashville: Abingdon, 1979), pp. 49–65; Edward Schillebeeckx, *Christ: The Experience of Jesus as Lord,* trans. by John Bowden (New York: The Seabury Press, 1980), pp. 159–164. The distinc-

tion is useful in exposing inauthentic extremes in the Christian life. But the distinction does not in itself show how faith and the exercise of freedom in love are integrated.

XI. MINISTRY IN A MISSION CHURCH

1. Bernard Cooke, *Ministry to Word and Sacrament: History and Theology* (Philadelphia: Fortress Press, 1977), pp. 193–199.

2. For a treatment of the offices of ministry, and thus a study of ministry that is more narrowly circumscribed than that of Cooke, see Edward Schillebeeckx, *Ministry: Leadership in the Community of Jesus Christ*, trans. by John Bowden (New York: Crossroad, 1981).

3. This is not to deny that all doctrinal theology is a practical discipline. Christian theology always emerges out of the life of the Christian community and reflects back upon it. But while in many cases this relevance is not explicitly drawn to attention, it is inescapable in a theology of ministry.

4. Cf. *supra*, Chapter IX.

5. One could say that this is an expression of the general thesis running through the whole of Gustavo Gutiérrez's *A Theology of Liberation: History, Politics and Salvation*, trans. and ed. by Caridad Inda and John Eagleson (Maryknoll, N.Y.: Orbis Books, 1973).

6. This theme is a fundamental principle in Segundo's theology that colors the whole of it. See the opening pages of *The Community Called Church*, trans. by John Drury (Maryknoll, N.Y.: Orbis Books, 1973) where Segundo poses the most basic question for understanding the Church in terms of its function in the history of the human race. "The primary preoccupation of the Church is not directed toward its own inner life but toward people outside. Unlike other organizations founded for the benefit of its own members, the Church is a community sent to those who live, act, and work outside its own narrow limits." "That is why it is so critically important, in trying to frame the Church in its proper context, to begin by asking the meaning of its insertion in the history of the human race to whom God's universal plan is directed." *The Community Called Church*, pp. 81, 82. "The Church was established in the world to benefit the rest of humankind." Segundo, *The Hidden Motives of Pastoral Action*, trans. by John Drury (Maryknoll, N.Y.: Orbis Books, 1978), p. 136. In Segundo's *Evolution and Guilt*, trans. by John Drury (Maryknoll, N.Y.: Orbis Books, 1973), one sees an evolutionary framework influenced by Pierre Teilhard de Chardin as the cosmic context or setting for his view of the role of Christianity in history.

7. The obvious exception here is the ministerial activity of the missionary who is sent beyond the borders of the community. But even here the traditional goal of the missionary was to effect conversion and thus draw people into the Christian community.

8. Gutiérrez, *A Theology of Liberation*, pp. 265–272. For a statement of the theme in political theology, see Johannes Metz, *Theology of the World*,

trans. by William Glen-Doepel (New York: Herder and Herder, 1969), pp. 115–124.

9. Segundo, *The Community Called Church*, pp. 78–86.

10. Segundo, *The Community Called Church*, pp. 78–86, 89–91; *Grace and the Human Condition* (Maryknoll, N.Y.: Orbis Books, 1973), pp. 50–55; *The Hidden Motives of Pastoral Action*, pp. 138–141. For Segundo Christianity is not meant to be a religion of the masses but the religion of an active minority. Unlike Karl Rahner who sees Christianity becoming a minority religion or sect in fact but not in principle, that is, this is not what it should be even if inevitably it must be, Segundo holds that this is what the Church should be. Because of this Segundo has been accused of "elitism" in his view of the Church and Christian life. It should be noted however that the term "masses" in Segundo's usage is not a purely sociological category. The distinction he is drawing attention to is not one of social classes. It is rather a distinction of attitudes and behavior. The term "masses" is "equivalent to inertia, passivity, non-liberty," which Segundo believes are contrary to the effects of the operation of grace and responsible membership in the church. See *Grace and the Human Condition*, p. 51. If there is an elitism in Segundo it is a moral elitism, one which cuts across social and economic classes and has nothing to do with intelligence or education. Its point is to stress the active quality of Christian life. For Rahner's position, see Karl Rahner, "The Present Situation of Christians: A Theological Interpretation of the Position of Christians in the Modern World," *The Christian Commitment: Essays in Pastoral Theology*, trans. by Cecily Hastings (New York: Sheed and Ward, 1963), pp. 3–37.

11. The goal of missionary activity is not understood today to be baptism of the masses for the salvation of their souls independently of a strong formation in the Christian faith and a genuine conversion that promises a certain quality of Christian life.

12. "The validity of the experiences embodied in Basic Ecclesial Communities will be recognized, and their further growth in communion with their pastors will be fostered." *Evangelization in Latin America's Present and Future*, Final Document of the Third General Conference of the Latin American Episcopate, No. 156, in *Puebla and Beyond: Documentation and Commentary*, ed. by John Eagleson and Philip Scharper, trans. by John Drury (Maryknoll, N.Y.: Orbis Books, 1979), p. 142. Cited hereafter as *Puebla*. See also Sergio Torres and John Eagleson, ed., *The Challenge of Basic Christian Communities*, trans. by John Drury (Maryknoll, N.Y.: Orbis Books, 1981), and Thomas G. Bissonnette, "Comunidades Eclesiales de Base: Contemporary Grass Roots Attempts To Build Ecclesial *Koinonia*," *The Jurist*, 35 (Winter-Spring 1976), pp. 24–58.

13. "We affirm the need for conversion on the part of the whole Church to a preferential option for the poor, an option aimed at their integral liberation." *Puebla*, No. 1134, p. 264.

14. The theology of Gustavo Gutiérrez, especially as it developed after his book *A Theology of Liberation*, has been centered on the reality of the situation of the poor, so that the very concept of "the poor" has become a primary

religious symbol. This is reflected especially in his collection of essays *La Fuerza Histórica de los Pobres* (Lima: CEP, 1979).

15. "In Latin America the Church must continue to move from the side of the powerful to the side of the poor." Ronaldo Muñoz, "Ecclesiology in Latin America," *The Challenge of Basic Christian Communities*, p. 153.

16. Cooke, *Ministry to Word and Sacraments.*

17. Cooke, *Ministry to Word and Sacraments*, p. 214.

18. Cooke, *Ministry to Word and Sacraments*, p. 214. Also p. 204.

19. Segundo's so-called "elitism" should be adjudicated within the context of this tension. Cf. note 10.

20. Exactly what the Gospel has to say concerning the secular or non-religious sphere is an open question here. The statement here does not imply that faith communicates empirical knowledge concerning secular reality. The point is simply that the Gospel does have bearing on the meaning and the direction of the exercise of human freedom in every sphere of existence.

21. See Cooke, *Ministry to Word and Sacraments*, pp. 214, 390, for reflections that lead in this direction.

22. Cooke, *Ministry to Word and Sacraments*, p. 204. Commenting on the ministry of the word, Cooke feels that the direction of this ministry outside the Church is primary. "'Ministry of the word' can refer, of course, to the Christian community's communication of the word of God to non-Christians or to the sharing of that word within the Christian church. The first of these two is in a sense more ultimate, since the Christian community has been given the gospel in order to preach it to 'every creature.'" *Ibid.* p. 324.

23. This double relationship is a question of fact but also one of principle. The content of the Christian message teaches this double relationship, of love of God and love of neighbor, the latter principle implying a transforming function in the world. See Ernst Troeltsch, *The Social Teaching of the Christian Churches,* trans. by Olive Wyon, Vol. 2 (New York: The Macmillan Company, 1931), pp. 999–1000.

24. The phrase "outside the Church" thus corresponds with the term "world" which has this double sense in Christian theological language. "World" refers both to that part of the human race that is not Christian and to whom the message of God in Jesus Christ is intended insofar as it is universal, open and addressed to human existence itself. "World" also refers to the whole sphere of human existence and activity, and as such it is in the Church and the Church is part of it.

25. Cooke, *Ministry to Word and Sacraments*, p. 206.

26. "Decree on the Missionary Activity of the Church," No. 36, *The Documents of Vatican II,* Walter M. Abbott, ed. (New York: Herder and Herder, Association Press, 1966), p. 623.

27. Cf. Schillebeeckx, *Ministry,* p. 68. These principles are amply developed by Cooke both historically and theologically. They flow from a concrete historical, genetic and developmental view of the Church. See *Ministry to Word and Sacraments,* especially Chapters 7, 14 and 26, pp. 187–214, 320–339, 509–520. The point which Cooke makes is simply that ministries in general,

and hence the offices of ministry, emerge out of the common life that constitutes the community. Negatively, the corporate ministry of the Church and the variety of ministries in the Church did not and do not derive from a single or an official ministry. "The corporate ministry of the church is . . . a commission that pertains to all baptized Christians including those also designated for specialized ministries. This common ministry of the community does not derive from the special ministerial function of the bishops; instead, the episcopacy is one of the special ministries that exist to sustain and nurture the corporate ministry of the church" (p. 203).

28. Karl Rahner, *The Shape of the Church To Come*, trans. by Edward Quinn (London: SPCK, 1974), pp. 57–58.

29. Cf. Cooke, *Ministry to Word and Sacraments*, pp. 325, 327.

30. Cooke, *Ministry to Word and Sacraments*, pp. 206–207.

31. Cooke, *Ministry to Word and Sacraments*, p. 326.

32. Cf. Johannes Metz, *Theology of the World*, pp. 107–111, for criticism of the privatization of Christian faith. Cf. also his *The Emergent Church: The Future of Christianity in a Post-Bourgeois World*, trans. by Peter Mann (New York: Crossroad, 1981), for an extended criticism of the Church in the west for its middle class character.

33. Metz writes that "it is our contention that theology, precisely because of its privatizing tendency, is apt to miss the individual in his or her real existence. Today this existence is to a very great extent entangled in societal vicissitudes; so any existential and personal theology that does not understand existence as a political problem in the widest sense of the word, must inevitably restrict its considerations to an abstraction." *Theology of the World*, pp. 110–111.

34. Schillebeeckx, *Ministry*, pp. 72–73, with special reference to the ministry of leadership of the Eucharist.

35. Cooke, *Ministry to Word and Sacraments*, pp. 196–197.

36. John A. Coleman, "The Future of Ministry," *America*, 144 (March 28, 1981), 245.

37. For a fundamental definition of and reflection upon the principle of stewardship see John Calvin, *Institutes of the Christian Religion*, ed. by John T. McNeill (Philadelphia: The Westminister Press, 1960), Bk III, Ch. 10, pp. 719–725, esp. p. 723.

38. Cooke, *Ministry to Word and Sacraments*, p. 107. For a review of the theological arguments justifying the Church's intervention in the political, economic and social orders, see John A. Coleman, *An American Strategic Theology* (New York/Ramsey: Paulist Press, 1982), pp. 10–25.

39. On the notion and epistemology of a contrast experience, see Edward Schillebeeckx, *God the Future of Man*, trans. by N. D. Smith (New York: Sheed and Ward, 1968), pp. 136, 153–154, 164. This notion is developed further in Schillebeeckx's *Jesus: An Experiment in Christology*, trans. by Hubert Hoskins (New York: The Seabury Press, 1979), pp. 621–622.

40. This statement is a commonplace in theology today. Religious faith perception engages the transcendent dimension of human consciousness and

does not provide information of an empirical nature about the world. But it does not follow from this that revelation and faith's perception have no bearing at all on secular human activity. Such a position is represented by Friedrich Gogarten in *Despair and Hope for Our Time,* trans. by Thomas Weiser (Philadelphia/Boston: Pilgrim Press, 1970). What Gogarten is nervous about is an abdication of reason in social planning and the danger of religious fanaticism. While one may agree that faith does not provide any information about this world, since this belies the very epistemological structure of faith, still at the same time what faith does perceive about human existence has some bearing upon rational social planning. Gogarten's position is based on one or two false assumptions. The first is that human consciousness can be compartmentalized. In a single consciousness what is perceived at one level cannot be totally divorced from perception at another level. And, secondly, Gogarten implicitly assumes that world planning can be accomplished by value-free technological reason, or that all those who employ technical reason are not influenced by ultimate concerns and values that ultimately are objects of faith.

41. For an analysis from a religious sociological point of view of this tension between the ideal and the actual on the social level, between a religious vision of a social order in tension with an actual social order, and how this religious vision comes to bear on social planning, see Coleman, "A Church with a Worldly Vocation," in *An American Strategic Theology,* pp. 38–56, esp. pp. 38–42.

42. Cf. note 40. Cf. also Joe Holland and Peter Henriot, *Social Analysis: Linking Faith and Justice* (Washington, D.C.: Center of Concern, 1980) for a fine concise primer in the necessity and logic of sociological analysis and research in dealing with ministerial problems of a social nature.

43. Coleman gives six criteria or norms governing the manner of the Church's intervention into the public social arena in *An American Strategic Theology,* pp. 27–31.

44. Cf. Coleman, *An American Strategic Theology,* pp. 31–33, 38–56. Cf. also Cooke, *Ministry to Word and Sacraments,* pp. 205–207, 392–393, on this autonomy of the laity in this applied ministry.

XII. LIBERATIONIST SPIRITUALITY

1. Juan Hernández Pico, "La Oración en los Procesos Latino-americanos de Liberación," *Christus,* 44 (December 1979-January 1980), 85.

2. Leonardo Boff, "Contemplativus in Liberatione: De la Espiritualidad de Liberación a la Practica de Liberación," *Christus,* 44 (December 1979-January 1980), 66.

3. The development here is that of Jon Sobrino, "Espiritualidad de Jesús y de la Liberación," *Christus,* 44 (December 1979-January 1980), 59–61.

4. Gustavo Gutiérrez, "'Drink from Your Own Well,'" *Learning to Pray,* Concilium, 159, ed. by Casiano Floristán and Christian Duquoc (New York: The Seabury Press, 1982), p. 38.

5. This Christological approach to spirituality is most consistent in the theology of Jon Sobrino. See, for example, the following works: Jon Sobrino, "General Features of the Christian Life from the Standpoint of Christology," *Christology at the Crossroads,* trans. by John Drury, (Maryknoll, N.Y.: Orbis Books, 1978), pp. 388–395; "Espiritualidad de Jesús y de la Liberación," *Christus,* 44 (December 1979-January 1980), 59–63; "The Prayer of Jesus and the God of Jesus in the Synoptic Gospels," *Listening,* 13 (Fall 1978), 189–213; "Christian Prayer and New Testament Theology: A Basis for Social Justice and Spirituality," *Western Spirituality: Historical Roots and Ecumenical Routes,* ed. by Matthew Fox (Notre Dame, Ind.: Fides/Claretian, 1979), pp. 76–114; "Following Jesus as Discernment," *Discernment of the Spirit and of Spirits, Concilium,* 119, ed. by Casiano Floristán and Christian Duquoc (New York: The Seabury Press, 1979), pp. 14–24.

6. Segundo Galilea, "El Rostro Latinoamericano de la Espiritualidad: Las Fuentes Histórico-sociales de la Espiritualidad," *Christus,* 44 (December 1979-January 1980), 69. If the symbol of grace were identified with that of the Spirit, one could also interpret Juan Luis Segundo's view of the Christian life as determined primarily by the theology of the Spirit. However the term "spirituality" does not play a large role in Segundo's writings. See Juan Luis Segundo, *Grace and the Human Condition,* trans. by John Drury (Maryknoll, N.Y.: Orbis Books, 1973), pp. 86–94, and Alfred T. Hennelly, "Towards a Spirituality of Liberation," *Theologies in Conflict: The Challenge of Juan Luis Segundo* (Maryknoll, N.Y.:. Orbis Books, 1979), pp. 140–156. It should be noted that these several approaches are not exclusive of one another. For example, Jesus is the principle for discerning the direction of the movement of the Spirit, and a following of Jesus is empowered by the Spirit. In some degree all of these several approaches appear in all of the authors cited.

7. Galilea, "El Rostro Latinoamericano de la Espiritualidad," pp. 69–71. This ecclesiological approach to spirituality dominates Gustavo Gutiérrez's *A Theology of Liberation: History, Politics and Salvation,* trans. and ed. by Caridad Inda and John Eagleson (Maryknoll, N.Y.: Orbis Books, 1973), esp. pp. 203–208, 287–306. Cf. also the discussion of the Christian life in terms of the function of the Church community being a sign to society and thus requiring a sign morality in Juan Luis Segundo, *A Community Called Church,* trans. by John Drury (Maryknoll, N.Y.: Orbis Books, 1973), pp. 78–86.

8. Gutiérrez, "'Drink from Your Own Well,'" p. 41.

9. Gutiérrez, "'Drink from Your Own Well,'" p. 41.

10. Sobrino, "Espiritualidad de Jesús de la Liberación," p. 59.

11. Hennelly, *Theologies in Conflict,* p. 31. Hennelly is in turn summarizing the themes of the spirituality of liberation theology presented in Segundo Galilea, *Espiritualidad de la Liberación* (Santiago: ISPAJ, 1973), pp. 8–10. Other enumerations of the characteristics of liberation spirituality congruent with the five elements presented here are given by Gustavo Gutiérrez, "'Drink from Your Own Well,'" pp. 39–44; Leonardo Boff, "Contemplativus in Liberatione," pp. 67–68.

12. "What is happening today in Latin America is too new and too harsh for it not to call a certain type of spirituality radically into question." Gutiérrez, "Drink from Your Own Well,'" p. 39. Cf. also Segundo's analysis of the Christian life demanded today in contrast with the classical statement of Thomas à Kempis' *The Imitation of Christ* in Segundo, *Grace and the Human Condition,* pp. 86–94.

13. Boff, "Contemplativus in Liberatione," p. 66.

14. Sobrino, "The Prayer of Jesus and the God of Jesus in the Synoptic Gospels," p. 211. Also Sobrino, "Espiritualidad de Jesús y de la Liberación," p. 63. The passage on the final judgment in Matthew 25 is frequently invoked by liberation theology at this point.

15. Gutiérrez, "'Drink from Your Own Well,'" p. 40.

16. Gutiérrez, "'Drink from Your Own Well,'" p. 40.

17. Boff's "Contemplativus in Liberatione" develops a view of liberation spirituality within the context of this tension. Cf. also Segundo Galilea, "Liberation as an Encounter with Politics and Contemplation," *The Mystical and Political Dimension of Christian Faith, Concilium* 96, ed. by Claude Geffré and Gustavo Gutiérrez (New York: Herder, 1974), pp. 19–33.

18. Sobrino, "Christian Prayer and New Testament Theology," p. 89. This theme is developed throughout this entire article.

19. Gutiérrez, "'Drink from Your Own Well,'" pp. 39, 42. Liberation theology also consistently stresses that the Kingdom of God which Jesus preached and to which the Christian life should be dedicated is a social concept and not merely an individual-personal reality.

20. Many of the ideas developed here have been presented in Roger Haight, "Institutional Grace and Corporate Spirituality," *Spirituality Today,* 31 (September/December, 1979), 209–220, 324–334; "Spirituality and Social Justice: A Christological Approach," *Spirituality Today,* 34 (December 1982), 312–325.

21. This statement should not be understood as undermining a real and genuine experience of transcendence or the validity of the Christian experience of hope in an absolute and transcendent future. But these experiences too are radically conditioned by our this-worldliness and historical solidarity. Transcendence can only be experienced through the world, and hope for the future can only subsist on the basis of some experience mediated in the past and present.

22. Thus, for example, even Marxist atheists have a spirituality in the most basic sense of the term. See José Miguez-Bonino, *Christians and Marxists* (Grand Rapids, Mich.: Eerdmans, 1976), pp. 133–142. In fact Marx's dialectical materialism was not a denial of the role of human consciousness and freedom in the determination of the future. Cf. Nicholas Lash, *A Matter of Hope: A Theologian's Reflections on the Thought of Karl Marx* (Notre Dame, Ind.: University of Notre Dame, 1982), pp. 88–124. But in principle such a denial would be in virtue of conscious reflection and freedom, that is, the activity of the human spirit.

23. Gutiérrez, *A Theology of Liberation,* p. 204.

24. This view of Christianity and the Church is formulated most clearly and persuasively in terms of an existential notion of tradition by Maurice Blondel, in "History and Dogma," *The Letter on Apologetics and History and Dogma,* trans. and ed. by A. Dru and I. Trethowen (New York: Holt, Rinehart and Winston, 1964), pp. 221–287.

25. For this reason psychological sciences and techniques are extremely important in training for Christian ministry since they are a tool for Christian ministers to understand and meet the personal freedom of each person ministered to on the level of his or her individuality.

26. See F. Mallet [Maurice Blondel], *Qu'est-ce que la foi?* (Paris: Librairie Bloud & Cie, 1907) for an analysis of the act of faith that criticizes the theology of faith after Vatican Council I, but integrates it into a more integral existentialist context.

27. On the one hand, religious experience of God implies obligation and duty before God. On the other hand, the full consideration of ethical obligation in a concrete matter of practical concern leads one back to religious and theological presuppositions. See James Gustafson, *Ethics from a Theocentric Perspective,* I, *Theology and Ethics* (Chicago: The University Chicago Press, 1981), pp. 70–71, 131–132.

28. This distinction between spirituality and ethics is taken from James P. Hanigan, "Militant Nonviolence: A Spirituality for the Pursuit of Social Justice," *Horizons,* 9 (1982), pp. 7–22.

INSTRUCTION ON CERTAIN ASPECTS OF THE "THEOLOGY OF LIBERATION"

1. Cf. *Gaudium et Spes,* 4.
2. Cf. *Dei Verbum,* 10.
3. Cf. Gal. 5:1ff.
4. Cf. Ex. 24.
5. Cf. Jer. 31:31–34; Ez. 36:26ff.
6. Cf. Zec. 3:12ff.
7. Cf. Dt. 10:18–19.
8. Cf. Lk. 10:25–37.
9. Cf. 2 Cor. 8:9.
10. Cf. Mt. 25:31–46; Acts 9:4–5; Col. 1:24.
11. Cf. Jas. 5ff.
12. Cf. 1 Cor. 11:17–34.
13. Cf. Jas. 2:14–26.
14. Cf. Acta Apostolicae Sedis 71 (1979) pp. 1144–1160.
15. Cf. AAS 71 (1979) p. 196.
16. Cf. *Evangelii Nuntiandi,* 25–33, AAS 68 (1976) pp. 23–28.
17. Cf. *Evangelii Nuntiandi,* 32, AAS 68 (1976) p. 27.
18. Cf. AAS 71 (1979) pp. 188–196.
19. Cf. *Gaudium et Spes,* 39; Pius XI, *Quadragesimo Anno:* AAS 23 (1931) p. 207.

20. Cf. nos. 1134–1165 and nos. 1166–1205.

21. Cf. Puebla Document, IV, 2.

22. Cf. Paul VI, *Octogesima Adveniens*, 34, AAS 63 (1971) pp. 424–425.

23. Cf. *Lumen Gentium*, 9–17.

24. Cf. *Gaudium et Spes*, 39.

25. Cf. Acts 2:36.

26. Cf. 1 Cor. 10:1–2.

27. Cf. Eph. 2:11–22.

28. Cf. Puebla Document I, II, 3.3.

29. Cf. Lk. 10:16.

30. Cf. John Paul II, Address at the Opening of the Conference at Puebla, AAS 71 (1979) pp. 188–196; Puebla Document, II P, c. 1.

31. Cf. John Paul II, Address to the Favela Vidigal at Rio de Janeiro, July 2, 1980, AAS 72 (1980) pp. 852–858.

32. Cf. Puebla Document, II, c. II, 5.4.

33. Cf. *ibid.*, IV, c. 3. 3.1.

34. Cf. *ibid.*, IV, II, 2.3.

35. Cf. Paul VI, Profession of Faith of the People of God, June 30, 1968, AAS 60 (1968) pp. 443–444.

INDEX OF TOPICS

341

INDEX OF NAMES